D1547070

VIA FOLIOS 85

Pioneering Italian American Culture

PIONEERING ITALIAN AMERICAN CULTURE
ESCAPING *LA VITA DELLA CUCINA*

Essays, Interviews, Reviews

of and by

DANIELA GIOSEFFI

with an Introduction and Notes

by

Angelina Oberdan

BORDIGHERA PRESS

Library of Congress Control Number: 2013932249

Cultural Studies • Women Studies • Literary Studies • Non-Fiction

Cover illustration by TK Multimedia

Heartfelt thanks to Angelina Oberdan for her editorial assistance.

Printed in the United States.

Published by
BORDIGHERA PRESS
John D. Calandra Italian American Institute
25 W. 43rd Street, 17th Floor
New York, NY 10036

VIA Folios 85
ISBN 978–1–59954–059–7

Dedication

This book is dedicated to
my daughter, Thea (Gioseffi Rinaldi) Kearney;
my friend Angelina Oberdan;
padre caro mio Daniel Donato Gioseffi;
madre cara mia, Josephine Gioseffi;
sorella cara mia, Camille Gioseffi
— and to all women who wish to be free
to pursue their creative instincts and succeed
at their art, regardless of nationality, culture, or creed.

I owe thanks to my friends
cari amici Dr. Allan B. Rubin, Dr. Lionel B. Luttinger,
Maurizio Edwards, Alfredo de Palchi, Angelina Oberdan,
and my publishers Fred Gardaphe, Paolo Giordano, and
Anthony Julian Tamburri, for their supportiveness and
encouragement and to all those in the Italian American
community of writers, herein, who have offered
their encouraging understanding and appreciation.

Acknolwedgements

Permission to reprint selections in this collection has been acquired from the following sources to which the author is grateful. Contact these sources directly for reprints of individual selections

Cateura, Linda Brandi. "Homage to Astarte, Goddess of Earth," *Growing Up Italian: How Being Brought Up as an Italian American Helped Shape the Character, Lives, and Fortunes of Twwenty-four Celebrated Americans,* ed. Linda Brandi Cateura (New York: William Morrow, 1987).

Cavalieri, Grace. "Pointing Beyond Language," a review of *Word Wounds and Water Flowers,* by Grace Cavalieri, published in *Poet Lore* (1996). Transcribed interview of Daniela Gioseffi from *The Poet and the Poem* Webcasts from the Library of Congress (2008).

Corso, Paola. Interview of Daniela Gioseffi from "Does Your Fiction Need to be Stretched? Five Authors Describe the Magic of Magical Realism in Expressing Emotional Truths" published in *The Writer* (2007).

Di Maio, Dina. Interview of Daniela Gioseffi published in *Small Spiral Notebook: A Venture into Something Literary* (2004).

Di Pasquale, Emanuel. A review of *Going On: Poems,* by Daniela Gioseffi, *VIA* (2001).

Gioseffi, Daniela. "Breaking the Silence for Italian-American Women: Maligned and Stereotyped," *MS. Magazine* & *VIA* (1993); rpt by permission of the author.

___. "Diane Di Prima: Pioneer Woman Poet of Italian American Heritage, An Inspirational Force of the 1970's Feminist Movement," *The Paterson Literary Review* (2010–2011); rpt by permission of the author.

___. "Forging into the American Mainstream since the 1960s: On Being a Woman Writer with an Italian Name," *Breaking Open: Reflections on Italian American Women's Writing,* ed. Mary Ann Vigelante Mannino and Justin Vitiello (West Lafayette, IN: Purdue UP, 2003); reprinted by permission of the author.

___. Excerpt from "Introduction." *On Prejudice: A Global Perspective,* by Daniela Gioseffi (New York: Doubleday, 1993); rpt by permission of the author.

___. "Is There a Renaissance in Italian American Literature?" *MultiAmerica: Essays on Cultural Wars and Cultural Peace,* ed. Ishmael Reed (New York: Viking, 1997); rpt by permission of the author.

___. "Have You Really Read The Fortunate Pilgrim? and Lately? A Feminist's View of the Creator of the Infamous *Godfather.* Re-thinking Mario Puzo in the Age of the Sopranos," *VIA* (2003); rpt by permission of the author.

___. "Josephine Gattuso-Hendin, Novelist and Scholar: *The Right Thing to Do & The Fortunate Pilgrim*: Comparable and Equally Iconic of Our Italian-American Culture," *VIA* (2008); rpt permission of the author.

___. "A Non-Conformist Italian Poet in New York City: A Retrospective Essay on Alfredo de Palchi's Poetry," ItalianAmericanWriters.com (1999), and republished in *Homage to Alfredo de Palchi,* ed. Luigi Fontanella (Stony Brook, NY: Gradiva, 2011); rpt by permission of the author.

___. Reviews of Italian American authors published in *The Paterson Literary Review, Rain Taxi Review of Books, Small Press Review,* and *VIA*; reprinted by permission of the author.

___. "What Would Your Immigrant Father Say About the World According to Tony Soprano?" ItalianAmericanWriters.com (2003), and partly on a New York Times blog; rpt by permission of the author.

___. "Why I Became a Professional Crooner at Fifty-Seven: A Personal Essay on Frank Sinatra," *VIA* (1999); rpt by permission of the author.

___. "Why Stereotyping of Italian Americans Persists," presented at the John D. Calandra Institute of Italian American Studies Conference in 2008; printed by permission of the author.

___. "Fishing in the Mainstream for Italian American Poets," Reviews of Italian American Authors, previously published in various journals/periodicals, i.e. rpt by permission of the author.

Grillo, Jean Bergantini. "Arrivederci Kitchens: Four femmine forte shake up the Madonna Myth," *IAM: National Magazine for Italian-Americans* (1976).

Hendin, Josephine Gattuso. A review of Gioseffi's *Blood Autumn, Autunno di sangue: New & Selected Poems, VIA* (2007).

Magistrale, Anthony. A review of Gioseffi's *Wild Nights! Wild Nights! The Story of Emily Dickinson's "Master," Neighbor and Friend and Bridegroom, Gentle Read Literature* (2010).

Massimilla, Stephen. A review of Gioseffi's *Symbiosis: Poems, Rattapallax*

Misurella, Fred. A review of Gioseffi's *In Bed with the Exotic Enemies: Stories, VIA* (1998).

Morreale, Ben. "Eyes For Seeing Inward," a review of Gioseffi's *In Bed with the Exotic Enemy, Small Press Review* (1998).

Oberdan, Angelina. "Emily and Me: A Conversation with Daniela Gioseffi about Gioseffi's novel—*Wild Nights! Wild Nights!*: The Story of Emily Dickinson's 'Master,'" *Sugarmule* (2010); rpt by permission of the author.

Puccio, Valerie. "Daniela Gioseffi on New Mother Earth," *Phoenix* [Brooklyn, NY] (10 Apr. 1979): 2.

Soucie, Lily Lona. A review of *Women on War: Essential Voices for the Nuclear Age from a Brilliant International Assembly,* ed. Daniela Gioseffi, *VIA* (1990): 180–82.

Stampino, Maria Galli. A review of Gioseffi's *Word Wounds and Water Flowers, Italian Americana* 17.5 (1999): 228–29.

Table of Contents

INTRODUCTION

by

ANGELINA OBERDAN

How Daniela Gioseffi, Feminist and World Peace Advocate, Escaped la vita della cucina to Pioneer Italian American Literary Culture

by ANGELINA OBERDAN

Jerre Mangione and Ben Morreale cite Daniela Gioseffi, in *La Storia: Five Centuries of the Italian American Experience,* as "perhaps the most celebrated author of Italian American background [...], thanks to a profusion of national performances, readings, interviews, and publications in which she has participated."[1] This collection of prose writing by and about Daniela Gioseffi reveals how she escaped *la vita della cucina*—the symbolic "kitchen-prison" of women according to Italian Old World mores—to become an influential voice in Italian American culture, promoting the Italian American literary renaissance.

In the more than fifty years that she has been publishing in the mainstream, Gioseffi has been a dedicated activist for sociopolitical justice, environmental sanity, women's rights, and freedom from prejudice for all ethnic groups. Gioseffi's numerous accolades prove Mangione and Morreale's statement: she has been awarded an American Book Award; grants from the New York State Council on the Arts of the National Endowment for the Arts; a Pen American Center Short Fiction Award; a Lifetime Achievement Award from the Association of Italian American Educators; OSIA's NY State Literary Award; and the John Ciardi Award for Lifetime Achievement in Poetry. Her fourteen successful books of poetry and prose have firmly cemented Gioseffi's place in literature. Yet, Gioseffi calls herself, with a laugh and a smile, a "jackass of all trades," but this self- effacement connotes her achievements. She has done what those with many interests dream of doing: investigated, practiced, and critiqued many art forms.

Featured on Veteran Feminists of America's website[2] in 2009, Gioseffi has been a prominent voice in American mainstream magazines since the 1970's; her work has appeared in widely distributed periodicals such as *MS., The Nation, The Paris Review, Chelsea Literary Review, Poetry East, Prairie Schooner, American Book Review, Poet Lore, Rain Taxi Review, and Library Journal,* as well as *VIA: Voices in Italian Americana* and *Italian Americana.* She has given presentations throughout the country and abroad and appeared on National Public Radio, the BBC, and network television. In 1996, Gioseffi won the Sydney Sulkin Prize from *Poet Lore* for her reviews of poetry. Laurels such as those mentioned exemplify the range of Gioseffi's knowledge, and there is much to be learned from her writings in varied genres, including the pieces in this book.

---

[1] See Mangione and Morreale's "The Writers: 1960–1990," *La Storia: Five Centuries of the Italian American Experience* (New York: Harper, 1993) 422–50.
[2] For more information about Veteran Feminists of America, visit vfa.org.

Under "Gioseffi, Daniela" in *The Italian American Experience: An Encyclopedia*,[3] George Guida, currently president of the Italian American Studies Association (formerly known as the American Italian Historical Association), most succinctly describes her heritage and her significance in the Italian American literary community:

Pioneer Italian American women writer and social activist, Daniela Gioseffi has occupied an important place in American culture since the early 1970s. A renowned poet of the Italian American and woman's experience, Gioseffi has also achieved notable success as a novelist, playwright, editor, lecturer, educator, broadcast journalist, actress, and singer. Born to an Italian immigrant father and a mother of mixed heritage, Gioseffi has crusaded for social justice in America and around the world. At 21, she went to work as a journalist and activist in Selma, Alabama (WSLA-TV), at the height of the Civil Rights Movement. There she helped integrate Southern television. Her activism led to her arrest and subsequent abuse at the hands of the KKK or Alabama authorities, an experience she reconstructs in the story, later a stage play (Off-B'dway in Greenwich Village adapted to the stage by Luciana Polney), titled *The Bleeding Mimosa* (1991).

Upon her return from the South, Gioseffi moved to New York City, where she began her career as a poet. Since the late 1960s, she has been published in numerous anthologies and journals such as *Antaeus, Italian Americana, The Nation, Paris Review,* and *Voices in Italian Americana.* Her first collection, *Eggs in the Lake,* appeared in 1979; her second, *Words Wounds and Water Flowers,* in 1995. The poems of both volumes, while lyrical, address a host of complex social and political issues—from racism to sexism to the ravages of war to the threat of global nuclear destruction—with unfailing "poetic vision."

A number of her best poems express the frustrations and joys of being Italian American. Several merit mention here: "Bicentennial Anti-Poem for Italian American Women" from *Eggs in the Lake*; and "Unfinished Autobiography," "For Grandma Lucia La Rosa, 'Light the Rose,'" and "American Sonnets for My Father" from *Words Wounds and Water Flowers.* All but the last of these poems explore the connections and effects of anti-Italian American prejudice and the repression of women in the traditional Italian American family.

Gioseffi's other endeavors have complemented her copious literary output. She has presented her work on National Public Radio, the British Broadcasting Corporation, and Canadian Broadcasting Corporation; taught creative writing and intercultural communications; and lectured throughout the United States and Europe on world peace and disarmament. While continuing to champion these causes, Gioseffi has taken a leading role in the ongoing Italian American literary and cultural renaissance. Her work and presence have inspired writers of all backgrounds to strive for cross-cultural understanding.[4]

[3]See Guida's "Gioseffi, Daniela," *The Italian American Experience: An Encyclopedia,* ed. Frank J. Cavaioli, Salvatore J. LaGumina, Salvatore Primeggia, and Joseph A. Varacalli (New York: Garland, 2000) 267–68.

[4]See Guida's "Gioseffi, Daniela (b. 1941)," *Italian Amererican Experience: An Encyclopedia,* ed. by Frank J. Cavaioli, Salvatore J. LaGumina, Salvatore Primeggia, and Joseph A. Varacalli (New York: Garland, 2000) 267–68.

In the last sentence, Guida implies how far-reaching Gioseffi's work is and how she has inspired the work of so many others.

In gratitude, it is important to look at how some major personal and cultural circumstances and events in Gioseffi's life directed her on this path of activism and influence. As Catherine Giambanco Vignale writes in an essay titled "In Search of the All Italian American Woman of Letters," "Daniela Gioseffi is one of those few women who has been able to overcome discrimination, cultural pressures and expectations and found a voice as an Italian American woman of letters." Whether Gioseffi was guided by these events or reacting to them, they were the obstacles Gioseffi had to overcome, as the saying goes, to escape *la vita della cucina.*

Clearly, Gioseffi has escaped the stereotypical Old World role of the female, but "escaping *la vita della cucina*" isn't rhetorically precise; in so much as the "kitchen" symbolizes the Italian American family, Gioseffi didn't leave it. Indeed much of Gioseffi's activism and work can be viewed as tending a larger kitchen. While this is a stretch (the whole world isn't a kitchen), it is important to understand that by becoming an activist and a writer Gioseffi didn't abandon her familial heritage. Rather, she was greatly influenced by it. In her essay titled "Forging into the Mainstream Since the 1960s," Gioseffi writes, "My immigrant Italian forbearers made me who I am for worse or for better, and I can never deny that rich heritage of passionate emotions—the suffering and joy that art portrays—which I learned early on from my Old World Italian family." She attributes the enthusiasm of her activism and the vigor of her writing to her ancestral Italian roots.

While escaping *la vita della cucina* implies dissention against the patriarchy of the Italian American family, Gioseffi's life and work are a tribute to her grandfather, Galileo Gioseffi, and her father, Donato Gioseffi. Galileo Gioseffi was a strong influence on her, and she writes that

> From him I learned to question and rebel; Grandpa Galileo was an iconoclast who loathed the Church's hypocrisies and medieval dogma. His rebellious attitude rubbed off on my father, and then onto me. No doubt the prejudice my father suffered in America inspired me to join the Civil Rights Movement in 1961, at which time my writing turned to journalism for a spell.[5]

Gioseffi credits her grandfather for her activism, but she was also greatly influenced by her father, for whom her admiration is a repeated element in her writing.

About her father's impact on her career, Gioseffi writes, "Despite my feminism, I have to say that my Italian patriarchal father's love of literature—his tenacity to fulfill the American Dream—was my greatest inspiration to being a writer" ("Forging into the Mainstream Since the 1960s"). When Daniela was a child of ten, her father began reading canonical masterpieces to her in a dramatic, operatic voice—for example Cervantes' *Don Quixote* and Shakespeare's *Romeo and Juliet.* These dramatic readings of great literature were a strong encouragement for her to achieve a Master of Fine Arts in Drama. She herself presents

---

[5]See her essay, "Forging into the Mainstream Since the 1960s," included in this collection.

captivating readings with appropriate bravado as a result, always achieving much audience approval. Gioseffi writes:

> Since my father had always dreamed of becoming a writer, my writing has been an attempt to fulfill his dream for him. I can still picture him sitting with his back to us, hunched over his typewriter, forgoing the glories of a sunny afternoon, trying when he could, between the duties of his full-time job as a chemical engineer, to become a writer.[6]

The influence of both her father and her grandfather shows that Gioseffi has not defied the patriarchy of her family but rather that she has fulfilled its expectations by rising beyond some of its more confining ones.

In the same way, Gioseffi's life and work do not condemn the more traditional roles of the women in her family; rather, by escaping *la vita della cucina,* she has venerated them. In her most powerful essays including those herein, Gioseffi discusses how she viewed her grandmother, her mother, and her aunts as repressed: "their limitations and their need for liberation inspired me to write about women's lives" ("Forging into the Mainstream Since the 1960s"). This is also what motivated Gioseffi to fight for women's rights.

It is through her writing and advocacy that Gioseffi has in fact given a voice, if only a retrospective one, to the women of her family. As Valerie Puccio writes in her review of Gioseffi's performance poetry and first collection of poetry, *Eggs in the Lake,*

> To Gioseffi, Italians have always been freer in emotional expression. From their Renaissance beginnings, the Italians have celebrated a culture of art, music, poetry, and dance. They have always felt an ethnic pride concerning their romantic passions. Gioseffi evokes this emotional power well in her poetry performance.[7]

To Gioseffi, her performances and her poetry were not really an act of entirely escaping the kitchen; instead they were a way for her to make the whole world her symbolic kitchen.

As Grace Cavalieri—poet, playwright, and host of the Poet and the Poem, a widely distributed public radio show funded by The National Endowment for the Arts at the Library of Congress—wrote in her review[8] of Gioseffi's *Word Wounds and Water Flowers,*[9] "When I was young, passion was not fashionable. Most women I knew were like my mother—they never raised their voices, certainly wouldn't argue politics at the dinner table—in fact, most didn't even drive a car." The lines of the poems included in the essays of this collection, too, ring of Gioseffi's Italian heritage; Cavalieri states that they come "from the singing and

---

[6]Gioseffi elaborates on this in "Forging into the Mainstream Since the 1960s," included in this collection.
[7]See Puccio's "Daniela Gioseffi on New Mother Earth," published in Brooklyn, NY's *Phoenix* (10 Apr. 1979): 2.
[8]See Cavalieri's "Pointing Beyond Language," a review of Gioseffi's *Word Wounds and Water Flowers* published in *Poet Lore* (1996).
[9]*Word Wounds and Water Flowers* was published by Bordighera in 1996 as one of the first ten books published under the imprint of *VIA* FOLIOS.

dancing of women in the cadence of our ancestors who carried wheat to the Easter altars. Her [Gioseffi's] Italian antecedents inspire much in the body and rhapsody of her work. It is in the tradition of an Italian quality and spirit in poetry." By being unembarrassed about her femininity as in "The Fishblood of Woman" and "Blood Autumn," as mentioned by Cavalieri, Gioseffi imparts feminine strength. The poems in this collection are not just written from a woman's perspective. Cavalieri writes that the book also "has a male spirit; and for those who call the earth a woman, and the world a man, Gioseffi has a grasp on each." Maria Galli Stampino said in a review[10] of the same book, "Here is no tolerance for complacency or denial; this book lays siege to the reader's sensibility." Thus, through her uninhibited passion that transforms itself into inspiring manifestos, Gioseffi makes passion popular. While the women of Gioseffi's family were not able to express themselves, Gioseffi's poetry compels women who read her poems to express their own passion.

While the structure of the Gioseffi household may have been conventional, their religious beliefs were less so. Of her religion, Gioseffi writes,

I've always felt that my assertive feminism came from not having been raised Catholic, but Humanist Agnostic, by my atypical immigrant Italian father who was educated by the fruits of his own hard labor.... In any case, I've ended up a Mother Earth celebrant, but people always assume I'm Catholic because of my name.[11]

Unlike many other Italian American women, Gioseffi is not Catholic, and therefore, that she should assume a stereotypical woman's role in the kitchen was not reiterated by her religious beliefs. Perhaps this non-traditional aspect of her Italian American home helped Gioseffi to escape *la vita della cucina*.

As it is for everyone, Gioseffi was not only molded by her family; who she is and how she escaped *la vita della cucina* was greatly affected by her childhood in Newark, New Jersey. Of it, she writes,

I'd grown up in Newark, attending Avon Avenue School, an integrated public school, not far from where the Springfield Avenue race riots were to take place. Italian, Jewish, black ghettos all bordered on one another and were inextricably mixed in the school.

In fact, Gioseffi has a particularly poignant memory of her childhood friend, Silvy Jackson:

I'd been called a "nigger lover" in third grade for befriending a "colored girl," Silvy Jackson. We played hopscotch in the corner of the schoolyard away from the other kids. I remember having bonded with her because we were the only kids in our class who didn't have the thirty-five cents a week that other students brought in for milk money. She sat to my left in the back row next to me, and our eyes met in a smile, as the other kids were munching their graham crackers and drinking their milk. We

---

[10]See Stampino's review of Gioseffi's *Word Wounds and Water Flowers*, published in *Italian Americana* 17.5 (1999): 228–29.
[11]See "Breaking the Silence for Italian American Women," included in this collection.

bonded in deprivation, pretending fiercely, together, that we hated English graham crackers and milk.

Gioseffi elaborates on this in "Breaking the Silence for Italian American Women,"[12] which received more responses than other articles in MS. in 1994. She continues this story and recounts how she felt closer to her African American classmates because of their similar socioeconomic status than she felt to her other classmates in elementary school.

Because Gioseffi didn't have any female Italian American role models in her neighborhood, Gioseffi found feminine inspiration where she could. Edna St. Vincent Millay was one such heroine of Gioseffi's youth:

> The drama of her life, the fact that she won a scholarship to Vassar for a poem she wrote and her subsequent rise from poverty into the light of poetry really impressed me. It was a dramatic story like the ones my father told of his struggle to become educated and respectable from humble beginnings. But Millay was a woman and a feminist, and to see that a woman could work hard to become a writer and be respected for her work, really influenced me. She was such a great beacon to me, both her life and her craft with language.[13]

And it was one of Millay's poems that made Gioseffi aware that Italian Americans' plight for equality wasn't limited to Gioseffi's neighborhood. Millay's "Justice Denied in Massachusettes" is about the case of Ferdinando Nicola Sacco and Bartolomeo Vanzetti. Although Gioseffi wasn't alive in the 1920s, she repeatedly emphasizes the story of these two anarchists convicted of murdering two men during an armed robbery. After a series of trials and appeals, Sacco and Vanzetti were executed in 1927 by the influence of Judge Thayer, a bigot who dubbed them "dirty dagos" and "filthy guineas." This historical event had such an affect on Gioseffi because Millay wrote about it, and because it was one of the first incidents, publicly sensationalized in the news, of prejudice against Italian Americans. It grabbed Gioseffi's attention.

Provoked by prejudice against Italian Americans, the influence of her grandfather and father, and other variables, Gioseffi joined the Civil Rights Movement in 1961. She appeared on an all-black gospel show—which aired on WSLA-TV in Selma, Alabama—to enlist Freedom Riders. After her first Freedom Ride, Gioseffi wasn't arrested like other members of the ride. Later that evening, she was arrested, taken to the jailhouse, and raped by a deputy sheriff who was a member of the Ku Klux Klan. Unable to write about the experience for years, Gioseffi writes about it in "Breaking the Silence for Italian American Women" as well as in her short story, "Bleeding Mimosa."

---

[12]"Breaking the Silence for Italian American Women" is included in this collection.
[13]See "Forging into the Mainstream Since the 1960s."

It was around this time that Gioseffi became a feminist pioneer. Barbara J. Love's entry about Gioseffi in *Feminists Who Changed America 1963–1975*[14] discusses Gioseffi's feminist awakening and highlights her social activism:

> Her feminist awakening began in 1961 in Selma, Alabama, where she was a civil-rights journalist and activist. After appearing on an all black Gospel TV show announcing freedom rides and sit-ins, Gioseffi says, she was "arrested in the middle of the night and then raped—as a virgin of 20—at the station house by a deputy sheriff who was a member of the Ku Klux Klan."
>
> Her feminist awakening continued in 1966, she says, when she "almost died in childbirth due to doctor's errors." In the mid 1960's, Gioseffi began to give feminist readings and talks for WBAI-Radio NYC. In the late 1960s, Gioseffi's work began appearing in feminist poetry anthologies. At the same time, she joined New Feminist Talent and lectured on college campuses on "The Birth Dance of Earth: A Celebration of Women and the Earth in Poetry, Music, and Dance."
>
> She published *Eggs in the Lake,* a book of poetry that celebrated women's freedom and erotic power and won a grant from the New York State Council for the Arts. Her drama "The Sea Hag in the Cave of Sleep" was produced at the Cubiculo Theatre in Manhattan and also won a multimedia grant award from The New York State Council for the Arts.
>
> Gioseffi wrote *Earth Dancing: Mother Nature's Oldest Rite*; published *The Great American Belly,* a comic feminist novel about surviving divorce and raising a child alone; and toured England speaking on her feminist theories....

Clearly, Gioseffi's activism wasn't limited to a particular group of people; she fought for equality for everyone.

Michael Palma states in his announcement, "Daniela Gioseffi Wins John Ciardi Award for Lifetime Achievement in Poetry,"[15] that "[i]n keeping with the diverse talents of the man for whom it is named, the award recognizes contributions to poetry not only through original verse, but also in translation, criticism, teaching, and editing—all fields in which the late John Ciardi worked with great distinction." And the announcement continues by cataloging Gioseffi's "extraordinarily varied career":

> ...[S]he has worked professionally as an actress, singer, and dancer. She has had a number of her own theater works produced, including an adaptation of Turgenev's *Fathers and Sons* and a multimedia production entitled *The Birth Dance of Earth* (1972), for which she also composed the music. She created and maintains the website, *PoetsUSA.com,* which incorporates sites devoted to the poets of New Jersey and to Italian American writers. She conceived the idea for, and administers, the Bordighera Poetry Prize, which has so far enabled the publication, in bilingual, annual editions of fourteen volumes by Italian American poets.

---

[14]See Barbara J. Love's *Feminists Who Changed America 1963–1975* (Chicago: U of Illinois P, 2006) 175.

[15]See Michael Palma's announcement, "Daniela Gioseffi Wins the John Ciardi Award for Lifetime Achievement in Poetry" in *Italian Americana* 25.2 (2007) 170–71.

Her own published works include *The Great American Belly Dance* (1977), a novel[16]; *Earth Dancing* (1980), nonfiction; *Dust Disappears* (1995), translations from the Cuban poet Carilda Oliver Labra; and *In Bed with the Exotic Enemy* (1997), a novella and stories. She is also the editor of two anthologies, *Women on War: International Voices* (1988 & 2003, American Book Award, 1990) and *On Prejudice: A Global Perspective* (1993), both reflective of a commitment to social justice that stretches back at least as far as to the beginning of her career, as a journalist covering civil rights demonstration in Selma, Alabama, in 1961. She has received a PEN Short Fiction Award, a World Peace Award from the Ploughshares Foundation, and a Lifetime Achievement Award from the Association of Italian American Educators. Lines of her poetry have been etched in marble on a wall of Penn Station in New York, beside passages from Walt Whitman and William Carlos Williams.

Gioseffi has published five volumes of poetry, from *Eggs in the Lake* (1979) to *Blood Autumn: Poems New and Selected* (2006). From the beginning, she has produced poems in various modes with equal skill and intensity: social and political commentaries, as in the long title poem of *Word Wounds and Water Flowers* (1995), with its almost Whitmanesque sweep and verve; explorations, often mythically inflected and erotically charged, of the female principle; tender and often painful family reminiscences; and concentrated lyrics that celebrate the beauty of the outer and inner worlds. At times these separate components coalesce, as in the sestet of "As When Some Silenced Singer Hears Her Aria: A Sonnet for Vittoria Colonna":

> my tongue is loosed beyond a private caroling, my pen prances
> urged by mysterious love as if it had no part in what is sighed
> as Earth sings praises through me, my eyes are green sea,
> red skies, wildflowers, a child who dances
> well when loved beyond the pain of men's tribal wars, pride,
> threatened suicide, and bloody rivalry.

Even in this brief excerpt from Gioseffi's poetry that Palma includes in his announcement, we can see how distinctive an influence Gioseffi's Italian American heritage and her feminism has on her poetry.

Also a pioneer of the multicultural movement, Gioseffi writes that "[b]y the end of the 1970's, many Italian American writers had seen the light and knew that the multicultural movement was where they belonged if they were going to gain a foothold in American letters."[17] However, it was in 1979 that Gioseffi became aware that she was a pioneer in Italian American literature and really started to promote Italian American writing. She attributes this revelation to Ernesto Falbo, co-founder of *Italian Americana,* who told Gioseffi, after a poetry performance at SUNY-Buffalo: "You're one of only two or three Italian American women poets in this country. You're a pioneer!…"[18] Additionally, renowned vice-presidential candidate, US Congresswoman Geraldine Ferraro also recognized Gioseffi as a

---

[16]Gioseffi published her second novel after winning this award; it is titled *Wild Nights! Wild Nights: The Story of Emily Dickinson's "Master," Neighbor and Friend and Bridegroom* (Austin, TX: Plain View Press, 2010).

[17]See "Is There a Renaissance in Italian American Literature?" included in this collection.

[18]For Gioseffi's discussion of the story, see her essay, "Forging into the Mainstream Since the 1960s," included in this collection.

pioneer who would create a lasting impact on the Italian American community. After listening to Gioseffi read her poetry at a forum of the National Organization of Italian American Women, Ferraro wrote, "I enjoyed your reading of poetry. We are both pioneers of two different careers.... But I think your talent is a true gift."[19] Since then, Gioseffi has been particularly influential in promoting the Italian American literary renaissance[20]; she's made remarkable contributions to the community through her literary prowess. She edits and publishes *ItalianAmericanWriters.com*.

Indeed, Gioseffi is credited with founding the First Brooklyn Bridge Poetry Walk in 1971 based on Italian tradition. After reading about how Florentines proudly paraded Michelangelo's newly finished statue of David through the streets of Florence to celebrate the glory of their city-state and its art, she decided to celebrate the Brooklyn Bridge, the noted Eighth Wonder of the World, in her community of Brooklyn Heights, New York, by parading poems about the Bridge across its expanse with the assistance of a grant from The New York State Council for the Arts Creative Artist Public Service Program. The colorful placards that she and a friend hand-painted heralded the names of poets who'd written famous poems about The Bridge: Vladamir Mayakovsky, Garcia Lorca, Hart Crane, and also Walt Whitman who wrote "Crossing Brooklyn Ferry" before the bridge was built. Betty Kray, of the Academy of American Poets, copied the idea from Gioseffi and hosted a similar event to which the young Italian American poet, Gioseffi, was not invited; many of the accomplished poets Kray did invite—including Galway Kinnell, David Ignatow, and James Wright—read poems from the chapbook Gioseffi published at the first Print-Center as a program for her sponsored event. The Brooklyn Bridge Poetry Walk is now hosted by Poets House,[21] where Gioseffi is often a featured reader or a gracious host of various events some celebrating Italian American writing. Though Betty Kray of the Academy of American Poets is wrongly claimed as its inventor, Gioseffi is rightfully credited with inventing the First Brooklyn Bridge Poetry Walk by Richard Haw in his book titled *Brooklyn Bridge: A Cultural History.*[22]

Incidents like this—the co-opting of her creative ideas by people in the mainstream—at the beginning of her career were wounding to Gioseffi who's writing was emotionally passionate compared to that being written by her mainstream literary peers. The publication of The WASP Mystique by Richard C. Robertiello and Diana Hoguet[23] helped Gioseffi articulate why there is prejudice against Italian Americans and Italian American writers. She writes:

...their 1986 analytical text on the subject demonstrates that Latino, Italian, African, and Jewish-American styles of communicating—modes with passionate displays, talk

---

[19]This quote is from letter from Geraldine Ferraro to Daniela Gioseffi (27 Sept. 1985) included in this collection.
[20]See "Is There a Renaissance in Italian American Poetry? ..." originally published in *Multicultural America: Essays on Cultural Wars, Cultural Peace*, edited by the renowned African American poet/editor/novelist Ishmael Reed (Viking, 1997).
[21]An interview of the Poets House Executive Director, Lee Bricetti, is included in this collection.
[22]Haw's *Brooklyn Bridge: A Cultural History* was published Rutgers UP in 2005.
[23]See Robertiello and Hoguet, *The WASP Mystique* (New York: Donald I. Fine, 1987).

with gesticulation, animated body-language, folksy warmth and informality—were misunderstood by the "all-American" style of social behavior.... These polite inhibitions seemed to dominate literary styles, and particularly during my college years, they seemed to make any display of passion in poetry unacceptable.[24]

Gioseffi also pointed out in the late 1980s the lack of Italian Americans involved in PEN events.[25] She attributes much of the prejudice against Italian Americans to the mafia stereotype.

Of mafia stereotyping, in "Breaking the Silence," Gioseffi states:

I'll never forget how Norman Mailer, back in the '80's, told me I reminded him of Geraldine Ferraro, because I was a blonde Italian. I felt like saying, "Si,si signore, we all look alike!" He also said, publicly, at a PEN general meeting over which he presided as president, that Mondale shouldn't have gotten mixed up with Italians from Queens, implying that they are all Mafiosi, and he said it with aplomb, as if he thought himself very clever to declare Ferraro's unfounded Mafia connection the reason Mondale lost. Ferraro in grief has declared: "Again and again, they [the media] bore on that same theme: Because I am Italian, I or my family is suspected of being gangsters ... with no data to support the claim...." An editor in *The New York Times* was finally quoted in Richard Reeves column as saying, "The stoning of Geraldine Ferraro in the public square goes on and on, and nobody steps forward to help or protest."

And of course, Gioseffi is correct; Hollywood's creation of the mafia stereotype has made Italian Americans fearful of defending themselves, and many have come to believe the mafia stereotype and are hesitant to attempt to break down the Hollywood exaggeration or point out how overblown it is—especially after all the box office acclaim movies with mafia themes have achieved.[26]

It was during the Howard Beach racial attack that Gioseffi saw this—Italian Americans afraid to stand up for themselves—happen, and Gioseffi was upset by the image of Italian Americans that the Howard Beach and Bensonhurst incident when Yusef Hawkins was killed seemed to support, due to media portrayal of distorted facts. While discussing the incident in "Breaking the Silence for Italian American Women," Gioseffi points out how only the attackers in the community were publicized and how the people who helped, the women especially, were given no acknowledgement. These women called the police, tried to help Hawkins, and visited his home to express their sympathy. "Pizza Boycotts" were organized against the Italian American neighborhood.

Moreover, Gioseffi points out that in a similar situation where an Italian American was the victim, Italian Americans would not have banded together to protest the ethnic group associated with the crime. Indeed, she sites a rape of an Italian American girl that occurred in 1992 to show how Italian Americans are unjustly

---

[24]See "Forging into the Mainstream Since the 1960s."

[25]PEN is "a global literary community protecting free expression and celebrating literature." For more information, visit their website at www.pen.org.

[26]Over thirty-five such movies have been made since *Little Caesar,* a box office success of the 1930's starring Edward G. Robertson, the acclaimed Jewish actor, started the craze.

singled out as the root of all evil and rarely portrayed as victims in the media, even when they are. Gioseffi believes that Italian Americans need to understand how and why we are discriminated against so that we can better defend ourselves with the community pride that should be ours. In many ways, that is among the themes this text illuminates. It augments what Robert Viscusi's believed when founding the Italian American Writers Association (IAWA) in the 1990's. Viscusi has written extensively on the need of Italians to write their own stories, read each other and buy each other's books in order to keep from being "written" and portrayed wrongly by others. The motto of his organization is "Write and read or be written!" Gioseffi, a charter member, believes completely in Viscusi's and IAWA's tenant.

In the same vein, Gioseffi is adamantly against prejudice in all its forms. In 1986, years earlier, the then Governor of New York, Mario Cuomo wrote to Gioseffi, "... philosophical arguments and laws are not the only ways to end prejudice. Works of art with themes such as yours can also help bring about greater understanding among different groups."[27] Groundbreaking major press collections of world literature, Gioseffi's *Women on War: International Writings* and *On Prejudice: A Global Perspective,* have done just that; they have facilitated many different voices conversing about crucial topics endemic to war and prejudice. The compendiums were featured at the United Nations, received awards from the Ploughshares World Peace Foundation, and continue to be used extensively for tolerance teaching. Indeed, of Gioseffi's recent interview of the writer Sapphire, Grace Cavalieri wrote that "No one is better than Daniela Gioseffi at discussing race, sex and gender issues in literature...."

Gioseffi's edited collection titled *Women on War: Essential Voices for the Nuclear Age from a Brilliant International Assembly*[28] illustrates Cavalieri's comment. In her review of the compendium with its thirty-page introduction by the author, Lily Iona Soucie[29] admits that "Although I was born when World War II began, history's deadliest war, I hadn't been directly affected by the conflict, except for food rationing. Consequently, I wondered what I could gain from such a book...." Ultimately, Soucie discovers that there was much animosity towards Italian Americans during the war.[30] Soucie quotes Emma Goldman, whose essay titled "Patriotism as a Cause of War" is included in the collection: Goldman, writes

> Patriotism assumes that our globe is divided into little spots, each one surrounded by an iron gate. Those who have had the fortune of being born on some particular spot consider themselves better, nobler, grander, more intelligent than the living beings inhabiting any other spot.

[27]This quote is from Cuomo's personal correspondence with Daniela Gioseffi (21 Nov. 1986) included in this collection.
[28]Published by Simon and Schuster in 1990 and rpt. as *Women on War: An International Anthology of Writings from Antiquity to the Present* by the Feminist Press, 2003..
[29]See Soucie's review of *Women on War: Essential Voices for the Nuclear Age from a Brilliant International Assembly,* edited by Daniela Gioseffi, published in *VIA* (1990): 180–82.
[30]Gioseffi's poem titled "'Don't Speak the Lanuage of the Enemy'" comments on the situation of Italian American's during World War II.

Soucie concludes this quote by stating, "We no longer can afford to see each country in isolation but must see all nationalities as part of the larger human family." This is exactly want Gioseffi is attempting to do with this collection. As a woman with an Italian American surname, she understands that we cannot isolate ourselves, not even in our communities or neighborhoods; instead, as a woman from a hyphenated background, in *Women on War* Gioseffi tries to unite all ethnicities in understanding against war and for peace. As Soucie reiterates, "the patriarchal structures and values we've inherited and that dominate the world encourage compartmentalizing and are a major cause of war," Gioseffi has gathered the voices of women from around the world who explain how war affects their lives economically, physically, and spiritually.

Women on War was greatly applauded by those in the mainstream. Doris Jean Austin published a review of the original American Book Award winning edition of the multicultural compendium in *The New York Times* on January 7, 1990; she wrote:

> Seldom has literature more earnestly argued for world peace than in this international anthology, an eloquent response to global violence that features the work of more than 200 women-social scientists, journalists, novelist, poets, essayists and ordinary citizens. *Women on War* allows the reader to open to almost any page and capture a brief yet concise historical episode, a poem or an excerpt from a novel. This is a book one hopes will be translated into all of humankind's languages.

Gioseffi shows by her example and this collection, that it's by escaping the woman's limited role of homemaker, as defined by a patriarchy, that civilization can move beyond war in a world of nurturing cooperation.

The brilliant scientist Carl Sagan wrote of *Women on War*:

> This is a book of searing analyses and cries from the heart on the madness of war. Why is the half of humanity with a special sensitivity to the preciousness of life, the half untainted by testosterone poisoning, almost wholly unrepresented in defense establishments and peace negotiations worldwide?

As Sagan understands, Gioseffi was inspired to give women of the world a voice against the horrors of war, because women's voices on the subject are rarely heard or listened to. The book, reissued in 2003 by The Feminist Press, with a longer introductory sociopolitical analysis has become a women's studies *classic* now *inprint* for over twenty-five years since it's first Simon & Schuster edition in 1988.

One of the most appealing aspects of Gioseffi's pioneering for Italian American women, and women in general, is that she's not a man-hater, nor is she a woman who neglects the kitchen entirely. She loves to cook nourishing meals for friends and family. In fact, Gioseffi is an adoring mother and grandmother who travels to New Jersey for a few days every week to help cook for and tend to the needs of her grandchildren and family.

Fred L. Gardaphe, author and distinguished Professor of Italian American Studies at the John D. Calandra Italian American Institute of Queen's College of CUNY, states in his essay "Mythologies of Italian America: From Little Italys to the Suburbs" that an Italian American woman, like Gioseffi, can only become a writer "by directly challenging the forces that attempted to keep her tied down in traditional roles." These traditional roles for an Italian American woman are defined as wife, mother, and cook; and this symbolic "standard of the kitchen" was emphasized in the lives of most Italian American women of Gioseffi's generation. Indeed, her educated and inspirational father, Donato Gioseffi, though he encouraged his daughter's reading, would often bemoan being a father of three daughters who had "no son to carry on the name." He would often ask Gioseffi, when she was in high school, "What does a woman need to go to college for? She will only be married and have babies, so why bother with a higher education?" Gioseffi's sisters, therefore, chose secretarial courses, but Daniela was inspired by her father's struggle for a higher education. She defied the norm and worked her way through Montclair University in New Jersey by checking coats and hats, delivering groceries and prescriptions, babysitting, and waitressing to become the first woman of her Italian family to attain college and university degrees.

Daniela Gioseffi broke the mold of many women of her generation. She did not aspire to be like her mother or her Italian aunts who were all factory seamstresses and housewives—with little ambition beyond providing for their families in their Newark ghetto milieu.[31] With this, and the inspiration of both her grandmother's vivid storytelling and her father's work ethic and tenacity, Gioseffi escaped *la vita della cucina*, and yet, she managed to remain a good homemaker and cook for her family and to be an attentive mother and grandmother, while writing and presenting her books to the world. As she recounts in various essays and interviews herein, she had to overcome many obstacles after breaking free of patriarchal Italian expectations.[32]

Gardaphe believes that the struggles an Italian American female must go through can attribute to the strength of their writing:

> Italian American female writers are struggling against the constraints placed on them from both inside and outside of their ethnic culture. Add to these cultural constraints the usual issues of negotiating one's place in the vast array of English and American literary history and the struggle to find a style, a voice, a publisher and one begins to see why becoming writers is so difficult for Italian American women.

Gardaphe goes on to write that successful Italian American female writers, like Gioseffi, who have "taken on this double burden [...] [have] showed us best how to get this done." Because of all that Italian American women must reconcile to become writers, they have, in some ways, done it better than Italian American men, and without having to portray the gangster stereotype that Hollywood demands of Italian American men.

---

[31]Gioseffi writes about this in "Forging into the Mainstream Since the 1960's," included in this collection.

[32]Gardaphe, Fred. *Italian Signs, American Streets: The Evolution of Italian American Narrative* (Durham: Duke UP, 1996).

Indeed, Gioseffi's poetry is highly esteemed by other Italian American writers. Fred Misurella, Professor of American Literature at East Stroudsburg University, PA, writes of Gioseffi:

> this Italian-American writer has given uncompromising voice to the individual spirit, seeing, yearning, and deserving, yet unsatisfied. Her poetry, non-fiction, and fiction have engaged readers with humor, sensuality, and thought. Few, if any American writers of the twentieth century combine her sense of wonder in such a unique, poetic, and dramatic fashion with a realism grounded in complex daily experience.[33]

In the same vein author Josephine Gattuso Hendin, *Tiro A Segno* Professor of Italian American Studies and Professor of English at New York University, wrote that

> Gioseffi's poetic personae are not only what Emerson called "the world's eye" but also its consciousness, body, and voice. In the vivid compressions of her poetic imagery, belief comes alive as physicality. Sociopolitical oppression is experienced as felt pain or outrage at injustice. Idealism about love, creativity, and art are instantiated in the bittersweet position of the woman writer caught between the claims of family and the pull of writing.[34]

As Hendin noted, Italian American female writers examine reality without ignoring their heritage or relying on it but rather by accepting who they are and where they come from in a humble manner.

Of course, Gioseffi doesn't only write poetry, and her prose has also been commended by Italian American authors. As Fred Misurella wrote in his review[35] of Gioseffi's *In Bed with the Exotic Enemy,* Gioseffi's voice "combines the all-encompassing embrace of a Whitman with the metaphysical wit of John Donne," and she "offers a collection of sixteen stories and a novella that, page after page, maps the gulf of loneliness and frustration between individuals whose souls aspire to flight while their bodies remain firmly planted on earth." This collection begins with the short story titled "Bleeding Mimosa" (previously mentioned), where Gioseffi relates a story similar to her own experience about a young journalist in Alabama who is raped by a cruel, racist police officer, a member of the Ku Klux Klan. Her story, "Donatuccio Goes to School in America," is similar to the historical story of her father's arrival in America. Ben Morreale writes that in this story,

> Gioseffi brings to life, through the eyes of a boy, the Italian immigrants experience crossing the Atlantic at the turn of the century, and their fierce anxiety awaiting entrance to the new country. At Ellis Island the boy and his mother are to be met by their father who has come down from Schenectady. However, the boy has been infected with a fever, and he is put in quarantine for a month; the father is simply told to come back in thirty days.

---

[33]See Misurella's review of *In Bed with the Exotic Enemy: Stories,* by Daniela Gioseffi, included in this collection.

[34]See Gattuso-Hendin's review of *Blood Autumn, Autunno de Sangue,* included in this collection.

[35]Fred Misurella, review of Gioseffi's *In Bed with the Exotic Enemy: Stories,* published in *VIA* (1998).

In this story, Gioseffi has captured that anxiety that seized so many immigrants as they were examined that often many jumped into the sea upon hearing that they had to return to Italy after being bottled up in ships fit more for cattle than human beings.

However, not all the stories in this collection are so closely connected to Gioseffi's biography. The book ends with a novella, "The Physic Touch," about a three-armed man, a former circus freak, and a gorgeous prostitute—star-crossed lovers whose story is thoroughly captivating. Of the novella, Fred Misurella wrote:

> I recommend it for its strange pairing of characters, its absolute believability, and for the pathos and humor that make it one of the great pieces in the novella genre. A prostitute and a three-armed man fall in love, largely out of convenience, but as they live together and improve their lives, the love, physical at first (his third hand, after all, provides added technical dexterity!), evolves into a deeply felt affection and commitment.... Gioseffi raises the level of these two characters' lives to a high plain of passion and thought, where the conflicts of soul and body, fate and personality intersect with cool, poetic beauty. Then the final lines, a yin and yang of opposites: "Where the darkness copulates with the light, the world is born again in the dawn of every morning ... as one body pours light into the darkness of another, pours hard full lit meanings into the dark wet hollows of dreams."

As does Misurella, Morreale comes to an apt and celebratory conclusion in his review[36]; he writes that "[a]nyone interested, in the psychological novel, the historical novel, the ethnic novel and a novel that speaks to the ear, *In Bed with the Exotic Enemy* will read a novella and short stories that bring the past and present to vivid life."

Professor Mary Jo Bona of Italian American Studies at the State University of New York, Stony Brook, discusses, in her article "Recent Developments in Italian American Women's Literary Traditions," the affirmation of ethnicity that inspires many Italian American women writers, including Gioseffi.[37] These Italian American women writers "neither cast off cultural background as a provocative area of literary treatment nor solely utilize the story of Italian America as the means to explore the development of the self." There are a multitude of "American" topics that have been spun in an Italian American light by female writers of Italian heritage.

Especially in her creative work, this is what Gioseffi does: she doesn't deny her heritage nor does she rely on it. She forges a path for herself in a manner similar to Lawrence Ferlinghetti (poet and creator of City Lights Bookstore and its associated press) who said about one of Gioseffi's manuscripts, "I can see why you've been published extensively, perhaps more than any other Italian American poet. It was a pleasure to read your book."[38] Early in her career, Gioseffi was a

---

[36]See Morreale's "Eyes For Seeing Inward," a review of Gioseffi's *In Bed with the Exotic Enemy,* published in *Small Press Review* (1998).

[37]See Bona's "Recent Developments in Italian American Women's Literary Traditions" in *Claiming a Tradition: Italian American Writers,* ed. Mary Jo Bona (Carbondale, IL: Southern Illinois UP, 1999) 163–98.

[38]This quote is from a personal letter from Lawrence Ferlinghetti to Daniela Gioseffi (12 Aug. 1984) included in this collection.

finalist in the Yale Series of Younger Poets, judged by Stanley Kunitz; in The Pitt Series of Poets, judged by Muriel Rukeyser (1972); and in the Academy of American Poets Walt Whitman Award, judged by William Meredith (1975). Her poetry still has the energy that poet and former Professor of Literature at Purdue University Felix Stefanile saw in it when he wrote:

> What a marvelous energy your book, *Going On* has! The poem, "The Young Girl" is so small and so powerful. The pathos and menace of "August When Spiders Spin." "Watching American Television" with its bold mixture of anger and detail heat up the poem.... I could go on.... Your idiom is contemporary, and at the same time universal.[39]

Versatile Gioseffi has the ability to discuss growing up in a Newark Italian ghetto as fluently as she writes of AIDS in far-off Africa. Her poems become a mingling of personal and worldly experience in which the reader questions, doubts, and praises these together and separately.

Her emotional range is much larger than many other writers. Cavalieri is correct in saying that "Gioseffi is one of the school of strong epic poets. Few women take on the page like a Ginsberg or a Whitman. Sometimes her voice is full volume, full tilt, strapping, and vigorous, then it reels with tenderness...."[40] Gioseffi's own definition of good poetry is this:

> Good poetry is a heightened, imagist, surreal or plain, but concentrated use of language that *releases* emotion and tells universal truths in order to bring humans together as one race struggling with the glories of life and the horrors of war's destruction and the finality of death. Along the way, poetry constructs the idea of God as love, which is truth as beauty or beauty as truth, as Keats and Dickinson explained in their poems. Poetry solves all the riddles of life and its meanings as much as they can be solved by the human mind, spirit, and imagination. Good poetry is meant to release emotions that are universal for the purpose of sharing human experience.

Phillip Appleman, a highly accomplished poet and editor of the definitive edition of Charles Darwin's *The Origin of Species,* said, "Anyone who thinks that a poet cannot write about important, serious contemporary subjects without the burden of rhetoric should take a lesson from Daniela Gioseffi," and with this as her working definition, she is able to write truthfully about a variety of subjects.

Gioseffi fluently examines the themes of Italian American literature including communality and family. In her poem, "If You Could Keep Only One Small Purse of Things," she meditates on what the title suggests: the small things people keep in remembrance. The first stanza begins,

---

[39]This quote is from Stephanile's personal correspondence with Gioseffi (28 Nov. 2001) included in this collection.

[40]See Cavalieri's interview of Gioseffi, transcribed from *The Poet and Poem,* and included in this collection.

> there would be your daughter's picture in a locket,
> your husband's shirt with his smell nestled into it,
> some dried sprigs of lavender to sniff
> from your dead mother's garden.... (lines 1–5)

The items reflect many of the aspects of the Italian American family including children, marriage, the impact of the mother as well as the necessity of gardens and herbs.

While the speaker is able to name concrete things that symbolize meaning, it is also clear that "there's so much / you could live without" and relying on the tangible for memories is conventional, yet superfluous (lines 7–8). As the poem continues to meditate on the small kept items, the meditation turns to loss:

> Still, time slowly steals all we need.
> Finally, there's almost nothing left.
> So some of us choose to give away
> even our great grandmother's silver mirror.... (lines 18–21)

Whether things are given away or not, memory fades, and death comes. No one can hold off death, like the loss of memories, by keeping a purse of things that represent family and life. This contemplative poem grieves over the loss of family, of memory.

When it comes to tradition, myth, and allegory in general, Italian American female writing differs somewhat from the writings of their male counterparts. The allegory of Italian American female writers, and particularly Gioseffi, is a story about the role of women within the traditions as well as their desire to break free of them and *la vita della cucina*. Professor of Italian American Studies, Mary Jo Bona observes that one feature "of *italianità* [which] gives Italian American writing its distinct ethnic flavor... [is] [a]n emphasis on the strength and inspiration of grandmothers and mothers." Because this tradition has much to do with sexual subjugation, enforced wifehood, and childbearing, the allegories used by Italian American female writers tend to include a distinct physicality.

Gioseffi's poem, "Vases of Wombs," is loaded with mythical meaning through her sensual description of a woman's body. The poem is dedicated to the *Venus of Willendorf*, one of the earliest representations of the woman's body. The sculpture exaggerates the female body to exemplify pregnancy or fecundity.[41] This statuette offers the first ideal image of a womanly earth mother, and the poem continues to reflect on the feminine form through its allusions.

The structure of this poem, like the Venus of Willendorf, centers itself around the torso of a fecund woman. The first stanza begins with a contemporary feminist's mixed feelings about her female form:

---

[41]For further information on *The Venus of Willendorf*, see "The Venus of Willendorf: Exaggerated Beauty" (2006).

> For a long time,
> I've thought about this body of mine
> with agony, with curiosity, and dreams
> of caressing lovers and children.

The poem continues as the narrator reverts to the distant past for understanding: the speaker's raised arms become that of an Etruscan priestess (line 6). However, even as the speaker's arms represent an Etruscan euphoria, they are still used "to pray and protect hunters," the men who have recognized her as their protector (line 7). The next image, of hips curved like a Greek vase, is something the speaker recognizes as her own attractiveness to men because she can hear "the blood flowing through them," and she is aware of their power (line 8–10).

While the speaker values her fertile form, she condemns her feminine buttocks because: "they've held me to the earth while others fly and inhabit high shelves of libraries" (lines 12–13). Her female body is a dilemma, i.e. "biology as destiny," that has grounded her and kept her from having or writing books placed on the important shelves of libraries. In simpler terms, her body is valued over her intellect. Viewing the metaphor with a Roman slant, in Ovid's *Metamorphoses,* people who were turned into birds are those who have achieved some metaphysical state as in the story of Ceyx and Alcyone's dedicated love for each other.[42] The female speaker feels she cannot reach any ethereal state because her hips, her body for childbearing, have chained her to the earth, and yet she ends by celebrating that she has become a garden, a place for earthly beauty.

In being so planted in her place, the speaker's body is available for men to accept from it what they need. "Men accept mead, soma, / nectar from my hands, / blood from my womb, / crystals from my eardrums...." While the speaker willingly gives nourishment as a woman, the men want to enslave her like a trophy: "In return, they try to pierce the heart / that ticks between my thighs / pinning me to the bed like a butterfly..." (lines 19–21). In this sexual subjugation, men act in the same way her own form does in the previous stanza; they hold her to the earth and do not let her fly. After sexual subjugation, "[t]hese breasts and buttocks swell / until they're all that's left of me, until / I'm melted into earth and planted as a garden" (lines 24–26). The speaker and her body become fertility; she is not a whole body anymore but only the reproductive parts and the earth itself, with which she identifies, that will be asked to continue reproducing even as it is used and abused. This condemnation of being merely an object of fertility is realized through the imagery of the poem. The poet is able to allegorize the plight of the Old World Italian American woman who is purely a childbearing homemaker ensnared in *la vita della cucina* through her use of mythic allusions, even as she herself escapes into a New World mode of being a social justice activists and an author of published books.

At the same time, she does not completely reject her patriarchal Italian heritage. In "Orta Nova, *Provincia di Puglia,*" Gioseffi describes returning to her father's *piccolo villagio della Puglia* and meeting the villagers. These villagers

---

[42]For the story of Ceyx and Alcyone, see Ovid (1994).

"nod knowingly, / when in talking of you, (*padre mio*) I must leave the table to weep— / alone in the restroom, looking into the mirror / at the eyes you gave me, the hands so like yours" (lines 29–33). Gioseffi feels an internal connection with the people of her father's community, and she questions which land, Italy or America, is truly her home as many transplanted ethnic Americans born of immigrants might (line 40).

Because of the conflicted duality of Gioseffi's identity as an Italian and an American, she is able to reflect upon her dual-ethnicity through the experiences of the immigrant population that preceded her. In her poem, "Don't Speak the Language of the Enemy," she describes the perils of being an Italian immigrant during World War II in America. Posters with that saying were displayed throughout the country during World War II and the Italian native tongue or dialect was greatly suppressed. While the mother tongue is an essential language—resonating with the poetry of home and heritage and relied upon to unify people and their communal beliefs—it has also, according to Robert Viscusi (President of IAWA and professor at Brooklyn College), been referred to as "a cursed tongue" as recently as the 1980's, because of the nefarious reputation given it by the folly of Mussolini.

Yet, the Italian immigrant community of Newark where Gioseffi grew up, depicted by her in "Don't Speak the Language of the Enemy," is so inherently Italian in its daily life that forbidding its language destroys pride of family and ancestral heritage and downgrades self-concept or identity, as Viscusi also explains. Gioseffi's poem adds emotional depth to understanding the plight of the first generation Italian in America who felt displaced and persecuted, fleeing one difficulty in Italy only to gain another in America.

Lawrence Di Stasi wrote, in his history *Una Storia Segreta,*[43] about the disgraceful incidence of concentration camps for Italian Americans like those for Japanese Americans during WWII in the United States and about the destruction it wrought upon immigrant and naturalized citizens of Italian background. This stain on American history is now better known than when Gioseffi was young, but it is still not widely understood by the Italian American populace and much less so by the average American. Gioseffi's poem toured with Di Stasi's *Una Storia Segreta: When Italian Americans were "Enemy Aliens"* exhibit, which he shepherded to more than fifty states nationwide, spearheading the movement to pass national legislation which would officially acknowledge what had long been a secret of history. Indeed, on November 7, 2000, the legislation known as "The Wartime Violation of Italian American Civil Liberties Act," was signed, Public Law 106-451, by President Clinton.[44]

The images of Gioseffi's often quoted poem "Don't Speak the Language of the Enemy," exemplify the ethnic ambiance that remained in the neighborhood even when the language of its immigrant population was repressed: an old man plays his mandolin, stale bread is ladled with tomato sauce to feed a poor family, the fathers are working hard laborious jobs while poorly clad children play in the

---

[43]See DiStasi's *Una Storia Secreta: The Secret History of Italian American Evacuation and Internment During World War II*, with a forward by Helen Barolini (HeyDay Books, 2001).

[44]For more information, see *LawrenceDiStasti.com.*

street. Yet, the tone in the last stanza of the poem becomes ironic when considering that many Italian immigrants could only speak in an Italian dialect while feeling pride in their new country:

> the raggedy guineas can speak no other,
> and so they murmur in their rooms in the secret dark frightened
> of the camps where people like them are imprisoned
> in the new land of golden opportunity. They whisper of Mussolini's
> stupidity—stifling the mother tongue, wounding the father's pride,
> urging their children to speak English by daylight,
> telling each other, "We are Americans. God Bless America!"

The poem shows lucidly the difficult situation and complex mentality of Italian American communities during the Second World War. It's a main reason why the children of these immigrants never learned to speak fluently the original language of their parents.

Yet, all the poems in Gioseffi's most recent collection, *Blood Autumn, Autunno di Sangue,* are accompanied by their Italian translations. The choice to publish a bilingual collection of her works demonstrates Gioseffi's attempt to reclaim her Italian heritage and have empathy with her forbearers.

Accomplished poet, Donna Masini, professor of creative writing at Hunter College of the City University of New York, wrote:

> Empathy is what we hear through Daniela Gioseffi's poems. Hers is the compulsion to witness and report back to us. In the shadow of all the world's violence, she calls for nothing less than the redeeming power of love—erotic love, mother love, community love. Here while "chairs of state are arranging themselves in *isms* of death," these poems come as urgent dispatches....

This is a sentiment that Maria Mazzioti Gillan shares with Donna Masini regarding Gioseffi's work. These poems or "urgent dispatches" are in much of Gioseffi's writing, and they are a call to struggle against prejudice and discrimination wherever it is found.

Professor Robert Viscusi wrote that Italian Americans "need Daniela Gioseffi to recall what speaking the language of the enemy was like." We need her to continue reminding us why we should defend our ethnic heritage. In reading the works in this collection, we are reminded of the richness of our heritage and the many reasons why it should be defended and preserved. Gioseffi has done much more to promote Italian American writing and the legacy contained within it. After serving on the advisory board of *VIA: Voices in Italian Americana,* she founded the Annual $2,000 Bordighera Poetry Prize for bilingual book publication with Italian poet, Alfredo de Palchi.

Of the prize, Anthony Tamburri wrote, in "Bordighera Press Celebrates Twenty Years of Publishing: 1990–2010," In 1998, Bordighera Press launched the Bordighera Poetry Prize, which is generously funded by the Sonia Raiziss-Giop Charitable Foundation (where Alfredo de Palchi is a trustee) and founded and administered by Daniela Gioseffi. Each year a "distinguished judge" decides on the winner from a bouquet of twenty or so finalists. The winner receives a prize of $1,000 and book publication in soft and hard cover bilingual editions. The multi-purpose goal of the prize is to recognize American poets of Italian decent and, at the same time, keep alive the contract between both cultures—Italian and American—through the Italian translation. This is just one example of how Gioseffi continues to promote and inspire Italian Americans through her legacy. In 2009, she was honored—by popular vote—during October Italian American Cultural and Heritage Month on the website, *Thirty-One Days of Italians*—as the most loved literary figure of the year.[45]

This collection of prose writings by and about Daniela Gioseffi shows how she has embraced and promoted her Italian heritage while escaping *la vita della cucina*. It begins with reviews of Gioseffi's writings by prominent Italian American authors so that readers who are less familiar with her creative work can acquire a sense of it. Also, reading a selection of reviews of her work provides a sense of the community of Italian American writers and scholars. Next, the interviews of Gioseffi are useful in understanding her worldview, and in all of them, she reminds us of the value of her heritage and ours. She tells stories of her grandparents and parents, emphasizing how hard they labored and how much they dreamed. A captivating storyteller, even when discussing her multimedia performance piece, "Birth Dance" in Jean Bergantini Grillo's interview of her, she transitions to narrating her cultural heritage. Through her narratives, we come to know her ancestors, who serve to remind us of ours.

Because Gioseffi's grandparents' and parents' labors never completely fulfilled their American dreams, Gioseffi examines the world that opposed their fruition. She explains the pain of how the Mafia stereotype perpetuates discrimination against Italian Americans, and she explains how pitting ethnic minorities or subcultures against each other serves to distract the public from larger sociopolitical and economic issues. She also reminds us of Italian American forbearers who were heroic in their accomplishments—Filippo Mazzei, Marconi, Maria Montessori, Frances (Vinciquerra) Winwar, Grazia Deledda, Enrico Fermi, Enrico Caruso, Vito Marc Antonio, and Joseph Tusiani, who brought forty Italian classics into English for an American audience, to name just a few.

By recounting her experiences in the feminist movement during the 1970's, in addition to discussing her involvement with the dawning of the multicultural movement, we discover the extent of her wider audience. Her interviews are also significant, because we learn of her reasons for writing her novels[46] and poetry from her own perspective.

Gioseffi's essays represent the breadth of her knowledge about literary culture. Her personal essays discuss her experiences as an Italian American female writer in an Anglo-Saxon male culture. In essays like "The Love of Italy in Emily Dick-

---

[45]For more information on the *Thirty-One Days of Italians,* visit: <http://home.earthlink.net/~31italians/id56.html>.

[46]Gioseffi speaks about *The Great American Belly Dance* in Linda Brandi Cateura's interview of her. She speaks about *Wild Nights! Wild Nights! The Story of Emily Dickinson's "Master,"* and *Neighbor and Friend and Bridegroom* in my interview of her, also included in this collection.

inson's Poetry: Emotional Symbolism and Womanly Rebellion," she explores the relationship between American nineteenth-century intellectual culture and Italian in addition to understanding contemporary Italian American culture and its relationship to American society.

An esteemed literary critic and reviewer, in her essays about the work of other Italian American writers—Diane Di Prima, Mario Puzo, Josephine Gattuso Hendin, Lawrence Ferlinghetti, Helen Barolini, Alfredo de Palchi—as well as a compendium of her collected reviews of Italian American poets, "Fishing for Italian American Writers in American Waters," she supports the conclusion regarding a renaissance in Italian American Literary Arts in "Is There a Renaissance in Italian American Literature? ..." that was appreciated by the African American editor and author Ishmael Reed and anthologized in his *Multicultural America: Essays on Cultural Wars, Cultural Peace.* Others of her personal essays focus on complex reasons that result in stereotyping of Italian Americans as well as the truth of their accomplishments.

In the final section of this book, "Gioseffi's Interviews of Prominent Italian American Women Who Are Movers and Shakers of American Literary Arts," Gioseffi demonstrates that Italian American women—particularly Grace Cavalieri (of *The Poet and the Poem radio show from the Library of Congress*), Lee Briccetti (Executive Director of Poets House), Noreen Tomassi (Executive Director of the Center for Fiction), and Jane Ciabattari (Former President and Current Blog Editor for the National Book Critics Circle)—have succeeded in escaping *la vita della cucina* to rise above the Old World image of Italian American women and achieve prominent positions in American letters.

These essays, interviews, and literary critiques of Daniela Gioseffi, edited together in one volume, can reach a wider audience as her creative writing has already. Erica Jong wrote in a letter to Gioseffi: "My heart goes out to you and I applaud your work.... I, too, get tried of the prejudice against Italian American writers.... It's good to know that there are sisters who care and who support your struggle."[47]

Again, as Governor Mario Cuomo wrote to Gioseffi: "...Philosophical arguments and laws are not the only way to end prejudice. Works with themes such as yours can also help bring about greater understanding among different groups."

And, as Geraldine Ferraro wrote to Gioseffi: "We are both pioneers in different careers ... but I think your talent is the true gift."

This compendium exemplifies how a pioneer woman of Italian American heritage forged a way into the American mainstream culture to escape *la vita della cucina* and promote the image of her immigrant forbearers. It strives to inspire others and hopes to promote—by drawing attention to one—the voices and writings of Italian American women and men, in general. Daniela Gioseffi's example demonstrates how we have and can succeed in being accomplished contributors to American culture and its more compassionate and enriching elements and sensibilities of tolerance and understanding.

---

[47]This quote is from a personal letter from Erica Jong to Daniela Gioseffi (24 Apr. 1986) included in this collection.

PART I: COMMENTARY & REVIEWS ON
THE WRITINGS & PERFORMANCES OF
DANIELA GIOSEFFI BY VARIOUS
ITALIAN AMERICAN AUTHORS

Daniela Gioseffi on the New Mother Earth

by Valerie Puccio

The Queens College Italian American Club, 1977

Did you know that Italians are thought to be the most passionate people in the world? Anyone can tell you that dealing with passions daily isn't easy, but Italian poetess and priestess of the Earth Mother, Daniela Gioseffi, manages to deal with hers in an admirable fashion; she makes art out of them. Gioseffi writes poetry and novels. She also performs Mid-Eastern dances, plays the African lyre and the Middle-Eastern drum, sings songs, and tells stories in a multimedia performance titled "The Birth Dance of Earth: A Celebration of Women and the Earth in Poetry, Music and Dance." She has toured the country with this creation made of her original costumes, sewn by herself, her own choreography, musical compositions, poetry, and song.

Gioseffi came to the College last Tuesday as a guest of the Italian American Club in celebration of Italian American Week on campus. Her poetry-performance was held in House 26 where the audience was offered a comfortable couch, pretzels, potato chips, soda, and a radiant smile.... The warmth and generosity emanating from Gioseffi's performance made everyone feel like close friends. During the hour, Gioseffi read from her book of poetry entitled, *Eggs in the Lake.* She also read from other female writers such as Edna St. Vincent Millay, Emily Dickinson, and Sappho. She talked about her feelings, played her instruments, shared her ideas, and ended the hour with a birth dance, a Mid-Eastern Baladi or Egyptian dance of life.

Calling herself "A Celebrant of the Earth Mother Speaking in the Age of Plutonium Waste," Gioseffi preached a celebration of life through an awareness of the environment. The earth to Gioseffi is feminine, erotic, and life giving, providing food and supplying energy, as she makes clear in her poem, "The Earth is Feminine in Most Languages," which deals with the emotional freedom and creativity of the life force of women. Gioseffi believes that the female is representative of Mother Earth. She supplies the nutrients, the food, and the nurturing instinct necessary to create life.

Gioseffi understands that "all of life is erotic." She begs us to revel in life's sensual pleasures, to "feel the wind on our faces, enjoy the colorful sunset, and taste the delicious ripe peach." She asks that masculine and feminine traditions become balanced to form a universal acceptance of caring emotions and sensitivity to human needs. Men should be able to cry; women to feel strong and reasonable. To Gioseffi, Italians have always been freer in emotional expression. From their Etruscan beginnings to their Florentine and Venetian Renaissance, the Italians have celebrated a culture of art, music, poetry, and dance. They've often felt an ethnic pride concerning their romantic passions for *La Dolce Vita.* Gioseffi evokes these emotions well in her poetry performance. Her smile is full of love and genuine pleasure. Her dance is vibrant, erotic, and exciting. Her words are stirring, sharp, and real. In her poem, "You Are a Mediterranean," Gioseffi speaks of her heritage as a passionate Italian struggling to be accepted in a more somber and staid Anglo-Saxon American culture:

Nerves Can't reach
passion that spills on floorboards.
You're a wild insomniac
and want a warlock to come to you
in the night with evil magic
and say stop trying to do what is proper.
You are a bat who clings upside down
in a corner, of the daylight and flies
in the dark while the rest are asleep.
You want to assassinate memory
but you need rest from this body
that offers no ecstasy
except through clenched teeth.
No purity to reach
No virginal dawn to wait for and rape,
you pace in a ferment.
You take your voice in your arms
and rock it to sleep.

Two Reviews of *Word Wounds and Water Flowers: Poems by Daniela Gioseffi*

1. by Grace Cavalieri, 1996

When I was young, passion was not fashionable. Most women I knew were like my mother—they never raised their voices, certainly wouldn't argue politics at the dinner table—in fact, most didn't even drive a car. The movies of my childhood featured lovable, cute women who always got the man after singing and dancing their ways into our hearts. But while I was young, women writers were in the process of their own becoming, and now on the shelf of the 90s, we finally have a line-up of strength and eloquence in literature: Denise Levertov, Adrienne Rich, June Jordan, Toi Derricotte, Ruth Stone, Marilyn Hacker. The list can, thankfully, go on and on, finally too long to quote on the page; and, we must add to that list Daniela Gioseffi.

Gioseffi has been in the field for over thirty years as a peace activist, radio commentator, and poet. Her *Women on War: International Voices* (Simon & Schuster, 1990) won an American Book Award. Her novel, *The Great American Belly* (Doubleday), was optioned by Warner Brothers. Her fiction, *Daffodil Dollars,* won the Pen Syndicated Fiction Award; and among other literary achievements, *On Prejudice: A Global Perspective* (an anthology published by Anchor/ Doubleday, 1993) won the *Ploughshares* World Peace Award and was presented at the UN. Now, a new collection of her own poems is out, since *Eggs in the Lake* (BOA Editions, 1977)—her first.

Gioseffi is one of the school of strong epic poets. Few women take on the page like a Ginsberg or a Baraka, or a Whitman for that matter. The long historical poem is an ambition fueled by the stamina of the writer more in love with opera than sonnet—that kind of poet termed "athlete of God."

Fitting for its content is the title of this book: *Word Wounds and Water Flowers* (*VIA* FOLIOS 4, 1995). The work itself seems bruised by its creation, coming out of the bright blue spot of her wounds, making them something to walk through, to talk about, to use, to rebel against the void, to shake those among us who will not listen and do not care—a vulnerability that says water flowers will blossom in spite of all. The title poem is an eight-pager. It's a plea for our commonality; an attack on all who will still separate us by gender, race, etc. Those of us who "remember the 60s" will remember this kind of cry, stirring the crowd, before the crow went home to surf the web in a virtual reality.

Gioseffi's work has an obvious political agenda, yet is not reductive. It is—for a beginning description—every bit a woman's work. The lines are from the singing and dancing of women in the cadence of our ancestors who carried wheat to the Easter altars. Her Italian antecedents inspire much in the body and rhapsody of her work. It is in the tradition of an Italian quality and spirit in poetry.

There is an unembarrassed presentation of a female perspective in "The Fishblood of Woman": "All blood is red so that we can see it, / and anger is read /

so that we can know it...." Then the menopausal bleeding in the poem "Blood Autumn" mixes with the memory of autumn, the blood of a creature hunted in the autumn woods, and compares the dying of color to a woman who does not go quietly into age.

In the poem "Unfinished Autobiography" we have the biographical detail of Gioseffi's life:

> I'm a "Jersey girl" who grew up, part Polish war orphan
> part Jew
> half Italian immigrant
> daughter of a lame "guinea gimp,"
> who was a poet dying of the word, "empathy"....

From another poem ("Ruby Throated Hummingbirds Are Gone") we find the resonance of a life deeply felt:

> A wounded love sprouts like a weed
> from the watery depths,
> uncultivated,
> flowers, white and purple, bloom,
> even in these days of dying/leaves.

Gioseffi's direct address to her father, the immigrant so disparaged as a man, uses her love to become a poet, to say: "You never understood America's scheme. / Your wounded dream, father, will never heal in me, ..." So there is the heritage, "the crimson apple of being," she hands to her own daughter and to us in this poetry.

The book presents a woman who is unafraid of feminine imagery; yet, this is not a book of, singly, a feminine view. It has a male spirit; and for those who call the earth a woman, and the world a man, Gioseffi has a grasp on each. She takes on "the pockmarked earth" in a rage of power manufactured by passion. She's a warrior. However, the litany and indignity of *word wounds* (from the title poem): "Guinea, dago, spick, nigger, polack, wasp, mick, chink, jap, draut, russkie red, bastard, kike, bitch, macho pig, gimp, fag, dick, cunt, prick," could be attacked as rant. Her rhetorical verse verges on a shout at times. And to counter this criticism, we have to ask if the same voice used in the "parlor" should be the one used on the battlefield. I don't think so. In this long poem, the juxtaposing of the natural (all human, all natural) against the devastation by its opposites could not be held together within one single piece by a lesser poet. Sometimes it is full volume, full tilt, strapping, vigorous, then it reels with tenderness. All of this is found in the title poem—a bitter amalgam of personal history, political exegesis, a naturalist's prayer. Can someone do all this without tripping on her robes? Well, language still works best when in the context of strong conviction, and this is a woman at war. She has declared her cause and will use every word-wound weapon our computers can bear to make her meanings prevail.

Within this book, Daniela Gioseffi can, at once, stake various claims as oracle, innocent, free spirit, and crusader. Her poetry uses a "fairy land of angels, gods and goddesses…," and it is, at times, overly heavy with mythology. Her mission is for the ecological and against "men's tribal wars." This may be a clash of tones not all readers will like. It is mostly spectacular, vivid, and impressive. I do like the muscular approach to the well made poem. I do like the wail, the passion loosened, then a mastering, a control, combining unlike elements and making them work. I like Daniela Gioseffi's courage. I like the fact that she has declared lyric warfare in a book that shows multidimensional sides to a poetic reach. We could say she is a child of Walt Whitman and Edna St. Vincent Millay. But I am certain Thor was in charge of this wedding.

2. by Maria Galli Stampino, 1995

Daniela Gioseffi's inspiration is nourished by her being a woman and the daughter of Italian immigrants. Her poetry thus sounds diverse, earnest, and deep. It is attuned to nature (including the poet's own physicality), as well as to daily events that provoke her anger, concern, and involvement. The very title of her collection reveals the nature of these poems: *Word Wounds and Water Flowers,* the two phrases linked by a conjunction. No space separates the hurt of the wounds and the healing power of water, or—to be more explicit—the power to kill and the power to regenerate. Also, the title intimates Gioseffi's ability to exploit the musicality of words and phrases in novel ways: the alliteration of the first three nouns is broken in the fourth; then it resurfaces, surprising and delighting the ear.

Gioseffi uses a direct language, at times a stark one. She wants to stir her readers' concern and outrage over contemporary issues. But precisely because she feels an urge to act, her tone is never desperate: far from it. Not only is there room for improvement in such disparate fields as gender relations, pollution, and racism; a moral duty exists to be engaged and make one's voice heard. Here is no tolerance for complacency or denial; this book lays siege to the reader's sensibility.

These poems do not ring hollow at the core. Her attention to nature and her feeling toward the "other" among humans strike deep chords in our feelings.

Luckily her upbringing instilled concurrent ideals: the necessity to act, the necessity to write. Gioseffi does not "declare" or decline into solipsistic utterance. She transmits what it means and feels like to be a woman, a mother, a wife, a friend, a daughter, and granddaughter, a human being concerned about injustice and violence anywhere.

So the book becomes in effect a call to action, even while individual poems are a soothing recall of the past, or a vision of a better place. Similarly, words can hurt and heal, depending on use. They harm, for example, when employed as taunts:

> These are the word wounds,
> roots of mushroom clouds to rise
> from the pockmarked earth:
> "Guinea, dago, spick, nigger, polack, wasp, mick chink, jap, frog, kraut,
> russkie red, bastard, kike,
> bitch, macho pig, gimp, fag, dike, cunt, prick." (58)

In these lines, the poet's voice subsumes that of her Italian ancestors as well as that of any hyphenated American smitten by such insults. But this list—a long list to little poetic effect—lacks the power (not to mention the grace) of other passages in which Gioseffi conveys her roots.

Take a short poem like "Guilt Is a Gift That Is Given." The first stanza explains what guilt is: a "gift" passed on from generation to generation, an expression of love, caring, and blood. The second delineates the ties that bind Gioseffi to her father: blood and filial piety. Thus a central concept to the Italian American culture is brought to life lyrically to be sympathetically imagined by all those readers who might not be familiar with it. At the same time, "guilt" and "blood" are freed from the negativity usually associated with them in main stream society. It is as if a reader were able to perceive not just the positive aspects of guilt and blood, but their centrality in an American culture so close and yet so far apart from his/hers. In such instances lie the power, vigor, and fascination of these poems. They speak an American language, but they profoundly reflect Gioseffi's gender, age, and ethnicity.

A Review of Women On War

by Lily Iona Soucie, 1990

Daniela Gioseffi, *Women on War: Essential Voices for the Nuclear Age from a Brilliant International Assembly* (Touchstone/Simon & Schuster 1988. Re-issued in a new edition with a longer Author's Introduction (Feminist Press, 2003).

When I first picked up *Women on War,* I wondered what women would know about war, which seems to be a man's "game." Although I was born when World War II began, history's deadliest war, I hadn't been directly affected by the conflict, except for food rationing. Consequently, I wondered what I could gain from such a book. However, after reading it, I realize one cannot live in this world and not be affected by war.

Several survivors of World War II are quoted in *Women on War.* Natalia Ginzburg (Italy), in a piece entitled "The Son of Man," says,

> There has been a war and people have seen so many houses reduced to rubble that they no longer feel safe in their own homes, which once seemed so quiet and secure. This is something that is incurable and will never be cured no matter how many years go by.... Once the experience of evil has been endured, it is never forgotten.... We shall never be at peace again. (112)

Gioseffi's book is not only timely but essential reading. The world is at war, as Margarita Chant Papandreou points out in her article "Global Feminism for the Year 2000." Violence escalates in American neighborhoods and in other countries officially not considered to be at war. "The huge international arms traffic, the immense budgets of defense departments, the fleets travelling the world through international waters, the 40 or more local wars that are waging now: we are on a war system" (339).

Toyomi Hasimoto (Japan) poignantly captures the aftermath of war when she describes what it was like for a single bomb to wreck a peaceful and happy family. Along with her husband and three-year old son, she experienced severe injuries as a result of the bombing, leaving the child blind in one eye, the husband chronically ill and unable to work again, and Toyomi the sole support of the family. But the tragedy did not end there: she had four children after the war ended, and each one of them suffered a serious reaction from the enduring effects of radiation. In Toyomi's words:

> There are many others for whom the atomic-bomb sickness remains a constant source of pain and despair or an ever-present threat. Only people who suffer from this kind of illness can know its full terror.... It is the duty of those of us who have lived through the hells of the atomic bombings and the years of agony following them to proclaim our experiences so that war and its evils can be recognized for what they are and abolished from the earth. (216)

45

Over and over, whether from this century or another, Greece or South America, known or unknown, women have insisted that wars must end. If anyone doubts the writers' conclusion, after reading this book, the skepticism will be erased. The earth cannot sustain the brutality wars and other acts of violence say, "To sound off with a cheerful 'give me liberty or give me death' sort of argument in the face of the unprecedented and inconceivable potential of destruction in nuclear warfare is not even hollow; it is downright ridiculous" (25).

Nationalism and patriotism create many unnecessary conflicts. Several of the writers insist that these attitudes are outmoded and that a more encompassing vision must be embraced of one world undivided. Ann Druyan (USA) says,

We have to expose the delusion of nationalism for what it is, one of the early symptoms of the mass psychosis of war. We have to know what we are talking about so that no bomb salesman can intimidate us with the jargon of science or technology. (34)

Emma Goldman (USA/USSR) picks up on this theme. She says,

Patriotism assumes that our globe is divided into little spots, each one surrounded by an iron gate. Those who have had the fortune of being born on some particular spot consider themselves better, nobler, grander, more intelligent than the living beings inhabiting any other spot. (119)

We no longer can afford to see each country in isolation but must see all nationalities as part of the larger human family.

However, the patriarchal structures and values we've inherited and that dominate the world encourage compartmentalizing and are a major cause of war. Papandreou, quoted earlier, says, "The connection between militarism and sexism is of great concern to us. Patriarchy is a system of values of competition, aggression, denial of emotion, violence" (338).

Consequently, eliminating wars will require subverting and transforming such structures, making them more humane and responsive to basic human needs. But to do this, one needs to not only feel, but feel passionately.

Helen Caldicott (Australia) started the "Women's Party for Survival" because

It's the women who cry. Now I'm not excluding all mothering men. But, you know, women are very passionate, in fact, they very often drive men crazy because they're so passionate and emotional. It's appropriate to be emotional.... It's appropriate to be passionate about our survival. (291)

Not only must we feel, but we need to change our basic assumptions, find a replacement for war. Margaret Mead (USA) says that war is "just an invention, older and more widespread than the jury system, but nonetheless an invention" (134).

A new attitude about war and replacing structures that makes it attractive—to perpetuate its existence (war means big money for military contractors)—will require each of us, women and men, "all people of all beliefs, political persuasion, colors, creeds, and races" (Caldicott 34), to do the work of peace. So eloquently stated by May Britt Theoria (Sweden), "The work of peace is not reserved for politicians and experts. The work of peace calls for everyone" (65).

While the task of ending wars will involve us all, many writers quoted in this book believe that women have a particular mandate to counter the destructive course we are on. They find hope in the inroads made by women's liberation movements but realize that more and more women are needed to infiltrate the structures we've inherited, political and otherwise, without losing what has been recognized as feminine values (nonviolence, caring, nurturing, non-oppressive personal and institutional relations).

Most importantly, as Karen Malpede (USA) expresses, "We need new rites, new myths, new tales of our beginnings, new stories that speak of new options open to us. The task before us is a task of the imagination, for whatever we are able to imagine we will also be able to become" (132). Denise Levertov, an American poet, takes this idea one step further in the opening stanzas of her poem, "Making Peace":

> A voice from the dark called out,
> "The poets must give us
> imagination of peace, to oust the intense, familiar
> imagination of disaster. Peace, not only
> the absence of war."
> But peace, like a poem,
> is not there ahead of itself,
> can't be imagined before it is made,
> can't be known except
> in the words of its making,
> grammar of justice,
> syntax of mutual aid.
> A line of peace might appear
> if we restructured the sentence our lives are making,
> revoked its reaffirmation of profit and power,
> questioned our needs, allowed
> long pauses.... (326)

I recognize that *Women On War* is designed to give women a chance to speak. ...

Though there are also many male activists with a desire for peace, I appreciate Gioseffi's motives in anthologizing women's voices. They have not had enough opportunities to be heard over the years and may bring a perspective the world needs. So many female voices joined together in protest could initiate the peace Denise Levertov describes. To realize the power of such voices is indeed essential in this nuclear age.

Two Reviews of *In Bed with the Exotic Enemy*
The Fiction of Daniela Gioseffi

Daniela Gioseffi, *In Bed with the Exotic Enemy: Stories & Novella* (NC: Avisson, 1995).

1. by Fred Misurella, 1997

In a voice that combines the all-encompassing embrace of a Whitman with the metaphysical wit of John Donne, Daniela Gioseffi offers a collection of 16 stories and a novella that, page after page, maps the gulf of loneliness and frustration between individuals whose souls aspire to flight while their bodies remain firmly planted on earth. In a story called "The Exotic Enemy" Gioseffi's character says,

> Yes, I'm sixty-six ... and I know now that erotic ideas are like flashy lights turning on in heads that echo from mouths and shine up secret places, and people can be greedy in their groins and ugliness can come even from the beauty of nubile bliss. Sex can be ripped from the blood as if the body were not a house of green moss, a vase of kindness, a space for greed set alight from the dark by the glow of hand on hand.

Time passes, the flesh decays while hopes take flight, even as the human spirit continues to desire. The exotic enemy of the title is someone wanted, yet someone unattainable, primarily because of physical, social barriers that create barren spaces between us.

In the first story, "Bleeding Mimosa," a young journalist participates in the 1965 march on Selma, only to be reviled, jailed, and raped by a local law officer with no capacity for social or sexual love. In "A Yawn in the Life of Venus," a young woman rises from her bed, stretches in the morning light, and takes coffee while reflecting the various ideals and frustrations of the men and women in her life who think about her with love and desire but can neither possess nor fully encompass her. Each has different ideas, memories, and images of her, so their reflections, gathered in the narrative, form a modern, cubistic portrait of a traditional mythic, as well as erotic, image.

"Rosa in Television Land" also presents a clash between tradition and modernity. A seventy-two-year-old woman who works in a chocolate factory to support herself and her ailing sister earns more money in one day performing for a television commercial than she does in a month at the factory. But her earnings come at a price. She recites her lines ("Uma always use Ultragrip ona my dentures to enjoy my family pic-a-nicks!") before a table full of meats and foods such as her family only dreamed of when they sailed to America from Apulia. Then she watches, puzzled and horrified to see the table of sumptuous food dumped into garbage bags uneaten.

These divisions—between desire and satisfaction, tradition and modernity—recur frequently throughout this book and may, I think, form the connecting literary motif of Daniela Gioseffi's writing. Her wide range of interests—poetry, short stories, the novel, anthologies, and music, as well as active participation in ecological and social causes—animates almost all these stories, but never at the expense of narrative art. Complexities and mysteries of human character and behavior form the crux of every dramatic situation in the book, and social issues such as racial hatred, sexist behavior, moral intolerance, and bias concerning physical appearance serve as background and context for, as Milan Kundera sees it, a fiction writer's one true subject: the investigation of human character and the possibilities of human existence.

In this book, Daniela Gioseffi conducts her investigations with insight, wit, and, above all, compassion, always in clear, energetic prose. The final story in the collection, a novella entitled "The PsychicTouch," demonstrates these qualities with special clarity. I recommend it for its strange pairing of characters, its absolute believability, and for the pathos and humor that make it one of the great pieces in the novella genre. A prostitute and a three-armed man fall in love, largely out of convenience, but as they live together and improve their lives, the love, physical at first (his third hand, after all, provides added technical dexterity!), evolves into a deeply felt affection and commitment. He takes up work as a bartender, his three limbs making him famous as a quick, showy mixer of cocktails, and she attends classes in literature and writing. But one night when she goes to the bar to see him, they glance at each other as he performs and for the first time see themselves and their love in a public, commercial context that illuminates and degrades their affair. Embarrassed by a shared sense of freakishness, they revert to self-loathing and an old despair that dooms their love. Moving swiftly toward a wrenching denouement, Gioseffi raises the level of these two characters' lives to a high plain of passion and thought, where the conflicts of soul and body, fate and personality intersect with cool, poetic beauty. Then the final lines, a yin and yang of opposites: "Where the darkness copulates with the light, the world is born again in the dawn of every morning ... as one body pours light into the darkness of another, pours hard full lit meanings into the dark wet hollows of dreams."

For more than thirty years this Italian American, pioneer writer has given uncompromising voice to the individual spirit seeing, yearning, and deserving, yet unsatisfied. Her poetry, non-fiction, and fiction have engaged readers with humor, sensuality, and thought. Few, if any, American writers of the twentieth century combine her sense of wonder in such a unique, poetic, and dramatic fashion with a realism grounded in complex daily experience. *In Bed With the Exotic Enemy* gathers an important part of Daniela Gioseffi's lifelong work. It deserves the attention of all readers: Italian Americans, feminists, social activists, and, most of all, artful, literary thinkers. It is a first rate collection, and I recommend it. After all, you and I form the elusive exotic enemy of the title.

2. by Ben Morreale, 1998

Daniela Gioseffi's stories and novella *In Bed with the Exotic Enemy* continues a long writing career that brings to life a variety of experiences of the past century filled with haunting characters.

In the opening story, "The Bleeding Mimosa," she tells of a young woman who leaves her home in New Jersey to take part in the Freedom Riders demonstrations in Selma, Alabama. Within the story, she speaks of ethnic relationships not often seen or talked about.

Her vision is wide and, in "Donnatuccio Goes to School in America," Gioseffi brings to life, through the eyes of a boy, the Italian immigrants experience crossing the Atlantic at the turn of the century, and their fierce anxiety awaiting entrance to the new country. At Ellis Island the boy and his mother are to be met by their father who has come down from Schenectady. However, the boy has been infected with a fever and he is put in quarantine for a month; the father is simply told to come back in thirty days.

In this story, Gioseffi has captured that anxiety that seized so many immigrants as they were examined that often many jumped into the sea upon hearing that they had to return to Italy after being bottled up in ships fit more for cattle than human beings.

In "Beyond the Spit of Hate," Gioseffi puts herself in the shoes of a Black nursing aid caring for Mr. Helms, a hateful old man. With this story and others, she brings about a loving reconciliation of races, showing that love can be stronger than hate. The roots of this story take one back to the Ancient Greek-Sicilian philosopher Empedocles who warned the world that the struggle in this world will always be between Love and Hate.

The young nursing aid creates a plan and over a period he reconciles with the old man and a friendship develops. The young man goes on to become a doctor to care for white and black poor. In his work, he remarks, "… all pupils are black and corneas white and all eyes for seeing inward as well as out…" and concludes "when I think this way, tears come and I smudge them all over my face, making my black skin shine, washing away old Helm's spit, again and again."

There are stories of teenagers battling their sexual emotions all in portraying ethnic relations that give character to people in her stories. It is through relations (as in life) that Gioseffi creates her living characters. There are women in films looking to better their careers. Many of the stories, too, are metaphors that make us see what it means to be alive in the many varieties and problems life presents one with. In "The Psychic Touch," a man has a third arm, which is very helpful to him, but an embarrassment in life. He attempts to hide it, to no avail. He finally cuts it off.

Daniela Gioseffi is a poet, a novelist, critic, and playwright. Among her many books are *Women on War* and *On Prejudice: A Global Perspective.*

In her *Word Wounds and Water Flowers,* a collection of her poems, she evokes her grandmother:

I remember
grandma
got out of bed
in the middle of the night
to fetch her husband a glass of water
the day she died
her body wearied
from giving and giving and giving
food and birth.

Her novel *The Great American Belly Dance* was praised by Pulitzer Prize winning author Larry McMurtry in *The Washington Post,* as "filled with energy and irresistible writing."

Anyone interested, in the psychological novel, the historical novel, the ethnic novel, and a novel that speaks to be heard, *In Bed with the Exotic Enemy* will read as a novella and short stories that bring the past and present to vivid life.

Going On: Poems, a Review

by Emanuel Di Pasquale

Daniela Gioseffi, *Going On: Poems* (*VIA* FOLIOS, 2001).

Neither passive nor dreamy, Daniela Gioseffi is fully alert to life's necessities and reads on the page like a strong epic poet—a Whitman or a Ginsberg—but she can also lapse into short musical lyrics. In her latest book, *Going On*—a collection of fine-tuned lyricism and philosophical observances, Gioseffi writes:

> Now is the time of spiders, snakes, and mushrooms
> not simply pretty wild flowers, bergamot, blue chicory
> ....
> The earth is dry with dread
> like the thirst I have for love
> the touch upon my head by my dead father's hand.

Both Nature and Man/Woman are starving for life. As in her first collection, *Eggs in the Lake* (Boa Editions, 1979), Gioseffi embodies a female force. A feminist who loves men, she is a child of nature who loves the earth as Mother of All. Her music wakes us and soothes us; her philosophy stirs us: "… we grieve the gifts we are given always in transience… land can be made to blossom with fruit enough for all." Her idea of "Living Energy," so similar to Wilhelm Reich's scientific beliefs, drew me to her work: open-hearted, responsible, and all-embracing.

Her poems celebrate people and poets she has known—her daughter, friends, family—and awe of the natural world. Her daughter is connected to nature in the poem "Daphne," as are the people from her beloved father's home town in Italy. Her poems are sweet in temperament, never mean spirited though sometimes despairing and angry. There is a primordial sweetness that confirms God as living in the body and in the natural world of all of us. "I long to be free to sing with leaves full of birds / … arms become branches, supple homes for birds to sing."

Gioseffi's vision comes together in the poem, "The Plan," where she quotes from her father, Donato, a philosopher of Pulglia: "God is only the love that all of nature creates for us, and greed for unnecessary things is killing this beautiful life." The poem that follows crystallizes all the greater complexities of the poems that precede and come after it:

> The plan was for butterflies,
> bees and bats to suck among flowers
> gathering sweetness to live
> as they carried pollen, seed to ova,
> to bring fruit from need....

And, the lines from an earlier poem in the collection give a taste of her lyricism:

Bridal days and wedding nights of grace and youth
and doors opening in women...

We live in the shadows of immense hands
like death that will take our sex away....

... The last ghosts of Indians
are asking for food
in the amber waves of dying grain.

The poems must be read in their musical wholeness for full effect, but William Allen of *Chelsea* magazine was correct when he said: "Gioseffi wounds to litanize and heal." Her writing has been described by other accomplished critics and poets as "mythopoeic, visionary, healing, original and irresistible" and one cannot do better than to repeat those adjectives here.

A Review of Symbiosis, 2012

by Stephen Massimilla

In *Symbiosis,* her eleventh book, her fourth book of poetry, and first e-book (Rat-tapallax Press 2001)—we find Daniela Gioseffi at the height of her extraordinarily life-embracing career. Here fecundity and intensity, brilliancy and sincerity were created to create together. Judging from the deftness, luxuriance, and punch of her lyricism alone, one would be hard put to explain why Gioseffi is not yet quite a household name.

Still, *Symbiosis* is most arresting for its message. Seizing on destructive myths, from the Biblical claim to "dominion" over nature to "Darwinian theory" to the modern "technocratic imagination," Gioseffi counters with a call for "willful life" arising from "non-violent copulations" of cell and cell, woman and man, nation and nation, humankind and "The Big Blue Ball Wet With Sun." This vision is conceived as a mythic alternative: a return to the Great Mother Goddess "to be worshipped as in the beginning."

In confronting the sociopolitical issues that occasion her vision—school shootings, police violence, racism, imperialism, overpopulation—Gioseffi is never journalistic or self-righteous: her courage is unflinchingly honest. She recounts her own rape by a Klan member in Alabama, for instance, and in protesting the rape of the planet, she implicates self-absorbed poets as "powerful liars" who look the other way when they preach that "a poem should just be // not mean."

For all her Whitmanian amplitude and Dickinsonian incisiveness, Gioseffi joins the ranks of Neruda and Tsvetayeva as a champion not only of beauty, but also of truth. In a form now explosive, now meditative, now lyric, now satiric, now inspirational, she urges us both to face the enormity of the beast and to embrace life in its unfathomable potential "looking the tiger in the eye // within range // of still possible futures // throbbing with flowers, birds and words."

A Review of Blood Autumn

by Josphine Gattuso Hendin

Daniela Gioseffi, *Blood Autumn • Autunno di sangue. Poems New and Selected.* With translations by Elisa Biagini, Luigi Bonaffini, Ned Condini, Luigi Fontanella, and Irene Marchegiani. (Bordighera Press: *VIA* FOLIOS 39, 2007).

Daniela Gioseffi's *Blood Autumn • Autunno di sangue,* underscores the unique role Daniela Gioseffi has played in the Italian American canon and in contemporary poetry. Winner of an American Book Award and a recipient of a New York State Council for the Arts grant, Gioseffi continues to win accolades. *Blood Autumn,* a selection of new and familiar poems presented in English and, on facing pages, in Italian translation, has been named by *The Monserrat Review* among the "Best of Spring Poetry, 2006." Graced with translations by notable poets and writers, this bilingual edition not only doubles the musical range of Gioseffi's voice, but also brings together two traditions that link the deeply personal with the mythic and social in the intensity of lived experience. This collection makes clear that Gioseffi has mastered that fusion of being and poetry.

Gioseffi's poetic personae are not only what Emerson called "the world's eye" but also its consciousness, body, and voice. In the vivid compressions of her poetic imagery, belief comes alive as physicality. Sociopolitical oppression is experienced as felt pain or outrage at injustice. Idealism about love, creativity, and art are instantiated in the bittersweet position of the woman writer caught between the claims of family and the pull of writing. The poet's voice—whether passionate, ironic, or meditative—registers all, connecting the mythic and the daily. In some poems, the poet assumes the burden of judgment, of divining the proportions of feeling, meaning, and form we owe to the challenges of living. The meditative opening stanza of "Beyond the East Gate" introduces that task:

> I listen to the voice of the cricket,
> loud in the quiet night,
> warning me
> not to mistake a hill for a mountain. (28)

It is not the only task Gioseffi undertakes. An activist as well as a poet, Gioseffi takes on political strife in both the general struggle between the powerful and the vulnerable and in specific instances of oppression. She indicts the treatment of Italian Americans as enemy aliens during World War II, even as Italian Americans constituted that largest ethnic minority in the US Army. She brings a compassionate understanding to the impact of prejudice: In "Don't' Speak the Language of the Enemy":

> The poster pasted on the fence at the end of the block
> streaked with setting sun and rain reads:
> "DON'T SPEAK the LANGUAGE of the ENEMY!"
>
> But, the raggedy guineas can speak no other,
> and so they murmur in their rooms in the secret dark frightened.
> of the camps where people like them are imprisoned
> in the new land of golden opportunity. They whisper of Mussolini's
> stupidity—stifling the mother tongue, wounding the father's pride
> urging their children to speak English by daylight,
> telling each other, "We are Americans. God bless America." (36–38)

Gioseffi does not shy away from the politics of personal life that surface in conflicts between the claims of family and the pull of art. In the silence and guilt that follow leaving a daughter in the care of her grandmother, a poet-mother hopes her child will accept her poetry as a loving legacy. Every writer, and particularly every woman writer, will understand the depth contained in the poem, "Taking the Train Back to the City—for my daughter at three years old":

> What can I give you, unless
> I reach your private ears
> with poems from me.
>
> If I could push you in park swings forever through the airs of spring,
> but I can only hope, face to face
> with these cold blank windows,
> that you will not loathe whatever world of you
> is to come from the word whore in me. (52)

Gioseffi's poetic personae are registers of those intense experiences that link our connection to art with our bond with each other. In poems that take on the eternal struggles between all that is powerful and all that oppresses, Gioseffi achieves mythic power. She pits love against the force of negation ranging from violence in all its forms—from the erosions of aging and disease to death from war, gunfire or the brutality of nature.

The title poem, "Blood Autumn," is a tour de force, the work of an accomplished poet at the apex of her power. The poem uses the particular situation of a woman who hates violence joining the man she loves on a hunting trip. It brilliantly aligns the cycles of nature, human passages from youth to age, and the ebb and flow of power from male and female, on the axis of mortality itself. The poem's opening five stanzas tightly intertwine the beauty of nature with the violence of war, disease, gender differences and time. All are fleshed out in the memory of a hunt in the autumn-moment of middle age, in that season of vivid color and intense feeling before the barrenness of winter and death.

Memory of autumn, of menopausal bleeding
and blood from a creature you hunted
in the woods, oozed over a wet rock, you used
as a table in the brook, carving meat
from bone, skinning it down to red flesh,
as I squatted behind a stump, shuddering

at the killing I'd seen, crying secretly as I peed
and bled into the yellow leaf-soaked earth. I'd wanted
to go with you, in this awful autumn of aging,
I'd said I go bird watching, with binoculars
as you hunted with your shotgun.

Tired of my squeamishness,
of worries of bombs poised in silos,
warfare's germs bred in laboratories,
Chemicals stirred to deadly alchemy, genius

death—a lump flowering, a cancer blooming in my breast
to be removed next week by the surgeon's laser knife,
I wept in the hope of flesh as the deer trembled
to its death, first day of hunting season—fattened
against winter from summer's gathering, nibble by

nibble of wild berry, young shoots, lichen and wild fruit—
only to fall in a leap over the swell of forest floor,
into our dell, crunching leaves, in a flash
like the explosive splash of an osprey as it dives
into the lake to seize a fish from on high. (88)

Gioseffi's prowess in techniques of compression permits an interpenetration of nature, sexual politics, and the violence of disease, war, and the hunt. Blood flows through the human and natural world coloring life as it crests and ebbs. These dark intensities are relieved by the love that overarches the disparities between the bleeding woman and hunting man and are redeemed by the woman's acceptance of the inevitability of the winter and death that will come for them both. Her sibylline voice foretells that her man must deal with death by "controlling it," by taking life on his hunt for reassurances about his own prowess, but nevertheless understands his triumph in this quest as a necessary illusion:

I'd joined you in the hunt and saw the deer
coming toward us, my eyes and ears sharper
than your fading ones. I wanted you at seventy
to win, to feel young and strong again. (90)

The poem closes with her acceptance of her man as a fellow-sufferer from mortality and her forgiveness for his killing of the deer:

> I wept like a girl seeing the deer tremble
> and your old hands trembling, too, as you carved
> its heart out and I knew
> that you
> are saddened by your necessity,
> hurt like me by autumn's unbearable beauty. (89–92)

"Blood Autumn" demonstrates Gioseffi's extraordinary gifts as a poet able to align the many of facets of experience in a powerful celebration of life in all its tragic beauty. The collection as a whole underscores her breadth. It offers poetry of telling wit, erotic love, timely political points, and the ongoing interactions of mother and daughter that provides a plentiful feast. The Italian translations of Gioseffi's poems are by talented poets and writers whose work compels us to think of the Italian traditions Gioseffi's work suggests. Precise and elegant translations by Ned Condini, Luigi Fontanella, Elisa Biagini, Luigi Bonaffini, and Irene Marchegiani remind us of Italian traditions of storytelling. These include conveying meaning through dramatic, illustrative incident, using both the immediacy of nature and pagan, pastoral forms, and binding the real and the mythic so as to invest daily experience with larger meaning. Over the broad range of human experience and spanning the funny, the lighthearted, the sensuous and the serious, this collection offers a full menu of pleasures in both English and Italian. *Blood Autumn* • *Autunno di sangue* makes clear the enduring vibrancy and importance of Daniela Gioseffi's poetic voice.

PART II: CONVERSATIONS WITH DANIELA GIOSEFFI

Jean Bergantini Grillo

Interviews Daniela Gioseffi About **Shaking Up the Madonna Myth**

From "Arrivederci Kitchens: Four *femmine forte* shake up the Madonna Myth," *IAM: National Magazine for Italian-Americans,* 1976.

DANIELA GIOSEFFI is a surgeon of the soul. She is a poet, a playwright, and a multimedia artist whose sensitive performance-readings earned her praise as an "intellectual belly dancer."

Daniela thinks of herself as a sort of priestess of feminism. Her "Birth Dance," a combination of poetry and dance, is a celebration of the liberation of modern woman. The experience is both earthy and sophisticated, primal and intelligent, combinations that also describe *Daniela.*

The roots for this delightful mix originated, *Daniela* says, with her parents. *My father was born in Orta Nova near Bari,* she begins, d*ue to small pox contracted aboard ship, he and his mother had to bury his sister Raffaela at sea on their steerage passage journey to America. His family had been mayors and engineers of villages like Orta Nova and Candela, but my father was lame from a boyhood accident. He couldn't do heavy labor. He landed in America, a poor immigrant responsible for supporting a horde of sisters and brothers.*

He hungered for an education, and while operating both a shoe-shine business and a newspaper route, he not only put himself through college, but also won the highest awards given in science and the arts—a Phi Beta Kappa key and a Sigma Psi from Union College in Schenectady where his family settled upon arrival in America. Donato Gioseffi (called Daniel by an Ellis Island official) went on to work as a chemical engineer and played a major role in the development of the Sylvanias "Soft Light" and "the Blue-Dot for Sure Shot" for a corporate chemical laboratory, earning a pittances for his inventions patented by corporations.

His daughter remembers him as her inspiration. *From when I was very young,* she says, *he would read the classics to me ... Shakespeare, Cervantes. He had been ridiculed for his Italian accent when he came to this country, so he studied English and learned to speak it perfectly. He developed a beautifully clear voice, and I loved to listen to him talk about da Vinci, Michelangelo, Fermi.*

Her mother, on the other hand, was uneducated and unable to offer Daniela literary nourishment. What she supplied instead was an artistic bent. *My mother is your typical make-a-silk-purse-out-of-a-sow's-ear type. She painted well and has a great deal of creative energy.*

Daniela, now in her early thirties, has had her poems published in several important anthologies and literary magazines, including *The Nation* and *The Paris Review.* Her multimedia poem/plays have been presented off-Broadway, and she tours the nation's colleges under the sponsorship of a feminist talent agency, New Feminist Talent, that also handles Gloria Steinem and other prominent feminist speakers. But she is most pleased with the recent appearance of *Eggs in the Lake,* her first book of poems (BOA Editions, 1977). It is dedicated to her father and mother—Daniel and Josephine Gioseffi. Like many first-generation Italian Americans, she clings to her family roots.

61

Linda Brandi Cateura

Interviews Daniela Gioseffi About
Homage to Astarte, Goddess of Earth

From *Growing Up Italian: How Being Brought Up as an Italian-American Helped Shape the Characters, Lives, and Fortunes of Twenty-four Celebrated Americans, Mario Cuomo, Gay Talese, Geraldine Ferraro, Daniela Gioseffi, etc.,* ed. Linda Brandi Cateura (New York: William Morrow, 1987).

DANIELA GIOSEFFI is the only Italian American woman, with the possible exception of Diane Di Prima, to be widely published as a poet by established presses. Her poems have appeared in anthologies alongside the work of Emily Dickinson and Muriel Rukeyser. Her book of poems, *Eggs in the Lake* from BOA Editions, was praised both here and abroad, as was her novel, *The Great American Belly Dance* from Doubleday. For relaxation she plays, composes for, and sings lyrics to the lyre. A woman of forthright views, she speaks with no holds barred. In a world of resigned acceptance, she raises her voice in protest. This is what Daniela had to say when I taped her at her home in Brooklyn Heights, New York City, 1986. I've removed my questions for the sake of continuity.—*Linda Brandi Cateura,* New York.

DANIELA GIOSEFFI:

Women writers who are ethnic Americans, particularly writers with Italian names, have a hard time being validated in a society which is in population overwhelmingly Anglo-Germanic. For example, Frances Winwar, the novelist, was forced to change her name from Frances Vinciguerra, which translates "win-war," in order to publish in America. And what American remembers Grazia Deledda, the Italian woman who won the Nobel Prize for Literature in 1926? Not even the feminist movement has reclaimed her! And you won't find her mentioned in American texts on literary art. Somehow, if you are an Italian woman writer, you are not perceived as a particular ethnicity, or as a writer at all, in this country. No one ever says, "Gee, the discrimination has been hard for you," as they understand it has been for black women writers. There is a subtle discrimination of preference for an Anglo literary tradition here—without question. It involves a tendency to discredit other sensibilities. Helen Barolini, a writer whom I know, explains it all very eloquently in *The Dream Book,* an anthology of neglected Italian American women writers (published Schoken Books 1985). All the scholarship carefully documenting this discrimination against all "ethnic American" writers, with non-British, non-German, non-Irish sensibilities, is there, in her well-written introduction.

My writing is for the general reader. Hopefully I write universal themes. For example, one of my novels is a satire on American culture title *The Great American Belly Dance* (Doubleday 1977). The main character is Dorissa, an Italian feminist who performs all around the country, teaching everyone that the so-called "belly dance" was originally an Etrurian birth dance dedicated to Mother

Earth, in imitation of the birth contractions which bring life forth from the womb. Before the Virgin Mary came the Earth Mother goddesses of prehistoric times. Before patriarchal religion of God-the-Father took over, there was a ubiquitous earth-mother deity all around the Mediterranean Sea. Dorissa celebrates the Old Religion of Earth Goddess, whether she is the Roman Ceres, the Greek Demeter, the Egyptian Isis or the Phoenician Astarte, for whom the pagan Easter was named—the celebration of the fertile egg or feminine ovum.

I have a satiric passage in the novel where Mary, in a surreal dream vision, squats down on the earth and gives birth to a female messiah while she is performing belly-dance movements. I'm sure this might seem sacrilegious to some, but for me it is satire on patriarchal religions, which deem the female inferior. You know how we southern Italians are! We don't take the Church too seriously. We see it as operatic pageantry—having lived alongside the various popes, with their ancient corruptions, illegitimate children, massacres of the innocent, *and* what have you for centuries! As a woman, I cannot take Catholicism seriously. Christianity is one thing; Christendom is another. It is far too patriarchal and oppressive of women. There is a theory, which seems psychologically correct to me, that the celibacy of the priesthood, of men *only,* was institutionalized long after the founding of the Church, by either homosexual Medieval monks or misogynists. It was never deemed necessary in the Scriptures themselves. There is no mention of it in the Bible or in the words of Christ.

I've just finished another novel, called *Americans,* which *is* about Italians and partly about the roots of all ethnic prejudice in this country. And it is about my hope that America can overcome all such prejudices—against all groups of people non-Anglo or non-Germanic in their culture. But I wonder, as a woman with an Italian name, whether I will be able to find a publisher for it—even though I had very good reviews, both here and in London, for my other novel. It deals partly with my father's life as an Italian immigrant struggling for sustenance and respectability and the cruel discrimination he had to deal with. It also makes clear that ours is not the only ethnic group that suffered or is suffering.

Since it is not about Mafioso sensationalism, which is all Hollywood wants from us Italians, I wonder if America will be interested. We know how terribly the blacks and Jews have suffered, but the pain of Italians, Hispanics, Poles, Asians, and Native Americans is just beginning to be understood.

The largest part of our population is *overwhelmingly* English, German, and then Irish, with far lesser French, fourth, and the Italians, here, *fifth* in numbers. Besides, I read that 80 percent of Italians born here after 1960 are Italian and *something else,* as my daughter is Italian, Irish-German American. I myself am now married to a Turkish-Polish-American Jew. Perhaps this rapid assimilation explains the discrepancy in the population statistics.

The point is, as Alice Walker, a very fine black American author, has said, we are just beginning to understand "what it means to be an ethnic-American and a woman in a society that validates authenticity in neither."

Some years ago there was an article in *The New York Times* that was titled, "Bad Image Still Plagues U.S. Italians." Of course, it was referring to the Mafioso stereotype that haunts us, Hollywood-style. But you hear people who invoke the term *Mafia* using it for *all* organized crime of any ethnos, or never talking about that persistent Anglo-American institution the *Ku Klux Klan,* which did plenty of lynching of blacks, Jews, Catholics, Italians—anyone not of the all-American redneck image—right on through this century, *and is still at it!* Are Americans as upset about the Nazi party that persists among them as they managed to be about the idealistic so-called "Communists" during the McCarthy reign? The popular American mind is duped with such imbalances and prejudices.

Why does this American stereotyping of Italians persist when the great majority of Italian Americans, like other ethnic groups, are hardworking, ordinary people, not sensational criminals—when Italy has given the world so much culture, where the Renaissance took place to save the world from barbarous medieval bondage, where most of the great paintings of Europe are still housed and many were painted, where music flourished, giving the world the forms and instruments of the symphony? Italians gave birth to Da Vinci, Galileo, Vivaldi, and many great cultural heroes—Paganini, Marconi, Fermi, La Guardia, Garibaldi, and DiMaggio—and still the Mafia image persists to this day.

There is a theory of why it is so. It is the old tactic of divide and conquer. Keep ethnic groups—the "Rainbow Coalition" of American minorities—set against one another, while the wealth remains in the hands of the same few who have always controlled it. The bulk of the wealth in 1986 is still held by the same few, and it is distributed very much as it was in 1913, when my father first came from Italy. He came as part of the hordes mainly imported by profiteering steamship companies as cheap labor—to break up the labor movement, which was begun by immigrants who had arrived earlier.

It is so ridiculous for Jews or blacks or Italians or Hispanics to be set against each other when the bulk of American industry is militarized and the war-weapons industry is controlled by the executives of General Electric, Westinghouse, Bechtel, Lockheed, Honeywell, Grumman, Hughes, or what have you—all the big Pentagon contractors who are likely to blow us "ethnics" all to kingdom come with greed and the profit motive. In my estimation, *that's* the truly scary organized crime of our time: corporations like Union Carbide are poisoning people, and are not held accountable for their crimes. The most a corporation gets is a fine in dollars, which it can usually afford, but some little "ethnic" in a ghetto who steals a piece of bread is clapped in jail—and Hollywood throws up a Mafia sensational smokescreen to blame all crime on Italians and we sit and take it. Should we? How many Hollywood films are exposing the Ku Klux Klan?

It is all right for President Reagan to have advertised cigarettes, which kill, and been a television spokesman for General Electric, which builds the Mark XII deadly warhead (and to be a PR man for Star Wars) for which General Electric may get a big Pentagon contract, but Geraldine Ferraro, because she is Italian, and a woman, is highly criticized for advertising something relatively benign like Pepsi-Cola. It's a funny world, growing up Italian! I mean, Pepsi-Cola doesn't build the Mark XII warhead the way G. E. does, while it hypes with a slogan: "We bring good things to life." and the Mark XII warhead is the most deadly evil weapon in history—*sizzles billions in an instant.* Still, Ronald Reagan has gotten away, very well, with being the G. E. spokesman through the years—but look at the criticism of Geraldine Ferraro, in comparison!

That's why it is difficult growing up Italian in America! It is difficult for any ethnic group that doesn't fit the all-American Hollywood image. The American popular vocabulary is full of ethnic slurs—ugly pejoratives that we carry in the backs of our minds.

My father came from Apulia, on the Adriatic coast, across from Greece—a little village called Candela, because it looked like candlelight on a hill at night, a one-goat mountain village. His father, Galileo, was an artisan of the town, and his father before him, the mayor. In those days, a town craftsman was well respected. He handcrafted all sorts of leather goods and gold-leafed them in Florentine style. Unfortunately, when he arrived here in 1910, my grandfather found America had no use for craftsmanship. The Industrial Revolution had created the assembly-line shoe or purse. He was devastated to end up a shoe repairman, a mere cobbler, in a large city like Schenectady, and later in Newark, rather than a respected artisan of a small village community. He was soon frustrated and broken by America and put all his hopes for the American dream into his sons, my father being the oldest and, therefore, most burdened and responsible to *la famiglia.*

The name Gioseffi, by the way, was misspelled by an immigration officer, like so many names of immigrants from southern Europe, and the name became Josepha. There's no *j* in Italian. Later, my father researched the original spelling in his homeland. His Christian name, Donato, was changed to Daniel and so I am called Daniela, actually an Anglo-Saxon version of a Hebrew name. His real name was Donato Gioseffi.

His mother probably came from Naples; her mother definitely was Neapolitan. But we are not sure whether it was Naples proper or a village outside of the city. She was such a humble, gentle soul, Grandma Lucia from Naples. My paternal grandfather was a blonde, blue-eyed Italian, and there are many such. After all, the Swiss Alps are not so far away, you know—you can walk over the Alps. My father was blue-eyed, with very pale skin, like me. Some aunts and uncles are blue-eyed and some are brown-eyed. Grandma Lucia, on the other hand, was olive-skinned and had black irises, very dark brown eyes. Half the children came out olive-skinned, and the other half blonde and blue-eyed. Family legend has it that we are Greek Albanian Italians and that we are descended from the Etruscans, the truly indigenous people of Italy, the pre-Roman Italians. With our new ways of cracking language codes, I believe it has been discovered that one-third of contemporary Albania is ancient Etruscan. Many of the Roman edifices and amphitheaters we know were built over Etruscan ruins. The Etruscans were closer to the Greeks in civilization. They had a marvelous civilization. D. H. Lawrence admired them, traveled a great deal in Etruscan Italy, and wrote essays about the Etruscans and their lands.[48] Many feminists are interested in the Etruscans because their women

---

[48]See Lawrence's *Sketches of Etruscan Places and Other Italian Essays,* ed. Simonetta de Fillippis (Cambridge UP, 2002).

were equal to their men and the civilization was of matrilineal descent.

When my grandfather Galileo, who had arrived in America first, went to meet his family at Ellis Island, he was heartbroken to find that my father, Donato, was hospitalized with scarlet fever and diphtheria and that his daughter, Raffaela, had died aboard the ship of scarlet fever or diphtheria and had been buried in the ocean. He couldn't even read the English-language message an official stuck in his hand as he waited, pacing back and forth, wondering what had become of the family he had traveled miles for Schenectady to greet. "Your five-year-old daughter, Raffaela, died and was buried at sea," it said, in effect, "and your wife, Lucia, and son, Donato, are quarantined in the hospital. Come back in thirty days to see if you can meet them for entry."

Can you imagine my grandfather's sorrow—how devastated he was! Remember, many of the immigrants who arrived here diseased were healthy when they boarded the overcrowded steamships, but because of the close quarters and bad conditions aboard ship, they often contracted illness by the time they arrived at Ellis Island. Some died at sea. Very simply, the steamship companies were profiteering. They would go to the Old Country and advertise that the streets of America were paved with gold: "Buy your passage from us, and have all your dreams come true!"

What they were actually doing was overbooking, even in crowded steerage, and making big profits. They imported people like angleworms and gave them slop to eat. They gave them filthy conditions to travel in. They had to stay in overcrowded, disease-ridden cabin's below deck, with a stench and very little water to wash themselves and very little fresh water to drink. Water was rationed. On the deck, they sat in the rain and wind. "God bless America, land of liberty." They were imported like cargo by big industrialists for cheap labor to break the unions here. That is why we were brought over from southern Italy—not to give us freedom in the land of the free and the home of the brave. Sure, we were starving there, too, but at least under blue skies. At least we were not treated like worms, like cargo, like slaves. We were brought over in better conditions than black slaves, but many were indentured servants when they came. Somebody would make an illegal contract with them: "If you work for a penny a day, we will let you have a job over there." And there were a lot of immigrants using one another after they arrived. The ones who had learned to speak English used the ones who hadn't to make a profit from them.

Let us be realistic about this home of the brave and the land of the free, this land of "Bring me your poor, your tired, your huddled masses!" Though there is a grain of truth in that—hopefully someday this will *really* be the land of the free, free of ethnic prejudice and stereotyping, and maybe there is something here more hopeful than in Russia—the truth of the matter is that we were herded here to break the unions because the immigrants who were already here had wised up and started to unionize.

And there were lots of battles going on. People were still being shot down in the streets. The Vanderbilts or J.P. Morgans or Carnegies or whoever were fighting each other for control of the railroads or whatever and hiring guns to shoot labor leaders and one another, too. A lot of murder and violence was going on. As late as the 1920s in America, you still had Jews and Italians and blacks and Catholics being lynched by WASP Fundamentalists in the South. One of the few words that made its way back across the sea into the vocabulary of Italy's Italians was the word "lynch." They heard about how Italians and others in America were suddenly "lynched" for no reason, accused of nonexistent crimes.

My father was a miniature Horatio Alger. When he came here, he was lame—he had fallen in Italy and injured his leg—and couldn't speak English at all, but he graduated from Union College in Schenectady. He won honors in science at Columbia, too. This little lame Italian immigrant came from such poverty that sometimes he didn't have food to eat. At Christmas, the biggest present he ever got as a child was an orange, and on some Christmases there wasn't even an orange. He had a large number of brothers and sisters.

It's not well known that many immigrant Italians were starving in America. There was no Social Security, there were no pensions then, there was no unemployment insurance. They rarely applied to social services in any case, because there was a code of honor that you did not accept charity from anyone except your sons. This is part of the pride of the Italian male. Perhaps it's a noble characteristic. My grandfather would sooner starve than ask the government for money. So he was often starving. In Italy, you simply had a lot of children, and your wealth was your children. It was a way of life. They helped you work the land or run your business or whatever you did. Discouraged with life in America, because he was so discriminated against and had no friends or *paisani* or money, my grandfather became very ill. Then everything fell on my father, the eldest son.

You will not find American sons supporting their parents and brothers and sisters anymore. You don't find that kind of familial closeness. Two attributes of Italian American families are that the divorce rate is low and very few Italians put their old people in nursing homes. Even today, according to statistics, we still take care of our old in our own homes. In this, we are even more adamant than Jewish families, according to an article in *The New York Times,* in 1986.

As a boy, my father took care of the entire family. How did he do it? Every morning he walked six miles in the wind, snow, and sleet, and six miles every evening, delivering newspapers, and he was lame in one leg. He earned a penny apiece for each paper delivered. And he brought the pennies home to put bread on the table for his brothers and sisters. He also brought home baseballs to sew from the factory. The family sat around the kitchen table sewing baseball covers on the baseballs. Baseball was becoming a huge fanatical thing in America. It has become a multibillion-dollar sports industry. In a three-room cold-water flat, they sat every night by the cold stove, seven brothers and sisters, mother and father, sewing baseball covers at the table.

They sat in the kitchen, talking to one another, being together. My grandmother would tell them Italian fairy tales while they sewed the covers on the baseballs for a few cents apiece, or sorted and sewed other items doing whatever they could to earn money so that the family, *la famiglia,* could survive. And they stuck together and made it.

And yet my father was so anxious to be an American. This anxiety to become

Americanized on the part of many Italians is responsible, I think, for the continuing prejudice *because they have not fought to get rid of the prejudice.* How many of us kept a hold of our language? My father learned American history from A to Z, and who were the people he quoted to me as I grew up: Shakespeare and Lincoln! Not Dante, but the great English Bard, and the best President America ever produced if he'd lived long enough. He learned to speak perfect American/ English in a resonant voice. His diction was impeccable. There was no Italian accent. And while he was delivering newspapers supporting the seven children in Schenectady and his mother and father and bringing home food for the table, he worked his way through Union College, working in the library, working at night, never sleeping, almost, sleeping less than Thomas Edison. Not only did he put himself through college and feed *la famiglia* while he did it, he also earned Phi Beta Kappa and Sigma Psi. And it still brings tears to my eyes to say it.

He became a chemical engineer. Along with Dumont, he helped invent television in a garage. He invented "Sylvania Soft Light," and softened the incandescent harshness of early light bulbs to eliminate the eyestrain of factory workers. An inventor with a photographic memory, he once helped a whole class of fellow students pass an exam at Union College. The professor was a bore. The women sat knitting and reading magazines in class while the men slept. One day the professor announced, "We're having an examination tomorrow on the entire history of education."

My father went home, and sitting by the coal stove with young kids throwing things and making a racket in the kitchen (there was no other place to study), he memorized all the salient facts in the entire eight-hundred-page textbook. Next day, his friends sat near him to copy the answers and pass them onto to the next person, and so on, and they all passed the course on my father's brain. Perhaps, the boring professor deserved it.

By the way, what did my father get for the patents on his inventions working in the company laboratory? One dollar! The corporations used him. He died without a pension. Imagine how difficult it was for him, a handicapped person, to get that Phi Beta Kappa honor and to speak English as perfectly as others. Yet, he died without a pension, after all that hard work. He was too humble and easily taken advantage of.

My mother never managed to become educated and was kept "barefoot and pregnant." But she also worked in the factory, like most immigrant women. They were allowed to work in the factory, but not to have careers. They only thought of work as a way of putting bread on the table for the family, supplementing the income. They never thought of it as self-fulfillment.

I'm the first college-educated female of my whole family. When I was traveling around this country as a young poet, giving poetry readings, I met a Professor Ernesto Falbo at the University at Buffalo. He said, "Do you realize you're a pioneer? There are fewer of you than black or Puerto Rican women poets. You're one of only two known Italian American women poets in the country." He made me aware. There was just Diane DiPrima and myself in all the major press, feminist poetry anthologies of the 1970's. I was over the age of thirty when I became aware that I was the first woman in my big Italian family to go beyond grammar school. I was the first Italian American woman besides Diane Di Prima to make any sort of name in the history of American poetry.

On the positive side of the Italian ethnos is our love and respect for music, art, and food. They are also part of the warmth of the Russian peasant and other Eastern or Southern European peasants. You give all the food you have when a guest visits the house, and this is how you show your wealth—by putting your food out on the table, and you give it very generously. The kitchen is a place of cleanliness, where good things are created for the family. It is the center of the home. Even when the Italians got a little bit better off and everyone was working and bringing in a paycheck home from the factory, and all the kids were grown up, they would still meet for feasts in the kitchen.

My relatives spent much more time in the kitchen than in the living room. Unfortunately, Italian living rooms were often covered with plastic. They're such a strange thing to us. The southern Italians really didn't have a parlor in Italy, and they don't know what to do with it, so they display it like a museum for guests only. The house where my father grew up in Italy was one room with loft beds arranged around it and a brazier in the middle for chilly evenings. My grandparents lived in a tenement here, and when their children were all married, they kept the parlor to entertain guests. My grandmother was always scrubbing the floors, and everything was spotless in her house. On special occasions the family would gather there, and my grandfather would have his mandolin leaning against the wall and he would sing and play, and the family would join in the old songs. As he played, my grandfather would have some of his homemade wine, which he kept in a bottle in the icebox, with the ice chunk melting in a pan. And still my grandparents would have starved in their old age if my father hadn't helped them, because they had no Social Security or pensions. There was no welfare, and they'd have refused it. They wouldn't think of asking anyone but their son for charity.

Perhaps the Italian who has contributed the most to American political society was an early immigrant, a writer, and a close friend of Thomas Jefferson. His name was Filippo Mazzei. Translated into English, his work was read by Jefferson and had a big influence on his thinking. Mazzei's statement, "Tutti gli uomini sono di natura ugualmente liberi ed indipendenti," which translates, "All men are by nature equally free and independent." It's the foundation of democracy and was echoed by Jefferson in the Declaration of Independence. I think it's important for us to remember Filippo Mazzei, who influenced Jefferson, and the architecture of Monticello, too. We need to know that many of our democratic ideals were part of Filippo Mazzei's writings. Yet, do we ever hear of this early, influential, Italian immigrant in our discourse of American history?

Dina Di Maio

Interviews Poet, Translator, Author, Teacher— Renaissance Woman: Daniela Gioseffi

Published in *The Small Spiral Notebook: A Venture into Something Literary,* 2004.

DINA DI MAIO [DD]: I want to preface this interview by saying that as an Italian American female writer from New Jersey, I appreciate what you've been through and what I've learned from your poems. There isn't much out there in the way of Italian American literature though this is thankfully changing thanks to writers like you who paved the way, but how do you see the future of Italian American literature?

DANIELA GIOSEFFI [DG]: I don't think of what I write as "Italian American literature," *per se,* but universal poetry and prose for any reader. Yet, I am an American writer of Italian descent, and some of my works hinge on themes having to do with that heritage, but most are universal in spirit. At the same time, I kept my Italian surname rather than *Americanize* it to make a sociopolitical statement of pride in my ancestral heritage, and I've tried to help the community of Italian American writers to overcome the cruel stereotyping that has plagued Italian Americans in the media. I've served on the board of *VIA: Voices in Italian Americana* magazine as an advisor, and I founded the Annual Bordighera Poetry Prize, which is the only national publication prize for an American poet of Italian descent. I present it at Poets House in November of every year with Alfredo de Palchi. As a trustee of the Sonia Raiziss-Giop Foundation, Alfredo de Palchi co-founded the prize with me by supporting it with funding. There is a $2,000 prize each year shared by the poet and the translator who puts the Italian American poet into Italian, and there is bi-lingual book publication as reward, by Bordighera Press, the only press especially for writings by Italian American's in the USA. It was housed at Purdue University in West Lafayette Indiana, but has now moved to the University of Florida at Boca Raton with its editor and publisher, Anthony J. Tamburri.

There is currently a Renaissance of Italian American writing in America, and our women and men are blossoming forth with many books. There are many publications and activities, readings and organizations. Myself, Sandra Mortola Gilbert, Diane di Prima, and others have succeeded in paving the way for a whole new generation of our women writers, and Mary Ann Mannino of Temple University in Philadelphia will bring out a book of essays about that blossoming from Purdue University, 2003.[49] There are many works and writers to be found at *ItalianAmerianWriters.com,* which I founded, and much activity happening at the Italian American Writers Association (IAWA), too. There are several links to be found at *ItalianAmericanWriters.com,* including a large bibliography of our writings. There really are many books and works by writers of Italian descent flourish-

---

[49]See Mannino's *Breaking Open: Reflections on Italian American Women's Writing* (West Lafayette, IN: Purdue UP, 2003).

ing now. But I made my start in the mainstream of American literature, publishing in *The Paris Review, The Nation, Ms., Poetry East, Prairie Schooner,* and with presses like BOA Editions, Ltd.—an important, mainstream poetry presses—and with large New York publishers like Doubleday and Simon and Schuster. It certainly wasn't easy when I started publishing in the late 60's and early 70's, with such a long syllabic Italian name, but there are many writers of our background publishing now, and you'll find them on *ItalianAmericanWriters.com.*

[DD]: You've done so many things, including poetry, translations, plays, novels, teaching, and performance. You're probably best known for your poetry. What do you consider yourself?

[DG]: I've been a "jackass of all trades," or "a diamond of many facets," depending upon how you want to look at it. (Laughter.) I started as an Equity actress playing in Shakespearean and other classical dramas—touring with The National Players of Washington, D.C., all over the country. My MFA is in World Drama and playwriting. I've been a dancer and a jazz singer, professionally, touring and performing. I'm a painter and visual artist, too, part time. I've sold paintings and had shows. I started as a "performance poet" in the early days of Soho, and won a New York State Council for the Arts "Creative Artists Public Service Program" grant with which I created the First Brooklyn Bridge Poetry Walk in 1972—a multi-media event co-opted by Poets House since (and without giving me credit, too, I might add).

My first publication of note was a novel from Doubleday that was also published in Zagreb, and in London by New English Library. I toured all of Great Britain and her BBC radio and television stations discussing it with interviewers—a feminist satire titled *The Great American Belly Dance.* It was great fun and hard work being a novelist and a playwright, too, for awhile.

But first and foremost, I consider myself a poet. I've given thousands of poetry readings around the country and on National Public Radio, and I enjoy writing poetry better than anything. I've published four books of poetry, with BOA Editions, Via Folios of Bordighera Press at Purdue, and with *Rattapallax.com,* but I wish I'd spent more of my creative life concentrating on poetry. I think one is forced by our culture to focus very roundly on one form of art in order to be very well known in it. One isn't allowed to be a Renaissance person in our time. One is forced to specialize, yet I've had the varied experience of seeing my plays performed, my fiction published, reading my poetry far and wide and teaching in every sort of situation from public school to prison to university. I've spent a good deal of time writing criticism and publishing it far and wide, too, but poetry is my first love, so I like being called a poet. I've read poetry from Riker's Island House of Detention to the B.B.C. at Oxford. I've really released myself from an ivory tower and seen the world at every level and from many different points of view, from international book fairs in Barcelona or Miami to readings in Soho to Harlem or Scarsdale or the Academy of American Poets. I think it makes for a much broader view than being an academic poet alone—though I've worked in colleges and universities, too.

[DD]: You've written a lot about prejudice and ethnicity as well as race. You also worked as a journalist in Selma, Alabama in the 1960's. What was it like there and how do you see things in the U.S. in the 21st century?

[DG]: I have much despair about the current political situation. It seems that the current US administration is undoing so much of the good that was done in past. I was in Selma, Alabama in 1961, and the Deep South was not integrated then, and neither was television. It was a scary situation. I was menaced and abused by the Ku Klux Klan for integrating Selma's WSLA-TV station. There was a burning cross on the lawn one morning after I appeared on an all black gospel show announcing Freedom Rides and Sit-Ins as an intern journalist. But, the prejudice and cruelty I witnessed and experienced and the prejudice my father suffered as a young immigrant called "a guinea gimp"—drove me to fight against prejudice and to write *On Prejudice: A Global Perspective,* which won a World Peace Prize in 1993 when it was published by Anchor/Doubleday. My own experiences are written of in my short story collection titled *In Bed with the Exotic Enemy,* Avison Press, 1997. Also, "The Bleeding Mimosa," based on my experiences in Selma can be found at my website, *Gioseffi.com.*

[DD]: Your poem, "On Top of the Empire State," talks about a love/hate relationship with New York. I certainly feel this hate/love relationship with New York City as I imagine many people do. At the same time the city both welcomes, and it also excludes. Do you consider yourself a New Yorker, or are you still a "Jersey girl"? Why?

[DG]: Both really, as I've spent half of my life, mostly the first 24 years in New Jersey, and then 30 years in New York City, with a stint back in New Jersey in the Kittatinny Mountains way Northwest, near the Delaware Water Gap. I love the woods there, but I guess I'm really a New Yorker most of all by now, after over thirty years living here among the poets and the literary community. There is nothing like the international character of New York and her rich cultural life anywhere else on the planet. There is so much to part take of here. It's overwhelming, and yet, I love the woods, wild life, hiking, birding, sitting on a mountain ridge and watching the hawks fly. Waking to the songs of birds! When I'm in the city, I miss the country and visa versa. I feel a kinship with Jersey poets though, and so I founded *NJPoets.com.* So many poets have lived in Jersey or been born there from Allen Ginsberg to Stephen Dunn, Gerald Stern, Robert Pinsky, John Ciardi, Alicia Ostriker, C.K. Williams (who was born in Newark like me), and the list goes on and on. Even Norman Mailer was born there, and of course, Stephen Crane and Philip Freneau. Walt Whitman spent his last years in Camden. New Jersey is the Poetry State as I call her on my website of Jersey poets. When I lived in Northwest Jersey for a spell, I founded The Skylands Writers and Artists Association, and hosted readings with the help of the NJ Council for the Humanities. There plenty of poetry going on in that state, but no place is a rich in writers as New York City, I don't think. I love living in Brooklyn Heights were so many writers from Norman Mailer to Henry and Arthur Miller, W.H. Auden, Buckminster Fuller, and Flannery O'Connor have lived. I believe it is the prettiest part of the city, a tree-lined village of brownstone houses, which made up the first suburb of Manhattan. I see the East River, the Statue of Liberty, and Ellis Island where my father landed from Italy in 1913—from my roof deck. It is a fantastic view of the skyscrapers of Manhattan from here, and I think of my father's name inscribed on the Immigrants Wall of Honor at Ellis Island and realize its ironic that I can view that Island of Tears, *Isolde della Grime,* from my roof deck everyday or from the Promenade with its view of the East River and the great sweep of The Brooklyn Bridge—Eighth Wonder of the World. Seeing that *View of The Bridge* as in Arthur Miller's play, I suppose inspired me to create The Brooklyn Bridge Poetry Walk. I read Lorca and Mayakowsky's poems about her and Whitman's poems "Stand Up Towers of *Manahatta*" and "Crossing Brooklyn Ferry." These had their effect on me, and I feel very Chauvinistic about Brooklyn Heights, my home town for so many years now. Of course, Walt Whitman lived here too and worked on *The Brooklyn Eagle* newspaper, which still exists and publishes here.

[DD]: It's obvious in your writing that your father was a great influence on you, more so than your mother. Do you think that's true and if so, why? Do you think it has to do with feminism in a way? Maybe that you admired your father for certain things he was able to do that maybe at the time limited your mother being a woman?

[DG]: Yes, my father was the educated one who loved to read. My mother worked hard in factories as a seamstress, and like all my Italian Aunts, she never even went to high school or learned to drive a car or write a check, but my father worked his way through Union College and Columbia University, achieving Phi Beta Kappa and other honors. He delivered newspapers and shined shoes to do it, but he was a great lover of reading. I guess I chose to identify with his accomplishments rather than my mother's menial labors. He was the one who could do things out in the world, where my mother was homebound to female duties. He read me the classics Cervantes, Shakespeare, Dante, Rabalais. I sat at his knee at ten years old listening to *Romeo and Juliet* and *Don Quixote,* read with great histrionics, Italian passion and operatic feeling. He inspired me to want to write, and his compassionate nature has inspired the themes of my poetry.

[DD]: You're very active in supporting writers. You have websites for Italian writers, New Jersey poets, and women. Tell our readers a little about Skylands Writers and Artists Association. What is it, and why did you found it? What do you hope to accomplish with these endeavors?

[DG]: I've already said something about these endeavors, but I can add that I enjoy bringing writers together and facilitating their networking and enjoying each others' works. As artists we often have to be entrepreneurs of the arts and create our own opportunities and networks in order to make art happen. I worked early on for The-Poets-in-the-Schools movement. I was a charter poet with Poets-in-the-Schools, Inc., and I also worked for Hospital Audiences, Inc. bringing poetry and poetry workshops into public schools, prisons, senior centers from an early age. All that sort of communal activity inspired my founding literary prizes and running a not-for-profit organization as well as founding web sites for writers when the internet began to flourish.

[DD]: One of your poems will be engraved on an artist's installation on a renovated wall of Penn Station this year. When will that be done and which poem was chosen? Did you get to choose it?

[DG]: I believe it is already finished, but I'm not sure the installation is open for viewing yet. I haven't yet seen the marble etching myself, but it's in a newly renovated area. We'll have an opening soon in the Jersey Transit area of The 7th Ave Concourse of PENN Station, as part of an installation by Larry Kirkland Studios. It suits me to be etched in marble between New York and New Jersey, sort of symbolic of my life in transit and my verse is etched there with Walt Whitman's and William Carlos Williams's. Kirkland chose lines from the first poem in my first book of poetry, *Eggs in the Lake,* BOA Editions, Ltd. 1977, titled "Beyond the East Gate." It begins,

> I listen to the voice of the cricket,
> loud in the quiet night,
> warning me not
> to mistake a hill
> for a mountain....

Spiritually speaking, it's important not to mistake the hills for the mountains we have to climb in our lives.

Turning sixty was a mountain peak moment, and I've started down the other side of the mountain, but I still work and write and have dawning horizons to travel beyond. I've just published a new electronic book of poetry titled *Symbiosis* with Rattapallax Press, and it's available from BookSurge.com. That was a really new venture for me, but the future of poetry is on the Internet.

[DD]: Thank you for this interesting interview, Daniela.

[DG]: *Grazie* for your interest, Dina, and all good wishes for your new electronic magazine. *Auguri sempre* with all your endeavors.

Grace Cavalieri

Hosts Daniela Gioseffi on **The Poet and the Poem**

Transcribed from *The Poet and the Poem* Webcasts from the Library of Congress sponsored by the National Endowment for the Arts and the Witter Bryner Poetry Foundation, 2008.

GRACE CAVALIERI [GC]: This is *The Poet and the Poem,* from the Library of Congress, and I am Grace Cavalieri. My guest is Daniela Gioseffi. And she's the author of *Blood Autumn*; that's her sixth book of poetry, and fourteenth in all. Here she is, with an opening poem.

DANIELA GIOSEFFI [DG]: "Music Is a Child of the Grass"

> Your skin is translucent in the still air of this room.
> Clay is prerogative; eyes are derivative.
> We live in the shadows of immense hands
> like death that will take our sex away.
>
> Bridal days and wedding nights of grace and youth
> and doors opening in women.
>
> Music is child of the grass
> and teaches us the cost of frostbite.
> We can't separate the misunderstandings
> or wash dishes in the music box.
>
> We talk and spend the word on our burning hands.
> A cinder of a joke catches in our throat.
> You laugh to hold onto the hurrying waters.
> A fern is a fan that resembles a rainbow
>
> and the last ghosts of Indians are asking for food
> in the amber waves of dying grain.

[GC]: An American classic, Daniela Gioseffi. We are on location, in New York, in her beautiful studio, surrounded by the proper accoutrements for Daniela: her own paintings, her own drawings, her own sculpture, her books, the memories of all the great poets she has known, including Allen Ginsberg.

And I would just like to say that Daniela is the pre-eminent woman, literary activist, in America. What do you think I mean by that?

[DG]: Perhaps it has to do with the fact that I did an anthology called *Women on War: Essential Voices for the Nuclear Age from a Brilliant International Assembly,* and I did win the American Book Award for that, because it was the first international compendium of women's writing against war. And because I was a civil

rights activist from the age of twenty, when I was abused by the Klan. Also, I edited a world compendium of literature called *On Prejudice: A Global Perspective.*

[GC]: I remember that very well, and I think that what I've come to thank you
for is changing women from victims. So I'm here in your presence to say that's
something I want to go down in history with your name: you changed women
from victims to visionaries, and you're still doing it.

[DG]: I know that you too have been a proponent of women's rights with your
poems about Mary Wollstonecraft, and I've become very interested in free thinkers in particular. Right now, I'm working on a book about Emily Dickinson, who
was really a free thinker in her time. She resisted all of the born-again Calvinist
Puritanism of her day, and so I feel in the tradition of great American women
poets, with you, in that we are trying to see women as visionaries, and pay attention to their visions rather than just to their oppression, which we all know about.

This is a poem that I've written more recently. It doesn't exactly have to do
with that theme, but it does have to do with writing poetry, in general, and I think
it's something that most poets can identify with.

"Rejection Makes Wings with Each Little Death It Offers"

I've know rejection as much as you, and love
we've wanted escaped on a winged horse
who always flies higher exceeding grasp.

We've reached for love with words,
longed for love, wanting to live forever in books,
enjoying the attempt in those brief moments
when we knew we were alive. Words fell
into music that brought smiles to those
who love nuance, more than loud sound that blasts
the mind with dance. Yet, what we've swallowed of love
sticks in our throats with glue of longing, as love
happens only in moments that pass like Zen ripples
over our bodies growing old.

Eyes of envious gods peck at our moist
flesh; so we're not allowed to live forever,
but hope, perhaps, our songs could live on after us
to comfort mortality in new lover's eyes.

Some days we feel our words are mere trash
sitting at the curb in the rain, waiting to be collected
before it spills into the gutter and runs down
drains at the ends of streets into nowhere.

Most of the time, we're trying to love, and not loving,
but we're trying, and when we stop trying, we feel dead,

even as songs that live sting us with memories of lovers
who are gone with their words living on in longing for love,
so good, so pure, so full, so erotic with touch, once felt,
that it flees onto a page, and up flying higher
after that winged horse who always goes higher,
up and away into the land of Pegasus green pastures
where we can never go
until we meet our end chasing
after that heavenly tail.

[GC]: The voice of Daniela Gioseffi! I'm Grace Cavalieri. Did you hear the line, the music, the image, the scope?

Daniela was a dancer. She was a singer. She is an artist who has been on the stage, and I think all of that comes to the fore when I hear her work.

We want you to know that *Blood Autumn* is coming out from *VIA* FOLIOS, Bordighiera Press, this year, 2006. She has an e-book, titled *Symbiosis,* and many other books—*Women on War,* was issued again in new edition. Is it out now?

[DG]: Yes, it's in an all-new edition from the Feminist Press with all added writings, especially from the East and the areas of war that weren't covered in the first 1988 edition; Simon and Schuster did the first one from Touchstone, and now the new one is from the Feminist Press at The City University of NY, with all-new revised writings and a thirty page introduction to the world situation as it is today. I've added much more international writing, because there's much more translation now than there was in '88. And, we know a lot more about the women writers of other countries. We still don't know enough, but we know a good deal more than we did in 1988.

[GC]: And I know that you won a PEN Syndicated Story Award. It was for "Daffodil Dollars." You've written novels; you've written stories; you've written e-books. How do you manage to venture into so many paths swirling through various literary genres and not get vertigo?

[DG]: I suppose, I really don't think about it very much, because I started with an MFA in theatre and drama. My first pieces were plays. Then I went from plays to multimedia poetry for the stage. My first grant from the NY State Council on the Arts was in performance multimedia poetry. I created a stage-poem called "Care of the Body." It had dancers dressed as anatomy charts doing yoga while images flashed on a screen behind them, and a long poem audio played about the insane things humans have done to their own bodies through the ages, Egyptians binding their skulls, Chinese women binding their feet, Ubangi lips, etc. That was my first staged multimedia poem. I won a grant award in multimedia poetry. That encouraged me. Then I had a baby daughter, and found I couldn't go to rehearsals so much. I started writing poetry for the page at home.

[GC]: *Vagina Monologues* was really preempted long before; they just didn't know that you were way ahead of the game. Your writing has always been about the rebirth, replenishment, of women, and you use the body image succinctly to make spiritual points. There's a great deal about your work, however political, which is—as I say—deeply sexual. Is that what the critics say about you?

[DG]: Yes, but they say erotic and sensual without ever using any four-letter words. So it's erotic, but not what I would call "sexy," "dirty." Because I think the word "sexy" is an abbreviation of "sexuality." And so I'm more concerned with birth and death and how it's related to the body and how we are sensual creatures. We live through our senses; we have no life without seeing, touching, feeling, tasting, hearing.

[GC]: I feel that sensuality is the opposite of pornography because pornography is dehumanizing, and, as you say, sensuality is sending the poem out into the world with all of its faculties, its hearing, sight and smell. And we're going to *hear* another, right now.

[DG]: I think, after that discussion, I should read a poem called, "The Sea Hag in the Cave of Sleep." It's a longish poem of about six minutes, but it epitomizes everything we've just been talking about.

    "The Sea Hag in the Cave of Sleep"

> *For all the bold and bad and bleary*
> *they are blamed, the sea hags.*
> — James Joyce, *Finnegans Wake*

Words whirl her round in pools.
I cling by my teeth, grinding mountains.
She floats. I scream. She drops
through an eternity of light.
She floats again. I fall
calling for animals to warm her,
pleading with trees to feed me.

    Darkness fills her like a carbohydrate.
    Ponds ooze; crickets drone in black space.
    A snake slides over a rock;
    a seed is dragged to another grave.
    Human voices hum behind the stones;
    a vast lonely conscience
    strains to give itself a name.

The cave of sleep opens as she spreads her legs.
The father enters the iridescent dark
    from which he came.
Blocks of ice fall from his aging flesh. She turns to him

to marry him and be his mother again.
       When she turns again
she is his son. The shine of his skin slides
down her throat. Seaweed glides through my limbs.
       Kisses.
Kisses. Land and water come together
       in the mud of our lips
crawling with tongues that give touch to words.
He swims into me in clouds of semen.
Babies cry in our mouths. We float from the warm well
in aboriginal kisses.
       Lizards nestle in bushes
       hurting and loving leaves;
              sea birds peck at tortoise shells.
       She feels how wet the earth is,
       nearly all water.
       Since she first bled
       there's been a passion finer
       than lust, as if everything living were
            moist with her.
She knows the language of leaves
as an animal blessed with it.

       In the trees is a clue to everything
       and a happy one, like the genesis
       of estrogen. Ever since
       the first woman bled, plants cry when
       animals are murdered; hands think
       as bees emoting sweet sweat;
       apples are made for eating;
       even mathematics is glandular;
       an algebra of feelings.
       Only wars are waged in the guise of pure perception
       as though flesh were an alloy of aluminum,
       or an isolated element.

She takes off her dress;
she lifts off her breasts;
she has a talk with the sparrows
who inhabit my chest.
She is divided by contrary loves I have taken in.
When I open her legs a river of contradiction
       flows from me.
Her limbs are estuaries rippling toward my stomach.
She downs inside myself
longing for a god to speak to her from her lover's
       tongue,
as they explode together in whirlpools
       of sperm and ova
spinning against the silence.

When the baby came down out of her,
it felt thick between my lips,
squeezing out erect life. Its belly
passed her clitoris as it came with
its cries of semen squirting from me.
As its toes slid out,
I was female again.

A vast landscape accepts her with silence
as if it were my private garden
to gather stones from her sleep.
The phantom of age descends the staircase!

In the middle of the afternoon,
when light is blinding,
I am looking for a man with arms,
        tree-trunks.
fingers, branches to turn her nipples
green as spring buds. She waits outside myself, for him to welcome her in.
Or is it sleep, a peace deep as death,
she wants from him?
She puts on feathers like a bird
or chorus girl. He can't know which.

If he comes to her bed,
she'll be an orgasm of birds singing in wet leaves.
The mouth of my dream will be open forever.
I'll burst with a child, time hurdled from her throat.
She will paint a song beneath my eyelids
to sing into his sighs:

> *Down by the water*
> *silver-haired witches are dancing,*
> *down by the water,*
> *tossing their curls.*
> *Their breasts are eyes*
> *from which the sea rises.*
> *In their mouths the sea cries.*
> *They are kicking the sand*
> *made from our bones.*
> *Silver-hair witches*
> *down by the water*
> *singing and dancing,*
> *playing with bones.*

We take for each other
the place of absent gods.
We bargain for the eyes of fish

to swim in an underground stream
longing for no death.

These are our plum pits,
petrified and strung.
These are our beetles gleaming in coal.
We have come shining in ice from mud
trailing seaweed in our wings of bone.

We read; we write books;
from the deep spring of orgasm flowing in the flesh,
we erupt in cataleptic fits
as faith from the insane.
We will invent love until the sea closes in.

The phantom of age ascends the staircase;
a vast landscape accepts me with silence;
I gather stones from her sleep.

She has knitted him a shawl
and come to the frayed ends of history.
His fingers are no longer primal myths kneading her.

Sea and shore mix in one giant sex.

In the index of my womb, I find her face.
She is no spider queen after all,
She is a green beast with arms of sorrow.

Her whole body is a phallus.

I came out from between my own legs
into this world.

[GC]: That was called, "The Sea Hag in the Cave of Sleep." And that proves to us that feminist writing is not male bashing. Feminist writing and political writing do not have to be polemical; they can be lush. They can be filled with sensuality, and that's the interesting thing about your work, and I think where you have been the leader of a certain movement in America. I've been watching this for some time, and do you think I'm on the right track when I describe you?

[DG]: I feel very flattered by what you're saying and also very understood. "The Sea Hag was written for the stage" and first performed at the Cubiculo by actresses, directed by Maurice Edwards. I feel very good to hear you say what you've just said, because what I was trying to portray in poetic terms is the self-actualization of the woman: how the woman gives birth to herself, how we as individuals all give birth to ourselves, and how the male and female are symbiotic in their relationship.

[GC]: Is that what your e-book, *Symbiosis,* is about?

[DG]: Yes, very much about *symbiosis,* the male and female in cooperative balance as creators of life. New life ought to come from love. Because for me, as a free thinker, there is no god, but love, no anthropomorphic deity, and as Emily Dickinson said, "I loathe dogma." For me, to just look at the true nature of creation is religious experience: the beauty of plants and trees, the symbiotic relationships of biological life, for example, the lichen made of cooperating fungi and algae, and on up the ladder of creation to man and woman as makers of children. All the lessons of nature. They're there, and that isn't to say that there isn't the vultureism of nature, too. We need to be hard-nosed about it; we can't just think of pastorals with pretty flutes and dancing children. There's the need for bio-diversity and the wondrous phenomenon of atmospheric balance, and photosynthesis that gives life to all on earth. I just think that when we view the glory of nature, we don't need the dogma of religions, because nature teaches moral lessons and true emotion helps us know what's good and kind. Emerson says as much in his essays.

[GC]: Ah, yes. Let's hear another poem to that effect.

[DG]: Okay. Here's one that says something especially for us poets, Grace:

Rejection Makes Wings With Each Little Death It Offers

I've know rejection as much as you. The love
we've wanted escaped on a winged horse
who always flies higher exceeding grasp.

We've reached for love with words,
longed for love, wanting to live forever in books,
enjoying the attempt in those brief moments
when we knew we were alive. Words fell
into music that brought smiles to those
who love nuance, more than loud sound that blasts
the mind with dance. Yet, what we've swallowed of love
sticks in our throats with glue of longing, as love
happens only in moments that pass like Zen ripples
over our bodies growing old.

Eyes of envious gods peck at our moist
flesh; so we're not allowed to live forever,
but hope, perhaps, our songs could live on after us
to comfort mortality in new lover's eyes.

Some days we feel our words are mere trash
sitting at the curb in the rain, waiting to be collected
before it spills into the gutter and runs down
drains at the ends of streets into nowhere.

Most of the time, we're trying to love, and not loving,
but we're trying, and when we stop trying, we feel dead,
even as songs that live sting us with memories of lovers
who are gone with their words living on in longing for love,
so good, so pure, so full, so erotic with touch, once felt,
that it flees onto a page, and up flying higher
after that winged horse who always goes higher,
up and away into the land of Pegasus green pastures
where we can never go
  until we meet our end chasing
  after that heavenly tail.

[GC]: There's some Aphrodite in you, too. Let's have some more poetry. Set it up for us.

[DG]: Speaking of Aphrodite, that gives me a very good prompt. This is a recent poem, written many years after "The Sea Hag in the Cave of Sleep," and of course, I got the idea of sea hags from *Finnegan's Wake* by James Joyce, and that of course was a monologue, something you'll understand as a writer of plays. That was a very long monolog, and actually it was first produced as a play on stage, "The Sea Hag…," with three women with one old, one young, one middle-aged, all wrapped in the same seaweed costume as one three-headed woman saying the monolog. Here's a recent poem, just written last year, called:

"Old Aphrodite Rises from Her Porcelain Tub."

She thinks of how easily supple rose petals bruise,
how quickly flowers wilt. Naked,
kneeling in the tub, her bottom
rising as she bends, trying to rise –
she doesn't feel erotic, but assailable.

Does her aging body spurn her?
As she kneels balancing carefully –
to rise slowly with breasts hanging forward –
afraid of falling alone in her bathroom
where no one would hear her –
she doesn't feel sensual, or sensuous,
as she used to. She doesn't dream of sex,
or passion, ardor, or orgasm.

She remembers a news photo of a woman
kneeling as she's stoned by angry men, a story
of a woman made to kneel by her rapist,
a suppliant virgin sacrificed in ritual,
a woman bent over river stones alone
washing clothes – surprised by her violator,
a woman in a motel

kneeling over, dead in a pool of blood
as she grips her innards with the pain of an illegal abortion.

She doesn't dream
the substance of love poems
as she kneels and bends –
naked now and old – thinking
of all the women who have assumed
this suppliant pose, not only for men,
but for their war gods –
in whose names bombs are exploded over cities,
and land mines set to blow off legs
of children running after butterflies in meadows,
framers tilling fields to feed their families.

As she rises from the tub,
she wants to look upward,
raise her arms full of snakes and power,
raise them heavenward
as ancient figurines lift their arms
like magic wands spraying beams
from each spread finger.

She wants to invoke
the vast mystery of space
as a proud suppliant to all that lives –
arms thrust upwards, palms open to light.
Even if she's nothing more
than a temporal body
trapped inside her second of sempiternity
with tired heart weakening
as it beats inside her breast –
just an old woman rising
from the porcelain shell of her bath,
alone inside her small chamber
in a teeming city, looking upward
at the ceiling and the light over the sink.

[GC]: Daniela Gioseffi is a woman of social conscience. She's a feminist. She's been a theater person, performer, creator, and painter. I'm looking at all of her art objects right here. Her work is dialectic between what it is to be alive and an overview of the entire struggle. As a leader of the Italian American writers, I think that you're among the couple of names that will pop up as one of the *first* ones to publish widely in American literary books. So for the last 25 years, I have watched this movement where you have tried to take people who were in the corner, and brought them out center stage, and this happens because of your feeling for your own heritage. Tell us a little bit about your background. I think your father was a *politico*.

[DG]: My father was actually a very poverty stricken immigrant of the *Mezzogior-no,* a Pugliese who came to America in 1913, as a boy who couldn't speak a word of English. Absolutely poor! He had seven brothers and sisters. He supported them all through The Great Depression of the 1930's. His father was a shoemaker. My grandmother, Lucia, was very loving. I think we got much of our inspiration for storytelling and writing from *Nona* Lucia who used to tell Italian fairytales around the coal store in her cold-water flat in Newark. My father grew up extremely poor, but he worked very hard to put himself through Union College earning a Phi Beta Kappa and Sigma Psi, honors in both the liberal arts and sciences, as a youth, walking six miles every morning, on a lame leg, to deliver newspapers, six miles every evening, too, earning a penny per newspaper for *la famiglia,* and living on only pasta and beans, *pasta fagioli.*

[GC]: Sounds like soul food to me! So, he was very poor, but managed to be educated through extremely hard labors?

[DG]: Yes, he really worked terribly hard, carrying newspapers, delivery coal buckets, shining shoes, tending parking lots, shelving library books at Union College Library, selling newspapers from an early age to become somebody. He didn't have time to be politically involved. He was a chemist; a chemical engineer, and he invented *Sylvania Soft Light* and Sylvania's *Blue-Dot-for-Sure-Shot,* but he was working for a corporate lab so he never earned more than a dollar for the patents of his inventions though the corporation made millions from his ingenuity. He was very prejudiced against as a small boy; they would call him, "Little Guinea Gimp," or "Dago Dope," names like that. It hurt him terribly because he believed in "The American Dream." So actually, I'm much more political than he ever was; I found my own way to socio-politics as a result of the prejudice that he suffered. And that's what inspired me to do *On Prejudice: A Global Perspective* with Double-day publishers and to struggle to bring more knowledge about his heritage to the American people.

[GC]: *On Prejudice: A Global Perspective* won a World Peace Foundation Prize, I have to say, also. And, I always think of you as a daughter who was very much loved. Now where these stories have come from are just through osmosis over the years, but you were extremely devoted to your father; isn't that right?

[DG]: Oh yes, he was my inspiration in every way. He was so bound to teach himself English and get rid of his Italian accent that he read Shakespeare cover to cover while tending a parking lot, nights, putting himself through college. As I was growing up, at ten years old, he was reading me Shakespeare's *Romeo and Juliet,* Cervantes's *Don Quixote.* He read me a fair amount of classical literature. He had developed what we would call a beautiful broadcast-radio voice with General American Standard speech. He was only five-foot-six and lame and very sickly and thin, but he had the rich deep voice, of a broadcaster or classical actor. He was gifted with this operatic larynx, and he used to just hold forth so dramatically and passionately, reading Shakespeare and such.

[GC]: I know that your work, and perhaps, his inspiration has resulted in many awards for Italian American writers, publications, the Bordighera Poetry Prize from Bordighera Press. You have been a founder of that prize. *VIA* FOLIOS? What's that logo?

[DG]: *VIA* FOLIOS is an imprint of Bordighiera Press, published by Anthony Tamburri, Fred Gardaphe and Paolo Giordano. *VIA* FOLIOS is publishing *Blood Autumn* • *Autunno di sangue,* in biligual edition this year. It also published my second and third book of poems, *Going On,* and *Word Wounds and Water Flowers.* I went with that press, because I had some name recognition to help give it credibility in the mainstream, so I could bring more young American Italians into print. I started publishing first with BOA Editions in 1977. My first book *Eggs In the Lake* was in print for many years. In 1997—with the financial support of Alfredo de Palchi, trustee of The Sonia Raiziss-Giop Foundation—I devised an annual $2,000 Bordighera poetry prize for bilingual editions by Italian American poets.

[GC]: You've had books from major presses, which I think is pretty interesting, because many of us who have a pile in our closet have gone the small press route, but you seem to have been blessed by major presses as well, which is a good thing because of wider distribution. I'm reading a piece of paper here in my hand, which tells me about a new award, and I think that's the Lifetime Achievement Award given at Hofstra University.

[DG]: Actually, it was from the Italian American Educators Association, which is run by President, Vito de Simone, and awarded at Hofstra. He founded a festival there, every year, of Italian American poets at Hofstra University. I was the featured reader this past September, and I also won, in 2003, the Italian American Educators Award for Lifetime Achievement.

[GC]: And now for permanence, your verse is etched in marble on the wall of Penn Station, along with William Carlos Williams and Walt Whitman. Not bad. Not bad.

[DG]: I was thrilled by that etching! And, I've loved teaching. I worked hard at it for many years, first with Poets-in-the-Schools, Inc. in public schools all over the Metropolitan area, and with Hospital Audiences, Inc. also doing workshops in prisons, senior centers, nursing homes, hospitals, etc., and finally at various colleges and universities like Brooklyn College, CUNY, Long Island University, New York University's Publishing Institute, Pace University....

[GC]: Well, let's hear another poem.

[DG]: Okay. I've just become a grandma, and I was studying with Marie Ponsot. For the first time in years, I went back to studying poetry, and I thought, "Well, if I'm going to study poetry, I have to study with a woman older than me so that

I can look up to her. I took a class with Marie Ponsot, because I hadn't written in form and rhyme in years. She's in her 80's and was teaching us a form call a *tritina,* which was invented by a friend of hers, and I was about to become a grandma for the first time so I wrote,

> "Grandma's Reverie"
> — A Tritina for Marie Ponsot
>
> Why does the reverie of being a grandmother
> confer such a fresh and lavish thrill?
> It's not come by my particular will.
>
> I won't be the mother who tempers the will
> of this child in a Cimmerian age. A grandmother
> thrills at knowing life waltzes on incepting new thrill
>
> though most don't cognize their far ancestor's thrill
> or really know their great, great grandmother's will
> or who, if, or, what made her a grandmother
>
> loved. Being a *grand* mother, gives will to thrill.

[GC]: Tell us about the form.

[DG]: Well the *tritina* is half of a sestina, so to speak, and repeats words. It uses three stanzas, and the three words—"grandmother," "thrill," "will," in this case—are repeated in each stanza in different sequence. And then, after the three stanzas, all three words are used in a final line, separate from the three stanzas. And that's a *tritina,* which Marie Ponsot was teaching in her workshop. Actually I wrote another *tritina,* which I think is a bit smoother than this one, also dedicated to Marie Ponsot because she liked it.

I must say, I studied with her because here, at eighty-six years old, which (I think) she is now in 2006, she's still going on writing, getting prizes. It's wonderful. She's sort of the Stanley Kunitz for us women. Marie Ponsot keeps going on at eighty-six, still teaching, and writing, and publishing and winning prizes. So, I dedicated this to her as an example of someone to look up to and who gives us the strength and the will to go on, because we have to admit that our culture doesn't value its aging women, or its aging men perhaps, as much as it should. Although I think that the aging women have a harder time of it. So Marie Ponsot is a wonderful inspiration for all of us. Here's another *tritina* dedicated to her:

> "Lost Tree of Heaven"
> --A *Tritina* for Marie Ponsot
>
> Between my childhood house and the house next door
> was a strip of concrete where a lonely Ailanthus tree,
> older than the houses, stretched arms toward the sun,

and seemed to smile in my window, filtering sun,
especially when fresh spring air opened the door
letting in zephyrs to stir new leaves of the old tree,

and tiny aromatic white petals danced from my tree
as if it were given snowflakes from the sun
to sprinkle softly down on me, small in the open door

to heaven's door where I dreamed I'd live above the tree in sun.

GC: I love that one, and Daniela doesn't need a textbook because if you look around her place, we have anatomically correct paintings of flowers: wildflowers, domestic flowers. And they show up on the page I see. So, you know of what you speak; you know nature correct?

DG: Well, to some degree, yes. I believe like Emerson and Dickinson did, that nature is the proper study for us and that science is really for me a religion. The intricacy of natural creation is so phenomenal one doesn't need a religion beyond it's wonders, sort of as the Buddhist believe, or more accurately for me, The American Transcendentalists like Emerson or Whitman. It's so amazing the way we live in symbiotic relationships and how everything on the planet is related to one another and to everything else in the web of life on Earth. We're living in very dangerous times. The Age of Fossil Fuels and pesticides is destroying our very sustenance, and air, land and water for the children.

I recently appeared in an anthology called, *Only the Sea Keeps: Poetry of the Tsunami,* which was to benefit the thousands of people who suffered from the tsunami. Then, after all of those thousands and thousands of people died in a Middle Eastern tsunami, we were hit by Hurricane Katrina and all these other natural disasters—the earthquakes in Pakistan and India, in the Cashmere region, among others. It's clear to climatologists like Bill McKibben, worldwide, that we have got to really pay attention now to the fact that global warming is definitely upon us. I contributed three poems to a benefit anthology, called *Only the Sea Keeps,* edited by Judith R. Robinson, Joan E. Bauer and Sankar Roy, and available on a website called *PoetryforHumanity.org/.* The book is a memorial to the tsunami victims and raises some money for the survivors.

These poems were written in order to say something about natural disasters and about our need to see us as one huge interconnected humanity here on earth.

"The Dead for Whom We Sing"

Clear day, so cool, so bright,
the sunset seems to weep tonight
for they are dead and gone.

Lovely trees, green and serene,
sway with a dirge and weep
for they are dead and gone.

Shock makes gazers wipe their eyes,
as thoughts grow from the grave,
for they are dead and gone.

Sweet spring, full of new days and roses,
a time when wonder revives in us
with music that begins and ends with breath,
for they are dead and gone.

Only the spirit of love and loved one,
lasts beyond its season and never grows
cold though the whole world turn
to water or coal,
as all that dies, lives now and only
now
in us
who feel it, see it all before us
laughing and weeping
like the dead for whom we sing.

They make the longest demands,
because we die forever
and cannot live
or love
upon command.

"In This Vast Galaxy"

in this huge and bustling world,
you were given only a speck of time
in which to love—
in your aborted life, sister, bother,
father, mother, daughter, son.
You slowly burgeoned and sprouted
from your chrysalis to die too soon,
sweet trace of nectar on your lips,
as all of us,
delicate as butterflies,
gone too soon,
reigning too briefly to understand our power,
or our beauty
our scepter stilled, pen silenced,
just as we're fully bloomed.

"Earth Song"

We are the eyes
of leaves
We are the ears
of mud.

We see sunset and rise.
Hear bird songs and wind sighs.
We are the eyes
born of the sea.
We are living souls of Her.

In Her womb
there are no nations.
Her children are one rainbow of light.
We yield to Her.
We are the prisms of Her sight.

We breathe the breath
of one universal
ball of water
--one home to all of us.

She is the Mother of All.
She bears the son,
and is daughter and lover
to everyone born of Her seas;
there are no enemies.

GC: From *Only the Sea Keeps,* that is the voice of Daniela Gioseffi. And we're talking about feminism; we're talking about consciousness, and we're talking about poetry. And they all seem to go together. I feel there's no difference in the war that we have within ourselves, and the bridges that we try to cross to the world.

They say that women own the earth and men own the world. But I think you manage to put the two together. I think you said, "I'm not settling for this just being the Mother Earth thing. I'm not allowing the men to just be in charge of war and awards and movements. I think I'm going to combine them both in one lifetime.

DG: Yes, yes, I really don't feel like an angry feminist who's trying to make women behave more like men, but trying to reach some sort of symbiotic understanding, and these last poems I read are deliberately very simple. I meant them to be very simple. Very universal, and hopefully profound in meaning, as well as accessible to anyone who would read them. I was so thrilled that they were quoted in the preface to *Only the Sea Keeps* as a result, because I wanted them to be very accessible to all cultures.

We're living in a time—and I've been through my time of experiment, and abstract or surreal poetry—but I think we've come to a time where poetry in America has been quite abstract and the poetry most paid attention to was abstract expressionistic or language poetry for awhile. I think since 9/11, people are returning to more accessible poetry with socio-political content. That doesn't mean that it has to be rhetorical because one can write a bad love poem, just as one can write a bad political poem, but to raise some of these human issues to the spirit of poetry.

GC: What do you think is your own historical tradition? Other than observable science, which I see you've got from your father and the scientific bent, which I find in all of your work, but your own historical tradition. Do you really feel a sense of connection to Italy?

DG: Well, in the sense that growing up I've always heard the stories of Galileo, The Father of Science and his persecution by The Church, and my grandfather's name was Galileo, and we could not avoid knowing how superstition and the Church was trying to hold science back. Unfortunately, that's happening again in our time with those who want to deny the facts of Darwin's *Origin of Species*. Iconic poets like Walt Whimtan and Emily Dickinson who was—by the way one of our most scientific poets—knew better. Dickinson studied chemistry, she studied botany, she knew everything about flowers and birds and the chemistry of her day and she really, like Emerson—wrote that we don't need a church in order to worship creation. "Some keep the Sabbath/ going to church.' I keep it staying at home / with a Bobolink for a Chorister / and an Orchard for a dome...." We should get out and look at the natural world and study it, and not stay in the dark rooms of churches listening to dogma, but instead we should be studying science. That's the creation we should respect, and if there's a God, that's God's creation. We should pay attention to it in the sunshine, out in nature. That was the whole transcendental movement, which I think was the best part of our American history, and I want to be part of that tradition of Walt Whitman and Emily Dickinson, our two great poets. Since they both wrote in such differing styles, we, as American poets, have the right to write in any way at all from the very tight lyricism of a Dickinson to the long prosaic line of Whitman, to sing in a rhapsodic way or write in a sparse lyrical way. I do try everything, being the "jackass of all trades" that I am, having been a classical actress, so I come from the tradition of having for years recited Shakespeare, Racine, and Congreve and various classical playwrights, and then reading tons of contemporary poetry as well as nineteenth-century writers.

GC: How about another poem? Set it up for us.

DG: "As When Some Silenced Singer Hears her Aria." This is a sonnet in the Petrarchan style for Vittoria Colonna of Naples/Ischia. She lived from 1492–1547, and was the first European woman to publish a book of poetry. She was a friend of Michelangelo. And, the first European woman to earn a doctorate was an Italian woman as well. So this is a sonnet dedicated to Vittoria Colonna of Naples/Ischia, who lost her husband in a war when she was very young and in love with him. She spent the rest of her life writing sonnets about that love and loss.

"As When Some Silenced Singer Hears her Aria"

— A Sonnet for Vittoria Colonna
Naples/Ischia, 1492–1547

or creatures crawl riding foam to hurry back to salty home,
as oceans pound fruit to pecking pipers,
or shells keep tunes in ear-like chambers,
filled with sand and sea to roam
like songs rejoicing feathered nest and comb
as warm eggs crack chirping hunger, and a child slithers
forth to touch, smell, see, hear earthly cries and laughters
pushed suckling free from nurturing womb –

my tongue is loosed beyond a private caroling, my pen prances
urged by mysterious love as if it had no part in what is sighed
as Earth sings praises through me, my eyes are green sea,
red skies, wildflowers, a child who dances
well when loved beyond the pain of men's tribal wards, pride,
threatened suicide, and bloody rivalry.

GC: You're listening to Daniela Gioseffi and this is *The Poet and the Poem,* Library of Congress radio. Daniela writes powerful work, and she reads it with great power. Do you have a short goodbye poem or us?

DG: Okay, I'll read "The Young Child":

who chattered without stopping
lost among lizards,
leaps in my heart.

When she broke her glass hair-
ribbon all the shops in heaven
closed their doors.

In the silence of the snowy streets,
I hear a sad voice, mature
and cowering, calling
from a nearby alley, warning me.

I place my hand over my mouth
where the three silk stitches of her cry
smother dryly.

GC: This has been the voice of Daniela Gioseffi. This is *The Poet and the Poem,* from The Library of Congress, sponsored by the National Endowment for the Arts, because a great nation deserves great art. This is Grace Cavalieri, host, saying, "Goodbye until next time..."

Paolo Corso

Interviews Daniela Gioseffi Regarding Her Use of **Magical Realism** *in Her Fiction*

Excerpted from "Does Your Fiction Need to be Stretched? Authors Describe the Magic of Magical Realism in Expressing Emotional Truths," *The Writer,* 2007.

PAOLA CORSO [PC]: To begin, how do you define *magical realism?*

DANIELA GIOSEFFI [DG]: A story or poem written in the style of *magical realism* contains surreal or fantastical elements that happen within a realistic setting or circumstance. Characterizations are often realistic, but magical events happen that express an emotional truth. Properties of the fantastic and realistic are blended in one work.

One well-known visual example might demonstrate: The painting *Birthday*, created by Marc Chagall in 1915, contains some fantastic elements in a realistic and mundane setting. The man is floating in the air as he kisses the woman, who is surrounded by ordinary household objects. The couple is realistically portrayed as human figures in an indoor setting of chairs and tables and plates and cooking utensils. That the man's floating above the woman as he kisses her obviously represents the emotion the man experiences as he kisses the woman and hands her a birthday bouquet. One can't talk about magical realism without mentioning surrealism and symbolism as elements of the genre.

[PC]: Why did you gravitate toward this genre as a writer?

[DG]: I feel magical realism allows more emotional expression through symbolism, through magical elements that may be intrinsically believable but are never actually explained, leaving more room for readers' imagination to enter into a poem or story. Perhaps, too, there is more ability to explore sensory details when freed from strict reality. Cause and effect can be inverted and time collapsed.

[PC]: Describe your writing process and how you came to incorporate magical realism.

[DG]: I believe that reading profoundly affects one's writing. I read Italo Calvino, Alejo Carpentier, Jorge Luis Borges, Luisa Valenzuela, and the French symbolists Andre Breton, Charles Baudelaire, and also viewed Salvador Dali and Rene Magritte in painting, of course. My writing simply took on aspects of those I read and artists I viewed. I studied modern art and was influenced by it as well. The effects were all around me. Surrealism and magical realism were a part of my literary life. It came naturally to me as I wrote the poems in *Eggs in the Lake,* my first published collection (1977). It's a matter of expressing emotion through fantastical happenings, truths through surreal imagery, creating a mood with unreal juxtapositions in order to explain emotional truths— as in my stories, The Music of Mirrors, The Capitulation, The Fat Lady and the Snake Charmer, various surreal stories in my collection *In Bed with the Exotic Enemy* (1995). I especially use *magic realism* in that book in my novella, *The Psychic Touch.*

Angelina Oberdan

Interviews Daniela Gioseffi on Emily Dickinson, Her Novel
Wild Nights! Wild Nights! *and the Discovery of Dickinson's
Mysterious "Master," a Renowned Scientist*

Published in *Sugarmule*, www.sugermule.com 2010, on the occasion of her biographical novel's release.

ANGELINA OBERDAN [AO]: Throughout your publishing career, you've been interested in a wide array of topics: women's rights and middle-eastern dancing as well as international peace and the Italian American Renaissance in literature. You've written fourteen books of poetry and prose, and won an American Book Award for *Women on War: International Writings*.

What most recently influenced you to focus on Emily Dickinson, to write a scholarly essay about her life, and to write a historical novel about her possible romantic involvement with William Smith Clark, who could have been the "Master" figure of her poems and letters? I was interested when I saw that Robert Hass, a great lover of Dickinson, said that he liked the way you evoked Dickinson's life and times, and Galway Kinnell, who has also written about Dickinson, found the novel's nonfiction afterword "stunning, plausible, and convincing," as did Alice Quinn, Executive Director of the Poetry Society of America, another Dickinson fan. What brought you to the writing of *Wild Nights, Wild Nights: The Story of Emily Dickinson's Master* with its non-fiction afterword: "Lover of Science and Scientist in Dark Days of the Republic"?

Daniela Gioseffi [DG]: I based the drama of the novel on my non-fiction afterward.[50] I was so pleased that Robert Hass, Galway Kinnell, and Alice Quinn found my book interesting. As you know, Dickinson biographers have been debating that great mystery of American literature for over a century: Who was the mysterious "Master" figure of Dickinson's letters and poems?

While I was staying in the Emily Dickinson Room at the Wellspring Writers' Retreat in Ashfield,[51] I visited the Dickinson Museum in Amherst nearby and returned that evening to my room. I turned on my laptop, and, suddenly, out sang Emily's poem, "My River runs to Thee / Blue Sea Wilt welcome me?" which I'd set to music over twenty-five years prior. I hadn't played that song or thought of it in years, and it just sang out of my laptop by itself. I was shocked. It was a recording of Emily's poem that I'd composed and sang through the 1970's to my African harp (bought in Greenwich Village) at the budding of my own poet's career. That was in the days when I was among the first performance poets of New York's *avant garde* Soho "Happenings," or multi-media events. My earliest ventures into

---

[50]The nonfiction afterword, "Lover of Science and Scientist in Dark Days of the Republic: Solving the Mystery of Emily Dickinson's 'Master Figure,' 'Neighbor and Friend and Bridegroom'" was first pub. in the *Chelsea Lit. Rev.* 81 (2006): 109–41.

[51]The Wellspring Writers Retreat in Ashfield, MA hosts writers and artists. As well, Ashfield is the historical birthplace of William Smith Clark.

writing had been in playwriting and multimedia poetry for the stage. In fact of that, my choreo-poem, "The Sea Hag in the Cave of Sleep,"[52] was first produced off-Broadway at the Cubiculo Theatre in 1969 and '70. During those years, I was awarded a grant from the New York State Council for the Arts that I used to create and organize the first Brooklyn Bridge Poetry Walk. In addition, Marguerite Harris and I were once featured reading Emily's poetry for a radio show on Pacifica Radio, WBAI-FM in Manhattan, and I set some of Emily's poems to music to be performed with the African harp or lyre, particularly "My river runs to thee....

But—back to the day when I entered my writing studio—I'd not turned on that Mp3 audio file when it played out of my computer by itself. It was spring of 2003; I'd spent the day visiting the Emily Dickinson Museum, but I'd not even thought of that song. It played out of my laptop of its own accord! I'd just been reading, at the Dickinson Museum,[53] Ruth Owen Jones's article "'Neighbor—and friend—and Bridgroom—'...."[54] And in that surreal moment, it was as if a ghost had bid the music to play from my computer in the town where William Smith Clark, the "Master" figure of Jones's thesis, was born in Ashfield, Massachusetts.

[AO]: It sounds like that track playing from your computer was a supernatural sign of sorts. Do you believe in signs? Are you superstitious in that way?

[DG]: No, I would not call myself superstitious at all, but it was eerie to enter that room in the dark and have that old Mp3 file of a 1970's recording sing out, all by itself, from my computer. Since I'm not a believer in any occult phenomenon, I'm sure there's a scientific reason why this occurred. The laptop was turned on, and as I opened it that Mp3 on my hard drive was selected from hundreds of files and played out loud, all by itself. It startled and puzzled me. It made me think more intently about the powerful and erotic love that Dickinson speaks of in her poems and letters. It made me look more deeply into Jones's thesis about Will Clark and begin to read everything about the iconic poet's life I could get my hands on.

[AO]: Can you expand on that idea: on how hearing that particular poem playing from your computer made you consider the erotic love in Dickinson's poems and on how it related to Jones's thesis about Dickinson and Clark?

[DG]: I realized, for the first time, that the poem, "My River Runs to Thee" is a very intimate love song and an erotic beckoning; it seemed more than a mere hymn to nature or a divine creator. ED scholars do often find double-entendre in her love poems. Was the poem composed for nature's creator or for a lover? Or both? I noticed, too, that the combined words—"will" and "it" forming "wilt"—could be a deliberate pun on the nickname, "Will," made by Dickinson when "Will" Clark was traveling to Europe and at sea. In Jones's article, her thesis that

---

[52]See Gioseffi's *Eggs in the Lake*, fwd. John Logan (Brockport, NY: BOA Ed., 1979) 46–50.
[53]For more information on the Emily Dickinson Museum: The Homestead and the Evergreens, visit *Emilydickinsonmuseum.org.*
[54]Jones's article was published in *The Emily Dickinson Journal* 11.2 (2002): 48–85.

Clark was Emily's lover, or "Master" figure, is augmented by illustrating that Emily creates puns on "will" and "Will" throughout her poetry.

[AO]: So you became convinced that William Smith Clark was Emily Dickinson's lover, her so-called "Master"?

[DG]: Yes, the more I read, the more I realized that Jones's theory of Clark as the "Master" figure is the most plausible of all. After all, Will Clark was a great botanist, chemist, and geologist, and Dickinson's poetry is peppered with terms and concepts derived from those sciences. Botany was her concern as much as poetry. I'd only just discovered that Ashfield—where I was staying at Wellspring—was the hometown of Will Clark, Dickinson's probable "Master," when I went to the Dickinson Museum in Amherst that day. I found Jones's article in a reprint sold at the museum's bookshop.

As I've explained, when I entered my dark room, coincidently named the Emily Dickinson Room at Wellspring House Writers' Retreat, out of my laptop played:

> My River runs to Thee -
> Blue Sea - Wilt welcome me?
>
> My River waits reply.
> Oh Sea, look graciously!
>
> I'll fetch thee Brooks
> From spotted nooks -
>
> Say Sea – take me?

My voice singing it to my harp accompaniment sang out even though I'd not turned that audio file on. I simply walked to the desk, opened the lid of the laptop, and out played that music file. Ironic to say the least!

Anyway, I was there, living for three weeks, in the town of Clark's birthplace, a short distance from Amherst. I saw firsthand his humble beginnings compared to Dickinson's more opulent ones, and realized why her father would have forbade his daughter's marriage to the son of a more humble country doctor, so concerned with the family fortunes was he. I realized that they must have been star-crossed lovers like Romeo and Juliet, which happens to be the last thing Dickinson was reading before she died—just six weeks after Will Clark—and was buried in the West Cemetery in her family plot just a few yards away from Clark's family plot. I was haunted by what I began to see as a meaningful love song written to Clark when he was away at sea, and he was known to be away at sea around the time she wrote that lyric.

[AO]: Let's first discuss Dickinson's "opulent" beginnings. I've never had the chance to visit the Dickinson Homestead or the Evergreens. Would you describe them and how they affected you?

[DG]: The Dickinson Homestead, where Emily lived for much of her life, still stands alongside the Evergreens, her brother's home. The compound has been converted into a museum open to the public, and it is only a half hour's drive from the Wellspring House Writers' Retreat. At the Evergreens, I saw the parlor where Emily recited poems and played the piano to entertain friends at her sister-in-law's, Sue's, soirees. Her beloved nephew's nursery was recently opened to the public for the first time, too. I imagined Emily there and felt connected to the Dickinson Homestead that I'd visited a few times before, as well. I stood beside Dickinson's auburn paisley shawl draped across her antique sleigh bed and beside the Franklin stove in her bedroom. I saw the cradle in which she was rocked; saw the white, pique housedress she wore; saw the window by which she sat at a small writing table. It was the window from which she lowered cookies and cakes in a basket on a string to the children playing on the front lawn of her big, brick, Federal-style house on Main Street: the window from which she lowered notes to friends, to a groundskeeper, to a servant who hid them under his hat, as Jones surmises, and delivered them through the woods to Clark's servant. I learned that Professor Clark lived just up and behind her house, and I read the lines: "Behind the Hill – the House behind - / There – Paradise – is found!" I saw the back stairs that led up to her bedroom—which she called "The Northwest Passage"—the secret place where she may have had rendezvous in the dark with the "Sweet William" of her love poems. I began to imagine Emily's conversations with her "Master," and found myself doing that quite constantly.

[AO]: It must be a beautiful place—Amherst and the Dickinson Homestead— but can you clarify something for me? You visited the Dickinson Homestead and the Evergreens in Amherst, Massachusetts, but you stayed at the Wellspring House in Ashfield, Massachusetts, correct?

[DG]: Yes, the Wellspring House is located in Ashfield, a village that played a role in Massachusetts's history. William Smith Clark's cousin invented a more powerful telescope there, and some of the first advances in photography happened there, in that small New England town in the foothills of the Berkshires about a half hour north of Amherst, Dickinson's town. The old Clark farmhouse, where William Smith Clark was born, is down Main Street from Wellspring House Writer's Retreat and around a corner across from St. Joseph's Church. I almost bought that farmhouse; when it was up for sale in 2005, I was still spending time at the retreat writing *Wild Nights, Wild Nights*, and enthralled with the story of Clark and Emily, but another buyer beat me too it.

[AO]: Really? You almost bought Clark's boyhood home?

[DG]: Yes, I wanted to buy the Clark family's farmhouse, but was too late. It still has a plaque by the front door announcing it as William Smith Clark's birthplace.

He became a well-known Civil War hero in the area and an important scientist. He founded the University of Massachusetts for agricultural science that was so important in Dickinson's day. Ashfield is also the home of Paris Press, the press that published Hart and Smith's *Open Me Carefully: Emily Dickinson's Intimate Letters to Susan Huntington Dickinson.*[55] That's the text that defends a presumed love affair between Dickinson and Susan Gilbert Dickinson, the poet's sister-in-law.

[AO]: And you don't agree with this proposition? You don't think Emily Dickinson had a homosexual affair with her sister-in-law, Sue Gilbert Dickinson?

[DG]: Well, not exactly. In their edition of Dickinson's letters, Hart and Smith slant Dickinson's correspondence in defense of their thesis; putting all of her letters to Susan Gilbert—and only her letters to Sue—under one cover makes Sue appear to be Emily's "Master" because Dickinson's other affectionate correspondence with friends and relatives is omitted. I said, "not exactly," because I've come to understand that Dickinson most likely did have homoerotic feelings for Sue Gilbert when they were young. Homoerotic friendships were common and the norm between friends in the antebellum period, and homosexuality—as we think of it today—is a different matter. In any case, so many great artists, including Walt Whitman, have a bi-sexual nature, an ability to identify with either sex. Shakespeare had to understand both Romeo and Juliet to write his convincing love story, and LeoTolstoy, the great Russian writer, certainly lived well in the mind and body of Anna Karenina, if you see what I mean. Like many great artists in her mental orientation, Dickinson was able to empathize with or to love anyone whose intellect or sensibility she admired greatly. The three "Master" love letters, however, talk of a man with a beard, and seem to be addresses to a male figure. I do think she admired and had homoerotic feelings for her girlhood friend, Sue Gilbert. However, she had these feelings prior to falling in love with William Smith Clark. And, as I've explained, homoerotic relationships were common in the antebellum period, whether consummated or not; women and men were very affectionate and loving toward same sex friends. They didn't think of these affectionate friendships as homosexual in the way we define such orientations in our own times. And now, even Abraham Lincoln is thought to have had such a relationship, too, unrequited or not. Also, Emily was "courting" Susan Gilbert in the romantic letters showcased by Hart and Smith, because she wanted her brother to marry Sue. She was imitating what she and Susan read in Romantic novels by the Brontë sisters and George Eliot, among others. In fact—because she desperately wanted Sue to become a part of her family, to marry her brother, Austin—it is likely that she was acting out the courtship that Austin was not properly performing in correspondence.

---

[55]See editors Ellen Louise Hart and Martha Nell Smith's *Open Me Carefully: Emily Dickinson's Intimate Letters to Susan Huntington Dickinson* (Ashfield, MA: Paris P, 1998).

[AO]: Why do you think Dickinson wanted her brother to marry Sue so badly?

[DG]: I think Dickinson saw that a marriage between Sue and her brother was more than a good match; it would also benefit her. Their marriage would provide her with a female intellectual companion, a role that was left vacant in her life and could not be filled by her mother, Emily Norcross, or her sister, Lavinia. Sue was pretty, admired, and intellectually astute, and she could provide the mental stimulation Dickinson needed. They read and discussed poetry and literature together, and women's issues, too. In the nineteenth century, women were segregated from male society—meant to stay in their place at home or in sewing circle or in Bible study classes (as Dickinson's father firmly believed)—, and consequently, intelligent women needed close friendships with each other. Edward Dickinson, Emily's father, wrote publicly about his philosophy that women were meant to stay at home. He thought it socially improper for women to publish their writings, and felt that women's education was meant merely to enrich the spiritual life of the family and help in the education of male children. My Italain father, though not religious, felt the same. That women were only meant to work at home for *la famiglia*. Especially because she was pressured by the restricting, rigorous beliefs of her father, Dickinson reached out to Sue and the intellectual friendship she offered.

[AO]: All in all, what effect do you think that Sue had on Emily?

[DG]: Susan Gilbert Dickinson ended up being essential to Emily's development as a poet. Her importance in Emily's life, as a seminal influence on the literary genius, is doubtless. Sue was an extraordinarily independent woman and an eloquent thinker. Without a strong woman friend like Sue, Emily might not have developed her prowess as a poet. It's clear that—although Emily might have projected a love affair onto Susan and might have had a "crush" on her when they were young—the act of putting all correspondence from Dickinson to Sue under one cover slants the view of their relationship. It makes Sue appear to be Emily's "Master" figure, because all the other affectionate and loving letters Dickinson sent to friends and relatives are omitted. She wrote affectionately to Abiah Root, Samuel Bowles, Elizabeth Holland, and several others. We have only one-third of Dickinson's voluminous correspondence, as most of it, including the very possible exchanges with Will Clark, was burned as she requested Lavinia to do upon her death. Lavinia burned her letters, but refused to burn the many poems she was amazed to find in Dickinson's bedroom drawer amidst them the three mysterious "Master Letters" which have been of great speculation among her biographers. It was Victorian practice to burn one's correspondence, so intimate in the days prior to telephones, computers, and e-mail. Scholars attest to how affectionately Emily wrote many of her female and male friends with imaginative and even erotic innuendo.

[AO]: Did Emily and Sue always get along so well? I think I read that they had their differences.

[DG]: You are more well read than most graduate students I've met, Angelina, and you have quite a thorough knowledge of American poetry yourself it seems. In fact, the two women did not agree on important issues of religion. They took differing spiritual paths. They even had a falling out prior to the death of Austin and Sue's son's death;[56] after which, the poet didn't visit the Evergreens for approximately fifteen years. Also, if Sue had known about Dickinson's affair with Will Clark, she would have frowned severely upon it, because Will was a married man. As a married woman, Sue would have taken offense, especially because Austin eventually strayed from their marriage to have an affair with another married woman.[57]

[AO]: So explain to me the thesis of your essay and your novel.

[DG]: Although Dickinson may very well have been smitten with Sue—which was transferred to her brother with a vicarious romantic ardor, enough to cause him to marry Sue—*Open Me Carefully* is only one part of the story. I do not believe that Sue is the bearded "Master" figure of Dickinson's "Master" letters and poems. The more plausible thesis is that proposed by Ruth Owen Jones. Jones argues that William Smith Clark—the first Ph.D. professor of botany, horticulture, and chemistry at Amherst College, the founder and first acting president of U. Mass —is the most plausible possibility of all. Jones gives much evidence for Clark as Dickinson's "Master."

[AO]: And why do you think it was Ruth Owen Jones who unearthed the identity of Dickinson's "Master" figure when so many literary scholars have failed to do so in their analysis of primary sources?

[DG]: Jones is a historian of the Amherst area, a guide at the Dickinson Museum, an alumna of the University of Massachusetts.[58] She lives down Amity Street from the Jones and Frost libraries—nearby the Dickinson Homestead—where much of the history of the town and its people is housed. She has served as President or Chair of the Amherst Historical Commission, and she's a gardener who researched the Victorian gardens of her town. These are the factors that allowed her to discover and note what others failed to. Jones's vantage point allowed her to mesh the chronology of Emily Dickinson's life to Clark's and to prove that Clark was a prominent member of the poet's village society and a business associate of her brother and father. Austin Dickinson and Clark had business ventures together: renovating the town commons and founding a water company. I agree with Jones that Clark, a formidable intellect of his day, may well have been the catalyst for Emily's ardent and romantic imagination. He believed in and

---

[56]Thomas "Gib" Gilbert Dickinson died in 1883.

[57]For more information on Austin's affair with Mabel Loomis Todd, see Polly Longworth's *Austin and Mabel: The Amherst Affair and Love Letters of Austin Dickinson and Mabel Loomis Todd* (Amherst, MA: Univ. of MA P, 1984).

[58]At the Univ. of MA, Jones had ready access to Clark's papers because he was founder and first acting president of the university.

preached women's right to an education, (and he encouraged his sister to write poetry) and some of Dickinson's few published poems appear in the same periodicals that include his essays. He also paid much attention to literature written by women and even wrote some reviews of what he read. It is more than likely that he was the intended recipient of Dickinson's love poems and "Master" letters. He fits better than any of Dickinson's other presumed lovers. Even Cynthia Griffin Wolff, in her careful study titled *Emily Dickinson*[59] concludes, as Jones and I do, that neither Reverend Wadsworth of Philadelphia, nor editor Samuel Bowles of The Springfield Republican, nor Judge Otis Lord were the intended recipients of Dickinson's letters to her "Master" figure—though she did have a correspondence and love affair, even a marriage engagement with Otis Lord later in her life, when the popular myth of her seclusion prevails. She never did lead all that much of a secluded life; her brother and sister and their children were always around the homestead as were field workers and day servants; her parents were always coming and going, and her father, a statesmen and lawyer, brought his associates to visit her parlor and dining room; also the Amherst College students were coming and going nearby, and her faithful maid, Maggie Maher was around, et cetera. Her life was less secluded than poets of our day who often live alone, day after day. And she actually published in the scribal sense sending her poems to more than forty correspondents.

[AO]: Can you tell me more about William Smith Clark? Describe him for me.

[DG]: He was lively, a great conversationalist and storyteller, a scientific innovator. Clark was far more known and accomplished than Dickinson was during her lifetime. However, he came from the home of a humble country doctor of Ashfield, and he was social climbing in Amherst where Emily's family was of the cream of Amherst's rural village society. Dashing and charming, Clark taught the poet's favorite subjects at Amherst College, next door to her home. He was among the first professors of science of that venerable New England institution of higher learning to invite women to attend his chemistry and horticultural lectures. Clark believed that women had the right to an education and—unlike Dickinson's father—to a profession as well. Having traveled in Europe, he used affectionately Italian style greetings, hugging and kissing, and he wrote affectionate letters to his students with a tone similar to Dickinson's, which was unlike the more reserved correspondence of her brother and father. The members of the Dickinson family, though fiercely loyal to one another, showed no physical affection, and they were laconic in the Calvinist New England demeanor. During his travels, Clark observed styles of behavior alien to Amherst's Victorian Society. When he returned from his travels, he was somewhat of a shock to Amherst's rural aristocracy with his affectionate and lively demeanor. I can imagine him nurturing Emily Dickinson's love of gardening, her plant conservatory, and herbarium! He had large greenhouses and developed them for the village. He brought exotic plants back

---

[59]See Wolff's *Emily Dickinson* (Reading, MA: Perseus Books, 1998).

from the Orient. I'm sure he nurtured her poetry, too.

[AO]: Didn't you mention earlier that Will Clark also fought in the Civil War?

[DG]: Yes, Clark went off to fight in the Civil War because he was a staunch anti-slavery activist, and he left Amherst just around the time when scholars agree that there was a period of trauma in Emily's life that inspired her richest outpouring of poetry, the period in which she sewed her most finished verses into fascicles.

[AO]: In the book, you demonstrate that there's evidence in Dickinson's poetry to support the argument that Clark was her lover, her "Master." But what is the evidence in her "Master" letters that supports this theory?

[DG]: Actually one of Jones's important points is that it's suspicious that Clark, such a well known personage around and about Amherst and a business associate of Dickinson's father and brother appears only twice in Dickinson's surviving correspondence of which approximately only a third is estimated by biographers to have been preserved. One can surmise that Clark, the eminent botanist and horticulturalist of the town is conspicuously absent from the gardening poet's correspondence because of expurgation. All references, but two, were likely destroyed to avoid a scandal between the two most eminent families of the town: the Dickinsons and the Willistons. The affair, if disclosed, would have disrupted the society of the village and the functioning of Amherst Seminary, so central to the village's welfare and economy. Both Squire Dickinson and Squire Williston served on the board of the seminary that was then in transition into a college that taught the sciences, and Will Clark was married to Williston's adopted daughter, Harriet Richards. It would have been a scandal, upsetting the friendship between two eminent trustees of the seminary, as well as ruining Clark's career as a professor of science whose father-in-law was an important benefactor of the seminary. Sam Williston financed a new building and laboratory for Amherst Seminary of which Dickinson's father was a longtime treasurer and trustee. As you know, Emily's grandfather had founded the college.

The "Master" with a beard in the "Master Letters" is mentioned as someone with whom Dickinson walked in the meadows with her dog, someone close who seems to have lived in Amherst and been involved with flowers and horticulture. Clark was the chief botanist of the town and lived in a house behind a hill in back of her homestead, a house with many gardens and greenhouses; Emily wrote, "Behind the Hill - the House behind - / There - Paradise - is found!" of Clark, who she called her "Neighbor - and friend - and Bridegroom" in another telling poem. There is much evidence of Will Clark in Dickinson's texts if they are studied closely. For example, when Will Clark went off to fight in the Civil War, she wrote: "The Red upon the Hill / Taketh away my will -." Many other textual clues are rampant, especially mentioning the elements of the sciences that Clark taught at Amherst College.

[AO]: Could you tell me a little more about these two families?

[DG]: Sure, these two families—the latter into which Clark was married—were the leaders and builders of Amherst society and its livelihood. As you know, Amherst College was founded by Samuel Dickinson, Emily's grandfather, as a Puritan seminary meant to produce evangelical missionaries of the Calvinist faith. Samuel Williston, Clark's father-in-law, was the wealthiest benefactor of Western Massachusetts and served as a trustee of the university along with Dickinson's father, Edward. He funded the building of the science laboratory where Clark taught (upon his return from Gottingen with his European Ph.D.)., Austin, Emily's brother, later served as a trustee and treasurer of Amherst College, just as her father had. Clark married Harriet Richards Williston, and I can imagine that Clark married Harriet, nicknamed "The Queen," in order to advance his ambitious career, especially after Dickinson's father, Edward, might have spurned him as Emily's suitor. He rose from humble beginnings on the wings of his intellect and charm, and he did become one of the most important botanists of his time. Clark and Harriet lived across a wood behind the Dickinson homestead and northwest of it—around the corner so to speak. Also Emily's niece, Martha Dickinson, was born the same day as Clark's daughter and went to school with her. I bet Emily baked ginger cakes for the children Martha played with, including, no doubt, Clark's daughter, and she likely sent flowers to his wife, upon her convalescence, too. Harriet, nicknamed "The Queen" had several children, some of whom died. In fact, I think Dickinson's verse confirms this idea:

> Could - I do more - for Thee –
> Wert Thou a Bumble Bee –
> Since for the Queen, I have –
> Nought but Bouquet?

[AO]: I love her poems, even her short ones like the one you just recited.

[DG]: Of course, that's why so many literary scholars and poets are enamored with Dickinson's mind and imagination and are extremely curious about "the clock that made her tick." Italian poetry readers love her work, too, and she's been thoroughly translated into Italian and other European languages as well. She produced precise and eloquent verse, and publication did not seem to be her goal. "Publication - is the Auction / Of the Mind of Man -" she wrote disparagingly. Though it appears that publication didn't concern her, Dickinson's writing was read by many intelligent minds and was circulated in the scribal sense. Though it was not officially published, there are at least forty known recipients of her poetry, as I mentioned earlier.

[AO]: Do you think having an audience was necessary for Dickinson? Do you think she would have written so much without an audience?

[DG]: I don't think she could have written such fine work for herself, alone, as some people want to believe. She had lovers, friends, and readers who read her work with interest, and she was acquainted with important editors of her day: Thomas Wentworth Higginson of *The Atlantic Monthly,* Samuel Bowles of *The Springfield Republican,* Joshua Holland of *Scribner's Magazine.* And she was a reader of the best women writers of her day: Elizabeth Barrett Browning, the Brontës, George Elliot, George Sand, and probably Margaret Fuller and Lousia May Alcott, and perhaps Madam de Staël of an earlier day. Barrett Browning's novel in verse, *Aurora Leigh,* was very important to her. And of course she read Emerson, Hawthorne, Shakespeare, the *Bible,* and much other good literature. Reading is the best teacher of writing, but she was also communicating with living beings, very intensely, all of her life. In fact, Emily was far less isolated than many women poets of our time. She was rarely without correspondents or family, and a popular poet and novelist of the day had been her school chum, Helen Hunt Jackson, and in later life when they were reunited, Jackson encouraged her greatly. At the Dickinson Homestead, Emily's her sister, Lavinia, occupied the bedroom across the hall from hers, and they were in close consort all of their lives. The Irish maid, Maggie Maher, and the handyman, Tom Kelly, were readily available. Austin and Sue, with their son and daughter, lived next door. And many of the college's professors, including Will Clark, and their students came and went from her prominent father's household. Clearly, the idea of Dickinson's isolation has become much exaggerated, and I feel it's unfair for young scholars and poets to be made to feel that she wrote so well in a vacuum without feedback.

[AO]: And how do you combine Dickinson's poems, her letters, the historical facts, and the romance to create an effective portrayal of the love between Dickinson and Clark?

[DG]: I've peppered my novel with many of her poems having to do with the drama of her love affair with Clark and some of her public domain letters. I've used the earlier versions of the poems, now in public domain, for reasons of expensive copyright. Her texts help to dramatize the novel. I've attempted to approximate the story of Dickinson's and Clark's profound love and common interest in science—particularly botany, horticulture, chemistry, and ornithology—based on fact. Dickinson admired imagination. She dwelt in "possibility" which was her word for poetry and its powers. And she's one of our most scientifically aware poets. The theme of my novel involves Dickinson and her "Master," Clark, as part of the American Enlightenment, the Transcendental Movement led by Alcott, Emerson, and Fuller that brought America out of the Puritan Age of Iron and the dictates of Calvinist dogma into the light of scientific truth and the Age of Darwinian ideals— proving we're all one human race from the same genetic beginnings. Darwin's motive was *anti-slavery* at its core: to prove we're all descended from the same primates and the same gene pool. My life has been devoted to the cause of civil and human rights, in both my activism and my writing. I also spent five years writing and editing, *On Prejudice: A Global Perspective,*[60] Dickinson was of an anti-slavery society as was Clark. I bring that out in my book about them. They were great Americans of the cultural and scientific nineteenth-century enlightenment of our nation.

[AO]: That's a much different idea of Emily than I was taught in school. As I remember it, she was always portrayed as being a recluse. In fact, I think many people don't understand that a poet can be social. They believe poets needs to be solitary to write well.

[DG]: Poets need solitude in which to write, and Dickinson often spent time alone in her room at her desk, but the idea of her seclusion has been magnified into an exaggerated myth. It's wrong and cruel to teach young poets that they can write well and create sterling poetry without an audience, in total solitude without intellectual stimulation, because Emily Dickinson did so. She was quite social, a "Belle of Amherst" in her youthful days. She was often part of a very peopled world even in her later years when she refused to leave her father's grounds. She had intelligent and well read people whom she knew would read her poems, at least forty correspondents who read her work, some the finest literary editors of the time, Thomas Wentworth Higginson of *The Atlantic Monthly,* Paul Bowles of *The Springfield Republican,* Joshua Holland of *Scriber's,* and his wife, Elizabeth, one of her closest friends. Her well-read Norcross cousins, close correspondents with whom she lived for several months in Cambridgeport, Boston, became part of Emerson's literary salon. Helen Hunt Jackson, a well-known and popular poet and novelist of the day, was her old school chum in Amherst, and later in life when they were reunited, Jackson told Dickinson that she was a great poet and insisted on publishing her in an anthology of poetry, titled *A Mask of Poets.* Jackson wanted to serve as Dickinson's literary executor, but she died before she could. Dickinson only consented to anonymous publication in her lifetime, because she was the aristocratic daughter of a well-known statesman, a federal congressman, and a state senator of Massachusetts. The Dickinson name was known and prestigious in the Pioneer Valley, and it wasn't ladylike for women of her upper class station to publish. "Publication is the auction / of the Mind of Man," she wrote. Yet, I feel she fashioned her fascicles of poems for other eyes to read, especially those of her lover, Will Clark, who was a champion of women's right to an education and a published reviewer of women's literature. That's why her poems have passionate resonance; they had intended audiences in the scribal sense, within her correspondence and among her friends, despite her father's position forbidding her to publish publically. The myths about her reclusiveness are slanted and exaggerated.

[AO]: In addition to being a poet—among other things—this venture has turned you into a Dickinson scholar as well, hasn't it?

---

[60]See Gioseffi's *On Prejudice: A Global Perspective* (New York: Anchor/Doubleday, 1993).

[DG]: Yes. I've read just about everything written about her life and work. I've noted how much she saw Italy as the land of emotional freedom and bold creativity. When I started this phase of my life, I had a rough idea of her life in Amherst, and had bought into the mythology myself, and already knew some of her work by heart, but I've been studying it—her letters, the mores of her era—ever since spring 2003 when that lyric played by itself out of my laptop in "The Emily Dickinson Room" at Wellspring Writers Retreat in Ashfield—where, scientist, William Smith Clark was born thirty minutes from Amherst.

[AO]: In becoming a Dickinson scholar, what were some of the books you've turned to?

[DG]: I've studied Richard B. Sewell's, *The Life of Emily Dickinson*[61]; Alfred Habegger's *My Wars Are Laid Away in Books*[62]; and *The World of Emily Dickinson* by Polly Longsworth.[63] And I've read such works as *A Historical Guide to Emily Dickinson*[64] as well as subscribed—as a member of The Emily Dickinson Society—to *The Emily Dickinson Journal*. I've looked carefully at *The Master Letters of Emily Dickinson,*[65] and read through all of her poems and letters, several times. Once—in one non-stop sitting—I read all the way through R.W. Franklin's definitive collection[66] of all her nearly 1,800 known poems. After reading *My Emily* by Susan Howe,[67] I realized that Howe is correct in saying that there is much of Dickinson's poetry that is impenetrable and enigmatic, and that this is probably because the verses were never completed by the poet but sketched out as notes for a poem. I've concluded that, there is new meaning in many of her works, not seen there by Howe or others, if Dickinson's poetry is read by someone who accepts, even assumes, that Will Clark was her lover, her "Master." I could go on and on about all I studied to write my novel with a factual base, all the biographers, but let me simply say that much respected scholarship has entered my spirit and mind in the research and writing of what I hope is meaningful, historic, biographical novel based on its NON-fiction afterword with extensive bibliography. Dickinson became a bit of an obsession for me. I learned a good deal about nineteen-century America.

[AO]: You mentioned Richard B. Sewall's *The Life of Emily Dickinson*; what did you think of it? I know his book is well respected.

[DG]: Yes, and the "Emily" I portrayed in my novel, is more like the woman in the portrait at the back of Sewall's biography, earthy and assured; she's more wom-

---

[61]See Sewell's *The Life of Emily Dickinson* (Boston: Harvard UP, 1998).

[62]See Habegger's *My Wars Are Laid Away in Books* (New York: Modern Lib., 2002).

[63]See Longsworth's *The World of Emily Dickinson* (New York: Norton, 1990).

[64]See Editor Vivian R. Pollack's *A Historical Guide to Emily Dickinson* (New York: Oxford UP, 2004).

[65]See editor R. W. Franklin's *The Master Letters of Emily Dickinson* (Amherst, MA: Amherst College P, 1986).

[66]See Franklin's *The Poems of Emily Dickinson* (Cambridge, MA: Belknap/Harvard UP, 2003).

[67]See Howe's *My Emily* (Berkley: North Atlantic Books, 1985).

anly than the sickly, seventeen-year-old girl—as is portrayed in the well-known daguerreotype. I wrote my novel based on facts disclosed by Sewall, Jones, and others. My "Emily" is a mature hearty woman of quizzical and sardonic gaze who loves to ramble alone in the woods with her big dog, Carlo, in search of rare specimens of wild flowers. She's a woman with large, steady brown eyes that say, "I've lived for art and love alike. I have known carnal love. I'm the fully erotic woman of my love poems." I feel sure that Sewall would not have included the mature photo—with what she herself called, her "Gypsy Face"—in his book if he'd not strongly suspected it was a portrait of the poet at about thirty-three-years of age. Faces were important to Emily Dickinson; she kept portraits of George Eliot and Elizabeth Barrett Browning in her room. I feel strongly that she'd have wanted a more accurate view of herself as a mature woman. I invite all who are interested to study each feature in the photo in the Sewall biography and compare it with the youthful daguerreotype, taken at a time when the poet was sickly, just arisen from a long illness in bed. I've a feeling that those gifted with an eye for visual will agree with me that the mature photo is Dickinson with a slightly plumper face than she had at seventeen. The features match in distance between eyes, nose and mouth, hairstyle, earlobes, neckline, etc.

[AO]: I believe you've told me that you spent about five years writing and researching this novel. Why do you think you've become so intensely interested in telling what you believe to be Dickinson's more correct biography?

[DG]: I began to feel haunted by the spirit of an untold love story, and I think I wanted to understand, as a poet, what inspired the *most iconic* woman poet of my country. I found Dickinson's story to be quite different than the mythical one about a secluded spinster. The strange happening of her imploring love poem playing out of my laptop on inspired me to read more. The more I learned the more excited I became about telling a fascinating untold story of our country's greatest woman poet; *Wild Nights! Wild Nights!* my title, comes from her most erotic love poem. I wrote a novel that incorporated the facts verifying the identity of her "Master" as Professor Clark, botanist of Amherst College. It's a novel with a non-fiction afterword upon which the drama of the story is based. It augments Jones's idea that Will Clark was Dickinson's lover in her mysterious "Master" letters. After a life in American poetry, I was fascinated to understand the true story of Dickinson's life, what compelled her to write, and such erotic love poems, too.

AO: The more I know about Emily Dickinson, the more connected to her I feel— as I'm sure you do, also.

DG: I feel connected to her mind and spirit. I believe that she has more in common with other American poets than is portrayed by the myths surrounding her. Emily wrote of violets, daises, birds and bees, and she loved to walk in the woods as much as Thoreau did. She is one of our most scientifically aware poets. She sought to discover new elements of nature and to learn the truth of emotional powers. She observed sunlight and shadow, natural wonder, death and decay, and the beauty of her natural world. She found truth and beauty were *one* as did Keats. She understood Emerson's philosophy of "Nature" and "The Poet" in his seminal essays of the Transcendental Movement, inspired in him by his beloved teacher, Aunt Mary Moody Emerson and her insightful diaries.

In his essay, "The Poet," Emerson writes that rhyme and meter do not make the poem, but that the poem's contents must be organic to its style and form, and Dickinson was greatly influenced by this. She rebelled against Higginson's and Susan's attempts to make her conform to the traditional poetic style of her day with its obvious rhymes and meters. That a poem should first "mean" and then "be" would have been Emerson's creed. Emerson insisted that it is the thought that sends us into poetry, not the techniques of writing. He saw the ideal poet as a shaman of natural wonders and ethical behavior, as arising from human feeling and empathy more than from dogma.

Dickinson's verses were meant for oral delivery. She used elocution dashes— rather than punctuation— or so many of us Dickinson scholars believe. Young women of the day were trained in elocution and oral rhetoric, more than in discursive writing. School examinations were given and taught *orally* then, in a day when ink, paper and printing were expensive and good typewriters not yet invented. Also, human speech is overlaid on our pulmonary system. It's a product of our life's breath. We articulate with our exhaled breath. Punctuation comes from natural pauses in speech. Dickinson seems to have chosen a style of oral interpretation for marking pauses, not dashes, in her poetic texts. Her dashes, many scholars believe, are elocutions marks, not punctuation.

[AO]: You clearly feel connected to Dickinson aesthetically. What about religiously?

[DG]: "Poets All" was Emily's religion as it is mine. She was actually a transcendentalist who embraced a German sort of Pantheism, as did Ralph Waldo Emerson, William Smith Clark, her brother, and many of the other forward-thinking intellectuals of her time. There was a fervent movement among Dickinson's intelligentsia that decried the restraints of Puritanical Calvinist dogma that held scientific and social advancement back. Darwinism was being born and opposed by *literal* interpretations of scripture, just as in our own days of the Bush Administration and extreme, rightwing, born-again religiosity.. There was a so-called "Great Revival" sweeping the Pioneer Valley in Dickinson's day, just as fanatical religiosity is blooming in our time, fueling the "War on Terror." Dickinson, however, refused to be "born again" from her days at Mary Lyon's Calvinist Female Seminary until her death—unlike the rest of her family. Many fine writers of New England were rebelling against Creationism. Antidisestablishmentarianism was afoot. The separation of church and state was being codified. Emily did question her father's authority when it came to her beliefs, just as we feminists did in the 1970's and the anti-Vietnam War movement. Dickinson followed Emerson's rebellion against the tyranny of New England Puritanism—and into the light of

Transcendentalism— more like Buddhism with its non-theism— as in Emerson's, "Nature" and "The Poet." When the Aurora Borealis was seen in New England, it was imagined by many to be a sign of Armageddon. It helped spur Revivalism and Born Again Christianity (as the tsunami and Age of Terrorism have turned people toward Fundamentalist beliefs), Emily maintained her transcendentalist stance: hiding in the basement with a book of poetry and a candle when her father rounded up the family for church. I think of her poem:

> Some keep the Sabbath going to church -
> I keep it, staying at Home -
> with a Bobolink for a Chorister –
> and an Orchard, for a Dome –

I identify strongly with her inability to bear the religious hypocrisy she saw around her in Evangelical fervor. Putting religion before science is foolish, as even if you believe in a god, or follow one of the medieval religions that beget superstition and hypocrisy, creation is made of the truths of science and the natural world. Forward thinkers were espousing women's right to an education and human equality for all, in Emily's day just as the peacemakers are today. They abhorred the injustices they saw around them, especially in the slavery, often accepted by those who pretended to believe in Christ. Many then, also, ignored "The Sermon on the Mount," as they pillaged and fought and preached "fire and brimstone" over true charity and love. I think Emily must have read Hawthorne's "The Maypole of Marymount,' in which he argues against the evils of Puritanism and literal use of scripture in the "Age of Iron" as opposed to the Spiritual Enlightenment afforded by transcendental respect for the study of nature.

[AO]: Do you see many similarities between her plight and yours?

[DG]: Just as my life has been clouded by fanatical religiosity in the Age of Terrorism, so was hers emergent from the "Puritan Age of Iron," as Hawthorne called it. *The Scarlet Letter* is about religious hypocrisy and how it destroys truly humane character. Charles Dickens was writing of social injustice and moral truths as well, and was popular here in America then. I live in the shadow of misery created in my time by the last presidential administration that thought God led the U.S. to bomb and murder the Mid-East into "democracy" as insane Fundamentalist Muslims match his ardor for self-righteous tyranny. I had to hide from the attack on my city in 2001, as Emily had to hide in her basement on Sunday mornings to keep from being dragged to the parish church by her austere father. When Samuel Dickinson founded Amherst College, it was a seminary meant to fashion Christian missionaries who would fan out across the country and preach. Many ignored the essence of true Christianity, the beatitudes, for punitive ideas. This is similar to what our warmongering, military profiteering American administrations have done in our time as imperialist puppets of war industrialists and oil moguls. We need more *true prophets of human decency and kindness* and far fewer weapons profiteers. However, it's true that Helen Hunt Jackson and Mabel Loomis Todd understood Dickinson's poetry greatly. And, Sue Gilbert knew that Emily's poetry was original and insightful. She wrote a telling obituary about her sister-in-law that says much that's accurate. Dickinson should not be thought of as a lonely little wretch without a support system at all, but known by women who understood her work and encouraged it.

[AO]: That's largely how I feel. When it comes to my poetry, I really have a strong support system of women writers who understand my poetry, especially you and Amy Fleury.

[DG]: Probably the important women in Dickinson's life understood her better than her father, and some of the men, but certainly Sue Gilbert, Helen Hunt Jackson were an important support system, along with female writers she read. Mabel Loomis Todd, Austin's mistress, was utterly instrumental in preserving Dickinson's poetry for publication. Her sister, Lavinia, wanted to preserve it, but could never have done it without Mabel who went to Higginson, her first in-house editor, to bring it to posthumous publication. If it was Sue who nurtured her intellect early on, it was Helen Hunt Jackson, a successful writer and social activist of her time, who called her "a great poet" and urged her to publish. It was women—importantly Lavinia and Mabel Loomis Todd, and her niece Matty, and Mabel's daughter, too—whose commitment brought it to light. Higginson was instrumental as well, and shouldn't be blamed for her lack of publication during her lifetime. She didn't want to publish, because it was not ladylike for a statesman's daughter. She respected the father who sustained her and her family.

[AO]: What's your feminist take on Dickinson's situation?

[DG]: Girls were completely repressed then—even more than now in America. The women's suffrage movement was newly born. Her father was among the first of American men to believe that a woman deserved any education, even though he thought it was meant only for the graces of her home-life as a wife and mother. I grew up always hearing my Italian immigrant father longing for a son. He'd bemoan, "If only I had a son to carry on the name!" whenever we three sisters worried him. Women were just beginning to bloom out of their shells in Emily's day, and in mine, and much of the world's womanhood is still trapped in the Dark Ages. Birth control only became legal three years before I was born. My mother was of the first generation to be given the vote. And, oh, what a battle the movement for suffrage was! It took much suffering and endless activism—over a full century—from its inception to completion. My Italian Catholic aunts never even attended the state college three miles from home that I did. And when I did attend Montclair University, then a smaller college in 1956, it was against my father's best advice. Though he'd struggled for a good education and worked his way through degrees from Union College and Columbia University, his mantra was, "What does a girl need an education for? She only marries and has babies." Similarly, Emily Norcross, Dickinson's mother, and her sister, Lavinia, were content as homemakers who practiced housekeeping above reading or writing. Neither Emily nor I were interested in only households. "God save me from what women call Households!" she declared in a letter.

[AO]: Would you say that you feel connected to Emily as woman in addition to feeling connected to her as a poet?

[DG]: Emily was an internally, self-liberated woman for her time in her quiet way. She was not interested in the "dimity convictions" of gentlewomen. And even though my Italian immigrant father said to me, "Why should a girl go to college? It's a waste." he did help me a little with state college tuition only $95 per semester then, and he encouraged reading. He gave *mixed* messages, like Dickinson's father who was proud of her conversational abilities and intellectual refinements, but forbade her publication. I went to graduate school on scholarships and my father didn't try to stop me. I studied and read literature and science as Dickinson did, much on my own. She studied botany, biology, chemistry, ornithology, geology, literature, history much on her own, also.

[AO]: What other parallels do you identify with between your life and Dickinson's?

[DG]: Emily and I both lived during periods of war. I was born in the midst of World War II. Emily lived through the Anti-slavery Movement and the Civil War (which almost took her lover from her). I lived through the Civil Rights Movement— was nearly killed by the Ku Klux Klan. I lived through the Vietnam War. It almost took my husband, and my daughter's father, from me, though I was for much of my writing life without a husband.

[AO]: What about temperament? Do you think Emily's temperament may have been similar to your own?

[DG]: We're both a "middle child." We longed to please others: being neither the privileged older child, nor the beloved baby. Emily was born between her older brother, Austin, and her younger sister, Lavinia. She spent her life with them nearby. Her father is known to have valued his son's intellect most of all. He enjoyed Austin's wit and letter writing, more than he ever read Emily's poetry it seems. Emily was a fine gardener and a good baker, who loved to give gifts from her flower garden and her brick oven. They say liking to feed people well is a sign of a nurturing nature. People enjoy my cooking. Being known as a good cook doesn't have to make you less of a poet. Emily's townspeople knew her as a baker, a gardener, and a daughter of an important politician of Massachusetts. Only a chosen few knew her as a poet. If she'd had an affair with a married man, it would've been just as publically unknown as her being a great poet.

[AO]: That brings me to a point I wanted to make earlier. Even though I'm also a lover of nineteenth-century romance, even though I'm somewhat enamored with William Clark myself, it's difficult for me to imagine Emily Dickinson having an affair with a married man.

[DG]: I believe that Emily and Will fell in love *before* Clark was married. Also, when we think of Dickinson's life as devoid of marriage, we don't realize that there were few *eligible* men for her or her sister, Lavinia, in Amherst's rural aristocracy. There were five young women of Dickinson's social class to every eligible bachelor—a fact that literary critics who expound on her spinsterhood should be more aware of! The westward movement during the years after the Louisiana Purchase called away many of Amherst's eligible bachelors to Western business ventures. Civil War took more from her area.

Also, men whose wives had still-born infants, as Clark's wife had, were advised to leave their wives alone and deny themselves marital bliss until after pregnancies were over. Clark's wife was *often* pregnant; they had *eight* children, and two of his children died early on. No doubt he was afraid to go near his wife when she was in what was called "confinement." Pregnant women did not socialize and were advised to stay at home in Dickinson's day. Carriage, buggy, and horseback rides were far more jarring and rigorous, along deeply rutted dirt roads, than car and train rides in our time.

If Clark was a married man and Emily was his "Mistress" as he was her "Master," this would not have been so uncommon, even in Victorian times. In fact, her cousin, Maria Whitney, was likely Samuel Bowles' "mistress" and intellectual companion, just as Mabel Loomis Todd was her brother's mistress. Victorians were never as Victorian as we sometimes imagine them to have been. There was plenty of straying outside marriage. The Reverend Beecher, originally of Amherst, was caught in an affair with a married woman of his parish at the Plymouth Church here in Brooklyn Heights where Abraham Lincoln gave a famous antislavery speech in New York. Beecher's affair was the talk of the town and newspapers. Affairs between married people really weren't as unusual as one might imagine then. Christopher Benfey's book, *A Summer of Hummingbirds: Love, Art, and Scandal in the Intersecting Worlds of Emily Dickinson, Mark Twain, Harriet Beecher Stowe, and Martin Johnson Heade*,[68] has much to do with scandal among the American intelligentsia of the day. Mabel's and Austin's affair is the subject of a book by the Dickinson scholar, Polly Longsworth. Mabel's husband Todd, a professor of astronomy at Amherst College was a real womanizer, and drove Mabel to seek solace with Austin Dickinson, just as Austin was probably denied marital bliss by Susan Gilbert who had good reason to fear childbirth before the time of contraception. Her sister Mary died miserably giving birth to a baby who also died. Childbirth was a dangerous, often gruesome event. Childbed fever was rampant before the age of antibiotics. I think Dickinson's mother was never

---

[68]See Benfey's *A Summer of Hummingbirds: Love, Art, and Scandal in the Intersecting Worlds of Emily Dickinson, Mark Twain, Harriet Beecher Stowe, and Martin Johnson Heade* (New York: Penguin, 2008).

healthy again after the birth of her sister, Lavinia. Biographers know Dickinson's mother had a difficult childbirth with Lavinia. Emily as a small child heard the screams. She and Susan not doubt discussed fears of childbearing.

[AO]: So, Austin Dickinson's mistress, Mabel Loomis Todd, was responsible for the publication of much of Emily's poetry. Could you tell me more about her?

[DG]: Many don't realize it was Austin Dickinson's illicit amore who saw to the editing and publishing of Emily's first volume of poetry. Few poets or readers of Dickinson are aware that it is Mabel's drawing of Indian Pipes, one of Emily's favorite wildflowers, that graces the cover of the first edition of Dickinson's poems. Mabel, though she came to sing and play the piano in Dickinson's parlor while Emily enjoyed listening from upstairs, never got to meet in person.

Even though Emily is supposed to have died of Bright's disease or kidney failure, it's odd that she died just six weeks after Clark, while reading "Romeo and Juliet," the story of star-crossed lovers. She marked the passage of Juliet's that reads, "I know an apothecary...." Ruth Owen Jones, the historian of Amherst, who inspired my novel, makes this point. Clark is said to have died of a broken heart. Perhaps, Emily did also. People she loved died during the last few years of her life. Many died in those days from typhoid, cholera, scarlet fever, tuberculosis, and pneumonia. Death was a real constant in her life. It was not a mere *psychological obsession* as some critics who fail to read medical history claim. Death was a reality all around her to be dealt with philosophically. At least five of her best friends died before she reached the age of fifteen years, and the only portrait that people accept of her as authentic is one taken of her at about seventeen just after a severe illness that nearly pulled her into death's dominion with some of her closest schoolmates. She lived with a cemetery outside her window until the age of fifteen when the family returned to the previously mentioned Dickinson Homestead on Main Street. One thing most literary biographers often neglect to emphasize is the medical science of the times in which their subjects lived. There are few index entries on diseases in the most eminent biographies of the poet dealing with the issues that made her, as some critics write, "obsessed" with death in her poetry.

[AO]: That's a very important insight. Since we're nearing the end of our interview, is there anything else you would like to say about Emily Dickinson or about your novel?

[DG]: Yes, I want to thank you for your interest, because I see that you're an accomplished reader and writer yourself, especially for a woman of your age. I want to explain that I relived Emily's life in my mind in order to understand my own life as an American poet as well as hers. She was born of white Anglo-Saxon rural aristocracy in a small village in Massachusetts, in the 19th century. I come from Greek-Albanian-Italian and Polish-Russian-Jewish immigrants, and was born in the 20th century in a big city, but we're both American women poets of a liberal and rebellious bent. Dickinson was a transcendentalist rebelling against the Puritans. She made poetry her means of worshipping nature and all creation. I'm a *progressive, eco-feminist humanist*, a Free Thinker, as I believe Dickinson was for her time. She was a "Lover of Science and Scientist in Dark Days of the Republic," as I call her in my non-fiction afterword to *Wild Nights, Wild Nights*. Knowing her story makes her poetry more accessible to me, and I am enamored of studying the truth of science, too. I feel her frustration, her passion, and empathize with it, but that is what good poets do, *create empathy*. I was unable to get her likely affair with William Clark Smith out of my head. Why she took over my mind and imagination so, perhaps has to do with that inexplicable Mp3 audio file of "My river runs to thee..." playing out of my laptop all by itself in the Emily Dickinson Room at Wellspring Writers' Retreat in Ashfield, birthplace of Will Clark, just after my visit to the Dickinson Museum in Amherst. I felt compelled to write about her with the realization of Ruth Owen Jones's discovery of her mysterious "Master" figure. I believe, after much research into Dickinson's life and texts that Jones is correct. I hope I've created a little additional empathy for the truth of the poet's life and the profound meanings in her poetry, her love of science over religious dogma. It's such an important theme for our time when creationists are again attempting to deny the truth of Darwinism and rightwing politicians, supported by religious fanatics, are ignoring climate change and global warming. To tell a finer truth about this iconic American woman poet was my mission.

[AO]: I think you've succeeded in doing so. Thanks, Daniela.

PART III: PERSONAL AND POLEMIC ESSAYS
BY DANIELA GIOSEFFI

by Daniela Gioseffi

ℱ ORGING INTO THE AMERICAN MAINSTREAM SINCE THE 1960S: ON BEING A WOMAN WRITER WITH AN ITALIAN NAME

Published in *Breaking Open: Reflections on Italian American Women's Writing,* ed. Mary Ann Mannino and Justin Vitiello (West Lafayette, IN: Purdue UP, 2003).

Forging into the mainstream of American poetry with the Italian name "Daniela Gioseffi" was not an easy thing to do in the 1960's. I realize I was a bit like a Tarantella dancer trying to perform a classical ballet, but that fact hardly occurred to me—naïve and blithe spirit that I was then! My Italian-born father's deeply passionate nature, his ability to empathize with other's sorrow, joy, and longing—even when they were characters in poetic dramas and romantic novels—much inspired my writing. His histrionic sensibility was not in the stereotypic style of "all-American" educated culture. Perhaps, as an immigrant daughter, I felt I was among the misfits whose family manner or mode of expression was frowned upon, or completely misunderstood in those literary circles dominated by T.S. Eliot recitations and modes of understated angst.

Richard C. Robertiello and Diana Hoguet in their 1986 analytical text on the subject, *The WASP Mystique,*[69] demonstrate that Latino, Italian, African, and Jewish-American styles of communicating—modes with passionate displays, talk with gesticulation, animated body-language, folksy warmth and informality—were misunderstood by the "all-American" style of social behavior. Robertiello and Hoguet conclude that this emotional restraint has caused much neurosis in ethnic peoples, and sometimes in white Anglo-Saxon Protestants themselves. These polite inhibitions seemed to dominate literary styles, and particularly during my college years, they made displays of passion in poetry unacceptable.

At the same time, it seemed there was a kind of "passion envy" afoot in "all American" life and art, the sort of fascination which had made Hollywood characters like Valentino fascinating for my father's generation and which would make Al Pacino, Robert De Niro, and John Travolta fascinating in later decades. I recall that a student-poet named Frances Vanderbilt Whyatt—in workshop sessions, which I attended early on at The Poetry Project at St. Mark's Church in the Bowery—wrote a poem titled, "The Passion Through Daniela's Window," in response to my work. I was embarrassed by a quality I had not realized others saw in my writing. In any case, the Italian operatic style in which my father read literature to me as a child motivated me to write poetry and caused much of my work to have an emotionalism and dramatic content.

---

[69]See Robertiello and Hoguet, *The WASP Mystique* (New York: Donald I. Fine, 1987).

My identification with the drama of my father's immigrant struggle against prejudice and discrimination was strong because of the feeling with which he related the painful stories of his youth. His family, like many others in southern Italy in the early part of the century, came to the United States to escape poverty and hunger, only to be met with bigotry. His father, Galileo, sought his fortune, as so many men of his *Mezzogiorno*[70] village did then, in the New World, later sending for his family via steerage passage. My father and his family were to be met with much prejudice and snobbery in their attempt to Americanize themselves and assimilate.

I inherited my love of literature from a poor, hardworking, immigrant father who had struggled to achieve an education. His dramatic quoting of Shakespeare to me as I grew was, and still is, an important influence on my themes and style. He'd memorized the Bard's plays while tending a parking lot at night, and working his way through Union College with an ambition to learn the English language better than his American tormentors. Felix Stefanile,[71] an Italian American poet, has told me he deliberately portrays workingmen's themes in classical, formalist style. Like my immigrant father, he wanted to use perfect English and metric form to portray ordinary lives.

My father's first American teachers and his classmates had cruelly mocked his immigrant speech when he'd first arrived through Ellis Island in 1910. With very hard work and study, he amassed an extensive English vocabulary and spoke with eloquence. He wanted to use language better than his American classmates. He admired Abraham Lincoln, and believed in the log-cabin mythos of Lincoln's life—"the American Dream." That dream forged my ambition as he read to me such authors as Cervantes when I was ten years old, and Shakespeare's *Romeo and Juliet*— weeping with me at the finale. He loved Italian Renaissance painters whose work he would show me with pride in color-illustrated and much-treasured books he'd labored to buy. He was very proud of being an Italian and always told me anecdotal narratives of the lives of Leonardo Da Vinci, Michelangelo, Fermi, Caruso—those whom he considered to be the great Italian *men*. However, he never mentioned a woman to admire in his stories of Italian accomplishment!

Since my father had always dreamed of becoming a writer, my writing has been an attempt to fulfill his dream for him. I can still picture him sitting with his back to us, hunched over his typewriter, forgoing the glories of a sunny afternoon, trying when he could, between the duties of his full-time job as a chemical engineer, to become a writer. "American Sonnets to My Father" in my second book of poems, *Word Wounds and Water Flowers* (VIA/Bordighera 1995) written the year he died, 1981, is dedicated to him. It honors his struggle to be an American and tells of how I've attempted to fulfill his desire to be a published author. I managed to win a scholarship to the Edna St. Vincent Millay Colony for the Arts the year he died, and while there, walking alone in the woods, grieving his loss—he forever so dear to me—I wrote, "American Sonnets for My Father":

---

[70]*Mezzogiorno,* literally meaning "midday," is used to refer to southern Italy and sometimes connotes stereotypes of southern Italy, including notions of poverty, illiteracy, and crime that still persist today.
[71]Stephanile (1920–2009) has won many prizes for his poetry and work including the Emily Clark Balch Prize (*Virginia Quarterly Review* 1972) and the John Ciardi Award for Lifetime Achievement (*Italian Americana* 1997). In reference to Stefanile's collection of poetry, *The Dance at Saint Gabriel's* (Story Line P 1995), Dana Gioia wrote that "To say that Felix Stefanile is the most significant living Italian-American poet does not do justice to his achievement."

You died in spring, father, and now the autumn dies.
Bright with ripe youth, dulled by time,
plums of feeling leaked red juices from your eyes,
pools of blood hemorrhaged in your quivering mind.
At forty, I climb Point Pinnacle, today,
thinking of you gone forever from me.
In this russet November woods of Millay,
I wear your old hat, Dear Italian patriarch, to see
if I can think you out of your American grave
to sing your unwritten song with me.
Your poetry, love's value, I carry with your spirit.
I take off your old black hat and sniff at it
to smell the still living vapor of your sweat.

You worked too hard, an oldest child of too many,
a lame thin boy in ragged knickers, you limped
all through the 1920s up city steps, door to door
with your loads of night and daily newspapers, each worth
a cheap labored penny of your family's keep.
You wore your heart and soles sore. At forty,
not climbing autumn hills like me, you lay with lung disease
strapped down with pain and morphine, hearing your breath
rattle in your throat like keys at the gates of hell.
Your body was always a fiend perplexing your masculine will.
You filled me with pride and immigrant tenacity. Slave
to filial duty, weaver of all our dreams, you couldn't be free
to sing. So be it. You are done, unfulfilled by song except in me.
If your dreams are mine, live again, breathe in me and be.

You never understood America's scheme.
Your wounded dream, father,
will never heal in me, your spirit mourns forever
from my breath, aches with childhood memory,
sighs for my own mortality in you,
which I, at last accept
more completely than ever when we
laughed together and seemed we'd go on forever –
even though we always knew
you would die much sooner than I
who am your spirit come from you.
Remember, "a father lost, lost his!" you told us,
preparing us with Shakespearean quotation
and operatic feeling for your inevitable death.

Good night, go gently, tired immigrant father
full of pride and propriety. We, your
three daughters, all grew
to be healthier, stronger, more American than you.
Sensitive father, I offer you this toast,
no empty boast, "I've never known a man braver!"

The wound that will not heal in me
is the ache of dead beauty.
Once full of history, philosophy, poetry,
physics, astronomy, your bright, high flying psyche
is now dispersed, set free from your tormented body,
but the theme you offered, often forlorn,
sheer luminescent soul, glistened with enough light
to carry us all full grown. (9–10)

Yet, my immigrant father with all his passions, and despite his sensitivity, had told me it was a useless endeavor for a female "meant for cooking and bearing children" to go to college. It was the men of my generation who left the home to achieve as professionals, not the women. When I dared to defy my father by going to college, I commuted only a few miles from home to a state institution in Montclair, New Jersey.

The message I heard from my father—that a daughter was less than a son— drove me into a feminist rebellion. I began to read such feminist sociopolitical critiques as those written by Emma Goldman,[72] and I fondly quoted her declaration, "If I can't dance, I won't join your revolution." I also greatly admired Isadora Duncan's[73] rebelliousness.

This made women's themes important in my early work, particularly my first book, a novel *The Great American Belly* (Doubleday 1977). It is a comic feminist satire that deals with an Italian American heroine, named Dorissa Femfunelli, who travels the country performing a feminist ritual dance celebrating childbirth and women's nurturing ways. Dorissa—a Goddess worshipping eco-feminist— rebelled against patriarchal religions and her Italian father. At the same time, she was always anxiously seeking his approval.

In addition, an early poem of mine, entitled "Belly Dancer," was used at the end of my novel to show the triumph of the birth-dancing heroine, Dorissa Femfunelli. The poem celebrates womanly powers and the ability to bring new life into the world, and it's titled "Birth Dance, Belly Dancer":

An Etruscan priestess
through whom the earth speaks,
enters veiled; a mystery moves toward the altar.
Unknown features, shadow of death, of brows,
of eyes, mouth, lips, teeth of the night,
navel hidden, mysterious circuit,
electrical wire of the first cries
thrust from the womb.
Silk veils hover over her,
turn with a whirling gestures
—the moon glows in her belly.

---

[72]Goldman (1869–1940) was an early figure in the women's rights movement, birth control history, and the free speech movement. She supported anarchism and lesbian rights.
[73]Duncan (1877–1927) was a dancer, ahead of her times in all aspects of her life, and is created with the creation of modern dance.

Her navel winks in an amorous quiver.
Amazing belly that stretches large enough
to let a life grow. She glides, dips, shimmies,
thrusts one hip, then another.
The music breaks. Pain fills the drum. She
falls to her knees, doubles over, leans back on her heels
as her stomach flutters, rolls with contractions, upward,
downward. She raises her pelvis, arching, widening.
Arms rise like serpents from her shoulders,
beat, caress, nip, shimmer the air with rhythmic
pulse. At last the bloody mystery emerges,
inch by inch the head presses through the lost hymen.
Her pain works into a smile.
as the decked and bejeweled mother
pushes out her ecstasy.
Formless fluid shot into her,
molded, fired in the secret oven,
emerges, a child crying: it lives!
Its voice rings in her finger cymbals.

She rests her body, slowly rises from the earth.
Her breasts fill with milk. She shakes them:
these are milk; I am life; I give food!

Woman, whose nerve-filled clitoris
makes her shiver, ecstatic mother, dance with a fury
around your circle of women.
Spin out the time locked in your own womb,
bloom from your uterus, Lady of the Garden.
The moon pulls you, crashes waves on the shore.
Undulate the branches of your arms in the wind,
Goddess of Trees, of all living things.
Your flesh is not defiled by
men who can't contain your mystic
energy of woman. Belly
that invites life to sleep in you,
breasts of mortal ambrosia,
Amazon groin that lit the hearth,
altar, oven, womb, bread, table, Earth
Mother, pagan witch of magic birth,
from whom all suck leaves that flow
through the body's blood,
cave of your sex, our home,
moon of earth, Great Mother! (180–82)

Thus, the poem portrays an ancient folk ritual performed by women as a birth dance in imitation of birth contractions. The performance of the belly dance was a primitive Lamaze type of exercise to prepare women for natural childbirth—the quintessential feminine dance of life and birth—counterpart to the male "war

dance" or "dance of the hunt." It became a café spectacle after being put on display at the Chicago World's Fair in 1893, but had been a folk art ritual of the
Middle East and the vineyards of Italy and Greece.[74]

"Belly Dancer" became an important part of the theatrical performance "The
Birth Dance of Earth: A Celebration of Women and the Earth." It was a choreo-
poem with music and dance that I performed on campuses and in theatres around
the country, travelling from Miami to Milwaukee, San Francisco to Buffalo. During the performance, I danced, with other women joining in at the *finale*, joyously
celebrating woman's birth-giving and nurturing abilities. The tour culminated in
a performance at the Brooklyn Museum where the leading feminist artists of the
day featured their works, including the debut there of Judy Chicago's famous
installation, "The Dinner Party."

If my father had taught me that women were only meant for bearing children,
I devised a liberating way of celebrating the fact, and making it a feminist ritual.
My poem on the belly dance was published by *MS. Magazine* in a centerfold
spread, titled "The New Dance of Liberation." My earliest publications in those
first issues of *MS.* were what encouraged me to persist in these womanly themes
down to the present day as the Feminist Press prepares to reissue my international
anthology of women's writings, *Women on War: An Anthology of Writings from
Antiquity to the Present* (2003).[75]

Early on in the 1970's, I also created an experimental, dance theatre and poetry
piece, with visuals, titled "Care of the Body," which won me a grant from The
New York State Council for the Arts. I used the grant to create the first "Brooklyn Bridge Poetry Walk,"[76] a multimedia street theatre piece with David Amram,
famed jazz flutist, as Pied Piper, and poets reading poems about "The Bridge." We
walked over "The Eighth Wonder of the World," Hart Crane's "harp and altar of
the fury fused," reading Lorca, Mayakovsky, Walt Whitman, and others through
megaphones. We carried hand-painted placards I'd adorned with poets' names.

Seeing mine as the only Italian name on the list of grantees for the State Council on the Arts that year, had given me license and ambition to forge on in *that*
mode or form. It was a great impetus to my sticking with writing as a career.
I'd based the "Brooklyn Bridge Poetry Walk" on an Italian Renaissance custom
expounded by Florentine historians. The people of Florence, for example, are
known to have paraded Michelangelo's statue of David through their streets to
celebrate its creation. Also, Italian street fairs where an experience of my youth
when huge sculptures were carried through ghetto thoroughfares to celebrate
saints' days with festivals. Such influences explain why much of my early work
was performance poetry for theatre and street theatre.

I chose to acquire my higher degree in world drama, not poetry; all of this
bravado for performance, I believe, came directly from my father's, Donato's,
operatic way of storytelling. I had wanted to be an actress, and had acted early on

---

[74]See Gioseffi's *Earth Dancing: Mother Nature's Oldest Rite* (Harrisburg, PA: Stackpole Books, 1980).
[75]The first edition was *Women on War: Essential Voices for the Nuclear Age from a Brilliant Assembly*
(Simon and Schuester, 1988).
[76]The "Brooklyn Bridge Poetry Walk" is now hosted by Poets House.

with Helen Hayes and Ann Revere in Brechtian and Classical dramas. I also wrote a playlet, titled "Daffodil Dollars." Again, the theme was women's empowerment. I was a part of the early experimental poetry scene in New York's Soho—creating "happenings" or multimedia poetry events involving performance, music and dance. From there, I made a slow segue from poetic drama and theatrical performance to poetry for the page.

Although my feminist writing takes delight in all aspects of women's lives, the women in my family—my grandmother, my mother, and my aunts—seemed to be bound to the home, the kitchen, and the sewing-machine and did not seem to find much joy in being women. I viewed them as repressed; their limitations and their need for liberation inspired me to write about women's lives. I wanted to release them from the patriarchal culture in which I was raised where only men's opinions were voiced because they were the only opinions that mattered. Half of the human race, the nurturing less warlike half, was excluded from important and worldly decision-making.

My poetic monologue, "The Sea Hag in the Cave of Sleep," which tells of the sexual and mothering adventures of three women of different ages, was produced off-Broadway from 1968 through 1972. The "sea hags," characters inspired by James Joyce,[77] represented my Italian aunts and grandmother telling the stories of their struggle as women in a male-dominated world. They tell of how Pandora and Eve are blamed for all the troubles in men's lives, and all the while macho ways are causing destructive conflicts, famines and other brutalities that follow war. The poem ends with the lines: "I come out of my own legs into this world," which is meant as an affirmation of women's self-actualization. Woman is born of woman, and that's a different phenomenon than being man born of woman.

In tribute to this, and to Grandma Lucia (my father's Neapolitan mother), I wrote a poem which seems to embody all that was self-sacrificing and limiting for women in a patriarchal culture and performed it at *Casa Italiana*, Columbia University, in 1978 at the dawning of the current Italian American renaissance in literature. The poem, titled "Bi-centennial Anti-poem for Italian American Women, 1976," is not only dedicated to my grandmother—Lucia La Rosa or "Light the Rose"—it was also inspired by Ernesto Falbo. Falbo had been in the audience at one of my earlier readings at SUNY Buffalo, a reading of mine where, afterwards, he said to me, "You're one of only two or three Italian-American women poets in this country. You're a pioneer. There are fewer of you known than Black or Puerto Rican women poets." Through this statement, he inspired the following, "Anti-poem for Italian American Women," 1976, now called "For Grandma Lucia La Rosa: Light the Rose" in later years:

> On the crowded subway,
> riding to the prison to teach
> Black and Puerto Rican inmates how to write,
> I think of the fable of the shoemaker

---

[77]The sea hags appear in Joyce's *Finnegan's Wake* (Faber and Faber 1939).

who struggles to make shoes for the oppressed
while his own go barefoot over the stones.

I remember Grandma Lucia, her olive face
wrinkled with resignation,
content just to survive
after giving birth to twenty children,
without orgasmic pleasures or anesthesia.
Grandpa Galileo, immigrant adventurer,
who brought his family
steerage passage to the New World;
his shoemaker shop where he labored
over American factory goods
that made his artisan's craft a useless
anachronism; his Code of Honor
which forced him to starve
accepting not a cent of welfare
from anyone but his sons;
his ironic "Code of Honor"
which condoned jealous rages of wife-beating;
Aunt Elisabetta, Aunt Maria Domenica, Aunt Raffaella,
Aunt Elena, grown women huddled like girls
in their bedroom in Newark, talking in whispers,
not daring to smoke their American cigarettes
in front of Pa;
the backyard shrine of the virgin,
somber blue-robed woman,
devoid of sexual passions,
to whom Aunt Elisabetta prayed
daily before dying in childbirth,
trying to have "a son"
against doctor's orders, though
she had five healthy daughters already;
Dr. Giuseppe Ferrara, purple heart veteran
of World War II, told he couldn't have a residency
in a big New York hospital because of his Italian
name; the Mafia jokes, the epithets:
"Wop, guinea, dago, grease-ball."
And the stories told by Papa
of Dante, Galileo, Da Vinci, Marconi, Fermi, Caruso
that stung me with pride for Italian men;
how I was discouraged from school,
told a woman meant for cooking and bearing
doesn't need education.

I remember
Grandma
got out of bed
in the middle of the night
to fetch her husband a glass of water

.

the day she died,
her body wearied
from giving and giving and giving
food and birth. (7)

Though I devoured Nancy Drew mysteries in grammar school like any all-American girl, in my teens I discovered Edna St. Vincent Millay. The drama of her life, the fact that she won a scholarship to Vassar for a poem she wrote and her subsequent rise from poverty into the light of poetry really impressed me. It was a dramatic story like the ones my father told of his struggle to become educated and respectable from humble beginnings. But Millay was a woman and a feminist, and to see that a woman could work hard to become a writer and be respected for her work, really influenced me. She was such a great beacon to me, both her life and her craft with language. I was pleased to find how Millay had marched for Sacco and Vanzetti. Her poem, "Justice Denied in Massachusetts," is a tribute to the Italian immigrant struggle in America. Her example as a liberated woman and her involvement with social justice inspired me greatly.

My father didn't teach us Italian, not for lack of pride in it, but perhaps because he'd experienced so much prejudice for being an Italian immigrant. It's a little re-membered fact that there were concentration camps for Italian immigrants in the United States during World War II, similar to those in which Japanese immigrants were unjustly incarcerated. I remember a poster I saw in my ghetto neighborhood as a child living in the Ironbound section of Newark. I wrote this poem as a result. It explains why I, born during World War II, am not fluent in Italian. It's titled "Don't Speak the Language of the Enemy" it toured with Lawrence Di Staci's exhibit of *Una Storia Segreta*:

"Don't Speak the Language of the Enemy!"
reads the poster at the end of a gray alleyway of childhood
where the raggedy guineas of Newark
whisper quietly in their dialects on concrete steps
far from blue skies, olive groves or hyacinths.
Bent in a shadow toward the last
shafts of sunlight above tenement roofs,
Grandpa Galileo sadly sips homemade wine
hums moaning with his broken mandolin.
Children play hide-and-seek
in dusty evening streets as red sauce simmers,
proverbially, hour after hour, on coal stoves,
garlic, oil, crushed tomatoes blended
with precious pinches of salt and *basilico*—
a pot that must last a week of suppers.
The fathers' hands are ugly with blackened finger nails,
worn rough with iron wrought, bricks laid, ditches dug, glass etched.
Wilted women in black cotton dresses wait in quickening dark,
calling their listless children to scrubbed linoleum kitchens.
In cold water flats with tin tables, stale bread is ladled with sauce,

then baked to revive edibility. Clothes soak in kitchen laundry-tubs,
washboards afloat. Strains of opera caught in static
are interrupted by war bulletins.

The poster pasted on the fence at the end of the block
streaked with setting sun and rain reads:
"Don't speak the language of the enemy!"

But, the raggedy guineas can speak no other,
and so they murmur in their rooms in the secret dark frightened
of the government camps where people like them
have been imprisoned in the New World.
They teach English to their children by daylight,
whispering of Mussolini's stupidity--
stifling the mother tongue, wounding the father's pride,
telling each other, "We are Americans. God bless America!" (36–39)

In addition to the time period I grew up in, my grandfather, Galileo Gioseffi, was also a great influence on my life and writing. From him I learned to question and rebel; Galileo was an iconoclast who loathed the Church's hypocrisy and his rebellious attitude rubbed off on my father, and then onto me. No doubt the prejudice he suffered inspired me to join the Civil Rights Movement in 1961, at which time my writing turned to journalism for a spell. My father so admired Galileo Galilei, The Father of Science, and so he never raised me as a Catholic. That was a saving and liberating aspect of my life, and may be why I am among the first Italian American women to write and publish in the mainstream of American literature.

I became a television journalist in Selma, Alabama on WSLA-TV during the days of the Freedom Riders and lunch counter sit-ins. Because television programming was not integrated in Alabama in those days, I was beaten and sexually abused by the Ku Klux Klan for making an announcement on an African American gospel show. There were burning crosses and broken watermelons on the lawn of the television station the next morning. It took me many years to write about that incidence as I wanted to spare my father the truth. He never knew what happened to me, and I was ashamed of it, too.

I was over fifty when I finally published "The Bleeding Mimosa," a story about my rape and abuse at the hands of the Ku Klux Klan. Luciana Polney, a younger Italian American woman writer, adapted it well for the stage, and it was produced at the Duplex Theatre in New York City's Sheridan Square in 1994. It was a very liberating experience for me to view my story acted out by others. I watched the scenes between the immigrant father and the American daughter; the conflict in those scenes—to be a good daughter, and at the same time, to struggle to overcome prejudice toward liberation—was my conflict. I felt healed as I saw it played out to a survivalist's conclusion. I don't need to tell you how it brought copius tears to my eyes to watch Lucianna's dramatization of my story, "The Bleeding Mimosa." It saddened us both that no Italian Americans of The Italian American Writers Association attended that play. We are not so good, or weren't so good then, at supporting each other's endeavors. It greatly discouraged Lucianna and she left the Italian American scene to find better support elsewhere.

Now, as I've reached the age of sixty and look back over my career as a writer, I can clearly distinguish my influences. My Italian father—his passionate nature, his frustrated desire to be a respected writer in America, the prejudice he suffered, the reading he taught me to love, the education in literary art and science which he worked hard to acquire—was a large influence on my tenacious desire to forge my way into the mainstream of American letters.

On the other hand, my Grandmother Lucia's subjugation to my grandfather's will; my coming from an immigrant family which rebelled against the Church's ways, but in some measure upheld its patriarchal values; my own rebellion against Old World ways, seeking for truth and anarchistic liberation from the past; my desire to keep my father's surname and strive for acceptance as a daughter who could not be a son, as a woman who wanted to make a loving father proud: *all* these factors had a profound influence on my drive to become the first educated woman of my family, and my striving for an accomplished voice imbued with feminist themes in American literature.

My immigrant Italian forbearers made me who I am for worse or for better, and I can never deny that rich heritage of passionate emotions— the suffering and joy that art portrays— which I learned early on from my Old World Italian family. Despite my feminism, I have to say that my Italian patriarchal father's love of literature—his tenacity to fulfill the American Dream—was my greatest inspiration to being a writer. Sandra Mortola Gilbert, Diane Di Prima, Josephine Gattuso Hendin, and I—we feminists of that 1970s era—have I hope, offered some impetus to the women who began to publish later. The following poem says it all for me. It was written when I finally made the pilgrimage back to my father's village of origin, Orta Nova, near the Gargano—the spur of the boot—not far from Bari, in 1986, five years after his death. The poem is titled after the village, "Orta Nova, Provincia de Puglia":

"Land of bright sun and colors,"
you're called in *Italia—*.
near Bari and Brindisi where the ferry
for centuries has traveled the *Adriatico,*
to and from the "Glory that was Greece."
Orta Nova, city of my dead father's birth.
How strange to view you, piccolo villaggio,
with ladybugs, my talisman, landed on my shirt.

They show me your birth
certificate--"Donato Gioseffi, born 1905,"
scrawled in ink, on browning paper.
When I tell them I'm an author, first of my American family
to return to my father's home, I'm suddenly "royalty!"
They close the *Municipio* to take me in their best town car
to an archeological dig near the edge of the city.
There, the Kingdom of Herdonia, unearthed with its brick road

leading to Rome, as all roads did and still do,
back to antiquity's glory! Ladybugs rest on me at the dig
of stone sculptures the Belgian professor shows me. I buy his book,
"The Kingdom of Herdonia: Older Than Thebes."

Ah, *padre mio*, the taunts you took as a thin,
diminutive, "guinea" who spoke no English
in his fifth-grade class
from brash Americans of an infant country!
You never returned to your ancient land where now the natives,
simpatici pisani, wine and dine me in their best
ristorante. I insist on paying the bill. They give me jars
of *funghi* and *pimento* preserved in olive oil--their prize
produce to take back home with me. They nod knowingly,
when in talking of you, I must leave the table to weep--
alone in the restroom, looking into the mirror
at the eyes you gave me, the hands so like yours
that turn the brass faucet
and splash cold water over my face.

For an instant, in this foreign place, I have met you again,
Father, and have understood better, your labors,
your struggle, your pride, your humility,
the peasantry from which you came to cross the wide
sea, to make me a poet of New York City.

Which is truly my home?
This *piccolo villaggio* near Bari, with its old university,
the province where Saint Nicholas's Turkish bones are buried,
in hammered-gold and enameled reliquary,
the province of limestone caves full of paintings older than those of Lescaux,
this white town of the Gargano, unspoiled by *turisti*, this land of color
sunlight and beauty. This home where you would have been happier
and better understood than in torturous Newark tenements of your youth.

This land of sunlight, blue sky, pink and white flowers, white stucco houses,
and poverty, *mezzogiorno*, this warmth you left to make me
a poet from New York City, indifferent place,
mixed of every race, so that I am more cosmopolitan
than these, your villagers, or you
could ever dream of being. This paradoxical journey
back to a lost generation
gone forever paving the way
into a New World from the Old. (57–58)

by Daniela Gioseffi

ℬREAKING THE SILENCE FOR ITALIAN-AMERICAN WOMEN: MALIGNED AND STEREOTYPED

Published in *MS.* magazine in 1994, this article Received More Favorable letters in Response than any other article in *Ms.* that year.

My internship at WSLA-TV in Selma came to a climax when the Klan burned a cross on the lawn of the studio, after I'd appeared, a white spokesperson, enlisting Freedom Riders, on an all Black gospel show. Hardly realizing it, I'd dared to integrate Deep South television. The town was racially tense with "Sit-ins" at lunch counters and "Freedom Riders," riding on the wrong ends of segregated buses. Non-violent actions for civil rights were often the cause of raids and riots then. Following Rosa Parks' example, black and white students from the SNCC rode one morning on the wrong end of a bus seething with summer heat and racial tension. It wasn't the first ride for many, but it was for me. Afterwards, with other integrated demonstrators, I'd taken a drink at a water fountain marked with a sign: "Colored," in Tepper's Department store on Selma's Main Street.

Demonstrators on our particular ride were immediately arrested. They assumed that I wasn't booked and jailed because I was blonde, blue-eyed, and young, but my arrest came later in the evening—when I tried to enter my boarding house on a dark deserted street. A deputy sheriff, with his pistol drawn, whisked me away in his squad car, warning me to shut up or he'd shoot me for resisting arrest. "No one'll be the wiser if I do. Ain't none of your big shot niggers or Northern lawyers around to protect you!" he said. He laughed with satisfaction as he cuffed my wrists behind my back. The sheriff's office was the only law for miles around. We were alone in his unmarked police car on the way to the jail. He reached over and squeezed my left breast hard. "You're nice lookin' for such a piece of nervy Northern guinea trash. Your Papa must be the dumbest guinea goin' to let you come down here all alone. Maybe he's really an upstart Jew was an I-talian name. I heared they's lots of Jews in Italy. Your folks is probably a couple of Commies like them Jew lawyers who come down here tellin' us what to do."

I spoke, quietly, remembering the non-violent tactics I'd learned: don't anger your adversary with your defense. "People are people. We all have feelings."

"Niggers ain't people. Our preacher said the Holy Bible says so! I got no reason to think they is. And neither is guinea nigger lovers. We've lynched a few Jews and guineas down here, too, ya know? We got a whole big bunch of you dirty dagos all in one swoop in Lou'siana once not too many years ago! That burnin' cross left at your damned rebel T.V. Station was fair and final warnin'. I gave you one more chance. Then you went 'round drinkin' from nigger water fountains, too. Can't figure how you isn't greasy like them wops that run that pizza parlor in Birmingham? How come you got blue eyes like that Sin-a-tra crooner who dances with chimpanzees, like Sammy Davis, on your Northern T.V.? You oughta stay up there singin' on television, where your kind belong!"

Later, in the jailhouse, I pulled away from his explicit advance and infuriated him. "You got lots of nerve commin' down here to follow upstart niggers around my town!" My head hit against the brick wall of the cell as the deputy pushed me to the cot. "You piece of guinea trash!" Tall and muscular, he stood over me in the dingy cell as he unzipped his pants. I understood that I wasn't to be a Rosa Luxemburg or a Fanny Lou Hammer, but an unknown casualty.

Now, at fifty one, when I hear a recorded speech by Martin Luther King telling of non-violent resistance, equality for all, I ruminate, watery eyed, over those years of hope when we believed and sang, "We Shall Overcome," blacks and whites, together with Jews, Italians, British, Irish... Americans. The fervency of youth in the early sixties, when I was innocent, and virginal, and hardly knew I could die or be seriously hurt by bigotry! It wasn't that I was brave, just terribly naïve. I began my writing career, at twenty-one, as an intern journalist on Deep South television, which wasn't integrated in the early sixties anymore than were buses or lunch counters. Actually a New Jersey State College kid, in 1961, I'd travelled to the South for the summer, to work for WSLA-TV in Selma, where I was thrilled to have been hired to work on television by a Northern contact. I'd grown up in Newark, attending Avon Avenue School, an integrated public school, not far from where the Springfield Avenue race riots were to take place. Italian, Jewish, black ghettos all bordered on one another and were inextricably mixed in the school. There was plenty of racism in Newark, but it didn't seem unusual to me to live and work among blacks. I'd been called a "nigger lover" in third grade for befriending a "colored girl," Silvy Jackson. We played hopscotch in the corner of the schoolyard away from the other kids. I remember having bonded with her because we were the only kids in our class who didn't have the thirty-five cents a week that other students brought in for milk money. She sat to my left in the back row next to me, and our eyes met in a smile, as the other kids were munching their graham crackers and drinking their milk. We bonded in deprivation, pretending fiercely, together, that we hated English graham crackers and milk.

Now with menopausal hot flashes, I'm a graying blonde, who rides the New York subways at night with looks of hatred coming at me from tired nightshift workers who think I'm the enemy—who don't stop to think who might be who, or realize that we all suffer from hate and stereotyping. All are grieving, the whole earth bleeding now like a giant Selma mimosa blossom, spinning lost in greed and hate.

Over thirty years since that horrible night in Selma, with a quarter of century in the peace and social justice movement, and six published books to my name, I'm still not sure I exist as an American with a name like "Daniela Gioseffi"—too many vowels or syllables for most citizens to roll trippingly from their tongues. Yet, I'm grouped together with "white Europeans" as a privileged class. There's little acknowledgement of the subtle form of prejudice that still plagues Americans with my kind of ethnic name.

Having lived most of my life amidst the world of professional writers in New York, I have to relate this issue of ethnic prejudice in terms of my career. Writing for me, as for people of color, is a continuing fight for cultural identity. I look at the roster of the PEN American Center and recognize about five or six Italian female names and not many more male ones, among the thousands there. Do I ever see an Italian name on the brochures of the Academy of American Poets with its token Jewish, black, and Asian visages? It makes no sense to me, to lump all European American whites in a privileged class.

In my case, as a second generation Italian-American woman, there are no critically acclaimed role models in U.S. literature to aspire to or network with in an "ole gal" circuit. Frances Winwar, who was forced to change her name from "Francesca Vinciguerra," in order to publish her many biographical novels, is as much forgotten here, despite her prolific career as a novelist, as is Grazia Deledda, who was the second female writer—after the Swede, Selma Lagerlof—to win the Novel Prize for literature in 1926. Accomplished Italian women writers like Maria Mazziotti-Gillan, Diane Di Prima, Helen Barolini, Sandra Mortola-Gilbert, Barbara Grizutti-Harrison, Phyllis Capello, Josephine Gattuso, Lucia Maria Perillo, Patricia Storace, and Dorothy Barresi are fairly invisible on the American literary scene, despite their achievements and growing numbers. Few, educated in America, would have the opportunity to know of role models like Vittoria Colonna, Marchesi di Pescara (1492–1547), who was the first European woman to publish a collection of poetry and be widely read. Such writers were invisible to me, along with my Italian-American women contemporaries, as I attempted to forge my way into American letters. Only after forty, did I become aware that other women of my background were writers, and so there was a double bind in the fight for my identity as both a woman and an Italian one. Feminists don't need to hear how important role models are to one's aspirations. Vittoria Colonna, Grazia Deledda, or Frances [Vinciguerra] Winwar, who published many successful books throughout the 1940's and '50's in America, would qualify as "Lost Women Writers" in the PEN American Center, Women's Committee Events, if that series ever included an Italian American woman.

When I've tried to broach this subject, moreover, it's usually been poo-pooed by generally enlightened feminists, let alone establishment males. I'm made to feel like a "brazen fool" for even suggesting that there might be a little inequity when it comes to "wops" who get blamed by Hollywood for all the crime in the country.

Harvey Shapiro, head of the PEN Events Committee, made me feel awful, six years ago, when I suggested the "Writer in New York PEN program, featuring Black, Jewish, Asian, and Hispanic writers might include an Italian-American writer—especially, given the fact that New York contained the highest concentration of our population. He replied condescendingly, and I'm quoting exactly from my diary of that period: "Then let them write some good books!" Mr. Shapiro didn't even let me get around to suggesting a man like Gilbert Sorrentino, Lawrence Ferlinghetti, Ben Morreale, Jerry Mangione, or Joe Papaleo, for example, all of whom wrote a good deal about New York neighborhoods, let alone a woman of my ethnos. I wouldn't imagine suggesting that I had a novel, nicely reviewed by Larry McMurtry in *The Washington Post,* which contained New York scenes, among my five published books at the time.

These literary infractions might seem minor to those not struggling to make their living as writers in America, compared to the blatant prejudice that still surrounds people of my ethnos. Even my brother-in-law who's a learned Jewish professor at a major Ivy League university, when I mentioned, inadvertently, what a small minority population Italian-Americans were, as we viewed New York City from a roof top one evening, said "That's hard to believe, the way THEY control everything." A comment he would have taken as anti-Semitic if I'd said it about his ethnos. I've discovered that most intelligent and educated, even sensitive, people to say nothing of equal opportunity grant applications—don't realize that I'm of a minority which was lynched by the Ku Klux Klan, along with black and Jews, all through the earlier part of this century. Hardly anyone remembers the mass hysteria murders and lynching of Italian that took place in New Orleans in 1891 and continued as far north as Colorado well on through the 1920's. Or, the execution of Sacco and Vanzetti[78] by a verdict handed down by the bigoted Judge Thayer of Massachusetts who was known to have dubbed the labor activists, "Dirty dagos!" I knew a brilliant physician, Giuseppi Ferrara, now deceased, who was barred from a residency in a New York hospital, in 1933, because of his Italian name. Few remember that there were quotas on Italians attempting to enter Ivy League institutions, regardless of their qualifications and ability to pay, just as there were on blacks and Jews. The general prejudice toward Italian Americans is not made much of any more than Sacco and Vanzetti are remembered now—even though progressive intellectuals of the time like Edna St. Vincent Millay marched and wrote her memorial poem, "Justice Denied in Massachusetts," in defense of them.

Few are aware, and perhaps, Italian Americans themselves, are ashamed to remember, that in certain Southern states, Italians were segregated in schools and blue laws made it as unlawful to inter-marry with a guinea, wop, or dago, as a Jew or Negro. Such facts are hard to remember amidst other overwhelming horrors like the wholesale slaughter of Native-Americans, or Black slavery, or the Nazi Holocaust, and the continued suffering of so many other groups, like Hispanics or Asians, under the onslaught of ongoing prejudice against, and between, ethnic groups.

Remember how not long ago, Geraldine Ferarro, in her attempt to run for the vice presidency with Walter Mondale's campaign, was unjustly connected in the American mind with the Mafia, just as Mario Cuomo was in an ethnic slur delivered by Bill Clinton, Governor of Arkansas, in January 1992. Also, Commissioner Catherine Abate suffered a similar slur even more recently. Many readers might still, at this date, find it hard to disconnect an Italian politician from this cruel ethnic stereotype. When Ferraro was smeared with *Mafiosa* innuendo, the stories in *New York Magazine, The New York Post, The Wall Street Journal* were prominent, but when she and her family were completely absolved—after a painstaking search by nearly every investigative reporter in the country, especially those

---

[78]Ferdinando Nicola Sacco and Bartolomeo Vanzetti were anarchists convicted of murdering two men during a 1920 armed robbery. After a series of trials and appeals, they were executed on August 23, 1927.

working for the Republican campaign, her complete absolution from wrong doing or Mafia connection was likely to be found on page sixty, rather than page one. I still meet intellectuals, well-read ones of both sexes, who think she lost the election because she was a *Mafiosa*.

In terms of Mafia stereotyping, I'll never forget how Norman Mailer, back in the '80's, told me I reminded him of Geraldine Ferraro, because I was a blonde Italian. I felt like saying, "Si, si, signor, we all look alike!" He also said, publicly, at a PEN general meeting over which he presided as president, that Mondale shouldn't have gotten mixed up with Italians from Queens, implying that THEY are all Mafiosi, and he said it with aplomb, as if he thought himself very clever to declare Ferraro's unfounded Mafia connection the reason Mondale lost. Ferraro in grief has declared: "Again and again, they [the media] bore on that same theme: Because I am Italian, I or my family is suspected of being gangsters ... with no data to support the claim...." An editor in *The New York Times* was finally quoted in Richard Reeves column as saying, "The stoning of Geraldine Ferraro in the public square goes on and on, and nobody steps forward to help or protest."

The media has been so good at creating a Mafia innuendo that Italian-Americans are afraid to step forward and defend themselves from the slur. Hollywood has succeeded in making many of us suspicious of our own kind, disarming our self-defensive zeal, and so the stereotyping persists. We are not so good as Jews and Blacks at defending ourselves from cruel stereotyping, because wherever and whenever we group together for support, people whisper, "Mafia." This idea is verified by an article, "Scholars Find Bad Image Still Plagues U.S. Italians," written by Walter Goodman, reporting on a conference held at Columbia University, in *The New York Times* in October 1983. Though nearly all of the infamous "Murder Inc." was Jewish, Jewish organizations do not let the media get away with lumping them all together with Louie Lepke or Legs Diamond, the way Italians continue to be stereotyped by the image of Al Capone.

Even enlightened women's reproductive rights advocates of the eighties didn't seem to notice that Reagan/Bush were cavorting with "Born Again Right-to-Lifers" like Falwell, as much as they feared Italian-American politicians would be opposed to reproductive rights because of their supposed, stereotypic, traditional Catholism. This was so, though Ferraro and Cuomo—themselves Catholics— were more aggressively outspoken than most political defenders of the individual's "right to choice" and the idea of the *separation* of church and state.

I've always felt that my assertive feminism came from not having been raised Catholic, but Humanist Agnostic, by my atypical immigrant Italian father who was educated by the fruits of his own hard labor. He put himself through Union College, Phi Beta Kappa, and Columbia University, selling newspapers, shining shoes, and carrying coal buckets. In any case, I've ended up a Mother Earth celebrant, but people always assume I'm Catholic because of my name. Yet another stereotype put upon Italians.

As late as the summer of 1989, nearly thirty years after my time in Selma, I picked up *The New York Times Book Review* and saw an article on J.D. Mc-Clatchy's book, *Whitepaper: On Contemporary American Poetry,* and was it

"White!" and Anglo and Saxon and nearly all protestant and male. Harold Beaver, a visiting professor at the University of Denver, began his review of McClatchy's discussion of American poetry by referring to "the vast patchwork" of American poetry that Mr. McClatchy attempts to deal with in his book, *Whitepaper.* Then, he goes on to discuss the poetic voice, defined in Wordsworth's sense as "a man speaking to men." Once again, we "guineas, niggers, kikes, polacks, spikes, chinks, and twats" hardly existed in a treatise analyzing why American poetry is so dull, academic, and suburban.

The battle for recognition of the multicultural quality of America goes on, keeping us all divided and conquered as we reach for a piece of the dwindling pie in the sky. Now that the Russians aren't coming we're told, "The Muslims are!" or "The Japanese are ruining our economy!" to continue our compliance with war machine economics—just when our human resources should be going to save us from the disappearing ozone layer, or the erosion of our civil and human rights, let alone our dwindling arts foundation. Flag burning amendments get played up in the media while civil rights get run down in the courts. But, as an Italian-American who can hardly speak Italian, just as Native-Americans are forced to write their plight in English, I witness the language of my roots dying out and think about how Italy has no colonies speaking her tongue and puzzle over putting the whole rap on old *Cristoforo Colombo* like he was a Mafioso that ran the world, especially as he sailed for Spanish kings who were Hapsburg Teutons. Every time Columbus's name is mentioned, at any rate, someone says, "Leaf Erickson got here first." Can't Italians have a parade once a year without everybody protesting it's right to be? Why pin all of the rancor on Columbus for starting the demise of multiculturalism? He died a pauper in prison anyway. And no one calls him by his Italian name, "*Cristoforo Columbo,*" either.

One Tyrrhenian Sea group of pre-Roman Italians were the Etruscans who inhabited a strip of coastal land from Tuscany downward. Etruscan culture was much admired by D. H. Lawrence[79] and many feminist scholars, too, for its egalitarian treatment of women. Etruscan women shocked Roman men by attending public events with their husbands, rather than remaining sequestered as Roman women were forced to do. Indeed, the Etruscan statue of a woman and man as equals was often used as a symbol of the feminist movement in the early seventies when Etruscan culture enjoyed notoriety among feminist writers who appreciated its custom of matrilineal descent, and circular, rather than rectangular, architecture, among other qualities.

From *Saturday Night Live* to Hollywood, right up until today's presidential campaigns, to misconceptions of the Howard Beach and Bensonhurst incidents, Italian Americans continue to be stereotyped and scapegoated, even as their cuisine, fashion styles, music or art are touted as "in." We are excluded from manuals on racial and ethnic etiquette, and along with Poles, we are still the brunt of "dumb" jokes, even in "polite" company. If Italian Americans are occasionally

---

[79]See D. H. Lawrence's *Sketches of Etruscan Places and Other Italian Essays,* ed. by Simonetta de Fillippis (Cambridge UP, 2002).

stereotypically *Moonstruck,*[80] portrayed as families screaming over spaghetti dinners, they are more often portrayed as syndicated gangsters as in *Prizzi's Honor*, Academy Award Film of the 1980's.[81] Just a few years ago, speaking of racist stereotyping by Hollywood, *Prizzi's Honor* portrayed only Italians, Poles, Jews, Hispanics, and Blacks as criminals. All the police were Irish or British. Even a progressive satirist like Woody Allen felt perfectly fine stereotyping Italians as Sicilian Mafiosi, in another Academy Award winning film of the 80's, *Broadway Danny Rose.*[82] This was a fact acknowledged in a review by Katha Pollitt[83] in *The Nation.* It's the only time I can remember seeing Italian-Americans defended from stereotyping by someone of a different background. Not only are not all Sicilians in the Mafia, but not all Italian Americans are Sicilian—no more than all Africans are Zulu; all Irish, Catholics; all Jews, Israelites; or all Asians, Chinese. Italian women don't all have hair on their upper lips and stir a pot of spaghetti sauce as their main occupation, anymore than all blacks love watermelon or all Irish are drunkards. Neither are our women all the passive girlfriends or wives of mobsters, and neither are we the only prejudice folks in town, as media sensationalizing of biased-crimes in Brooklyn would lead us to believe.

Media coverage of the Howard Beach racial attack left most Americans under the misconception that the chief perpetrators of the biased murder crime were Italian youths of an Italian neighborhood. But, an Englishman by the name of Jon Lester, born and bred in South Africa, was the main assailant convicted of manslaughter in the death of the Black teen, Michael Griffith, along with Scott Kearn and Jason Ladone of the mixed neighborhood. But, "Howard" [not "Luigi"] Beach has become, in the American mind, an "Italian" neighborhood synonymous with prejudice and biased crime. "Pizza boycotts" were instituted by Black community leaders, and today few literate people, or college students, with whom I come in contact daily, are aware that it was Jon Lester, not even born in America, let alone an Italian-American, who led the attack. Few recall, also, that an Italian woman, Maria Toscano, gave testimony that helped to convict the teenagers who were found guilty.

Nearly no one, it seems, remembers, Elizabeth Galarza, an Italian woman, who ran down from her upstairs apartment into a street where gunfire was heard, and tried to resuscitate Yusuf Hawkins—in the infamous Bensonhurst incident. The murder of Yusuf Hawkins, on August 23, 1989, was no Kitty Genovesi situation. Eleven phone calls were made to the police from concerned community residents who heard the disturbance outside their homes. Elizabeth Galarza instinctively responded to Hawkins's need for help, without regard for her own danger. Seeing Hawkins—the black youth lying wounded in the street—from her upstairs window, she ran down into the street where a gunshot had been heard, to

---

[80]See *Moonstruck,* directed by Norman Jewison (MGM, 1987).

[81]See *Prizzi's Honor,* directed by John Hurston (ABC Motion Pictures, 1985). It was nominated for eight Oscars in 1986, and Anjelica Huston won "Best Actress in a Supporting Role" for her portrayal of Maerose Prizzi.

[82]See *Broadway Danny Rose,* directed by Woody Allen (Orion, 1984).

[83]For more information about Pollitt, visit www.thenation.com/authors/katha-pollitt.

be of assistance, leaving the safety of her apartment. She called for people to dial 911 for an ambulance and comforted Hawkins, holding him, trying to keep him alive and hopeful as the ambulance was on its way. But, there is not one entry concerning Elizabeth Galarza's act of human decency to be found in all the articles that appeared on the Bensonhurst incident in the computerized library periodicals index, Infotrac, which includes listings from *The New York Times, The Wall Street Journal, The Christian Science Monitor, The Washington Post, The Los Angeles Times,* and 960 assorted academic journals, too.

One can't easily find a media reference to the six Italian neighborhood women who visited the Stewart/Hawkins home to offer their sorrow and empathy: Nancy Sotile, Eddie Bonavita, Teodolinda Mallace, Rita Schettini, Rosa De Guida, and Rosalie Campione.

"These women stepped forward willingly as volunteers, where the men didn't step forward quite so easily, to keep peace in the community during the crisis situation of the marches led by Sharpton," explained Jack Spatola, Principal of a Bensonhurst school and a community leader working to save the youth of his area. "Italian ghetto kids have the third largest drop out rate in the city, next to Hispanic and Black youths," Spatola says. Everything reached a crisis level, and the women served as peacemakers, on the streets in the school and in the churches. Some of them attended the Hawkins's funeral in East New York among thousands of Black mourners, Nancy Sottile, Eddie Bonavita, and Teodolinda Mellace, with myself, Frank Barbaro, Father Arthur Minichello of St. Dominic's parish, and other Italian-American clergy. We went to pay respects and offer our sincere outrage, sorrow, and sympathy for the terrible loss and senseless murder.

Michael McQuillan, Advisor to the Brooklyn Borough President's Office for Racial and Ethnic Affairs offered his observation: "In my experience, as I work in the neighborhoods, whether it be Bensonhurst or Canarsie, wherever, women are often more willing to speak frankly about ethnicity. They reach out with a spontaneous sense of empathy for the suffering of other people, perhaps because the reality of the experience of sexism in a male dominated society contributes to their empathy for the plight of, for example, people of color in a white dominated society."

Rosalie Campione, a college student of Bensonhurst feels wounded by the major media portrayal of her home turf as a place of unadulterated bigotry. Rosalie helps to run a Bensonhurst Tenant Counseling Program for Displaced Homemakers—women who have lost a job or a mate through widowhood or divorce, or who imply wish to improve their job skills and self-image. The program, though run by The Federation of Italian American Organizations of Brooklyn, accommodates women of every ethnic background—Asians, Russians, Jews, blacks, Hispanics—to their job rehabilitation services.

"I went to F.D.R. High School, the one attended by the boys involved in the Bensonhurst crime," Rosalie says, "At F.D.R., I had close friendships with Latinas, Blacks, Irish, kids of every sort of background." Rosalie and her friend, Frances Failla, were among three Italian young people to represent Brooklyn at a gathering, titled "Youth Speaks Out," held at Long Island University and aired on NBC. Rosalie said:

Most of the attendees from the five boroughs were blacks or Hispanics, and when they heard we were from Bensonhurst and the word "Bensonhurst" was mentioned, they booed us, without knowing anything about us, or even giving us a chance to explain the truth of the murder of Yusuf Hawkins. My friends and I felt terrible about the murder. Joseph Fama, who was convicted of the shooting, was an older dropout with problems. I think he'd even had a serious head injury at one time. He wasn't a part of the high school Mondello crowd of neighborhood kids. Gina Feliciano, a Hispanic-Italian, had told Mondello that a group of her black and Hispanic friends were coming to her birthday party and were going to beat up Mondello and his friends. Yusuf Hawkins came down the street with his black friends to buy a used car in the neighborhood, and Mondello's crowd thought they were the Blacks coming to beat them up. They were waiting outside of Gina's apartment on the day of her birthday party. There were two black kids in the neighborhood crowd, too. One of them, Joseph Russell Gibbons, admitted to bringing the softball bats to where his group of White neighbors was gathering to defend their turf. Those foolish machismo guys thought they were defending their neighborhood, or something. Most of us girls aren't like that. We make friends across racial boundaries. We don't have such a sense of territory. People are just people to us. The guy who brought the gun to the scene was unfortunately a retarded boy with problems, and none of the others knew he had a gun with him when he suddenly shot Yusef Hawkins. It is tragic, a terrible tragedy…

Rosalie explained.

Most Americans are unaware that the *machismo* "Black Hand" or "Mafia" (a word now used generically for all syndicated crime of every ethnos) began in Southern Italy as an indigenous peoples' vigilante to protect the women and land from rape and pillaging, as many foreign invasions swept over Southern Italy from Naples to Sicily. Though most Italian-Americans come from Southern areas, particularly Sicily and Naples, as my grandmother did, my grandfather was from Puglia, a small village near the Gargano, an area where limestone cave paintings older than those of Lascaux have been discovered. Few Americans realize what a mixture of cultures the Italian peninsula encompasses with invasion by the French, German, Spanish, and Phoenician armies. Teutonic Lombards and Gaelic tribes and Northern Africans are all mixed together with Albanians, and Yugoslavians, as well. The Italian Renaissance, because of Venetian trade with the East, integrated many elements of Eastern culture bringing them Westward throughout Europe. The *oud* became the lute, and the swirling Mandela patterns of Eastern spiritual meditative art were incorporated into the Italian Baroque and Rococo forms that spread throughout European culture, just as the Asian rice noodles Marco Polo brought from China became Italian forms of wheat flour pasta. All cultures are inextricably mixed when you study them, and that is why prejudice is so insane. We all began in the heart of Africa, anthropologists and geologists and other scientists tell us, in any case. We are all the same human family, more alike than different. Words like Caucasian, Negroid, Mongoloid are useless classifications. I teach, in intercultural communication, that these are bigoted terms in themselves, implying prejudice.

"Divide and Conquer" was a tactic I saw used in Selma, just as it is used in South Africa today, where it's called, "Divide and Rule." Throughout history, those making profits from a war machine have laughed all the way to the bank, while poor ethnics at the bottom of the money ladder have been set at each other's throats to distract them from the real criminals. Now, Italians seem to be the scapegoat for all organized crime, as well as all biased street crime, too. Mario Puzo starved writing his earliest novels and his best, like *The Fortunate Pilgrim,* about ordinary, hardworking Italian immigrants, until he gave Hollywood *The Godfather*—the sensationalized Mafia image, which it wanted to market—just like *Amos and Andy* or *Little Black Sambo,* or *Steppin Fetchit* were marketable images that fulfilled the majority's prejudice. We don't need to be told how wrong it is to stereotype any whole group of people—including white Anglo Saxon Protestants—as more heavily prejudice than other groups. Every group contains enlightened individuals, a Jane Addams or Lucretia Mott, and extreme elements, too.

There was an Italian American girl of 15 years raped by two black men, on January 15, 1992, in the Marine Park, Midland area of Brooklyn. She was on her way to school when she was accosted and forced at threatening gun point into a car, raped, sodomized, and robbed, and then dumped by black men who used racial epithets. Since she was a minor, the press withheld her name. It was simply mentioned as a biased crime. She was classified as white, so no one made a big deal that this was a black crime perpetrated on an Italian American child. I think of how no Italian Americans will march on an African American neighborhood to protest the biased crime of the rape of that 15 year old Italian American girl—and of all the crimes of prejudice now taking place between this and that group in New York and elsewhere around the nation and the world, the Neo-Nazi groups here in the U.S. and in Germany and Europe with their swastikas on Synagogues and Catholic Churches, their acts of hate, and I get very depressed. Still, I know from dealing daily with young people and people of all kinds that most of us are decent, and even if we have awful stereotypes from Hollywood and television in the backs of our minds, we would never act upon them or go so far as to hurt or murder someone based on these ghosts of prejudice about others. But, the major media wants us to believe that we are all hideously prejudice, because big Pentagon contractors sit on the boards of major media conglomerates, and there's weapons profits to be made in dividing and conquering. Which came first the chicken or the egg? I think the media encourages prejudice with its sensationalized reporting. We don't hear about the good and decent people who are doing things to combat prejudice.

It's important to acknowledge that blacks, Jews, Native Americans, and also indigenous peoples everywhere often have had the worse of it in recent history, but we Italian Americans have suffered and are suffering, too. We women need to be wise to the old "Divide and Conquer" tactic. I keep hearing from Women's Studies scholars who tell me that there's no money for women's studies programs since Allan Bloom's *The Closing of the American Mind* was on the Best Seller list. And the civil rights I got bashed for trying to help institute are being eroded along with the rights I thought I gained over my female body, let alone my Italian name. I try to think of how many millions of people live and work together, and walk together, and ride together peacefully every day in big urban centers of mixed races and ethnic complexions. We don't marvel enough at the peace and decency that we are capable of. The little acts of heroism performed by an Elizabeth Galarza, for example. Such people, especially women, are forgotten. History is such a blood bath of hatreds fueled by warlords and weapons manufacturers that we become cynical of what our species is capable of. But, deep down, I believe that we shall overcome, and I am glad, even still, that I stood up for what was decent in Selma long ago. I'm sorry that the lessons of the past have to be constantly relearned. The rise of Neo-Nazism, the KKK gaining power, is the saddest phenomenon on earth today. It's happening just when we all need to pull together to divest from the war machine, to save Mother Earth, the only tear drop of love and laughter afloat in cold dark space.

by Daniela Gioseffi

⊘ₙ Prejudice: Ethnicity, Identity & the Literary Canon

From the introduction to *On Prejudice: A Global Perspective,* by Daniela Gioseffi, World Peace Award, The Ploughshares Fund: CA. Presented at the United Nations: NY, 1993.

> *History counts its skeletons in round numbers.*
> *A thousand and one stays at a thousand,*
> *as though the one had never existed:*
> *an imaginary embryo, an empty cradle,*
> *an ABC unread,.... no one's place in the line*
> *.... We stand in the meadow made of dead flesh,*
> *and the meadow is silent as a false witness....*
> *where corpses once sang with their mouths full of earth....*
> **—Wislawa Szymborska, Nobel Laureate, Poland**

Racism and ethnic conflict are again playing an intensified role in our dangerously over-militarized world, just as in 1944 when W.E.B. Du Bois wrote "Prospect of a World Without Race Conflict."[84] Du Bois knew what was happening to the Jews in Hitler's Germany, and he drew analogies between the dynamics of prejudice operating in that super tragedy, and others, like the genocide committed by 18th century slave traders—in which over 10 million Africans were estimated to have died in bondage enroute to *just* the Caribbean Islands. Du Bois knew what all 20th century *humanist* sociologists concerned about the bogus science of *Nazi "eugenics"* were attempting to demonstrate. There is no primary physical or biological difference between Jew and German, African, European, or Asian, as all so called "races" of humankind are inextricably mixed, stemming from the same genetic pool originating somewhere over 250,000 years ago in the heart of Africa. We were all born of the same natural creation. Without earth and without water in combination, in short, without *mud* from which all seeds and living creatures grow, there would be no life anywhere on Earth. This is, of course, not an "Afrocentric" view, but biogenetic fact, having nothing to do with cultural values from any particular nation or with value judgments of any kind. It is ironic that neo-Nazi skinheads, or Ku Klux Klan defamers, talk of "mud people" as a pejorative term, since without the fertile mud of creation, no life could exist on Earth....

"Me! I'm not prejudiced! I don't need to study prejudice! I'm free of it, or I suffer from it, so what do I need to learn about it?" We might tell ourselves. "All women and men are created equal. Prejudice is terrible! I already know

---

[84]See Du Bois' "Prospect of a World Without Race Conflict" in the *American Journal of Sociology* 49.5 (Mar. 1944): 450–56.

that!" But we should be very wary of the belief that there is nothing more to learn about the nature of prejudice. It's clear—as psychology explains—that none of us can be perfectly free of social prejudices, those subtle stereotypical reactions to surnames or cultural backgrounds or skin tones or eye slant or nose width and breadth or sexual orientation that are jumbled in the haunted attic of our psyches, causing us to make prejudgments of people before any evidence is in. As Charles Lamb—a nineteenth-century anti-Semitic English essayist—admitted in "Imperfect Sympathies"[85]: "For myself, earth-bound and fettered to the scene of my activities, I confess that I do feel the differences of mankind, national and individual.... I am, in plainer words, a bundle of prejudices--made up of likings and dislikings—veriest thrall to sympathies, apathies, antipathies...."

Indeed, one of the most common themes of literature through the ages has been that of prejudice from Leo Tolstoy's *Anna Karenina*[86] to Isaac Babel's "Karl Yankel"[87] or Chekhov's "Rothschild's Fiddle"[88] to James Baldwin's *Notes of a Native Son*[89] or Toni Morrison's *The Bluest Eye*.[90] World literature is replete with examples to support this premise of the theme of prejudice and no culture holds a monopoly on it. The vague unspoken suspicions we live with concerning each other, causes us to visit "the sins of the fathers" upon each other. We are certainly aware of the human rights crimes committed upon blacks by whites and gentiles on Jews, but are we aware that prejudice goes the other way too and destroys much human potential—especially now when all humanitarians of every culture and background need to unite to save Earth from imminent climate catastrophe?

Are you a Jew who is suspicious of all Germans; or a black suspicious of all whites? Or a woman who feels superior to all men? Or a homosexual who feels superior to heterosexuals? Are you an Asian who feels Europeans, especially *all* Americans de-scended from them, are inferior? Are you a person of African descent who hates or envies mulattoes? These are subtler reactionary prejudices less explored or articulated by the media, yet each requires a dissertation in itself. Say that you never subtly sus-pect all Irishman of drinking too much; all Blacks of being better rhythmic dancers or having more savage libidos; all Latins of harboring intense animal sexuality and being "hot tempered"; all Jews of being industriously stingy and overly bookish; all Italians of being connected to syndicated crime; all Japanese of being suspiciously unctuous or high I.Q'd; blondes of being dumber or having more fun; and brunettes of being capable of more manipulative evil—and one can conclude you weren't born on this planet. We need to face the fact that we all have stereotypic reactions *in subtle ways*, more subtle than these examples, but they exist because the human mind must general-ize in order to think and name things, and thusly things become symbols of themselves.

---

[85]See Lamb's, "Imperfect Sympathies," *London Magazine* (Aug. 1821).

[86]See Tolstoy's *Anna Karenina* (Oxford World's Classics), trans. by Louise Maude, Aylmer Maude, and W. Gareth Jones (New York: Oxford UP, 2008).

[87]Babel's "Karl Yankel" is trans. by Peter Constantine in *The Complete Works of Isaac Babel*, ed. byNathalie Babel (New York: Norton, 2001).

[88]Chekhov's short story is included in *The Steppe and Other Stories* (Oxford World's Classics), trans. by Ronald Hingley (New York: Oxford UP, 2009).

[89]See Baldwin's *Notes of a Native Son* (Beacon P, 1984).

[90]Morrison's *The Bluest Eye* was originally published by Washington Square P, 1972.

Count Alfred Korzibski pointed out, long ago, that "Cow 1 is not Cow 2" with his *Manhood of Humanity*[91] and science of General Semantics, but we cannot ever completely free ourselves of making subliminal generalizations about the "otherness" of the other. Language communication depends on generalizing concepts into denotative words. My friend is a Lithuanian German woman, and she is brunette, and I am a Slavic Jewish, Greek Italian with Ethiopian ancestry and blond, but without seeing us, most people would guess our hair color to be the opposite. Some whites have large noses and full lips, and some Blacks have small noses and thin lips. Some Jews look like Germans or Spaniards or Arabs or Italians, and Koreans and Vietnamese do not want to be mistaken for Japanese or Chinese. There are subtle differences in every being, unique from every other being, and still, despite the many mixtures in all our roots, we generalize about our nationhood, or cultures, or see ourselves as separate from others of other skin tones. We even manage to get "coloreds" and "blacks" separated and divided from each other in hierarchies of privilege in South Africa, in order that those possessed of the laws and the land might rule those who are dispossessed of their birth right. Blacks complain, too, that they discriminate among themselves according to skin shades, and ethnic Jews complain that over assimilated "WASP-ish" Jews look down upon them. Italians in America have come to be suspicious of each other, because of media sensationalizing of "Mafia connections," and are afraid to congregate to defend themselves against this cruel stereotyping. Aided by the media such stereotyping of ethnic groups as criminals is a means to divide and conquer them, as Indian scouts of one tribe were recruited by European settlers to help defeat other native tribes, and Black African slave traders of differing tribes sold their own people to European slave traders. A few assimilated Jews sold information about ethnic Jews to Nazi sympathizers in order to save their own skins during the Holocaust, just as Italian American male novelists and screen writers have learned to profit from Mafia stereotyping in a culture which will buy nothing else from them about their own people. These are desperate acts of the disenfranchised that amount to self-destructive race riots, which burn down the neighborhoods of the disenfranchised.

Stephen Jay Gould wrote of an interestingly subtle form of prejudice in *The Mismeasure of Man*[92] that after extensive ghetto riots during the summer of 1967, (in the U.S.) three (white) doctors wrote a letter to the prestigious *Journal of the American Medical Association*, stating that

> It is important to realize that only a small number of the millions of slum dwellers have taken part in the riots, and that only a sub-fraction of these rioters have indulged in arson, sniping and assault. Yet, if slum conditions alone determined and initiated riots, why are the vast majority of slum dwellers able to resist the temptations of unrestrained violence? Is there something peculiar about the violent slum dweller that differentiates him from his peaceful neighbor?

[91] See Korzybski's *Manhood of Humanity*, published by the Institute of General Semantics, 1950.
[92] Gould's *The Mismeasure of Man* was originally pub. by Norton in 1981.

We all tend to generalize from our own areas of expertise. These doctors are psychosurgeons. But why should the violent behavior of some desperate and discouraged people point to a specific disorder of their brain while the corruption and violence of some congressmen and presidents provokes no similar theory? Human populations are highly variable for all behaviors; the simple fact that some do and some don't provides no evidence for specific pathology mapped upon the brain of the doers. Shall we concentrate upon an unfounded speculation for the violence of some—one that follows the determinist philosophy of blaming the victim—or shall we try to eliminate the oppression that builds ghettos and saps the spirit of their unemployed in the first place?

Such subtleties of *determinist* attitudes operate even in the most civilized and educated circles, proving that the need for disseminating the truth about race and racial attributes persists even among the educated, though those who have a wide understanding of world history and culture are generally found to harbor less prejudice toward people of other cultures. This recent wisdom is causing some U.S. cities to require urban police to be trained in liberal arts. Studies show that education can succeed in helping us develop sensitivity and empathy for those of other backgrounds and cultures. Courses in conflict resolution and intercultural communication as well as a new multicultural approach to education are now being instituted, worldwide, in response to such studies.

Also, the need to foster the truth about racial attitudes has obviously given rise to a heated debate over multicultural curricula in the schools, as ethnic strife renews itself everywhere and the disenfranchised rise up out of their pain and claim the pride of their cultural accomplishments and the history of their resistance to oppression. Yet how many white children the world over have actually read Black slave narratives and understood the depth and breadth of slaveholders' brutality as history? How many have experienced narratives by cruelly colonized indigenous people telling of their lot—and their respect for the land and its resources--as actual history?

The raging debate among Eurocentrists and Afrocentrists and educators who helped to pioneer multicultural studies in the area of education is a ridiculous example of particularist exclusionism. Multiculturalists are considered too extreme by those conservatives who are angry Eurocentrists, or those avengers who are justifiably angry Afrocentrists. For an interesting revelation of culture and history, one might look at Martin Barnal's *Black Athena*,[93] a controversial but factual view on the issues. In 1990, Barnal helped to revive much forgotten and censored black history, which such black scholars as W. E. B. Du Bois, Frederick Douglass, Zora Neal Hurston, Langston Hughes, Lerone Bennett, Maya Angelou had been resurrecting for years within the Black community. Barnal did this within the same year that Diane Silvers Ravitch, an educator who has taught at Columbia Teachers College and served as a government official in education, was attacked by Afrocentrist and Eurocentrist alike. Ravitch presents a moderate view for all sides,

[93]See Bernal's *Black Athena: Afroasiatic Roots of Classical Civilization, Vol. 1: The Fabrication of Ancient Greece, 1785-1985* published by Rutgers UP, 1987. Subsequent volumes were also published by Rutgers UP in 1991 and 2006.

though the difficulty for such views is that they cannot correct heinous wrongs with enough passionate intensity to satisfy wounded avengers, even as they may cause less conflict in the present. And so, the heated argument between the Afrocentrists—with their justifiable anger—and "threatened" Eurocentrists continues. But, the debate does not change the truth of what W. E. B. Du Bois said, at the outbreak of World War I about the pillaging of Africa being an important element of the roots of European imperialism.

To understand the problems involved in the curriculum debate imagine—just for one example—a young person seated in a classroom, and imagine if that young person happens to be Jewish, and he or she is forced to read the following description, by Henry James, of a Jewish ghetto in lower Manhattan:

> I recall the intensity of the material picture in the dense Yiddish quarter.... There is no swarming like that of Israel when once Israel has got a start, and the scene here bristled, at every step, with the signs and sounds, immitigable, unmistakable, of a Jewry that had burst all bounds. That it has burst all bounds in New York, almost any combination of figures or of objects taken at hazard sufficiently proclaims; but I remember how the rising waters, on this summer night, rose, to the imagination, even above the housetops and seemed to sound their murmur to the pale distant stars. It was as if we had been thus, in the crowded, hustled roadway, where multiplication, multiplication of everything, was the dominant note, at the bottom of some vast sallow aquarium in which innumerable fish, of over-developed proboscis, were to bump together, for ever, amid heaped spoils of the sea.... The children swarmed above all--here was multiplication with a vengeance; and the number of very old persons, of either sex, was almost equally remarkable; the very old person being in equal vague occupation of the doorstep, pavement, curbstone, gutter, roadway, and every one, alike using the street for overflow.... There are small strange animals, known to natural history, snakes or worms, I believe, who, when cut into pieces, wriggle away contentedly and live in the snippet as completely as in the whole. So the denizens of the New York Ghetto, heaped as thick as the splinters on the table of a glass-blower.... The advanced age of so many figures, the ubiquity of the children, carried out in fact this analogy; they were all there for race, and not, as it were, for reason: that excess of lurid meaning, in some of the old men's and old women's faces in particular, would have been absurd, in the conditions, as a really directed attention—it could only be the gathered past of Israel mechanically pushing through.[94]

The Italians, "Negroes," and other "Aliens" described by Henry James in his essays on New York views of the Hudson, do not fare any better, and this is merely one example of many examples of bigotry in the canons of world literature, one might quote from esteemed writers like Ezra Pound, T.S. Eliot, Celine, Heidegger, that "minority" students might be forced to study in schools across the world which teach them nothing of their own cultural contribution to humankind. Indeed, even as authors, Mark Twain and William James (Henry James's brother) were decrying the U.S. war policy of genocide against Filipinos, Henry James was writing his biased descriptions of Blacks, Italians and Jews of Manhattan,

---

[94]The quotation is from James' *The American Scene* originally published in London by Chapman & Hall, ltd., 1907.

whom he called "Aliens." We continue to use the phrase "illegal alien" with its ethnocentric bias today to describe people who are forced to our shores by colonial imperialist war crimes on the part of our own governments. Culture is always a "mixed bag," of humane and inhumane artists. What good is a literary canon, as a symbol of "The Humanities,'" if it is full of bigotry and is not humanizing, but merely self-centered and decadent? Of course, censorship must be outlawed, but there are questions that need to be asked of people who construct curriculums. Isn't a black, Jewish, Latino, Italian, Cherokee or Sioux child better off reading one of the considered classic literatures of his or her own people? To gain the strength and pride in self that will serve him or her well through life! One can't help but agree with Amiri Baraka, African American writer and educator, and numerous others who have opposed the teaching of bigoted or narrowly cultured writers in the classroom--in favor of substituting writers who bring self-respect to children of all backgrounds. Especially since self-hatred or lack of self-respect, as has been discussed, leads to prejudice.

Yet, at this dangerous juncture, as we near the year 2000, after more than eighty centuries of art and human creativity, philosophy, music, poetry, social and biological science--we humans, considered the *paragon of animals* in our ability to think, named *homo sapiens, meaning wise or knowing animal,* persist, brutishly, in hating and killing each other for the colors of our skin, the shapes of our features, our places of origin on our common *terra firma,* our styles of culture or language, and most ironic of all our "religious" beliefs—despite the fact that all the great religions of the Earth teach the same basic tenant of The Golden Rule: "Do unto others as you would have them do unto you." Along with love and death, our literatures remain full of expressions of the experience of repression and oppression known as *prejudice,* "pre-judgement" of the worth of people based upon insufficient or erroneous evidence lacking in objectivity and factual data.

Prejudice in all its manifestations—xenophobia, ethnocentrism, sexism, andro-centrism, genocidal politics and militarism, environmental and social racism, cruel colonization and cultural destruction, crimes of cultural exclusionism and expansionism, imperialism, ethnic wars and hatred of each other—is still the major focus of our literatures, our history-making events, and our nightly news in the global village as the stars of our common galaxy, light years old, and our satellites, new since mid century, beam down into homes everywhere in the global village and teach us, daily, that we are all of *one* race, the only one we've found in the galaxy, *the human race.*

by Daniela Gioseffi

𝒲HAT WOULD YOUR IMMIGRANT FATHER SAY ABOUT "THE WORLD ACCORDING TO TONY SOPRANO?"

Partially published in a *New York Times* blog, 2002 and on *www.ItalianAmericanWriters.com.*

The over-riding issue regarding *The Sopranos*—and Michael Parenti, professor of history and sociology at UCLA, author of *Make Believe Media*[95] agrees—is that *The Sopranos*[96] takes attention away from the big, white-collar crime of the majority culture like the S & L Scandal or Enron debacle. The Savings & Loan Scandal[97] of over a decade ago was the largest robbery in modern history, still costing every family in American many thousands per year—yet it's hardly portrayed at all in the media, and its horrendous effects are ignored by dramatists. The focus on ethnic crime takes attention away from the environmental disaster or the current administration's fossil-fuel industrialists' war against our air, land, and water—an utterly vital legacy that belongs to all of us.

It's a way of focusing on us ethnics as the source of all crime and grime. Instead of America being forced to face a dramatization of the white-collar crimes that would save her from corporate thuggery, she's being diverted to dwell on *The Sopranos*, which offers a soap-opera with stereotyped ethnics. Although the popularity of this television series may have peaked, and the debate over it calmed down, the fact remains that it, and other dramas like it, continue to play on the media and be produced, and *The Sopranos* will be on cable or HBO for years to come and be continually marketed worldwide.

The Sopranos seduces as it demeans and stereotypes Italian Americans who are overwhelmingly nothing like this family of crime and violence—except that Italian Americans are, generally speaking, a passionately familial people. Italian filial feelings and loyalties are portrayed against a backdrop of low-life crime so as to destroy what is good in them. The show's popularity rests greatly upon the fact that Americans with their "WASPish" aspirations to false propriety suffer horribly from "passion-envy" and a thirst for displays of filial feeling combined with a lavish enjoyment of good food or nurturance, *la dolce vita.*

If television producers were to make such a popular, long-running series about Dillinger, a German American syndicated criminal, or one about Louie Lepke or Legs Diamond of Murder Inc., Jewish-American criminals, Germans and Jews

---

[95]See Parenti's *Make-Believe Media: The Politics of Entertainment* (Wadsworth Publishing, 1991).
[96]*The Sopranos* aired on HBO from 1999–2007.
[97]For a "Chrono-Bibliography of the S&L Scandal," visit the FDIC's website: *www.fdic.gov/bank/historical/s&l/.*

would be furious and insulted at the stereotyping of their people as thugs. You can be sure the Jewish Anti-Defamation League would not stand for it and would protest roundly.

But Italian Americans, in general, may accept the stereotype because they, too, have been sold a "bill of goods" by the Hollywood and television industrialists, and some of their own men have sold out their people. Italian Americans have come, because of a glut of such entertainment, to patronize the very stereotype that plagues them. There's always a grain of truth to every stereotype of an ethnic group, and an Italian mafia does exist, but in small measure compared to the mania of the myth. The same is true for a black mafia and a Jewish mafia and a Russian or Chinese mafia! None of them are as organized or internationally widespread as myth would have it. They affect far fewer lives than the Enron debacle, for or Wall Street criminality, for example. Certainly, in America today, we've witnessed through too much Wall Street criminality the exposure of a huge white-collar, corporate and syndicated crime. It's time to stand against ethnic scapegoating of all kinds in the decadent forms of Hollywood and the media. We need to see more Karen Silkwoods and films about heroic fighters of crime.

Would or should the Irish accept the stereotype of themselves as drunkards and liars? They seemed to have been very angry in the town of Limerick with Frank McCourt for his moving portrayal of the poor people of Limerick in his best selling memoir, *Angela's Ashes* (Scribner 1996), and he wasn't even attempting to stereotype the Irish.

Do African Americans enjoy being stereotyped as tall basketball players, Bojangles dancers, Aunt Jemimas, or Stephen Fetchits? African Americans and Jews have had the good sense to widely and fully belie such stereotypes and we should also.

Unfortunately, some Italians seem to relish the portrayal of characters in *The Sopranos*. Some young men like the idea of being seen as tough. Others think it's jazzy to be feared. Women identify with the suffering of the wives, daughters, and mistresses in the patriarchal soap opera. Perhaps, the power of the exotic characters drawn so sensationally in *The Sopranos* makes Italian Americans feel that any attention—to their style of food, dress, decor, music—is better than none.

Or, is it that Italian Americans themselves are fascinated by the exotic characterization that stereotypes them? Perhaps, they've even bought the silly idea that these characters are so welldrawn as to be analyzed for their behaviors? Or is it that the characters are finely drawn enough in their Italian aspects to draw us in so that we ignore the dark side of their criminality. Is it that we enjoy the Italian filial passions, food, wine, music, décor, ambiance so much that we "drink them up," even as we ignore the sensationalized, criminal stereotype, or its effects on our cultural well being? Haven't the best aspects or our post immigrant culture been used to invite us to the table of our own demise?

"Will there ever be an Italian American president if such an image continues to dominate the American mind?" I hear my dead Italian immigrant father sighing that question from his grave. Mario Cuomo would have made a fine president, one feels.

Those of us who are not sucked into this conundrum, who are sensitive to this narrow stereotyping of Italian Americans, are chastised for not getting "with the

program," but we are chagrined because this stereotype has occurred and succeeded more than any other ethnic stereotype in the Hollywood and television
industry. There is an *over-glut* of this image of Italian Americans without enough
countering images as frequently and constantly portrayed. Also, Hollywood and
television haven't accepted much else in the portrayal of this ethnic group because it found this one so lucrative. I still firmly believe, along with several other
scholars of our culture, that Italian Americans who enjoy this show are shooting
themselves in the foot. Jews read about the Jewish struggle. Blacks read about
the African American struggle in these United States, but Italian Americans do
not read enough about their own struggle or about the prejudice against them to
even create a big enough demand for good books about their everyday culture.
It's a theme we've heard for years and the main slogan of Robert Viscusi's Italian
American Writers Association: "Write and read or be written!"

Perhaps, the newly affluent generation is unaware that the largest mass lynching
in US history was of Italian American laborers in New Orleans in 1891? Have they
read Dr. Richard Gambino of Queens College on that subject?[98] (And, he's no relation to the Gambino crime family at all! We Italians all know him as a scholar who
started the current phase of our literary renaissance with the collection of essays
Blood of My Blood[99] back in the 1970's—a book that emphasised *La Causa*—as
some of us dub our mission to be understood as writers of a varied people.)

Mario Puzo—one of the best-known authors of our culture—starved writing
The Fortunate Pilgrim (Antheneum 1965) about ordinary, hard-working Italian
Americans, an excellent novel from which he couldn't make any money. And he
didn't make any money until he wrote *The Godfather* (J. P. Putnam's Sons 1969),
which is all that Hollywood wants from Italian American writers and actors since
that monumental movie and book success. Puzo admits that he never met a Mafioso and based the Godfather's main character on his mother, with her passionate
family ways of *la via vecchia*. It's the character of his mother whom he also portrayed in *The Fortunate Pilgrim*. That novel, though a literary success—in terms
of the reviews it received from every quarter—was never a best-seller or a Hollywood success. Puzo says he read up on the Mafia in newspapers in order to create a drama Hollywood would pay money for. He died saying that *The Fortunate
Pilgrim* was his masterwork and his favorite accomplishment, not *The Godfather.*
I recommend it as a very moving and marvelously well-crafted novel. It beats the
sensationalism of *The Godfather* by a long shot. We can all see our immigrant
Italian uncles and aunts and fathers and mothers in his true to life portrayals in
The Fortunate Pilgrim—a classic of American literature, dubbed such by learned
reviewers upon its publication. When *The Fortunate Pilgrim* appeared in 1965,
Puzo was called the Italian Bernard Malamud, the Henry Roth of Italian culture
in America, and plaudits reigned over his most literary work. Yet, his book never
found the readership it deserved. (By the by, feminists should note that women are

---

[98]See Gambino's book *Vendetta: The true story of the worst lynching in America, the mass murder
of Italian-Americans in New Orleans in 1891, the visious motivations behind it, and the tragic
repercussions that linger to this day* (Doubleday, 1977).
[99]See *Blood of My Blood* (Doubleday, 1974; rpt. by Guernica, 2002).

its main heroines.)

Actually, the first big box-office film about the Mafia was *Little Caesar,*[100] starring Edward G. Robinson, a very convincing Jewish American actor who more than once portrayed an Italian criminal for Hollywood. *Little Caesar* did so well at the box office, that many prototypes have followed, including the present day *The Sopranos.*

But, where are the accomplishments of other Italian Americans portrayed by Hollywood and television dramas? Enrico Fermi's dramatic attempt to save American GI's from the Nevada bomb tests is not portrayed anywhere. Toscanini's beating at the hands of Fascist thugs is portrayed nowhere, either. A New York politician, a champion of the people, Vito Marc Antonio's struggle to help all immigrants during the depression years is not portrayed anywhere. Mario Cuomo's stellar life story is a fine drama, as he rose from ghetto to successful lawyer to governor of New York State, but where's that in the media? Where's the story of Mother Cabrini and her dramatic struggle to help immigrants of all backgrounds, her self-sacrificing altruism? Where's the story of Filippo Mazzei, Thomas Jefferson's influential friend who gave Jefferson some of his democratic ideals? Where is the story of Grazia Deledda, Italian woman novelist who rose from a provincial girlhood to be Nobel Laureate in Literature? These stories need telling. These are the stories young Italian American writers can portray!

Very few uplifting portrayals of Italians or Italian Americans can be found in the media. There are many such of worthy Jews and African Americans, and rightly so! That is the problem: there is an *over-emphasis* on this particular stereotype, which even Italian Americans have begun to buy and consume as the main image of their own people. So brainwashed are we, and the entire world, on Hollywood's slanted portrayals. Hollywood influences can be good or bad, and unfortunately there's too much sensational violence with stunning special effects, and not enough heroic truths told about our true and real heroes of *all* backgrounds. America doesn't learn of her finest heroes well enough!

Michael Parenti's book, *Make-Believe Media,* fully explains this manipulation of all ethnics by the media— subtly meant to cover over and take attention away from the really big-time sociopolitical criminality in our time. Why isn't it portrayed that part of the Bush family fortune, as well as the Rockefeller fortune, comes from the Third Reich and I.G. Farben, a corporation that built forty death camps including Aushcwitz. Farben is now invested in large pharmaceutical companies involved in the G-nome project?" These facts are explained by John Loftus, President of the Holocaust Museum in Florida and former US Department of Justice War Crimes prosecutor.[101] Who knows such facts?

Why are there no popular dramatic portrayals of the cruel internment camps in the US during WWII for Japanese, *and Italian American* immigrants? Why aren't these stories big dramas for television moguls? That is the issue! They are certainly *dramatic* stories of big-time criminality and thievery on the part of the US government—but we don't see those portrayals for popular consumption. As

---

[100]See *Little Caesar,* directed by Mervyn LeRoy (1931).
[101]Loftus describes the connection between the Bush family and the Nazis in his September 2000 article titled "The Dutch Connection: How a famous American family made its fortune from Nazis."

everyone runs home to put their feet up and watch the intrigues of *The Sopranos*, Dick Cheney is refusing to hand over transcripts of the meetings he held with big moguls like Enron on the nation's energy policies, even though he has been asked by a lawsuit brought by the government's accounting department to do so. The focus is off the thievery on Wall St. and the fall of the economy, the surge in homelessness and joblessness. Wouldn't you imagine that Mr. George W. Bush's administration loves having "Tony Soprano" distract Americans from the big white-collar crimes of our time?

Please read Michael Parenti, our Italian Noam Chomsky, and his marvelous book *Make-Believe Media* to understand the concepts I'm attempting to convey. While you are at it re-read *Christ in Concrete* by Pietro Di Donato (Esquire 1937), about hardworking laborers of the thirties, a very dramatic and moving story, and ask why it isn't on television? Where is the television drama about the "Triangle Shirt Factory," in which so many ethnic women laborers perished, Italian, Jewish, Polish and Irish alike!

I'm a Greek, Jewish, Polish, *Italian* American with other ethnic mixtures! Italy is a multicultural nation like America. Italian Americans should take a good cue from African and Jewish Americans and read more of their *own* story in America, and their history of massacres and starvation by international powers that drove them from their homelands in the Old Country. The *mezzogiorno* was brutalized by northern powers in one of the largest genocides in modern history.

Finally, I'd like to quote Camille Paglia discussing *The Sopranos*[102]:

> It's not the Mafia theme that I detest, tired and pointless as that is after its canonical treatment in masterpieces like the first two *Godfather* films, directed by Francis Ford Coppola. It's the sickening combination of effeteness in conception and crudity in execution that no major media article on *The Sopranos* has even noticed much less analyzed.

Like Paglia, I find the characters really *caricatures* hoping to be intricate and not succeeding at being fully drawn. I find the good aspects of the series—the filial passions, food, wine, song, sentiment —used to *seduce us* into accepting our own defamation. *The Sopranos* and its terrible popularity stand against the fact of our being a varied people of many different abilities, styles, creativity, and professions—a people who have struggled upward in America from poverty with perseverance, hard work, education, and pride, and yes, honor! We are a people as perfect, or imperfect, as any— but where is our true honor or humanity so widely portrayed without the cloak of *stereotypic* criminality?

When I think of my own immigrant father's tremendous struggle to survive and make headway in America, when I think of his accomplishments against all odds, won through brutally hard work and education—I hear him moan from his grave at the popularity of "The World According to Tony Soprano." I hear him weep, asking

"Is this what I worked so hard for in America? Is this my Italian American pride?"

---

[102]Paglia discusses *The Sopranos* in her May 23, 2001 article titled "The Energy Mess and Fascist Gays."

WHY STEREOTYPING OF ITALIAN AMERICANS PERSISTS
IMAGINING THE NEW ITALIAN AMERICAN

Presented at The John D. Calandra Institute for Italian American Studies 2008 Conference.

One realizes that the subject of prejudice and widespread media stereotyping of our Italian American citizenry as gangsters, or *mafiosi*, has been dealt with *ad-nausea*. It's also understood that it's a frustrating subject that inspires sardonic jokes as Dr. Joseph Sciorra, Assistant Director for Academic and Cultural Programs at The John D. Calandra Italian American Institute of Queens College, the City University of New York, recently created on *www.I-Italy.org*, the blogosphere newly online for Empowerment of the US-Italy Community. Dr. Sciorra made satiric commentary regarding the criminal informant, Frank Fiordilino, former Bonanno mob associate, for decrying the glorification of the mafia in the media. According to *The New York Daily News*, Fiordilino said: "I apologize as well, especially to anyone of Italian background, by conspiring and utilizing our culture in the same manner the entertainment industry does with its stereotypes.... Hollywood intensified my love of that life, and in the process blindsided what being Italian meant."

Dr. Sciorra felt, at this juncture, a satire was in order, and rightly so, perhaps, for those who were quick to say, "Ah, here's our smoking gun!" Yet, Sciorra also goes on to quote Juvenal Anniballa, convicted as an alleged member of the Genovese crime family. Anniballa recalled: "It was spring of 1980, and I was finishing up at Brooklyn College when I decided to take this class on Italian-American literature with this professor.... he had us read *The Godfather*. You can sort of say I took the gun and left the cannoli. Now, I regret ever having read a book!"

Using a gangster's statement that his life of crime was inspired by a media stereotype is on one level laughable, and deserves satire. We all see such images of our Italian American selves portrayed in the media, and, of course, we do not all—indeed a very small percentage among us: .0025 percent out of 26 million, according to the U.S. Department of Justice—succumb to being criminals because of the stereotype. In fact Dana Gioia, former chairman of the National Endowment for the Arts, wrote me in 1985 that "I'm a little touchy about the Mafia, too.... [Mafia] movies have nothing much to do with the reality I've seen.... I've often noticed how differently Hollywood portrays Jews and Italians. We're the new 'niggers'— either comic or violent."

And, shouldn't we seriously ask ourselves how much evidence we can find that the stereotype which plagues us *does* effect the direction of our at-risk youth in what may well have become a self-fulfilling prophecy? Isn't a controlled study in order to be used as ammunition in our anti-defamation struggle against the guilty media? Should we ask ourselves why that controlled psychological study has not been thoroughly done? Wouldn't it simply require that a credentialed psychologist like Dr. Elizabeth G. Messina, for one example, interview a large number of incarcerated youths to question them as to how much the media stereotype has played a role in their decision to enter a life of crime or to participate in neighborhood gangs or mobs? Couldn't a questionnaire be devised, asking them how many of these media films and series they watched as youths and how they reacted to them? Would that supply an actual "smoking gun" for organizations like CARRES (The National Coalition Against Racial, Religious, and Ethnic Stereotyping) to approach media moguls with real blame and social responsibility for profiting at the expense of the Italian American community? Reports of such a study would make good headlines in newspapers and letters to program directors of popular media outlets.

Is it surprising that no such *controlled* study has been attempted, at least in major urban areas like New York, Los Angeles, and Boston? Distinguished Professor of Italian American Studies, Dr. Fred Gardaphe, seemed to feel it would be a worthy undertaking when he was recently asked about it by this author at The Calandra Italian American Institute in New York, in April, 2008—after this paper in earlier version was presented at the conference: "Italians in the Americas."

Dr. Elizabeth Messina, who has served as an Adjunct Assistant Professor of Psychology at Fordham University, and a faculty member in the Department of Psychiatry at Lenox Hill Hospital, New York, has written in, "Psychological Perspectives on the Stigmatization of Italian Americans in the American Media":

> A central psychological problem confronting Italian Americans in the United States today is the media's relentless stereotyping of them as criminals who are in some way connect to Mafiosi. These negative representations are controlling images because they are created and perpetuated by dominant social institutions to make the ethnic treatment of Italian Americans seem *natural* and *normative* .... Stereotypes of Italian Americans have strong negative connotations that reflect the history of this identity group.... There is now significant cross-disciplinary evidence that Italian Americans have occupied an ambiguous identity in American society as *stigmatized marginalized whites*. Unfortunately, research examining the psychological and social effects of ethnic racism, prejudice, and stereotyping related to Italian Americans is virtually nonexistent. Italian Americans still remain conceptually invisible in psychological and psychoanalytic research literature.

In addition to Michael Parenti—who discusses this subject in his book titled *Make Believe Media* and in his other works—officers of the Order of the Sons of Italy in America, including Dr. Milone of the Calandra Institute, have been collecting such statements by convicted criminals as those in Dr. Sciorra's article (above) for years, and have also worked on surveys gathering statistics on Italian

American ghettoized youth. Milione admits his studies are not definitive, but he says he has charted a spike in high school dropouts in neighborhood teenagers that correlates with the release of such films as *The Godfather* at the height of its popularity, or *The Sopranos* television series, at the height of its. This correlation, if proven true, is indeed vital, as it shows that certain of our male writers, directors, and producers are indeed creating a *self-fulfilling prophecy* by means of their media profiteering at the expense of their own community.

Years ago—when CARRES was founded by various Italian American organizations to "speak with one voice" in response DreamWork's *Shark's Tale* using Italian names and mafia implications to portray cartoon gangsters for a *children's* show—many statements came from various outlets implying a negative effect on Italian American youth. Gregory Kane of *The Baltimore Sun*, Terry Byrne of *The Boston Herald*, and Vicki Vasilopoulos, writing in *The New York Times* all wrote of how American society accepts the stereotype of Italian Americans as a matter of course, "like an addiction," said Kane. There was particular concern on the part of CARRES that the show was aimed at children in a developmental stage. Yet, one might add that such organizations have neglected in great measure, at least in the past, the writers of our culture who do not portray Italians in such a light. NIAF seems to embrace the likes of Rudoph Giuliani who perpetuates the stereotype like an "Uncle Tomaso," more than writers who belie the stereotype.

In terms of the need for a psychological study on the issue, as explained above by Dr. Messina, there was an interesting article by Professor Donald Tricarico of Queensborough College that correlated the tough guy Mafia stereotype of neighborhood macho youth gangs with media saturation. He portrayed and researched the so-called, "Guido subculture" of "Guidomobiles" that blare thunderous music from huge speakers, driven by guys with big gold chains and tee-shirts with rolled up sleeves showing bulging biceps, who cruise their neighborhood for "Guido-girls" with big hair and short miniskirts, trying to "score or find a fight." These teens, *a la* John Travolta in *Saturday Night Fever*, for one example, are of the sort who worship what Fred Gardaphe calls "the macho culture of death" in his book from *Wiseguys to Wisemen*. Tricarico implies that the popularity of the macho Mafia image in the media has influenced the so-called "Guido subculture" of these drop-out, gangster-style teens to exist, influenced into being by stereotypic portrayals overblown in the media. We know the media influences culture.

Why some social psychologist among us has not, in all these years of prejudice and stereotyping of Italian American males, actually performed a controlled study of interviews among men who have been incarcerated or belonged to neighborhood mobs or gangs is a wonder. This data would serve well for the sake of anti-defamation. It would give clear power to Italian Americans who join in letter writing campaigns such as those promoted by The Italian American One-Voice Coalition.

Dr. Jerome Krase explained in his presentation, in April 2008, titled "Italian American Politics: A Worm's Eye View," that Italian America has never coalesced and cooperated around a single ethnic issue as have Jews who cluster their political votes around the issue of anti-Semitism, or Blacks who form their body politic around the issue of racism. For one example, the election of Mayor Dinkins was much helped by the huge media blitz over the Yusef Hawkins case, one of the most media-driven stories of all time. The subtleties of the scorned love story of the mixed ethnic group attack, and the retarded teen who fired the gun that the rest didn't even know existed, never came clear in the major media. It was blown up as merely a racially biased crime that helped Dinkins win his election, when actually it was more of a story of thwarted teenage love and mistaken identity coupled with neighborhood *mixed-ethnic* gang mentality.

The fact of the Italian woman, Mrs. Galarza, who called 911, then rushed down into the street to give CPR to Yusef Hawkins and hold his hand as she waited for the ambulance to arrive—the woman who risked her life to come down into a street where she heard gunfire—hardly made the news amidst the stereotypical reporting of that incident and Mayor Koch's calling for "a pizza boycott" in order to divide and conquer the vote. Who among us can remember Mrs. Galarza's name and have written or researched her dramatic story? This author wrote of her in a *MS.* magazine article in 1994, titled *Breaking the Silence for Italian American Women*. That story received more positive letters to the editor from Italian American women than any other story *Ms.* published during those years— even though the editors of the magazine were *not* Italian Americans and it was a *mainstream* magazine, edited then my Robin Morgan.

Dr. Krase, when he spoke of Italian American political disunity, offered his thoughts on a panel organized by Ottorino Cappelli of The University of Naples, who has written a preliminary study with tables and figures on contemporary Italian American political elites in New York State, titled: "The Black Hole: Italian American Studies and Political Science" that corroborates Krase's thesis.

Some of our most prominent political figures from *both* sides of the aisle have publicly complained about this political disunity. Former Governor Mario Cuomo of New York of the Democratic Party, to this day, has refused to view or read *The Godfather*, as he feels a boycott of such works would serve us well, but one has never been fully instituted with political unity. Supreme Court Justice Samuel Alito, Jr. who lived for two decades in West Caldwell, New Jersey, an area defiled by the fictional Tony Soprano as his supposed home. During a visit to Rutgers University, Judge Alito complained that the hit HBO drama associated not only Italian Americans with the Mafia, but New Jerseyans, as well. Alito's comments about *The Sopranos*, which ended its infamous run last year, were part of a talk in which Alito lamented that there are too many stereotypes about his ethnic background, and he implied that political unity was needed to overcome them. The 57 year old Alito was actually born in Trenton and attended Princeton University, in New Jersey, before going to law school at Yale.

To demonstrate the disunity, among well known politicians on the subject, Republican Mayor Rudolph Giuliani has long proclaimed *The Godfather* his favorite movie and book. It's not surprising that *The Sopranos* was also a favorite of his. One wonders about the motives for his proclamation that the community should "Lighten up! It's only a TV Show!" when Mayor Bloomberg invited actors from the series to march at the head The Columbus Day Parade. Were Giuliani's motives based upon the fact that the producer of the gangster series, Brad Grey, was also the agent for Giuliani's sale of his book *Leadership* which profited him in the millions. Camille Paglia has correctly asked: Weren't the police and firemen, many of them, Italian-Americans, the real heroes of 9/11? Several of all backgrounds publicly disparaged the Mayor for not supplying them with proper equipment and salaries for their jobs. Several, indeed, blamed him for a large number of their casualties. The Italian American One Voice Coalition is only one group alienated by Giuliani who duly received it's 2007 "Pasta-tute" award.

Richard Capazzolo, former Police Commissioner of Westchester County, NY, and a lifelong Republican, and who is taken seriously by many members of the Italian American community, has for one, written an article titled, "Rudy, an 'Uncle Tomaso' Extraordinaire," outlining the many words and actions of the former Mayor of New York which demonstrate Giuliani's deliberate fostering of the Mafia image, including a recent campaign stop he made on the West Coast, in which he began his speech in his best *Godfather* voice: "Thank youse all very much for invitin' me here tuh-day ta dis meetin' of the families from dif-rent parts-a California." When Barbara Walters interviewed Giuliani on *20/20* she proffered, "Mr. Mayor, I understand you do a great impression of the Godfather." And Rudy complied in his now perfected Don Vito Corleone voice. Can one imagine Walters asking Mayor Bloomberg or Senator Chuck Schumer to imitate a movie version of Louie Lepke, Legs Diamond, or Myer Lansky of Murder, Inc. without The Jewish Anti-defamation League causing a tremendous media stir?

Isn't it time to stop allowing such disunifying politicos as Giuliani to serve in creating low self-esteem in us by perpetuating the mafia image to our detriment? His book *Leadership*, so disliked by most New York firemen and police, was sold by Brad Grey producer of The Sopranos for millions after 9/11. He has his motives for loving The Sopranos and telling the rest of us to "lighten up!" about the stereotype. Doesn't this disunity among prominent politicos underline Dr. Krase's thesis? Of course, it's common knowledge that Giuliani's father actually was an incarcerated criminal, and Giuliani built his career on overemphasizing himself as prosecutor of mob gangsters.

Our scholarly community seems no more united on the issue of "speaking with one voice" than our political one. In May, 2008, Fordham University in New York, hosted a large conference titled *"The Sopranos*: A Wake." It was an international conference of academic presenters, convened by Professors Paul Levinson and Al Auster of Fordham, David Lavery of Brunel University, London, and Douglas Howard of Suffolk Community College, and attended by academic fans of *The Sopranos* who took the series very seriously as *literary art* and who teach it, no less, in their classes. Among the professors who presented papers of supposed serious sociopolitical analysis were several Italian American professors who teach *The Sopranos* to their students *as literature* worthy of scholarly, critical analysis. Camille Paglia, would be appalled, as was I. Only *one* paper of the many presented, *only one*, was a protest of the stereotype.

It was amazing to see that with all the good Italian American literature one could chose from, these professors, many Italian, spend time and funding analyzing fictional mob characters who are basically murderous, disgusting stereotypes while they ignore Don De Lillo, Diane Di Prima, Maria Mazziotti Gillan, Robert Viscusi, Michael Parenti, and me for that matter. According to Camille Paglia, and Dr. Elizabeth Messina, among many other cultural and psychological critics, these characters are poorly written *soap-opera* types. Many realize that this decadent and degraded piece of pop culture has been hyped to a large degree in order to project all criminality on one ethnic group as a *lightening rod* to take attention away from the constant disclosures of larger, widespread cronyism on the part of corrupt government figures and Wall Street C.E.O's.

The social psychological studies of how many of our teens are influenced into a life of crime by the self-fulfilling media stereotyping could easily be done, and yet, where are those controlled studies in all these years of prejudicial stereotyping? They would be useful in an argument to media moguls who profit from our suffering. And, there's no doubt we continue to suffer in substantial ways from this stereotype.

Firsthand experience is a barometer of the larger society. This author with her grandson, in a park in Maplewood, New Jersey, this very year of 2008, heard the young mothers of the town blaming their high property taxes on an Italian Mafia *a la* Tony Soprano. Yet few Italian names were found on the greatly Irish and English township board, and the state has had non-Italian governors of late, Governor Whitman, for example, when taxes were just as high. This park incident recalled the memory of another telling firsthand experience at a time just after this author's immigrant father's death in 1981: awarded with a recuperative November stay at the Edna St. Vincent Millay Colony for the Arts, I began to write my father Donato Gioseffi's immigration story through Elllis Island.

I went to the local library in Lenox, Massachusetts, and searched the catalog for a category of "Italian American immigration or immigrants." There was no such subject heading. The librarian, straight-faced, directed that I try under the heading of "Mafia." Sure enough, there was a category "Mafia" in the card catalog, but *nothing* under "Italian American culture or immigration in 1981 in a New England library near the Millay Colony for the Arts where I was in residence.

An articulate public servant like Mario Cuomo suffered from the stereotype in his run or public office—the usual fate of an Italian politician. How many have written the drama of how he stood up against the nuclear-industrialists and really lost his chance at the presidency for refusing to allow Shoreham to open while promising to shut-down Indian Point, a facility that the Union of Concerned Scientists, and many public servants, believe daily threatens millions of lives in the greater Metropolitan area?

One doubts there will ever be an Italian American president, before there is or will be a Black or Jewish one, due to the use of this plaguing media image of all Italian Americans. Even Reverend Wright, Barack Obama's *former*, notorious minister, disparaged Italians with prejudicial ignorance, saying they were responsible for "lynching Jesus Christ *Italian-style* in Apartheid Rome" and that "they looked down their garlic and olive oil noses at Jesus for being poor." Yet no *major* media protest ensued as it did regarding his Anti-Semitic or unpatriotic statements. A fact that's easily checked!

Perhaps, because OSIA's statistical surveys, as well as other studies, show that 70 % of Americans, including Italian Americans, believe that if your name is Italian, you are connected in some way to a huge, mythological, international, criminal cartel known generically as the *mafia*! This Italian word has become so generic that it's used for all cartels of any background. Recently, a new television series piloted titled *The Cashmere Mafia* about some high-powered business women, a group of girlfriends who helped each other in classy big-business circles. They were Asian, WASP, and Irish, but it was titled the *The Cashmere Mafia* in a series something like *Sex in the City*, where the women were fashionably dressed in designer clothes.

Approximately 70% of Italian Americans, themselves, suspect each other of a Mafia connection, because they've bought into the media blitz of mafia mythology as a huge and powerful, international cartel guilty of being involved in everything from the assassination of President Kennedy to the covert murder of Marilyn Monroe. Those sad events were actually the subject of television documentaries in which the Mafia was *theoretically* implicated. The story of how Senator Estes Kefaufer falsely claimed the existence of a huge and dominating cartel is well documented in many texts as never existing on anything like the scale he supposed.

Surely we know by now that the Mafia of Al Capone, Lucky Luciano and such of the 40's and 50's has been dismantled and that John Gotti's influence did not spread so far and wide as the Mafia myth by the media would have us believe. Some of our authors were raised in neighborhoods where localized mobs prevailed, and one notes that they're the ones most readily involved in believing the overblown Mafia myth. Ironically, Mario Puzo wrote that he never met a Mafioso and that Don Corleon's character was based on his indomitable mother who served as the model for *The Fortunate Pilgrim's* Lucia Santa— a woman who labored fiercely to keep her children out of a neighborhood gang in Hell's Kitchen. That neighborhood thuggery exists in organized pockets cannot be denied, and that it exists in Sicily and Naples today in the form of a hideous *Camorra* as disclosed in *The Nation* and in a book by Roberto Saviano titled *Gomorrah: A Personal Journey Into the Violent Empire of Naples Organized Crime System*. There is organized crime today in America in larger numbers among the newer Russian-Jewish immigrants of the Brighton Beach area of Brooklyn, for example, but do popular series like the *The Sopranos* serve to take attention away from larger elements of ethnic and white-collar crime in our midst? That African American or Chinese drug dealers are operating at a larger percentage rate in their ghettos than Italian American gangs in the neighborhoods of our urban blight makes a symbolic series like *The Sopranos* a false lightening-rod that labels all crime and grime as merely Italian and attracts populist attention.

In attempting to shed some light on why the stereotype persists and is so difficult to eradicate, exposing the resultant problem of Italian Americans having a poor self-image or self-esteem must be addressed. Don't we often honestly suspect each other and ourselves of being thugs and thieves on some clandestine level? Certainly, one has heard of how Black youths insult each other with the "N-word" that the rest of us dare not speak, but how often do we, ourselves, look at successful Italian *nuovo-riche* business men in Armani suits and wonder about their mafia connections because of the media blitz that has characterized us? Hasn't the major media image succeeded in dividing and conquering us and weakening our self-defense and self-esteem?

Scholars among us, like Dr. Robert Viscusi in *Buried Caesars*, or Dr. Fred Gardaphe in *From Wiseguys to Wisemen*, or Dr. Richard Gambino, whom Viscusi quotes in his book, have a point when they say that the real problem is *self-esteem*, that protest hasn't gotten us far in thirty years of protesting, that we need to put forth *positive* images of the *new* Italian American of today, and bury the Caesars of yesteryear. We need to stop harkening back to only our great Renaissance heritage, which never really belonged to the great majority of immigrant children among us whose heritage actually goes back to the Kingdom of Two Sicilies, and not the Northern Italian Renaissance. We need to study the glories of that *Southern Kingdom* and claim them as ours, and better understand the historical roots of the "Black Hand" as a *vigilante* fighting foreign invaders and marauders for the purpose of arousing more self-esteem among us. We need to understand the massacres of Southern Italians and the cause of the poverty that drove our forebears here to America.

One hardly hears about the cultural greatness of the Southern Italian heritage that we need to promote for its finer elements. I note that among my Jewish New York friends, Sicily has now become a favorite vacation spot for its beauties. One notices that the so-called "Land of Color" of the *Mezzogiorno* and Pulia is now frequented by more *touristi* than before. People enjoy visiting the Gargano as a place of beauty where some of the oldest limestone cave paintings in the world can be toured and the relic of St. Nicholas can be viewed in Bari where one of the oldest universities can be found. But, even more than the *Mezzogiorno* of our parents' homeland, we need to promote the goodness of what we are today and have become. We need to go about positively creating a new image for and re-imagining the Italian American of *now* and the culture of Italian America that reaches beyond the immigrant paradigm that Fred Gardaphe discussed in his keynote speech at the Calandra Institute to inaugurate our April 2008 Conference.

We need to offer the dramas of lawyers, doctors, judges, teachers, musicians, scientists, painters, filmmakers, and writers of our *diaspora*, and yes, the hard-working blue-collar workers and masons and iron craftsmen and shoemakers, too. We need to begin to write and read about who we are today and promote the dramatic stories of our heroes and heroines recalling the dramas of Mother Cabrini, Arturo Toscanini, Enrico Fermi, Mario Cuomo, Susan Sarandon, Don DeLillo, or Nancy Pelosi and how they came to be who they are through hard work and tenacity and dramatic struggle. How about a popular screenplay about the tragedy of Mario Lanza, and how he was used and abused by Hollywood, how his passionate hot-temper and need to be thin destroyed him? I see a drama full of conflict in the life of Arturo Toscanini beaten by Fascists, even if he was an imperfect guy with a nasty temper and a hard disciplinarian of his orchestra. We need to write more of the novels that offer characterizations of *imperfect* heroes and heroines as Mario Puzo did in *The Fortunate Pilgrim* or Josephine Gattuso-Hendin did in *The Right Thing to Do—* two iconic books of our heritage that all of us should read and study more than the mythical characters of *The Godfather.*

In the introduction to *On Prejudice: A Global Perspective* (published by Anchor/Doubleday in 1993 and still used in many institutions of higher learning across the country), this author addresses the dynamics of prejudice: quoting several psychologists, anthropologists, and sociologists, like Gordon Allport, respected for his earlier widely studied book, *The Nature of Prejudice.* Robert Viscusi and Helen Barolini were included with essays, representing the Italian American issue, for the first time in a major mainstream text on prejudice, the first multicultural compendium to address issues of xenophobia of all kinds, including racism, ethnocentrism, instances of genocide, ethnic-cleansing, mono-cultural attitudes, homophobia, and all manner of prejudice, including stereotyping and scapegoating.

It was discovered that understanding psychological projection and scapegoating is vitally useful in our attempt to have a positive approach rather than a self-defensive approach to the problem that plagues us. Better self-esteem from a dignified, rather than a lowly self-defensive position can be fruitful and aid our efforts to write about and buy books and patronize plays and films about the true dramas of our ancestors and immigrant forebears and our own new contemporary story in America. *Self-esteem* is necessary before we can overcome discrimination and stereotyping.

Actors like Leonardo Di Caprio who do not indulge merely mobster roles to build their careers upon, as Al Paccino or Robert De Niro often have, are helping us to overcome the stereotype with their civic deeds, as well. Di Caprio promotes charitable and environmental causes that are multi-ethnic in nature. We need to join with all sorts of other anti-defamation leagues against *all* forms of prejudice towards all groups, as *On Prejudice: A Global Perspective* included *la causa* among the causes of Armenians, Jews, Blacks, Asians, Arabs, women, and gays in a more universal perspective on issues of prejudice in the mainstream.

We need to keep our united coalition of protest strong while we write, read, tell, and speak our true stories of Italians in the Americas. As professors of literature and culture, we need to teach books like *The Fortunate Pilgrim* by Mario Puzo or *The Right Thing to Do* by Josephine-Gattuso Hendin, rather than make room in our curriculum of Italian American Studies for *The Godfather*, or *The Sapranos*, regardless of their popularity. The history of *enduring art* is not the history of *popular taste*, and harbingers of culture need to resist popular tastes with sound substitutes rather than fall in with the lowest, common denominator.

We need to see that films like *The Godfather* or dramas like *The Sopranos* are popular fictions not just for their artistry, but because they provide a scapegoat for crime, a haven for psychological projection that rids the mainstream culture of its greater guilt. Psychologists and sociologists tell us that when a culture or a people or a person has a good deal of reason for self-hatred in recognizing its own greed and guilt, that greed and guilt are projected upon an exotic other. Psychological baggage is projected onto a group of people, who are different than our selves, in order to get rid of the pain of self-hatred.

One of our main problems in overcoming the prejudice that plagues us is that we have not succeeded in creating enough empathy for Italian American characters in the minds of the larger American society as Jewish and African American authors have. We have not been so good at portraying our imperfect struggle against poverty and discrimination as Jews have because, because for one real thing, we've not suffered anything as horrendous as a Holocaust in being made a scapegoat. Indeed, our Italy was infamously on the wrong side of that horrific World War. We are plagued by two big M's: the existence of a real mafia, and the fact of a foolish and fickle Mussolini. Those big M's in our path like an unyielding boulder make it hard to tell stories that create empathy in American readers. We have not survived anything as huge as the slavery of African peoples who were dragged here in slave-ships by the multimillions. It's more difficult, therefore, to create *empathy* for an assimilating and relatively successful group so constantly portrayed as criminal tough guys in love with the culture of death in the major media, but it can me done if we can create dimensional characters of feeling.

We have to ask ourselves why Jewish organized crime or Black organized crime is not so consistently and successfully portrayed by the make-believe media that Michael Parenti exposes in his wonderful expose *Make-Believe Media*. How many of us know and have read the books of our fine political commentator Michael Parenti as much as Jews have read theirs? Parenti is as insightful as Noam Chomsky and more entertaining to read with his sardonic wit. Even if crime and grim existed as part of our immigrant paradigm, we need to dramatize the stories of those who struggled against the white slavery of the early immigrant laborers, and those who struggled with great conflict against the neighborhood thugs. We need to create empathy in portrayals of real imperfect but triumphant heroes and heroines who will tempt readers of any background to know them.

In summary and conclusion, is it our *Omerta*—our code of silence—that has caused us not to tell the stories of white slavery of men, women, and children under cruel *padrones* that were part of our immigrant story. Why haven't we dramatized the human lives touched by *Una Storia Segreta* in a commercial novel or film that would move all Americans to tears? Is it because we keep to ourselves our own struggle and believe in the mafia mythology, or the custom of *omerta* allowing our selves to be scapegoats *because* of low self-esteem created by the conundrum of the mafia stereotype? Is it because we are not a good literary culture and do not patronize our authors who write our true stories? Is it because the first thing an Italian American museum does in its founding is invite a mogul from Wall Street, or a politician, rather than a great artist of words, or moving poetic power, to speak the keynote that inaugurates the museum of our *cultural* heritage? Is it because we fear to display our books, frightened that someone will think we're caught in a conflict of interest? Would a Jewish or Black conference exist without tables of books, bought and sold? Do we pay enough attention to our own literary heritage, the one that tells the true story? These are the questions repeated for emphasis.

Shouldn't we all dig up a copy of the fine psychiatrist, Dr. Robertiello's book, *The WASP Mystique*. His understanding of the oppression of ethnics forced to behave in the style of the dominant culture might set us free of self-hatred and shame. Don't we really need to stop patronizing the stereotypic images of ourselves as Rudolph Giuliani enjoys doing?

Getting our writing into the mainstream is our difficult task. We need more writers like Don De Lillo who are successful on the literary horizon at large, and that means we need to buy our writers' books. Why hasn't Vito Marc Antonio's dramatic story full of conflict been successfully sold as a screenplay? He was a public servant for *all* poor ethnics, not just Italians. Is it because Vito Marc Antonio's story isn't a commercial drama, or because we have not tried hard enough to write and sell it—because of our own low self-esteem and our own diversion towards the Godfathers and Tony Sopranos foisted upon us by the media? How much of our problem is our own fault in not writing and reading and publishing our own *true* stories with dimensional characters, neither saints nor villains? How many of *us* have read and bought, just for one old example, Mario Puzo's *The Fortunate Pilgrim* compared to those of us who have patronized *The Godfather?* These questions cannot be overemphasized.

How much of the stereotyping that continues is because of our low self-esteem and our acceptance of it, and how much is projection and scapegoating, and how much self-fulfilling prophecy foisted upon us by a few of our turncoat media profiteers? It is time to re-imagine and create the image of the *new* Italian American, neither saint nor sinner, but human being in conflict with his own striving and triumphant surviving in this imperfect democracy, a land of golden opportunity for *some!*

by Daniela Gioseffi

ᴡʜʏ I Bᴇᴄᴀᴍᴇ ᴀ Pʀᴏғᴇssɪɪᴏɴᴀʟ Cʀᴏᴏɴᴇʀ ᴀᴛ Fɪғᴛʏ-Sᴇᴠᴇɴ
A Pᴇʀsᴏɴᴀʟ Essᴀʏ ᴏɴ Fʀᴀɴᴋ Sɪɴᴀᴛʀᴀ, ᴄɪʀᴄᴀ 1993

First appeared in *VIA: Voices in Italian Americana,* vol. 1 (1999).

Because of Frank Sinatra, my success in poetry and writing was never quite enough to satisfy my Italian Ameican family. My old Italian aunts wept copious tears at the death of Mario Lanza, but I'm sure that Eugenio Montale's death went completely ignored by them. My Italian uncles survived World War II, to return home and dream of being Frank Sinatra, not John Ciardi or Felix Stefanile—or the plump operatic tenor, Mario Lanza either! Uncle Giuseppe survived the Battle of the Bulge, a broken man who never talked about the bloody bodies and agonizing deaths that must have surrounded him in that hideous war. Neither did he talk much of his inability to get a job with his Italian name, after the war, even with his Bronze Star. His sorrow was most expressed by his vocal renditions of Sinatra's sad love songs. He could imitate Sinatra's warbles to perfection. So could Uncle Michele, now a millionaire who lives far from *la famiglia*, and wants little to do with the faltering remnants of his old immigrant sibling brood with whom he grew up around a cold stove in Newark's Ironbound section. In his seventies, I'm sure he lounges at his Florida vacation home, dreaming that he is more like the "Chairman of the Board," "Old Blue Eyes," himself, Frank Sinatra. Uncle Michele actually did, and does, to a great degree, still resemble Sinatra—slender, blue-eyed, and slick in his suits and ties. He was, in any event, the Frank Sinatra of *la mia famiglia* all through the forties and fifties—his family's pride and joy as he worked his way through Bloomfield College at the suburban edge of Newark, where he was taught proper English and American manners—the manners with which he would succeed as a VP of the Dixiecup Corp.

Uncle Michele, became "Mike," a name like "Frank," in his navy uniform, in which he looked uncannily like Sinatra in *Guys and Dolls.* The photo on Grandma Lucia's mantle in Newark with Mike in his sailor-hat—jauntily atilt on his head like Sinatra's—meant a kind of American success! Sinatra's rise to fame and fortune by way of his passionate crooning represented the conquering of the American Dream with money and sex appeal, as well as a very Italian emotional quality to "The Voice"—a kind of smooth vocal passion, akin to popular operatic theater in Italy.

The original meaning of "enchantment" is a hypnotic spell that is sung, and who would say that Sinatra was not THE enchanter of all time? Ask yourself, can a poet enchant that way in America? The closest phenomenon we have to a Frank

Sinatra in American poetry is Galway Kinnell, but is that an Italian name? The bobby-soxer, teenage swoons over "Frankie" are legendary—as legendary as the young girls' swooning over Lord Byron during the age of English Romanticism. One of the earliest appearances by Frank Sinatra at the dawning of his soloist career at New York City's Paramount Theater in 1944 caused a Columbus Day riot. Over 30,000 young women, who were shut out of the sold-out performance, rampaged Times Square, broke shop windows, blocked traffic, and battled hundreds of policemen. Screaming, swooning women would tear the clothes from "Frankie!" We've all heard the legend, know the story, and have seen the newsreels. The "swinger with a swagger" crooned his enchantment for more than a half-century to sold-out seats. Yes, Sinatra *was* the Lord Byron of his time, more than W.S. Merwin or Galway Kinnell—for all of their swagger and good looks— and certainly more than John Ciardi or Felix Stefanile or any other poet of ethnic name could ever be!

What we realize the most is that Francis Albert Sinatra—the famous conqueror of Hollywood, who came to be known as "The Chairman of the Board" in that multi-million dollar industry—refused to change his syllabic Italian name to "Smith" in order to make it. He rose from *ghettohood* on the power of his warbles to enchant the nation and the world, and he would forever be the legend, the symbol of the American Dream that would inspire three generations of Italian boys to climb from the ghettos of the land on the music of their Italian wings. Many followed in his crooning footsteps, too: Vic Damone, Tony Bennett, Dean Martin. Even guys like Dominico Maduno from the Old Country made the transition back to the New World with their "*Volare*" warbles owed their success to "Frankie."

But, it was more than "Old Blue Eye's" voice that defined his success and his image. My father, Donato, who became "Dan" also resembled the young Frank at 28 years—not full of the big brawn of the Aryan oppressor. *Blue-eyed* and slight framed in his youthful photo that still adorns my wall, my father, the guiding-light and patriarch of our family, the object of our ancestral worship to this day, despite his intellectual aspirations and bookishness, also identified with "Frankie Sinatra" from Hoboken, New Jersey, my father's home state until his death in 1981 at 75 years. Though Daniel Gioseffi, our patriarch, would attain one of the first memberships by an Italian immigrant in an Alpha Chapter of Phi Beta Kappa at Union College in 1928, he, too, would dream more of being Frank Sinatra than Einstein or Ciardi. Why? Not just because Sinatra was king of the American Dream, but because his image was one of a tough guy who took no "crap" from any oppressor, Aryan, English, Irish or otherwise.

Sinatra, in his infamous Hollywood "rat pack" made himself close to other ethnics like Sammy Davis Junior and Dean Martin, even as he was hanging around with Peter Lawford of the Kennedy Klan. And, he was known as a snappy, womanizing tough guy who busted lips and broke hearts with reckless ease, romancing the likes of Ava Gardner and Anita Eckberg, Mia Farrow or even, rumor has it, Jackie Kennedy, the classy and fashionable First Lady herself. It was his confidence to be who he was and to keep his Italian name through it all that helped to give my uncles and father the will to go on through all the Mafia epithets, smears and pejoratives, like *wop, guinea, dago,* that plagued their generation of first generation immigrants. My white-haired grandfather, Galileo, never gave up his opera and his worship of Caruso and Verdi, but my uncles opted for Frankie with his very American drawl.

I can still see Grandpa Galileo with his pipe and homemade wine in hand—his ear fastened to the static-filled wooden radio in his cold water flat in Newark, on Magnolia Street, near Springfield Avenue (since burned down in the 60's race riots) trying to hear the thrilling notes of a Verdi opera through the sizzling sound waves. But, I also see my uncles in a back room of that flat looking into the mirror, straightening a bow tie, preparing for a date with an American girl, crooning a Sinatra love tune into the mirror.

And even more hidden in the back room of that cold water flat, I see my aunts with their hair rolled up in bobby-soxer style, crooning, very privately, that Sinatra tune, too, as they imagine what their date might say to them to win their favors. *Zia* Elisabetta, pretty and shy, sang with an emotional quiver that would make us all cry at our big Italian weddings. Shyly and hesitantly she'd take the microphone on the stage in front of the little hired band and croon, "I'll Never Smile Again" or later, "Polka Dots and Moonbeams," "Blue Moon" or "Mona Lisa, Mona Lisa, men have named you, you're so like the lady with the mystic smile," and we'd all weep and say, "*Mama Mia*, she belongs in Hollywood among the stars!" Sure "Mona Lisa" was a Nat King Cole tune and "Blue Moon," a Billy Eckstein one, but Frank Sinatra, "The Chairmen of the Board," had helped to open the door for ethnic singers and entertainers in America. He wasn't the only one, but his push to open that door was a very big one that Rudy Vallee and Bing Crosby can't completely claim with their English and Irish origins. Frank had embraced the African American jazz singer, and his kind, and opened a door into American culture, a defining influence, and one *other* than the one opened by Joe DiMaggio or Yogi Bara into the world of sports success and "*Bayssa Bolla!*"

I remember an African American friend saying to me in the early 70s, "There are only two ways a Black man can make it in this country: one is through sports, and the other is through entertainment." I agreed, reminding him that was true for Jews, Italians, Poles, and all ethnics just a decade or two before. None of them were welcomed at fancy hotels until entertainers of the power of Sinatra began insisting that not only they with their *nuovo riche* fortunes should be allowed to sign the registers of fancy hotels like The Astor or Hilton, but so should their fellow ethnic entertainers, like Sammy Davis Jr., be allowed to. Indeed jazz and pop music, along with sports, were the first integrating entities of American culture to so visibly force the issue of ethnic integration with the upper classes of English and German American aristocracy. And, it was the emotional qualities of these ethnic singers that transcended class and made them popular among rich and poor, human feelings being the same phenomenon at every social register. Sinatra was the Italian Paul Robeson, and he insisted on integration, too, most notably with Sammy Davis, Jr., as had Bing Crosby with Louie Armstrong. The voicing of emotions by such ethnic singers, emotions that are not allowed in polite Anglo-Saxon society, the sharing of joy and loss, sorrow and love, and that's what sold so well, not the intellectual content of the lyrics! These ethnic singers, Italian, African, Jewish American were giving a soulfulness to American popular culture and pioneering integration of classes and cultures at the same time. Their impact would be profound as they sang tunes by Gershwin, Rogers and Hammerstein, Cole Porter or Duke Ellington—now all "classic" Americana.

But, what did all this mean for me, an Italian American female, pioneering her way into American letters. It meant for one thing, that I would stubbornly refuse to change my long Italian name from "Gioseffi" to Josephs or Jones—despite my blue eyes and blond hair, despite my ability to pass for Irish or English if I'd wanted to! It meant that I would have a tough pride in my Italian American heritage, fostered by my uncles who took Sinatra's example and were ready to hit anybody who called them a "dirty guinea." Despite his anxiety to assimilate, my father kept a fierce pride in his roots, and I wouldn't be surprised that it was fostered in some part by the toughness of Sinatra's legendary pride. It meant that I, too, would forge ahead undaunted in the face of rejection and mafia epithets. It meant that success was possible in America, even with a long Italian name.

That is what Frank Sinatra has meant to me, and now that I'm in my senior years and have established myself with some measure of success in American letters as a poet, novelist and literary critic, it means that post-menopausally, I have returned to my original American Dream, the one fostered by delicate, shy *Zia* Elisabetta at those "gala" wedding affairs where we'd all dress up and she'd be our "Hollywood star" just for the day when she took that microphone by it's throat and warbled love tunes into our ears, and we'd all swoon and say, "She belongs in Hollywood or singing on the stage like Sinatra or Connie Francis, singing 'Mama!'" Or Louie Prima with "*Oh, la la, pesce, pesce baccula,*" containing all its hidden, erotic meanings. "Yes, Mama, the moon is on the water, and I want to catch a nice slippery, shining fish in the night, too!"

And, I want to be an enchanter, a better and more immediate enchanter than a poet: an enchantress who is a crooner, a jazz singer who reaps that ever-loving applause and acceptance from an audience like Sinatra did. So, I've returned to mainstream jazz singing, all those old Sinatra tunes, too, as well as the Ellington and Gershwin ones, and I'm giving concerts of Gershwin, Porter, Ellington, Mancini, Carmichael, everywhere, and singing in an elegant restaurant with bar. Here I am, the poet at fifty-seven, who doesn't even drink wine (let alone whiskey!), becoming a "saloon singer" like Sinatra was in his youth—all because of "The Velvet Voice"—that very Italian commodity that earns me more pleasure and relaxation, more immediate satisfaction, than all the dusty books that line my shelves. I love the smiles and applause that my easy listening crooning brings. I'm setting my poems to melodies and crooning them.

This is America, and people here don't love poets as well as they love crooners. They don't love professors and scientists as well as they love baseball players and movie stars, and I want some of that love and adulation, some of the immediate joy that a poet rarely receives—certainly not one with a syllabic Italian name. Witness the lack of fame for our best Italian American poets of my father's generation: John Ciardi, Felix Stefanile, Joseph Tusiani or Alfredo de Palchi! Lawrence

Ferlinghetti is the best known and most widely read, and even he never received a Pulitzer Prize or National Book Award! Why? Were these poets ever fellows of the Academy of American Poets? Were they given the National Book Award or the notoriety and worship given a T.S. Elliot, Jorie Graham, John Ashbery, or Richard Howard? Don't dare to think it has to do with their work!

So much for the insular world of American poetry, especially its decadent, esoteric Dadaist verse! I'm a crooner like Sinatra and loving it! Opera, after all, was the popular music of the peoples' emotions! Young women fainted over the emotion in the tenor's voice. Let it all hang out. I'm swinging, bopping and crooning the most American art of all—jazz—and having a ball. It picks up my spirits when the people applaud and come up afterward and say, "What a voice!" I feel sanctified by "Old Blue Eyes!" because I am a blue-eyed Italian who refused to give up her Italian name and who croons and dreams the unattainable "American Dream!" As a poet, despite some success in publishing six books of poetry, I feel like a prophet without honor in her own country, but as a crooner, when I hear that applause and "Oh, what a voice!" I can dream that I'm rising up to heaven on the wings of lyricism, even without a Pulitzer Prize!

"So, thanks to Frankie of Hoboken, from me, Daniela of nearby Newark, with my awards from the New York State Council for the Arts in poetry. I'm now crooning my Italian heart out, letting those Englishmen hear what real emotion and passion in the voice is all about! Call me a *mafiosa* if you like, but I'm just a singer with a harp or a heart, trying to get to the Heaven of Hollywood's, pie-in-the-sky America! Love me! Love my Italian voice!" I dream as I sing my lyrics into the night—fulfilling the hopes of my uncles and aunts who never understood American poetry so much as American popular music! Not one of them dreamed of being a poet, but they all dreamed of being Frank Sinatra, "Old Blue Eyes," "The Voice," "The Chairman of the Board" of Hollywood crooners, the enchanter of the American Dream, the tough guy who wouldn't change his name or give up, whose idea of love was to say, "If anybody ever hits you, call me!" And where did "The Great Sinatra," entertainer of all time and all seasons, ask to be buried, beside his parents Dolly and Martin in Cathedral City, in the plot of *la famiglia*, after all!

Frankie, "the way you wear your hat... the memory of all that, no no, they take that away from me," even if my name isn't Jones or Josephs, but "Gioseffi!"

by Daniela Gioseffi

MULTICULTURALISM
A RENAISSANCE IN ITALIAN AMERICAN LITERATURE?

From *Multicultural America: Essays on Cultural Wars and Cultural Peace,* ed. Ishmael Reed (New York, NY: Viking, 1997). Also presented at SUNY, Stony Brook, Italian American Studies Conference, 1997.

Most Americans are still unaware that the largest mass lynching in U.S. history was of a group of innocent Italian immigrant laborers in New Orleans at the end of the nineteenth century. There were blue laws on the books of many localities that forbade intermarriage with Italians and home sales to them, just as to Blacks and Jews. Discrimination against Italian Americans was rampant throughout the USA. Stereotypical Mafia films still abound from Hollywood and television, so that writing about ordinary Italian American people continues to be absent from the American consciousness. Most Americans are not ready to see our group as sufferers from prejudice, who might require some measure of sympathy. We're thought of as hardened criminals who can take care of our own, rather than ordinary people—with the added problem of being unrecognized as an offended minority.

By the end of the 1970's, many Italian American writers had seen the light and knew that the multicultural movement was where they belonged if they were going to gain a foothold in American letters. Despite the growing use of *political correctness* as a pejorative in a *reactionary* attempt to stop the dialogue that's begun in recent years regarding racism, sexism, prejudice, and the *opening* of the American mind and literary canon, most of our writers have joined the revolutionary movement founded by African American scholars. There's clearly a reawakening, or birth, happening in Italian American writing, as evidenced by several magazines and books recently published, which bear a definitive and self-proclaimed ethnic pride.

We "ethnic writers"—of many kinds—have swum up to the surface of U.S. literature, to find ourselves Americans of every kind. We've begun to listen to each other's poetry, relish each other's food for stomach and thought, glad to have survived the oppression of the WASP mystique, which up to now has plagued even the white Anglo-Saxon Protestant with an uptight stereotype.

As Richard Robertiello, the Harvard trained psychiatrist and author of *The WASP Mystique*, explained in his book:

Although a nation of ethnics, our established ethic is WASPishness, the standard by which assimilation is judged, while WASP conduct, for its part, was early on patterned on the model of the British upper class. Altogether, this has proved to be a very bad thing, making Americans WASP-worshipers, with an attendant devaluation and dilution of ethnic pride.

Robertiello wrote his book with a graduate student author and a WASP, Diana Hoquet, who had herself come to resent the WASP biases she was raised with. Jews who went into professional jobs tended to emulate the WASP mystique as they presented their case histories to Dr. Robertiello in his Manhattan practice, but Blacks and Italians, too, and other folk, made themselves miserable in their pursuit of WASPishness. The inferences of Dr. Robertiello's study were a cause for alarm, as so pervasive and pernicious was the mystiques that "even WASPs, wanted to be more like WASPs," and make themselves unhappy in their attempt to be so. But this was just before the dawning of the "multicultural" movement, and the American Book Awards given by the Before Columbus Foundation, and we are all wise today. Or are we?

There's no doubt that the very act of writing remains a fight for cultural identity, as Ishmael Reed explained in his book *Writin' Is Fightin'*, but Italian American writers—partly because of a fierce independence, somewhat because of the desire to assimilate, and mostly out of a fear of being dubbed Mafiosi if they tried to congregate—have had trouble organizing against the stereotypes that plague and pigeonhole them as spaghetti-sucking Mafiosi or "Guidos" who don't read or buy books.

But through the late 80's and 90's, the voices of real Italian Americans began to be heard; this included the publication of journals and books. Not only was *Italian Americana* refurbished, but a vital new literary and cultural review titled *Voices in Italian Americana* was born. Edited by Anthony J. Tamburri, Paolo A. Giordano, and Fred L. Gardaphe, it has quickly blossomed into a periodical read throughout the country. Just prior to founding *VIA,* the trio compiled a compendium, *From the Margin: Writings in Italian Americana* (Purdue UP 1991, 2000), which contained the work of many writers of note. And there are many other journals, such as *Differentia,* a review of Italian thought located at Queens College in New York, and *Fra Noi* of Chicago, to name just two. The publication of *Blood of My Blood* (Guernica Editions 1974, 2002), a widely read sociological commentary by Professor Richard Gambino, pioneered the current flurry of publication in the 90's.

And recently, the John D. Calandra Italian American Institute won a court decision that alleged discrimination against Italian American professors. The Calandra Institute had studied the problems of urban youth and discovered that Italian American teens had one of the highest rates of high school dropouts, statistically in the upper ranges with Black and Puerto Rican youth. Noting this fact, the Institute proceeded, under the leadership of Dr. Joseph V. Scelsa, to demonstrate that despite a large population of Italian American students, CUNY grossly shortchanged Italian American professors when it came to faculty recruitment and promotions. In November 1992, Judge Constance Baker Motley granted a preliminary injunction against the university, ending in a settlement, which in effect concluded that *civil rights are everyone's rights* and that federal statutes apply to Italian Americans as well as to traditionally defined minorities.

This was one of the most recent instances when Italian Americans were able to cooperate to defend themselves against discrimination. One might say that the spirit of labor organizers Sacco and Vanzetti was at least vindicated by Judge Motley's decision. Edna St. Vincent Millay and Edmund Wilson were a part of a progressive movement among American writers Sacco and Vanzetti, labor organizers, who'd called themselves "anarchists" against an unjust system.

But not until recently has there been any sort of successful movement among Italian American intellectuals to undo the ruthlessness of subtler forms of discrimination against them. The Calandra Institute sponsors a cable television show, *Italics,* which interviews Italian American literary figures and posts a rich calendar of varied cultural events throughout the Northeast. Dr. Robert Viscusi organized in 1991 the Italian American Writers Association (IAWA), which has established a literary salon and readings throughout New York City and in Greenwich Village where IAWA meets of a Saturday evening at Cornelia Street Café. Luciana Polney, playwright and poet, inspired the group to read at the progressive Nuyorican Café in the East Village, and interculturalism was encouraged. Activities began to connect more and more with the multicultural movement. In 1993, with Peter Caravetta, Robert Viscusi managed to institute a graduate course in Italian American literature at CUNY's Graduate Center in midtown Manhattan as well. Another first! Similar activities are blossoming in the Chicago area under the leadership of Fred Gardaphe and Paolo Giordano; for example, there was a series of readings sponsored by the journal *VIA* at the Caffe Trevi on North Lincoln Avenue in the windy city. Of course, Lawrence Ferlinghetti, the man who made publication of the Beat Generation poets possible with his City Lights Book Store and Press, was a pioneer of the current flurry of Italian American names in poetry, as was Diane Di Prima, who moved to the West Coast many years ago after her work in the 60's in New York. Ferlinghetti and Di Prima, like well-known poet John Ciardi, made inroads for the current Renaissance, if only by virtue of their surnames, as they were very much a part of the "mainstream" progressive movement in literature.

In 1985, Helen Barolini edited *The Dream Book: Writings of Italian American Women* (Schoken Books), showing how that group had been neglected even as they were producing a wealth of literature particular to their ethnic background. In her introduction, she cited forgotten role models like the Nobel Prize winner and prolific novelist, Grazia Deledda, who had been neglected not only by the male establishment but by the feminist canon as well. Barolini reminded us, too, of Frances Winwar, who was forced to change her name from Vinciguerra, in order to publish in America, and who was one of the most prolific American biographers of the 20th century. In fact, Winwar wrote the applauded bastion of feminism, *George Sand and Her Times: A Life of the Heart* (Harper 1945), still in print; but she has managed to be forgotten as an Italian American by American feminists, to say nothing of the male establishment.

Today, there's a press, Guernica Editions, founded and run by editor and author Antonio D'Alfonso, which has put out an entire line of Italian American poetry and fiction, including the recently published compendium of Italian American women's fiction, titled *The Voices We Carry* (1993), edited by Mary Jo Bona (Gonzaga

University), which brings together twelve authors of note from around the country.

So when, in 1991, a book of Italian American writings by both men and women appeared from the University of Purdue Press, the aforementioned *From the Margin: Writings in Italian Americana,* it spurred a storm of readings, reviews, and networking sessions among Italian American poets and writers of fiction and criticism.

For the first time in the history of the Academy of American Poets, Dana Gioia was able to publish a piece titled "What is Italian American Poetry?" questioning if such a thing existed. Though Gioia's short article, featured on the front page of the *Academy of American Poets Newsletter* (1992), wounded many by its omissions—particularly of prominent women poets—it was a first.

It created a controversy that led to a heated debate among Italian American writers, and it led to front-page piece, "Where are the Italian American Novelists," appeared on the cover of the *New York Times Book Review* (March 14, 1993) written by Gay Talese. One of the few big Italian American names on the New York and PEN American Center scene, Talese questioned whether there were any Italian American novelists beside himself—despite the fabulous plaudits, National Book Awards, and American Book Awards, received by many.

Because Talese's article implied that Italians were illiterate non-readers, it drew an angry reaction from our community of writers, and lists began to appear naming our accomplishments. The *Times* received a myriad of letters but printed none of the accomplished authors who named their ethnic brothers and sisters. A bibliography of fiction writers appeared in *Italian Americana's* Fall-Winter 1993 issue, along with answers to Talese's assumptive headline. Some the finest and most well reviewed among them are Carole Maso, know for *Ghost Dance* (Perennial Library 1986), *The Art Lover* (North Point Press 1990), *Ava* (Dalkey Archive Press 1993), and *The American Woman in the Chinese Hat* (Dalkey Archive Press 1994); Don DeLillo, National Book Award-winning author of *White Noise* (Viking 1985); Cris Mazza, winner of PEN's Nelson Algren Award and author of *How to Leave a Country* (Coffee House Press 1992); Philip Caputo's much-praised *Means of Escape* (HarperCollins 1998). The list goes on with names like Jerre Mangione and Ben Morreale, who aside from their fiction had just written *La Storia: Five Centuries of the Italian in America* (Harper Perennial 1993), a large history that had two lengthy chapters on writers, including myself, of Italian American background. Another book by Rose Basile Green, *The Italian American Novel: A Document of the Interaction of Two Cultures* (Fairleigh Dickinson University Press 1974), had in some measure answered Talese's question twenty years earlier. And Barbara Grizzuti Harrison's travel memoir *Italian Days* had been well received (Atlantic Monthly Press 1998).

New York and other cities began to blossom with Italian "pasta" salad and fashion boutiques, almost outnumbering the spaghetti and pizza parlors. Middle-class Italian chic was born across America. Italian American writers began to wonder and hotly debate—more than ever—why the few writers in the mainstream seemed to downgrade their own community of writers and its obvious audience. It seemed not to occur to some that if they kept denying the existence of fellow authors and audience, they were helping to perpetuate a syndrome of invisibility, broadcasting to publishers to refuse them further entry into the mainstream of American letters.

Of course, the issue is not merely one of surname, but cultural validation. As Fred Gardaphe wrote in *Italian Signs, American Streets: Cultural Representation in Italian/American Narrative Literature* (Duke UP 1996),

> The study of ethnic literature is more than reading and responding to the literary products created by minority cultures; it is a process that, for its advocate, necessarily involves a self-politicization that requires moving a personal item onto a public agenda.

Even with the current "Renaissance," we have yet to see the portrayal of "ordinary" Italian Americans, with their simple human struggles like everyone else's, enter the mainstream consciousness, as it seemed to for one brief shining moment in the 1930s during the labor movement, when *Christ in Concrete* (Esquire 1937) by Pietro Di Donato deeply wounded America's social conscience. Guernica Editions of Toronto is still the only North American Italian American press, even if it does sport a long list of fiction and poetry. And even if authors, including yours truly, have begun to win recognition by the American Book Awards and the progressive arm of the multicultural movement.

Today, *VIA* has become a magazine secure enough among its own to allow me to institute an intercultural "Guest Feature," which welcomes writers of other backgrounds. This is clearly a signal that many Italian Americans understand that they belong within the multicultural movement, proving, "We're all in this together." Still, there are those few who feel threatened by the fight against "Eurocentrism," thinking that it means to dispel the glories of the Italian Renaissance or the Etruscan legacy, along with the demise of the old "literary canon," which greatly excluded "ethnic" and "women's" literature (except for a few tokens, like Langston Hughes and Emily Dickinson) and which doomed many fine writers and artists to obscurity behind less worthy figures aptly dubbed "ole dull mouths" by Amiri Baraka: Henry James, T.S. Eliot, Ezra Pound, etc. And though snobbery is subtler than bigotry, it can have the same effect on the literary canon.

Perhaps we need to recognize that Italian Americans, in upholding the multicultural movement's ever-growing and changing "canon," are in a somewhat difficult position—different from other groups. After all, the Before Columbus Foundations, which gives the now coveted and respected American Book Awards, does belie Columbus, for years the central symbol of Italian American ghetto pride.

Many Italian American poets have begun to portray the irony in that problem, and *VIA* has published its first chapbook, by Robert Viscusi, *An Oration Upon the Most Recent Death of Christopher Columbus* (1998), a fabulously sardonic *tour de force* on the problem. Viscusi pictures Columbus—who after all died in prison having sailed under the Hapsburg Teutons for Spain, not Italy—as sitting in an ashtray, looking dejected. Viscusi then begins a dialogue with him which mounts irony upon irony for the Italian American, still stereotyped by the mass media as a "thug" or "Guido"—just as one-dimensional as any "Black Sambo" or "Aunt Jemima"—only with the added difficulty of being seen as the source of all underground evil in the world, as though CIA drug dealing, Pentagon germ warfare, S&L scandals *à la* John Keating, or the robber barons of old (Astor, J. P. Morgan, Rockefeller, Mellon, et al.) never existed (and that is to say nothing of the massive crimes of Exxon, Bechtel, Union Carbide or G.E....). Viscusi's epic satire declares:

> I look forward to the rise of the Columbian theology
> Columbus, it will teach, lived five hundred years
> in the character of a god
> once he died
> he acquired a new nature as a limit
> we study the theology of Columbus to learn
> what are the boundaries of enterprise.
> ...
> Columbus will inspire a cult of the carefully considered future
> and re-examined past....

Meantime, ghetto Italian Americans have had their only institutionalized celebration of ethnic pride, the Columbus Day Parade, downgraded, and this has caused some to react against the anti-Eurocentric movement, which seemed to say that Italians alone had invented *Eurocentrism*. Yet, in October 1994, Maria Mazziotti Gillan, a poet who took back her Italian name only around 1991 a few years ago, managed to found a center for multicultural activity on the campus of Paterson, New Jersey's Passaic County Community College. She brought ethnic poets from all over the country to debate the issues of a curriculum of diversity in a three-day conference which celebrated a multiethnic anthology titled *Unsetting America: An Anthology of Contemporary Multicultural Poetry* (Penguin 1994), edited with her daughter, Jennifer Gillan, who teaches at Bentley College in the Boston area.

Times have greatly changed since 1979 when, as a young poet, I was invited to give a reading at the State University of New York at Buffalo, and was approached by an elderly language professor of Italian, who said: "Do you realize that you are one of only two or three Italian American women to make any name for yourself at all in American literature? You are a pioneer!" For the first time in my budding career, I was forced to contemplate that my "Italian" surname might have anything to do with my struggle to make headway in American letters. Suddenly I searched for role models and found only one name, Diane Di Prima's, to look up to in contemporary letters. Hers and mine were the sole Italian female names included in any of the feminist poetry anthologies of the 1970s. Since then, a bevy of names has surfaced among our women writers, greatly due to the help of Helen Barolini's pioneering efforts. The professor who spoke to me after my poetry reading in Buffalo was Ernesto Falbo, who would soon pass away.

The current Renaissance in our literature includes too many names to mention here, but one that shouldn't be omitted is Grace Cavalieri. Poet, host, and commentator of a syndicated radio show from Washington, D.C.'s Pacifica station, *The Poet and the Poem,* Cavalieri has hosted most of the accomplished poets of *every* canon and built one of the largest audiences for contemporary literature in the country. She has published many books and is among the long list of Italian names now known in American letters.

And it is important to say these names: names like Ferlighetti, Ciardi, Sorrentino, Stefanile, Carnevale, Capello, Cavallo, Galassi, Romano, Gardaphe, Ciavollo, Maso, Mazza, Di Pasquale, DiPalma, Citano, DeLillo, Viscusi, Mazziotti, Tusiani, which are not associated with the stereotypical Hollywood Mafia story fostered by Gay Talese, Mario Puzo, or Frank Pileggi.

A few of our talented men made a fortune by giving Hollywood what it thirsted for to the eternal detriment of the rest of us. Ever since Edward G. Robinson in 1931 portrayed "Little Caesar" in a gangster film neither written, acted in, nor produced by Italian Americans, Hollywood hungered for Italian criminals, as though Dillinger, Boss Tweed, Louis Lepke of Murder Inc., or Legs Diamond were worth little box office compare to the exploits of an Al Capone. Still, to be fair, Mario Puzo starved writing his best and earlier book, *The Fortunate Pilgrim* (Antheneum 1965), relatively unknown to American readers to this day, as it portrays hardworking Italian immigrants in their ghetto lives rather than sexy thugs in dark suits driving black limos with blonde beauties as their gun molls. Puzo learned to give Hollywood the image it wanted from Italian American culture with *The Godfather* (G. P. Putnam's Sons 1969), and the rest unfortunately is history—a Hollywood image that plagues all peoples with Italian surnames and probably will unto eternity, regardless of how many men like Toscanini take their beatings from Fascist thugs in protest against bigotry and oppression. And this continues regardless of how many women like Viola Liuzzo die for demonstrating with Martin Luther King against the Ku Klux Klan of white supremacy.

There's the rub. Despite the flurry of activity among Italian American authors, despite their journals and prizes and modicum of fame, our culture has yet to experience the "ordinary people" of our immigrant struggle toward the American Dream. Maybe because that dream died, just as the second and more educated generation began to write about and explore our immigrant ancestors.

The closest we've come to being *charming* in Hollywood is to being *Moonstruck* bakers or bigoted pizza vendors. And no writer does a better job of explaining this phenomenon than Michael Parenti, the Italian American Ishmael Reed. Though not a poet like Reed, Parenti is an astute social commentator, particularly in his *Make-Believe Media,* which should be one of the bibles of the multicultural movement, as it proves beyond a doubt that we ethnics are indeed "all in this together."

Even if the shoe doesn't yet exactly fit, we're hobbling around in it—waiting for that big novel or screenplay in the sky that will set us free from stereotyping. Meanwhile, our fiction writers and poets are churning out stories. And as for me, at fifty-four years, I've begun to appear in textbooks used in the schools, like *Kaleidoscope: Stories of the American Experience* (Oxford University Press 1993), along with Zora Neale Hurston, Maya Angelou, Amy Tan, William Saroyan, N. Scott Momaday, Leslie Mormom Silko, Saul Bellow, Maxine Hong Kingston, *and* Nathaniel Hawthorne! So I know that I'm in this together with all writers of every burgeoning subculture.

Still, beware, *sorelle e figli* (sisters and brothers). "Divide and conquer" is still the tactic of the day. As for we Italians in 1997, even as Joseph Ceravalo, years dead, in a cover story in *American Poetry Review* is praised for his forgotten innovations in poetic style by Kenneth Koch, Ecco Press has published a new translation of Dante's *Inferno* by twenty writers, not one single Italian American or Italian among them. According to Dana Gioia—known for his translations from the Italian, as is Jonathan Galassi, like John Ciardi before him—not one single contributor to the Ecco publication has had a lifelong connection to Dante's language. Omission persists—even where the Italian culture is valued. But the Italian American Renaissance is palpable, even as the internal debate grows as to what exactly characterizes Italian American literature.

by Daniela Gioseffi

$\mathscr{H}$ave You Really Read *The Fortunate Pilgrim?* And Lately? A Feminist's View of the Creator of the Infamous *Godfather:* Re-Thinking Mario Puzio

Originally appeared in *VIA: Voices in Italian Americana,* 2003.

Mario Puzo's *The Fortunate Pilgrim* (1st ed. Antheneum 1965) is a well crafted and moving, if relatively forgotten, classic of American literature. As fine a novel by an American author as one can hope to read, it's rich in descriptive imagery of life in Hell's Kitchen along 10th Avenue on the West Side of Manhattan through the depression and wars years. Full of poetry and passion, *The Fortunate Pilgrim* is a greater book than *The Godfather* (1st ed. J. P. Putnams Sons 1969), so made of sensational Mafia mythology.

Though it holds all the craft and emotion of Pietro Di Donato's more currently embraced novel, *Christ in Concrete, The Fortunate Pilgrim* is truer in *character-ization,* and less subject to *bathos* and sentimentality. Its protagonist is a woman so finely drawn with love, awe, pity, passion, and fear by a male who understands her well, that even Shakespeare has not done a better job with *naturalistic* char-acterization of women. That dimension in Puzo's masterpiece is lacking in Di Donato's. The people created by Puzo's skillful prose are human down to their imperfections. They are full of love, uncontrolled emotion, doubt, longing, nasti-ness, and beauty. They stir the spirit with tears as well as smirks of recognition. Lucia Santa, Puzo's main character, is an amazing yet ordinary woman, larger than life, smaller than her monumental struggles to survive and bring her brood of children to fruition in the New Land. She is shrewd and fierce, yet lovable and drawn with empathy.

This is a book as real as the many immigrants who settled this land in the twen-tieth century and learned to survive by their wits, the one out of four or five who came through Ellis Island. It's a story of filial duty and sexual passion—the quali-ties of drama that stir people to love the television drama of *The Sopranos*—but without the heavy-hand of the Mafia stereotype that so grossly plagues the Italian in America. It is so much better wrought with real and very human characters worth our while than is *The Sopranos*. This is the true nature of the people who came to settle here with only the strength of their filial duty as a buttress against the hard labors of the New World, the miseries of tenement life from which they had to rise to save themselves. Yet, there is none of the mawkishness about their portrayal, which mars so many stories of that struggle.

The Fortunate Pilgrim is the true tale of the sacrificial lives of immigrant Italian women who put themselves second to their men—their husbands and brothers—in the scheme of hope for upward mobility, those mothers and older sisters who made their homes a place of survival for their children and younger siblings. This is the story of immigrant fathers who labored like dogs to support their families and provide for them against all odds. This is a novel of astute psychological understanding of sibling relationships and family order. It's a gem of craftsmanship that Puzo—to the very end—felt was his best novel.

Though it was heralded by laudatory reviews in major newspapers, Puzo confessed he earned nothing from it. When *The Fortunate Pilgrim* appeared in 1965, the author was called, "the Italian Bernard Malamud, the Henry Roth of Italian culture in America!" Plaudits in *The New York Times* and other prominent newspapers and periodicals reigned over his most literary work—yet the book never found the readership it deserved. It still, to this day, has not, even in our own community, compared to Di Donato's *Christ in Concrete*. This little book of Italian immigrant life in America is perhaps the finest ever put between covers by an Italian American male, and what a pity that Puzo is known better for the sensationalized myth he created with his bestseller, *The Godfather*. Even the characterization of the Don was based on Puzo's mother's personality, as the author explained in various interviews and in his 1997 preface to the re-issue of his earlier novel. As he wrote what was to become the world's best-selling novel, *The Godfather*, he said he heard his mother's voice in his head: "I heard her wisdom, her ruthlessness, her uncontrollable love of family and for life itself.... The Don's courage and loyalty came from her, his humility came from her, and so I know now that without Lucia Santa, I could not have written *The Godfather*."

Lucia Santa is the *real thing*, not based on myth, for Puzo said he'd never met any Mafiosi—as most of Italian Americans never have. He contrived his Godfather from newspaper stories of gangsters, combined with the real experience of his mother's character, her passion for *La Via Vecchia*, the old ways of duty and the old order of family she had brought with her from the Old World. Her rebellious son, Gino, is another character foil for her stubborn will to survive. He wants to live free of parental tyranny, and yet, he empathizes totally with his mother's struggle to keep the family afloat. No doubt Gino stands for Puzo himself in the novel.

1997 marked the 25th anniversary of the publication of *The Godfather* and the reissue of *The Fortunate Pilgrim*, but how many copies did the latter sell among Italians in America? That is the question to ponder. Perhaps, if our community of readers, critics, filmmakers, and actors had paid more attention to this fine seminal, classic, American novel, we Italians would have achieved greater success much sooner in literary art in America and fostered a better image of our culture in general. Puzo's chronicle of immigrants in depression-era New York City remains a relatively little known, or read, American classic of that society—one which would have served our people so much better than his later commercial success.

I challenge any feeling person to read *The Fortunate Pilgrim* without living through the lives of its characters and their complex relationships to each other, without weeping their tears or feeling their joys. This is a small masterpiece of a book to which we should all pay homage, and I admit that I had not really read it carefully before. I'd known of it and skimmed it, but I'd been too angry about the fortunes Puzo made on the Mafia stereotype to want to have anything to do with his books or the films based on them. This is one American feminist who has never seen or read *The Godfather* and who refuses to patronize it regardless of the praise it has received from film critics. The reader may think me stubborn and foolish, but I insist on defying the Italian American men who've made their fame and fortune from sensationalized stereotyping of their own kind.

Though a neighborhood mob exists on the fringes of immigrant life in Puzo's *The Fortunate Pilgrim*, it is not central to his book, and neither is it a huge international Mafia, which according to many fine scholars of history never really existed in the mythic proportions claimed by popular rumor. Its drama, furthermore, explains clearly why a neighborhood "Black Hand" based on a Sicilian *vigilante* came into being amidst the corruption of the New World run by robber barons and warring immigrant factions. Puzo demonstrates how such factions were set at each other's throats amidst laboring classes who served the rich and were exploited by them to live in poverty and rebellion. The mob on the fringe of this drama seems no more reprehensible than the Enron executives and Savings-and-Loan thieves who steal from the laboring classes and send their sons to war to die in order that the rich maintain their oil and nuclear investments.

The great irony for us feminists is that all that is interesting about *The Godfather* patriarch is in actuality based upon an indomitable Italian matriarch, Puzo's real mother! From a barren farm life in Italy to the cramped tenement life of Hell's Kitchen, Lucia Santa shines forth as the formidable spirit of her family's struggles in America where Old World values and ideas conflict with the New. This is one feminist—versed in women's literature—who has to admit that a male Italian has done a brilliant job of entering and understanding, with passionate sincerity, the life of an Italian mother of the immigrant generation. I recognize elements of my own grandmother, Lucia La Rosa Gioseffi, and my Italian aunts—Elissabetta, Elena, Maria-Domenica and Rafaella—brought to life in vivid language in the characters of Puzo's book. Perhaps, we feminists sometimes do such women a disservice by not understanding fully enough the choices they made given the possibilities that were open to them. They survived by cajoling their husbands and sons with feminine wiles and motherly demands into enduring their lives of hard labor for the sake of the family's survival.

Puzo understood that well when he created, with passionate realization, a heroine of great strength and human vulnerability, an earthy woman to be admired as the bulwark of her society, the pillar of her struggling immigrant culture attempting to fashion a humanity out of abject poverty—a fortunate, though unfortunate, pilgrim. Indeed, Puzo uses the word "fortunate" in his title with no small amount of irony. Lucia Santa knows when to be tough and when to be gentle. She's as real as the smell of olive oil, aromatic espresso, tomato sauce, garlic, harsh laundry soap, and scrubbed linoleum that permeates her tenement kitchen, the center of her family's life, in Hell's Kitchen as the Lower West Side of New York City became known in the thirties. This immigrant mother is the mortar of her small tribe and its survival amidst the degradation of tenement life in America.

She is a tragic and triumphant heroine, full of imperfect love, who sometimes uses a rolling pin to discipline her wayward and wild sons. Though the contemporary reader might not fully approve of her ways, one feels to the depth of one's soul how her brood depends with deep respect upon her motherly devotion. A twice widowed woman who has to be both disciplinarian father to her brood, as well as nurturing mother, Lucia is not drawn with sentimental tones or portrayed as perfect in her virtue. She provides a great character actress with a marvelous role in a screen drama. So why hasn't this film been *successfully* made, instead of *The Sopranos*, into a television serial drama? After all, the fortunate pilgrim, Lucia Santa Angeluzzi-Corbo, and her sons and daughter provide a stirring drama of sexual intrigue, filial feeling from fully drawn characters, and even a measure of violence from neighborhood mobsters, more true and real than the sensationalized fakery of *The Sopranos*—a success built on an overblown myth. Most importantly their struggle is analogous to that of all the working classes who suffer the corporate corruption of government today.

The episodes of *The Fortunate Pilgrim* have all the plot twists to maintain interest in an audience of any background from week to week, so why *The Sopranos* and not Puzo's masterpiece as a grand media success? The answer might very well be that the Mafia focus of *The Sopranos* provides a perfect scapegoat for all criminality in the American mind of our troubled times. In the age of S & L scandals, Wall Street debacles, and corporate white-collar takeovers of the government and media, these sexy Italian mobsters are a perfect distraction of the masses from the bigger government criminality of our era. The myth of a big international Mafia cloaks the truth of white-collar criminality permeating the problems of our lives.

Isn't that a possible explanation that we Italian Americans should be aware of? Shouldn't that realization fuel our continuing protest of this overblown stereotype? Why is Tony Soprano, an Italian guy, the very popular focus of crime in fictionalized television drama rather than Ken Lay of Enron or Dick Cheney of Halliburton and Bechtel or Henry Kissinger, nearly arrested and tried at Hague for many war crimes? And, how many of us are aware of the fact that when ex-Mayor of New York Rudolph Giuliani says, "Lighten up! It's only a television show!" his agent is Brad Grey, the producer of *The Sopranos* who brokered him a multi-million dollar deal for his book *Leadership*?

There's a conflict of interest of no small magnitude in Giuliani saying we ought to laugh off the criminal stereotyping of our people when his billionaire, media mogul friend, newly elected Mayor Bloomberg, invites the actors from *The Sopranos* to march with him in the Columbus day parade 2002—very likely by Giuliani's suggestion. We really do have to ask why Bloomberg didn't instead invite the new Under-Secretary of Management of the United Nations, an Italian American woman, Catherine Bertini—applauded for her ability to double the amount of refugees fed by the World Food Program with her executive efficiency and committed humanism. Why didn't he invite Nobel Laureate, Dr. Riccardo Gianconi, who had just won the prize in astrophysics that very fall? Why not invite Italian Americans of truly substantive accomplishment prominently in the news of that year, rather than mere actors in a fake television drama?

The answer lies in where his friend, Rudolph Giuliani, butters his bread on the backs of his own people. It lies in the motives of those who control the media, not simply in some natural law of supply and demand—for often a demand is engineered to suit a particular motive. Otherwise would people buy pet-rocks, black fingernail polish or kill for Cabbage Patch dolls? Puzo was sorely aware of this as he died still believing that his best novel had been short-changed by his American culture and his own ethnic people. Puzo knew he was—in a large measure—forced to survive by giving Hollywood what it demanded from him: an ethnic scapegoat for all criminality in America rather than a true portrait of his people.

We feminists need to realize, too, the vulnerability of laboring men so well understood by Lucia Santa. She has pride and respectability, as well as self-sacrificing attitude towards her children, and she insists on these qualities in her sons, as well. She is capable of selfishness in the service of her family, but pro-active and no servant of a man. She's a woman of strength with a deep understanding of the meaning of tough love and how we subsist through it. She has all the attractive qualities the Don of *The Godfather* and none of his criminality. There is no character in literature about who it can be better said, "Blood is thicker than water." No character makes us better understand duty to family than Lucia Santa: the innuendoes that peasant propriety compel, the rituals of family life, all that is good, necessary and important, earthy and real, made of sensual flesh and flawed nobility as she upholds her ideal of family honor. Her Old World value of filial duty is implicated in the tragic suicide of her eldest son so full of despair, caught in his dutiful life of stifling and unfulfilling labor at the railroad office. Filial duty is shown to have its downside in its possible destruction of individual fulfillment—especially in the role of the eldest son of an old style Italian family. The conflict of individual desire for New World fulfillment at war with Old World ideals of filial duty, *La Via Vecchia,* is one of the most constant themes of Italian American literature, and Puzo handles it very well.

Octavia, Lucia's daughter, is the perfect American foil of Lucia's character, a compliment to Lucia's strength and well-being. Octavia is a young woman of equal emotional value, with strong, practical sense who, unlike her older brother, saves herself from her mother's total subservience to *la famiglia* in order to have a taste of the finer things in life in the New Land: education, literature, theatre, books, and poetry. Octavia is a young woman who knows how to give tough-love to her siblings to aid in their survival, but who is not so willing or compelled—given her station in the family—to sacrifice herself so utterly to duty. In this drama, there is an advantage to being the younger daughter and not the older son—upon who responsibility weighed so heavily in *La Via Vecchia*. These are women who like beavers and bluebirds work hard to nurture and procreate life and salvage it from degradation, but Octavia has the sense to grab a bit of life for herself. Each character in Puzo's drama is carefully drawn, but it is clear that his greatest respect is for the women of his drama, something feminists might note.

Contemporary feminists should pay their respects to Lucia Santa Angeluzzi-Corbo and her proud, tough, and intelligent daughter, Octavia, for they are women for us feminists to reckon with and should not be defined by their self-sacrifice to their families. Such women with their cognitive strength and enduring capacity for nurturing—as well as their crafty instincts for survival—lived in what really wasn't a man's world at all. It was a world knit together as a fortress built with a combination of women's character strengths and devotion to family and men's backbreaking drudgery and loyal labor for their family's sustenance. In that immigrant culture of our parents and grandparents' days, the feminine style of nurturing in the home could not exist without the masculine way of the world in symbiotic balance. Times have changed to a large measure for American, and even Italian women, now, but this old truth is one we stand upon—one which allowed for fruition of our people in America.

Puzo's poetic prose is stunning in its evocative power and enriches the spirit with the sound, smell, taste, and sights of a sensual world—even finding beauty worth beholding in the ugliness of the ghetto—making us feel the energy of childhood as we enter the mind of Gino. Puzo's main male character, Gino, with boyish zeal, endures fathomless sorrow one minute and the thrill of carefree childhood the next—even in sailing his humble boat, a discarded stick, through the gutters of the ghetto, running after it with all the sheer energy of youth. The entry into Gino's mind provides some of the most poetic passages of the novel. Of muscular energetic body and grace, Gino has to bear the sting of being misunderstood by the world of adults who cannot fathom the longing to live, to run, to move, and to breathe free in a spirited young boy. It's as if Puzo had met my own Italian uncle, Galileo Gioseffi of Newark, a ghetto street urchin in his youth, so like Gino in his ways—always in trouble for his desire to jump and leap and run free of the weight of family and duty. Puzo uncannily enters the minds of the children in his story, and makes them breathe. His empathy for ghetto children is utterly palpable, and any ethnic person could identify with its universality.

His men are well drawn, too, with their sense of commitment to family, their strength and will, and their madness wrought of such impossible lives of miserable labor and dull duty to *la famiglia*. The brutality to which the immigrant workforce in America was subjected is vividly portrayed.

Indeed, Puzo brings to life the whole *villaggio* in daily motion—the entire ghetto, set on the Lower West Side of Manhattan around 10th Street through the nineteen-thirties and forties—with its diverse characters, so like those in a Fellini's *Amaracord*, and therefore so apt for a television drama. From the compromising doctor to the busy-body barber, from the frustrated wife to the gossiping *strega,* or brothel manager, from prosperous baker to the weary railroad worker: these people breathe full-blooded reality and are created with admirable poetic subtlety. The inter-connections of their laboring lives is brought home to the reader while the nobility of their pride and sense of decorum is experienced. The despicable weaknesses and likable strengths of their characters are clearly wrought by Puzo's psychological insights. These are the poor who fashion a life from toil and shrewd survivalist tactics, but who have a sense of duty and place, a sense of what is decent and good as well as tenable with compromise. They give and receive imperfect love as best as they can in Hell's Kitchen.

This is the true book of immigrant Italian America: neither sensational with "sexy" violence like *The Godfather* nor made essentially of saintly and sentimental laborers like Di Donato's wholly self-sacrificial characters in *Christ in Concrete*. Jewish and African Americans, Irish and Chinese children of this land will see their own strong and psychologically complex immigrant mothers and sisters, the male ancestors of their respective ghettos in the mirror of Puzo's women and men—so universal to the core of humanity.

I suggest we all dig up a second-hand, or library copy, of *The Fortunate Pilgrim* and relish with pride Mario Puzo's finest book. Then write to his publisher to reissue this truer classic of Italian America's immigrant life and buy it for our children to read. Perhaps, we should send copies to Brad Grey, producer of *The Sopranos* with suggestions for a serial dramatization. And, let our women—our brilliant feminist writers—give a bow to this male who unfortunately made his fortune from the Mafia stereotype, which we loathed in his later books. We might have to admit that if only Mario Puzo had enough readers for *The Fortunate Pilgrim* at the dawning of his career as a writer, if only Hollywood had chosen *this* book to make into a *brilliant* film, we might have real respect for his talent and gift as he knew where it truly lay as he died, still professing *The Fortunate Pilgrim* as his best work, regardless of where his great fortune had been made.

If like me, you never want to patronize *The Godfather*, if you insist upon principle that you will never view it or read it as the prototypical movie and novel that plagues our people—as I stubbornly have—you will be glad that you read *The Fortunate Pilgrim*. You might feel less angry at Puzo's monetary success as a commercial writer. You will see the terrible tragedy in his life as an artist whose best book is relatively forgotten and unread, and whose most sensational book brought him infamy, even as it won him riches and hurt his people. His tragedy is analogous to all our lives as writers in America as we only just begin to dig ourselves out from under the weight of a cruel stereotype no more deserved by our people than by any other group. According to statistical analysis by many fine academic scholars, there is no higher percentage of organized crime among our particular ethnic group than any other. Indeed when we fully look at white-collar crimes committed by the majority culture, we might be astounded at the smallness of its relative size. That is not a fact we ourselves easily realize after so much successful brainwashing and thorough scapegoating by Hollywood and television.

This novel of 254 pages in paperback, copyrighted in 1964, would endure among the American classics of the depression and war years—the settling of America by her immigrant workers—if only it were known and not forgotten and the sheer poetry of its prose heralded by those who should be reading and reviving it most: Italian Americans!

Finally, I repeat for passionate effect the theme of my humble and sorrowful *aria:* this is the book which should have been made into a successful movie for Americans to see and believe, not the bestseller of all time, *The Godfather*—with its sensationalized mythos and repugnant violence which paved the way for *The Sopranos* and so many other dramas like it.

In conclusions, I ask again: Aren't there sociopolitical reasons to ponder in our wondering why the film of *The Fortunate Pilgrim* with Sophia Loren as Lucia

Santa is hardly known? Is it only the skill of the director and the screenwriter that's involved? I want to replace the negative with the positive! This is the book that would better have created empathy for the plight of our very real forbears, our immigrant men and women. Those people upon whose very human shoulders we truly stand in this joyous and sorrowful New Land!

by Daniela Gioseffi

Ⅾ︎IANE DI PRIMA: PIONEER WOMAN POET OF ITALIAN AMERICAN HERITAGE: AN INSPIRATIONAL FORCE OF THE 1970'S FEMINIST MOVEMENT

Originally appeared in *The Paterson Literary Review* (Issue 2010–2011).

My recollections of and respect for Diane Di Prima and her work are very personal. Back in the late 1960's, I can recall reading her groundbreaking prose published in 1969: a fictionalized, erotic account detailing experiences among the poets of the Beat generation, titled *Memoirs of a Beatnik* (Olympia P 1969). I had just begun writing and publishing in literary magazines and had moved to New York City in the 1967. I learned of her unconventional life amidst the Beat writers of Greenwich Village in the early days of Allen Ginsberg's *Howl and Other Poems*, Jack Kerouac's *On the Road*, Amiri Baraka's *The Slave* and *The Toilet*, and Lawrence Ferlinghetti's *A Coney Island of the Mind*, and his City Lights Bookstore that published Di Prima's *Revolutionary Letters* in 1971.

I was very impressed with Di Prima's freedom. Here was a gutsy, brave woman, also a second generation Italian-American, unafraid of living her life with sexual freedom, undaunted in a world of mostly male artists, self-actualized and liberated enough from patriarchal Italian culture to be part of a very *avant-garde* movement in New York City, the Big Apple into which I was just sinking my baby teeth, trying to bite off a piece of my own poetry. If this Italian American sister, Diane Di Prima, could be a poet in such a cheeky urban scene, then maybe I could, too. I began to attend The Poetry Project at St. Marks in the Bowery—then the newest scene for poetry transplanted to the East Village from the West. There, I met poets from the so-called New York School of writers and artists, luminaries like Allen Ginsberg, Kenneth Koch, Ron Padgett, Joseph Ceravolo, Gregory Corso, Anne Waldman, Bernadette Mayer, and Ted Berrigan. Paul Violi, Allan Appel, Bill Zavatsky, and Rochelle Ratner were among other novices like myself whom I met there, and they were all also just burgeoning into their own lives as poets.

Importantly, Diane Di Prima, was the only other Italian name I would find, besides my own, in various feminist anthologies of the 1970's. In vain, would I search for other Italian American sisters in those mainstream, feminist poetry anthologies of the 1970's, and invariably *only* Diane Di Prima's name would come up comforting me with its vowel sounds. "I'm not alone in American poetry," I'd tell myself. There was another sister, *una sorella Italiana Americana*, out there in poetry land who had come from a similar immigrant heritage. Di Prima's memoir, *Recollections of My Life as a Woman The New York Years* (Viking P 2001) would later, also put those years into better perspective for me.

Shortly after my poem, "Birth Dance, Belly Dancer," had appeared in 1977 and my first volume of poems from BOA Editions, *Eggs in the Lake* (1979), was being published, I was interviewed on Pacifica Radio on the West Coast and met Peter Levitt who was poet friend and admirer of Di Prima's work. He gave me her book *Loba* to read, which first appeared as a work-in-progress in 1978. Peter Levitt offered *Loba* to me with enthusiasm because he declared its themes greatly resembled my own.

I was thrilled when I read *Loba* in its first edition. Here was a poet speaking my feelings, a comrade-in-arms, so to speak. I had survived a near-death experience in childbirth and was celebrating what the nurturing female force meant to the human race in its most primal sense as life-giver and preserver, Mother Earth, a feminine archetype to be venerated as the source of all, and so was Di Prima. As soon as I read *Loba*, I realized that Diane Di Prima would be sympathetic to my own themes, that we were more than just *sorelle Italiane Americane*, we were both involved with earthy and womanly premises and with celebrating feminine attributes and powers.

Back in 1978, I remember traveling to California, after I'd written my first novel, published the year prior by Doubleday, titled *The Great American Belly Dance*. I was riding high on my first major press publication. The novel had an Italian American heroine named Dorissa Femfunelli, and dealt with Dorissa's survival after a divorce through the inspiration of neo-pagan Goddess worship and ritualized feminist birth dancing. I'd begun to travel around the country in a poetry, music, and dance presentation, titled *The Birth Dance of Earth: A Celebration of Women*. My multimedia presentation demonstrated how the birth dance, a woman's sacred ritual of life and birth, had been degraded into a burlesque spectacle, though it had begun as a fertility dance in imitation of birth contractions. Not a belly dance, it was the quintessential feminine *dance of life* as opposed to the male *dance of war and the hunt*. The *birth dance*, dubbed the *belly dance* or *hootchy kootchy* by Mr. Bloom, an entrepreneur who brought Mid-Eastern dancers to the Chicago World's Fair in 1893, was really a women's folk ritual *dance of life* that had been co-opted and despoiled into a mere sexy spectacle. Thus, after being introduced to her work, I clearly realized a kinship with Di Prima's themes that celebrated womanly attributes and powers.

Actually, I would learn that many feminist poets were in those early and mid-1970's dealing with goddess themes, spurred on by various sociological and psychological texts like *Woman's Mysteries: Ancient and Modern* by M. Esther Harding of the C.G. Jung Foundation and Elaine Pagels's *The Gnostic Gospels* (Random House 1979, 2004) celebrating the feminine principal of spirituality in early civilizations. It was an era of feminist renewal. I would soon perform my "Birth Dance of Earth: A Celebration of Women and Poetry" at the Brooklyn Museum as one of the artists involved in the opening ceremonies of Judy Chicago's "Dinner Party," now a part of that museum's permanent collection in it's feminist art gallery. That era has now come to be called The Second Wave of Feminism, following the suffragette movement as it did by many years.

The themes of goddess mythologies were rampant among feminist artists of the day as we were being reborn to a new deliberate denial of patriarchal religions, just as our forebearers, women like Frances Wright, Lydia Marie Childs, Harriet Martineau, Susan B. Anthony, or Margaret Fuller had been generations prior. *Ms.* magazine had just begun and my first stories and poems were published in it, particularly *Eggs* which celebrated the *ova*, the basic feminine unit of life. My story, *Mrs. Prism's First Death*, about a repressed Victorian lady's first orgasm also appeared in an early issue of the same magazine. Posters proclaiming *The Discovery of the Clitoris* were hanging on the walls of women's art galleries in Soho, and American women were finding their erotic freedom and liberation from male dominance—something that Diane Di Prima had already done as an early pioneer of women's liberation.

Titled *Loba*, Di Prima's book, originally published, as has been mentioned, in 1978 as a work-in-progress, was hailed by many as the female counterpart to Allen Ginsberg's *Howl*. Being introduced to Di Prima's work-in-progress, gave added inspiration to my own quest. *Loba* would later appear in complete form with new material from Penguin's Poetry Series in 1998, but I would already know that for Di Prima, the *loba*, or "she-wolf" in Spanish, represented a quintessential feminine principal and an erotic force underlying female sexuality. I felt kinship with her in this from the start of my own budding career.

Unfortunately, it would be years before I would actually meet her in person at a reading of Italian American women poets in New York City in the 1990's, inspired by Maria Mazziotti Gillan. In those years Di Prima's work and my own would appear as features in various issues of *Ms.* magazine, then under Robin Morgan's editorship. My article, titled "Breaking the Silence for Italian-American Women," would follow an issue in which Di Prima was the featured writer. When Maria Mazziotti Gillan introduced us at a reading on the East Coast, I at last had my chance to tell Diane Di Prima in person what an inspiration she was to me and so many other women poets.

Customarily in mythology, the *loba,* or she-wolf, Di Prima's mythological figure, is labeled as a bone-gatherer and re-creative symbol of renewal or rebirth. Di Prima's opening poem, "Ave," is a tribute to the tacit, tormented women she commemorates as her "lost moon sisters." The *Loba's* main purpose is to gather and enliven that which is in peril of being lost forever. Di Prima's book, a series of poems, attempts to fulfill this primal purpose of the She-wolf, by assembling a renewed mythology of *Loba*, connected to the poet's identity as woman and author. *Loba* might be read as an autobiographical account of Di Prima's struggle to make her voice heard in a generation that was dominated by male poets, but, in a greater sense, *Loba* represents the primal voices of all womankind blossoming out of obscurity into a renewed strength, a rebirth.

Diane Di Prima's poems are especially concerned with women who have been robbed of their articulate strength. She questions:

How was woman broken?
Falling out of attention.

Wiping gnarled fingers on a faded housedress.
Lying down in the puddle beside the broken jug.
Where was the slack, the loss
of early fierceness?
How did we come to be contained
in rooms?

I thought also of how the she-wolf or *loba* gave birth to the grandeurs of Rome, how she suckled Romulus and Remus in Roman mythology.

Identifying, perhaps, also with the Goddess Diana of the Hunt, Diane Di Prima's creation of the *Loba* as a winning defender of women bespeaks her own ability to not only survive but successfully endure as a poet and a woman, and, for me, as an Italian American woman poet in particular. Di Prima was asking the same questions I and many other feminists were asking in those anthologies of the 1970's. How comforting it was to me to have an Italian-American *sorella* asking them with me and for me!

Though I started my poetic career in the late 1960's among the New York School poets of the Lower Eastside, I'd later decided, and perhaps to my detriment, that it was better to be an *independent* all around town, rather than adhere to any one school of poetry. I'd met other poets—like John Logan, Diane Wakowski, Joel Oppenheimer, Harvey Shapiro, Hugh Seidman, Galway Kinnell, Isabella Gardner, Robert Bly, James Wright, Willliam Heyen, Al Poulin, Jr., W.D. Snodgrass, W.S. Merwin, Robert Hass, John Ciardi, Nina Cassian, and D. Nurkse—, and I'd learned something from all schools, mainstream and fringe. But Diane Di Prima always remained on the horizon of my peripheral vision, and I heard often of her doings on the West Coast. Knowing she was still writing and thriving would always give me heart to go on, as she did, with her pioneering Italian woman's name in American literature.

Now, Diane Di Prima is Poet Laureate of her city of San Francisco, and it is a well-deserved honor—but I will always remember her earlier days when she wrote her first *Loba* poems, and before those, her early works, read in the coffee houses of Greenwich Village among the Beat artists and musicians of that era. I felt a comforting kinship with this gutsy, original woman, unafraid to venerate the feminine archetype as Goddess. Allen Ginsberg has said of her:

> Diane di Prima is a learned humorous bohemian, classically educated, and a twentieth-century radical. Her writing, informed by Buddhist equanimity, is exemplary in imagist, political, and mystical modes. A great woman poet in the second half of American century, she broke barriers of race-class identity, delivered a major body of verse brilliant in its particularity.

All through my career as a poet who published more and more, I would always feel comforted by her pioneering as an Italian American woman poet, the first so aptly named, by chance, *Di Prima* (of the first), and she would inspire me to forge ahead to be the next pioneer with an Italian American woman's name on the East Coast, soon to be met in poetry by other pioneers—Maria Maziotti Gillan, Donna

Messina, Pat Fragnoli, Mary Jo Bona, Maria Fama, and so many others—who have made their way into books and anthologies and helped me continue to be inspired to embrace my Italian American heritage, unafraid of my syllabic Italian name, because of my *sorelle della poesia*. Bless them and their pioneer, Diane Di Prima!

When Di Prima writes in *Loba*:

> I am you
> and I must become you
> I have been you
> and I must become you
> I am always you
> I must become you.

The she-wolf symbolizes the mythological force inside each woman and apart from her, an inner and outer being and presence of incantatory power. Though Di Prima "is" *Loba*, she must "become" *Loba*, and consciously manifest *Loba*'s spirit and ritualize her own identity simultaneously. For me as a *sorella Italiana Americana*, her lines have a very special resonance forever mixed with the word *corragio* in my memories as a youthful poet just come to New York City to forge my way into American literary art. I salute her in her fruition as Poet Laureate of San Francisco, and for all her accomplishments of a lifetime that offered inspiration to many women writers of our time.

by Daniela Gioseffi

$\mathcal{J}$OSEPHINE GATTUSO-HENDIN'S *THE RIGHT THING TO DO* AND MARIO PUZO'S *THE FORTUNATE PILGRIM*: COMPARABLE WORKS BY ICONIC AUTHORS OF OUR ITALIAN AMERICAN CULTURE

Presented at AIHA, New Haven Conference, 2009.

Josephine Gattuso-Hendin's novel *The Right Thing to Do* (David R. Godine Publishers 1988) is on a par with Mario Puzo's *The Fortunate Pilgrim* in its contribution to Italian American culture. The book is as well-crafted in its psychological character portrayals, as is Puzo's earliest and—in Puzo's own estimation—finest novel. Gattuso's book speaks to the heart of the immigrant predicament for women, with its protagonist, Gina, as much as Puzo's speaks of the immigrant experience for men with *The Fortunate Pilgrim's* main character, Gino, representing Puzo himself.

Gattuso-Hendin is not only one of our finest American Book Award Winning novelists, as is Puzo, but she is also a respected scholar in the mainstream of American literature. How many of us, within our own insular community, are aware of her major works of non-fiction and cultural commentary *Vulnerable People: A View of American Fiction Since 1945* (Oxford UP, 1978, 1979) or *Heart Breakers, Women and Violence in Contemporary Culture and Literature* (Palgrave Macmillian 2004)? Her groundbreaking books of cultural and literary analysis have been well reviewed in *Booklist, Library Journal, Publishers Weekly*, and *Kirkus Reviews*, to name a few mainstream outlets. The point is that the Italian American literary community should be aware of the widespread respect one of their major scholars and writers has received from American literary society. Gattuso-Hendin's contribution to the image of the Italian American writer reaches beyond our increasingly, inward-looking community.

Gattuso-Hendin's novel, *The Right Thing to Do*, effectively portrays both New York's Old World, Italian immigrant milieu, and a father's rage at his own powerlessness in the face of his child's desire for upward mobility and an American way of life. Gattuso-Hendin's novel is comparable in skill and importance to Puzo's, in the annals of Italian American literature. She speaks to the half of our humanity—our women—as profoundly as Puzo speaks to our men. She also underscores the tragedy of our immigrant men in The *Right Thing to Do*, as much as Puzo empathizes with our immigrant women in his most artful novel. Gattuso-Hendin's skill rests in her ability at naturalistic characterizations as adept as Puzo's in his classic and most important literary work, *The Fortunate Pilgrim*.

The great difference in the work of Gattuso-Hendin as our woman novelist and scholar is that she has not sold out her people, our *diaspora*, to the Hollywood and media thirst for slick, "sexy," and sensational Mafia stories, just as other of our women novelists have not—Helen Barolini or Tina DiRosa to name just two.

Mario Puzo, to his dying day, thought *The Fortunate Pilgrim* was his most artful and important literary work, and many critics have agreed. Puzo bemoaned the fact that *The Godfather* overshadowed it, because of its Hollywood sensationalism, to become the world's best selling novel of all time. He knew that he had damaged the image of his own heritage with the overemphasis on a Mafia story that he himself had never lived, but fabricated. *The Fortunate Pilgrim* was the truer story of his saga in America, but he had starved portraying the immigrant story devoid of the Mafia as center stage, in his most artful and moving work. In the preface to the novel reprinted by Random House, Puzo wrote about its first publication in 1965:

> I received marvelous reviews. But then came the next surprise: Nothing happened. I didn't become rich and famous. In fact, I was poorer than ever. I had to work two jobs instead of one.... I was furious, but only at myself. I rethought my whole life. Why should the public care that I put so much of myself into that book, so much care into each sentence? Why should my family care about my writing when it didn't earn my daily bread? ... . I concluded that I had worked ten years of my life in sheer self-indulgence. I thought myself that most despised figure in Italian culture, a "chooch"— that is, a man who could not earn a living for himself or his family.

Puzo goes onto explain:

> ...then came another surprise....to feed my family, I decided to write another best-seller. And to use some stories that my mother...told us as we were growing up. That book was *The Godfather*. It took me four years to write, still working two jobs. But it accomplished my aim. It is a bestseller, and this time I became rich and famous..... But there were more surprises to come. Whenever the Godfather opened his mouth, in my own mind, I heard the voice of my mother. I heard her wisdom, her ruthlessness, and her unconquerable love for her family and for life itself, qualities not valued in women at the time. The Don's courage and loyalty came from her; his humanity came from her. .... I know now, without Lucia Santa, [the mother in *The Fortunate Pilgrim*] I could not have written *The Godfather*.

Gattuso-Hendin's work, *The Right Thing to Do,* carries similar weight for our culture. It is the book that we can turn to for the portrayal of the immigrant father's tragedy and the daughter's struggle—just as Puzo's masterpiece portrays the immigrant mother's predicament and her son's tragedy. These two novels should be read as seminal and primary in any course of study featuring Italian American literature. They should be studied as emblematic of our Italian immigrant story. They have much appeal for second-generation offspring. They are both enduring and movingly dramas, told in artful, often poetic, prose, and they contain sardonic wit and honest self-knowledge. These books are not filled with one dimensional saintly characters, but real people.

Gina, Gattuso-Hendin's protagonist, is involved in intense conflict with her father, Nino Giardello, just as Gino, Puzo's protagonist, is with his mother, Lucia Santa. Gattuso-Hendin writes of Gina's attempt to gain freedom from the constricting paternity of Nino:

> the advantages she worked for weren't material or practical but psychic gains: to connect with something strong at the center of herself, to do something so well that the center took over everything; this was what she wanted.

In *The Fortunate Pilgrim*, the young Gino's desire to be free is consistently dramatized as is Gina's. Like her, Gino is always running away from the fetters of maternal control. In the following quote, there is similar psychological configuration as in the above quote:

> Gino turned around and went back toward Ninth, searching for rainbows in the gutter, he backtracked to the empty houses and found the rope dangling alone....Finally he reached the window and could see the street. The square frame for the window was only an empty stone socket. Gino stepped out onto the ledge, leaned out, and grabbed the rope. ... He pushed away from the ledge and for one glorious moment he had the sensation of really flying of his own will.

These children of immigrants are in a kind of love-hate relationship with parental forces: love for the nurturance and definition of the world that their parents supply and hate for the restrictions placed upon their attempts at self-actualization by the parental insistence upon *la via vecchia* of a ghettoized existence. The children long to be liberated into a greater American landscape of opportunity, while their parents cannot understand their desires and are utterly dismayed by their disobedience. Gina and Gino are mirror reflections of each other in "pursuit of happiness," while their parents, used to misery and toil, strive merely to survive the new land and its alienating ways, mocking their children's dreams for a better life, attempting to feed their own resignation and content with mere survival to their wayward offspring.

Gina and Gino have the "taste of poetry" in their spirits. Both are imaginative, bright, and clever children of unyielding, old fashioned, immigrant parents sincerely desperate to save them from what they see as the wild and immoral ways of an alienating New World culture.

Gina, in *The Right Thing to Do*, thinks to herself of her own and her mother's imprisonment under the yoke of a dominating patriarchal will:

> When you have to get along with a dictator, something inside you dies; there is never a free, easy, peaceful moment. What will he say? What will he do? If you go to the fruit store, you worry about getting back when he expects you and it spoils the conversation with women you meet. If you stay home, he crowds all your time, deciding what you should do, when you should do it, always interrupting with his needs. There was no closeness because he made himself such an object of fear it was impossible to be anything but angry or silent.

One finds Gino feeling the same way about Lucia Santa when, as a boy, he is constantly scolded by her possessive love, yet in the long run, Gino realizes that her fierce control was a mother's determination to hold the family together for the salvation of all. In the case of the Italian father, Nino, there is more pride than love felt by his child, it seems. Yet, in the end, Gina, in the last pages of *The Right Think To Do*, seems to realize her father's love for her when her cousin Vinnie, at Nino's funeral, says to her: "You'll never find anyone who cared for you the way he did." And Gina answers, "No, I won't." and finally she grants, in the end, as she views a landscape of freedom in front of her, that at last, she will someday write her father a symbolic letter of reconciliation.

Interestingly, it takes a funeral near the close of each novel to bring the children of these immigrant parents to the closure of a final peace with their parents. There are many parallels in the funeral scenes, one for the father, Nino, and one of the older brother, Larry.

Both immigrant parental figures of the respective novels, Nino and Lucia, are mirror images of each other bound to save their offspring from what they fear as the philistine ways of a new American way of life, and both succeeding well in alienating them and driving them away with their survivalist mindset. Both restrict their children's lives out of desperation and rage and alienation. Both are tragic in their attempts to love, and smothering in their desire to nurture with Old World wisdom, unable to resolve their concern for their offspring in the minds of their rebellious children. Both use stories of village life in their lost Italy to make their points.

Indeed, Puzo explains in his novel:

> It was a favorite topic, the corruption of the innocent by the new land.... *Figlio disgraziato.* Never could disobedience pass in Italy. The father would kill his arrogant son: yes, kill him. And the daughter? ...Ah, Italia, Italia; how the world changed and for the worse. What madness was it that made them leave such a land. Where fathers commanded and mothers were treated with respect by their children. ...Each in turn told a story of insolence and defiance, themselves heroic, long-suffering, the children spitting Lucifers saved by an application of Italian discipline....And at the end of each story each woman recited her requiem. *Mannaggia America!*—Damn America. But, in the hot summer night their voices were filled with hope, with a vigor never sounded in their homeland. Here now was money in the bank, children who could read and write, grandchildren who would be professors if all went well. They spoke with guilty loyalty of customs they had themselves trampled into the dust.

In Gina and Gino's struggle to realize their lives in America as the children of domineering parents imbued with provincial Italian customs, they encounter similar emotional conflicts within themselves. This conflict between parent and child is a major theme of Italian American literature of the last half of the 20th century, as feelings of familial duty contend with the need for self-actualization and freedom to participate in American society by casting off the restrictions of *la via vecchia*. The maternal and paternal love that second generation children are taught and reared with causes an interior battle, a love-guilt relationship within Gina and Gino. Note the character names that bespeak a female and male parallel in the longing to succeed in fulfilling the American ideal of "life, liberty, and the pursuit of happiness."

The ferocity of Nino Giardello and Lucia Santa in their battle to save their children from what they are sure is the evils of a lax and immoral style of life in The New World is a major psychological and emotional drama of our immigrant culture. The second-generation attempts to assimilate and gain prestige and respect, causes it to break free of the overly protective cocoon of *la famiglia* within which the parental yoke was tolerated to a much greater degree in The Old World. Mother and father were worshipped as the "ship of state" in an Italian family of old. Indeed, even today—as one visits cemeteries in Italy—like the one in old Urbino, a medieval town that became a seat of the Renaissance—one sees the blatant modern vestiges of "ancestral," or "tribal worship," evident in the modern grave monuments that are decorated with pictures of the deceased parent—icons to be prayed to and communed with as a spiritual guide even after death. Neither Gino nor Gina can quite fully escape these mores.

This reviewer notes that her own immigrant, Puglese father—a devote secularist—made trips to his immigrant parents graves to commune with them, in an interior dialog, long after their deaths. This custom persisted in him long after he'd been educated in American ways—spoke perfect American English and worked his way, with hard labors, through American institutions of higher learning, like Union College and Columbia University, to achieve degrees in both science, and the liberal arts, and earn a Phi Beta Kappa as among the first Italian immigrants to receive such academic honors. Vestiges of ancestral worship persisted despite his rejection of all organized religion.

Old World customs continue to exist even in third generation families where the influence of tradition, both "good and bad," dies hard against all contemporary ways—keeping novels like *The Fortunate Pilgrim*, and *The Right Thing to Do*, in print from their respective presses.

Josephine Gattuso-Hendin, unlike Mario Puzo, did not go on to write more novels as one would have hoped she would—though she is currently working on one. Her books of literary and cultural commentary are profoundly insightful, but she has not soiled her hands on selling out to Hollywood sensationalism and the Mafia image as too many of our male writers have with their memoirs and novels. She is not forced, as was Robert Viscusi or Fred L. Gardaphe, to analyze the Mafia syndrome as a *major* part of our Italian literary output and cultural image in America.

Instead, Gattuso-Hendin can speak to a larger American audience about violence in general in our wider American culture when she comes to her thoughtful conclusion in *Heartbreakers*:

> The emergence of violent women as iconic figures of modernity reveals a larger anxiety over change....Women in the real world remain the mainstays for family life [as in Puzo's *The Fortunate Pilgrim*, and *Gattuso's The Right Thing to Do*].... There is no widespread danger that hordes of women will suddenly turn murderous. But in serious literature, portrayals of violence underscore change, make a discontinuity with the past, and reveal an identity violence that nourishes destructive egotism and spawns unrest. Images of that instability fill civil society and coarsen our public discourse.

The emergence of remorseless, violent women in pop culture serves to deny the actual vulnerability of women, justify male violence, and project a world without sensibility that sanctions aggression.

That is the violent world of *The Sopranos* and other such popular television dramas that stereotype Italian Americans. Such dramas are popular for a parallel reason to the thesis that Gattuso-Hendin draws in *Heartbreakers*, stated above. Portrayals of ethnic criminality are lightening rods for the greater American international violence of white color criminals and corrupt, crony politicians also interested in the profit motive over all, just as are mobsters.

Finally, Gattuso-Hendin observes: "But it is the serious exploration of violence in contemporary literature that, through its major expression, bears witness to the social and personal costs paid by women for the dream of empowerment." The point here is that this fine novel, *The Right Thing to Do*, by a woman writer is not as celebrated by our culture as are those of male novelists who do us more harm than good with their constant Mafiosi dramas.

Josephine Gattuso-Hendin is a scholar and writer to be proud of as she explores larger horizons of literature. Her themes effect more directly the situation of women in our culture—and aren't we, at least, half of humanity, and the half with, perhaps, the most influence on the lives of coming generations in their struggle for freedom and empowerment?

The Right Thing to Do is a literary work that should be required reading in all courses of Italian American studies, along with Puzo's greatest work, *The Fortunate Pilgrim.* These are the portraits of our people that are real and true, not sensationalized for media profiteering. These should be the iconic books of our canon, and they are not the stories of *Wise Guys* or *The Godfather,* which have been lived by so very few of us. These are the more universally truthful novels that should influence our young and up-and-coming writers, infusing them with insightful literature of their heritage in America, the poetic and emotionally rich dramas of our Italian story, fostering empathetic understanding for our struggles in the New World. These are the books from which children of any immigrant background can garner wisdom.

Lawrence Ferlinghetti, Poetry's Entrepreneur, NOT "Poetry's Godfather"

Written in Response to *Poets & Writers'* Feature on Ferlinghetti, in *Poets & Writers Magazine* 2007.

How good it was to see Lawrence Ferlinghetti who has done so much for American literature, and who is widely read and respected for his poetry, featured with his syllabic Italian American name on March/April 2007 cover of *Poets & Writers*, but how sad to see him dubbed with the awful Hollywood stereotype of Italian Americans as "Poetry's Godfather?"

Even though Mario Puzo's *Godfather* is the bestselling book of all time, Puzo himself admitted he'd never met any Mafiosi and based the Godfather's main character, the Don, on his immigrant mother who is the heroine of his best novel, the one he himself thought was his finest work, *The Fortunate Pilgrim,* about ordinary, hardworking Italian immigrants. He starved writing that book despite its great reviews from fine authors because America always wants to dub us Italian-Americans with a *Mafiosa* stereotype—regardless of the fact that "since 1950, only 5% of the felons on the FBI's *Most Wanted List* have been Italian American." Additionally, "in a poll of American adults, conducted by the Princeton-based Response Analysis, Inc. several years ago, 74% said they believed most Italian Americans have some association with organized crime." And this is because of the huge bucks made by Hollywood and television industrialists who perpetuate this stereotype in television documentaries—including the PBS public television documentary, *Medicis: Godfathers of the Renaissance*— a television series some-what like *The Sopranos,* or even the children's movie, *Shark Tale,* in which the villain is a mobster shark named Don Lino, stupidly voiced by Robert De Niro in Hollywood Italian mobster style, and on and on *ad nauseum*. Mario Puzo died lamenting his inability to promote *The Fortunate Pilgrim* over *The Godfather*, as the image of the Italian in America, but the Mafia stereotype falsely overblown, mythologized, and manufactured, as it is, makes box office bonanzas.

How many Americans know that during World War II, 600,000 Italian Americans were identified as "aliens" and had their freedoms restricted? They were forced into internment camps, made to carry identity cards, obligated to relocate their lives and their children's lives.

This cruelty was instituted even while more than 500,000 Italian Americans were serving their country, fighting for and with the Allied Powers against Hitler and the Evil Axis. Unlike Japanese Americans, Italian Americans received no apologies or reparations until 1999 when the War Time Violation of Italian Civil Liberties Act was passed.

A fine writers' magazine like *Poets & Writers*, sensitive to problems of ethnicity, should avoid a stereotypic term like "Poetry's Godfather" for its implications on a venerable intellectual like Lawrence Ferlinghetti who has chosen to write with his father's full surname—which was for some time shorted to "Ferling." And because of this, Ferlinghetti has done much for us Italians by forging his way into American literary life with his syllabic Italian name on every one of the more than thirty books of poetry he's published— including *A Coney Island of the Mind,* which has sold over a million copies and is still selling— and with his influence in literary America as one of the owners of City Lights Bookstore, and, as the man behind City Lights Publishers. He truly is a prominent Italian American poet and businessman. It would have been so much nicer—and more appropriate—to see Lawrence Ferlinghetti dubbed "Poetry's Entrepreneur."

Born in 1919 in New York, Lawrence Ferlinghetti is a best selling poet of America to this day and a seminal figure of the Beat Generation that many believe could not have existed without his entrepreneurship. He earned a doctoral degree in poetry at the Sorbonne in Paris with a dissertation entitled The City as Symbol in Modern Poetry: In Search of a Metropolitan Tradition. After leaving Paris he moved to San Francisco. Ferlinghetti with Peter Martin started a magazine there called City Lights, titled after the Charlie Chaplin film. He and Martin established their enterprise on the second floor of a building on Broadway and Columbus in North Beach. They then opened a bookstore on the floor below as an additional venture, naming it after the magazine. The City Lights Bookstore became one of the most widely known bookstores on the planet, and still stands in its original location today, on a street named "Ferlinghetti" in recent times.

Ferlinghetti began publishing original books by himself and others under the City Lights logo. His Pocket Poets Series made poetry books inexpensive, and the small attractive paperback is still a common style today. Ferlinghetti published Allen Ginsberg's 'Howl' as Pocket Poets Number Four, and was tried on obscenity charges for this. He was declared innocent, a landmark victory for "free speech" that furthered the fame of City Lights Press and made Ferlinghetti instrumental in changing American mores toward a more progressive openness, helping to quell earlier hypocrisies.

In his definitive documentary, "Ferlinghetti," director Christopher Felver crafts an incisive, sharply wrought portrait that will reveal Ferlinghetti's true role as catalyst for numerous literary careers and for the Beat movement itself. Felver's one-on-one interviews with Ferlinghetti, made over the course of a decade, touch upon a rich mélange of characters and events that began to unfold in postwar America. As Felver explains in his description of his film and Ferlinghetti's life, these events include the publication of Allen Ginsberg's *Howl*, the divisive events of the Vietnam war, the sexual revolution, and this country's perilous march towards intellectual and political bankruptcy.

Since its inception in 1953, Ferlinghetti's City Lights Bookstore has become an iconic literary institution that embodies social change and literary freedom. Continuing to thrive for over five decades, it is a cornerstone of America's modern literary and cultural history. Felver's documentary explores the world of Ferlinghetti as San Francisco's legendary poet, artist, publisher and civil libertarian.

Ferlinghetti public and private life unfolded over nine remarkable decades. The poet's ideological identity began to coalesce soon after visiting the ruins of Nagasaki – just weeks after the devastation of the atomic bomb in 1945 – an event which Ferlinghetti says transformed him into "an instant pacifist." Ferlinghetti's newfound skepticism regarding the power of the state materialized into his unique brand of political activism shortly after he moved to San Francisco and made the acquaintance of Kenneth Rexroth. The political principles he infused into his poetry quickly spread throughout the world — even cited as one of the primary catalysts of the Velvet Revolution in Czechoslovakia.

The Beat Generation's rebellion could not have existed without Ferlingetti's level- headed sense and primary role as publisher, against the social conservatism of the 1950's He championed social awareness and permanently impacted the tone and character of American culture. It was Ferlinghetti's infamous censorship trial – for his publication of Allen Ginsberg's Howl in 1956 – versus the City of San Francisco that launched the social rebellion of the Beats into national consciousness.

By winning the trial, Ferlinghetti who stood alone as Ginsberg did not attend the trial, set a precedent that secured the First Amendment rights of publishing in this country and preserved the freedom of speech in literature. Ferlinghetti's industrious entrepreneurship set the foundation for successive generations of First Amendment activists: the musicians, poets, authors, and filmmakers who continue to protect our freedom of speech today. Felinghetti counted among his many friends and colleagues in literature Allen Ginsberg, Michael McClure, Billy Collins, Dennis Hopper, Robert Scheer, Dave Eggers, Diane DiPrima, Anne Waldman, and Pulitzer Prize winner Gary Snyder. The enormous social impact Ferlinghetti's legacy continues to have its effect on the American cultural scene.

Lawrence Ferlinghetti manifests what it means to be a rebel poet, a renegade publisher and a true bearer of the Whitman tradition. Despite being the bestselling poet in modern literature, his place in the history of American literature was not carved out by his pen alone. With his publishing house at City Lights, he has championed the writings of countless other writers and continues to turn successive generations on to poetry. Felver's film will educate the general public as to why Lawrence Ferlinghetti is easily one of the preeminent figures of modern political activism and very likely the most influential artist in the history of American literature since the 1950s. Now in his nineties, he remains productive to this day.

So please call him "An Entrepreneur Artist of American Poetry" and not "The Godfather," as that later title implies he did something illegal to become the great publisher and poet that he is. On the contrary, he has been one of the most hardworking and honest artists of the poem this country ever produced.

by Daniela Gioseffi

𝒜 Non-Conformist Italian Poet in New York City.
A Retrospective Essay on Alfredo De Palchi's Poetry:
Brilliant Flashes, Staccato Rhythms, and Emotional Power

First appeared in *Homage to Alfredo de Palchi* (Gradiva P; New York: Stonybrook UP).

Alfredo dePalchi's supreme independence from all literary movements has gifted him with a style all his own. Many fine Italian poets do not translate well into English, but de Palchi is not one of those. Though his staccato rhythms have more emotional power in their Italian originals, they come across well in English translation. De Palchi has been blessed with excellent translators and has published four bilingual collections; *Sessions with My Analyst* (1966, 1971) *The Scorpions Dark Dance* (1994) *Anonymous Constellation* (1997) and *Addictive Aversions* (1999) that have won him good reviews and recognition in the United States and England as well as in Italy where he is known, in good measure, as an "anti-poet." He's also produced many translations and spent years editing *Chelsea Literary Review*, and Chelsea Editions. When it comes to his own poetry, he is a non-conformist with a preference for a tight and terse lyricism. When it comes to America's iconic poets, he prefers the American succinct lyric mode of Emily Dickinson to that of Walt Whitman's loquacious prosody. He is a man who pretends to be much tougher than he is, as he has proven himself to be very altruistic, especially toward poets. He has helped to institute the Raiziss-DePalchi Translation Award at The Academy of American Poets, and the Annual Bordighera Poetry Prize for Bilingual Book Publication. Several other poetry publication projects have garnered his support as a Trustee of the Sonia-Raiziss-Giop Foundation. Alfredo De Palchi decries all establishment ideas of what the art of poetry must or should be. The language of his poetry is stripped of ornamentation. It is sharp and direct as well as colloquial. His verse is jagged and disjointed, and contains snatches of the unconscious mixed with conscious memory. It is composed in a measure like modern music. It comes from the gut of his being and does not substitute philosophic tenants for experience and emotion. It has the substance of a life deeply lived and felt, and a spirit fully disillusioned by the ugliness of human depravity. There is not one ounce of sentimentality in his poetry, though his passion for love and life and against injustice is palpable.

An Italian poet living in America, Alfredo de Palchi has always avoided conformity. For his individualism he paid a dear price in his teenage year. In his European homeland, his refusal to conform to the wishes of fascists who imprisoned him, caused him to be tortured during World War II in Legnago— a suburb of Verona where he was born in 1926. After the war, de Palchi was freed from the fascists only to fall victim to the partisans who in their communistic cadres inflicted grievous punishment upon the innocent young non-conformist— only just freed from imprisonment by fascists. These brutal and experiences in prison are the matter of the initial section of his first published book *Sessions with My Analyst.*

Titled "Remembering `45," this first section is made of thirteen monologues, speckled with interior colloquies, in a scalding sequence that exposes the beastly behavior man is so capable of in what the poet calls the "Paleolithic present." Drafted when the poet was only twenty-two years old, it was published in 1961, thirteen years later. The free verses are crisp and use the historical present with urgency in a stream of meanderings that bring back theme upon theme, always punctuated with a hopelessly felt Kafkaesque sense of guilt and existential despair. The poet lives in an inferno with no exit—in the deepest existential sense.

Imprisoned in Legnago, the teen-age Alfredo learned how despicable his townsmen could become under the dictatorship of Mussolini. Beaten by the belts and buckles of the sadistic guards who use their police power against the helpless, the poet remembers childhood wrongs, the abandonment by his father, the drowning of his pet dog by a sadistic boy, the abuse and contempt heaped on him, his own abuse of a rabbit when as a boy he handled one roughly as he drew it from a cage by its hind legs and heard it whimper. The whimper of the rabbit returns again and again like a litany of the damned and a reminder of guilt and cruelty, as the poet begins to picture "God the Father" as his own uncaring father, a godmurderer and killer like the fascist prison guards. The monolog of "Remember `45" is remarkably sustained in its intense despair and justifiable, angry cynicism. The lines move with kinetic action in brilliant flashes, experimental and flexible, yet fluid in a meandering stream of staccato passages.

The verses follow the young poets adventures with women and carry him from Paris to Barcelona to New York City. The poems have a lively sense of youthful abandon, mixed with an emotional sensitivity. They contain a poignant portrait of the poet's Italian grandfather, dying of cancer, the only father he ever knew— during The Great Depression years of his youth. The fleeting descriptions of great cities, Paris, Barcelona and finally New York, a city de Palchi love's and has lived in for many years, are palpable with spirited observations. His father, his God, his town, his country and the world have estranged the young poet and he is discordant with his revulsion and revolt. *Sessions with My Analyst* is a merciless exposure of de Palchi's probing of himself and his feelings of guilt and failure, yet it does not have the feeling of confessional poetry in the American mode about it at all. Rather the disjointed verses rage like a mutiny against injustice in a compulsive outpouring, begun in youth and finished in adulthood.

> My heat
> perverse bird
> at every summons to the light
> migrates
> to darkness.

The poet can find no refuge in Church or State, corrupted by corporate wealth that enslaves and makes robots of men in the marketplace:

> Into my
> hands in prayer
> I spit out my birth

He would commit suicide were he not driven by sexual appetite to pleasure in his own desire. His desires for women are fully explored in the poems that expose his physical drive in uncompromising terms. As L.L. Salomon wrote in the introduction to *Sessions with My Analyst* -- The book "is a work of art in which guilt complexes, adolescent fears and mature revulsion at the evil in man are deeply explored. Certainly no contemporary Italian poet of his generation can match de Palchi in these themes, as his dark and terrible past comes to life in these poems. He has lived in an inferno. He must forever

> thrust his
> dismal cargo forward
>
> under a light— alone,
> out of touch
>
> incommunicable –

The Scorpion's Dark Dance, Alfredo de Palchi second published book, was actually written prior to *Sessions with My Analyst*, while the poet was imprisoned in his youth, but not published until many years later.

Alfredo de Palchi's *Anonymous Constellation* is one long stream-of-consciousness, presented in the style of French symbolist poetry— with plenty of blank white spaces between the individual sections, or short poems, which wash through the poet's mind with stark imagery and cynical emotion. *Pour ce qu'il est tout insense* is the opening epitaph from Francois Villon— showing that the poet means to incense us with his ironic message – to slap us in the face with our own pretense at civilization. There's a thoughtful introduction by Alessandro Vettori of the University of Virginia which explains the poet's mission and why the style of the book is organic to its themes. The strongest section of the book comes in the middle when the poet leaps into concrete happenings, leaving the more abstract mode of existential nausea and despair.

Disgust and rage are expressed at corruption, greed, bigotry, hate, folly, human vanity, and the loneliness that is the human condition. These are de Palchi's themes as he takes us from the beginnings of our evolution through the vulturism of the animal kingdom to set us adrift in the far reaches of the stars. He is a poet longing for human perfectibility, calling us to awaken into humane conscience, aware of how power corrupts all in a self-aggrandizing universe where existence seems based upon the expediencies of survival and the necessities of nature.

Writing in his native Italian, de Palchi was translated into sharp-witted English by Sonia Raiziss—but the English translations are not quite as good as the Italian originals in tone and passion. The book is happily a bi-lingual edition and a cycle of poems not unlike his last, *The Scorpion's Dark Dance*, also translated by Raiziss, which won praise for its "dark exuberance, bright anger, cutting cynicism which hammers us to the other side of apathy." There is a Dantesque harshness and a Montalean sorrow, even as there are glimpses of redemption and self-insight that break through with a typically Italian, sardonic tone. De Palchi is a survivor of war and imprisonment by Fascist and Communists zealots, longing to find meaning in the violence and brutality that surrounds him and which nearly destroyed his youthful life. His earlier book, *The Scorpion's Dark Dance*, was a sharp contrast of surreal, existential rage with sensuous imagery. Nature's beauty bloomed forth in sticky, succulent contrast to the abstracted wit of a sardonic mind to offer its peace. The poems seemed to flow in a more driven sequence than in the current book. In *Anonymous Constellation,* the rage is more complete and encompasses nature, herself. The grass in the end covers all rot, corruption, murder, and massacre, but does not bring peace. Rather, in the later work, nature is a seductress tempting us to forget our horrors, a suspect beauty.

The poems intensify as one reads along. Perhaps, they are not arranged in the sequence in which they were originally written, but the highest points of the sequence come on pages 51-63. As one reads deeply into the book to capture its strength, a more concrete imagery leaps out of abstractions to ground the existential despair in everyday realities. An excerpt like the following—so much more powerful in the original Italian, too— is such a moment:

> They shot a black man
> in a fruit store,
>
> his tingling crinkled head
> lands in a crate of tomatoes....
>
> ...the crowd grumbles ....
> I shrug my shoulders, hurting at the thought
> of the crash in his own and at the sight of his face
> tinged with busted tomatoes
> — Is that blood?—
> — Eh, he's just a nigger –
> — says a dwarf clown.

This is followed by a section that states the central theme of the intensely streaming consciousness— which despite its cynical bite seems meant to bring us to a peace on the other side of despair and toward a more humane conscience. Only an idealist can become so disillusioned.

> ....the world grins under a fist
> we have opted for not weeping not helping

but looking away

when a body collapses
and walking off with the same indifference
we feel for the beast knocked out

by a car or a shotgun—
it's useless to pretend, everyone

is out for himself
and locked in him*self.*

And then the voice explodes into a flowering of truth that surmounts the every day world to become epic in proportion:

How can we swallow history, our
daily story, get used to enormous and
petty insults — under each fallen leaf a war
of insects and everywhere the rage
for survival: the mouse the rabbit
the cruising hawk attack
and the butcher's boy in his ferocious glee
lashing the ox and hungry for power....

This is de Palchi's ultimate sorrow. Yet, the poet's despair in *Anonymous Constellation* is full of heavenly aspiration, even in its existential nausea. The title poem gives the book a resonant aspiration, a respect for the mystery of self in relation to the cosmos, so unfathomable to one finite mind. Alfredo de Palchi suggests that each of us is his own "grand inquisitor" responsible for the love we can create within our own small society of friends and family. Within the walls of our own homes we may find love that transcends the bitter world. This is his finer message and *Anonymous Constellation* is a book worthy of many readers. Responsibility for human love and suffering is what the poet calls us to. In all his existential sorrow, de Palchi wishes to reach beyond himself to a greater understanding and humanity as he feels himself reeling in a vast universe, a mystery even to himself, an *Anonymous Constellation.*

Alfredo de Palchi's *Addictive Aversions* is a series of erotic poems divided into three sections, *Moments, Movements,* and *Mutations,* but it is more than merely erotic love that concerns the poet. As in the poet's earlier works, the book is one long stream-of-consciousness in the style of a French symbolist poem – with plenty of white spaces between the individual verses which wash through the poet's mind with stark imagery and contemplative clarity. Form follows function as the poems flow in a driven sequence and intensify as one reads towards the conclusion. Again de Palchi's fierce nihilism, and uncompromising lack of sentimentality—as in his other recent books, *The Scorpion's Dark Dance* and *Anonymous Constellations*—is at work to challenge our morality and bring us face to face with our animal natures.

These poems are about sexual obsession as part of the human condition of an ordinary man, but the question they pose is a deeply moral one that concerns the very psychology of our species. These poems bring us face to face with our existential despair in the midst of a baffling and unanswering mystery of creation.

De Palchi is both enthralled by sexuality and its pleasures and repulsed by the addictive grip in which it holds him. He is angered by his lack of control, his driving need, repulsed by his own animal nature. Though the visceral condition of being human holds orgasmic release as a pleasure, it also obsesses us with the need for orgasmic release. Obsession drives us through life more than our human will to rise above our animal natures and yet, as always, de Palchi longs for us to transcend our natures, to be aware. He challenges us to be better than mere procreative animals and longs to rise above his own nature. We will cheat, steal, and trespass the boundaries of honor in order to fulfill the addictive need that an enrapturing lover creates in us, he seems to say. But though, yet again, dePalchi's message is that there is no honor among men, only addiction, necessity, appetite, biological drive, there is a slim hope for a finer transcendence, if only one can find the incorruptible lover.

Alfredo de Palchi may see us as creatures in effect "raped" by our own sexual drive. He is both attracted and repelled by the life force— the addiction to the pleasures which repulses him, but there is no prudery here, and no religiosity, as the repulsion is more profound than Puritanical. It is a revulsion which is deeply philosophical as the poet seeks the light of reason in a Dante-like journey through his own pleasures, drives, and appetites, searching for a *raison d'etre* beyond them.

> I specify your body's insolence
> sometimes lyrical
> subterranean with childlike
> subterfuges, even your solar center
> devouring me seems to laugh.
>
> .... my existence interlocks with yours,
> morning and night but the intricate mood
> scares you because I am what you are
> and you are what I am
> joined in orgasmic nothingness –

Here again we meet with the existential despair of the poet who literally knew imprisonment and torture under both fascists and communists, finding dilemma at every turn. It is understandable why any sort of fanaticism is repulsive to him, including his own seemingly fanatical need of sexual release. Here is a poet angry and disgusted by the grip life has on him, the chemistry that defines him, the love that compels him. His mood is that of a *Don Juan in Hell*:
let's turn over the stone pocked with scribbles,

> worms, blanched with spermatozoa, molecules:
> such is the incessant beginning, the glimmer
> that locks us between the linear horizon and the leap—

De Palchi pictures erotic love like a rat gnawing at his throat, opening his arteries, causing him to spurt life. The poet wants to bring us face to face with the destruction wrought by man, because of his greed. He doesn't want to be drawn into this corrupted and corrupting world by blossoming life, the fruits of exploding seeds which force their voluptuous life upon us even as greed destroys nature's bounty and beauty, as in these lines:

> don't harden me
> with the stench of cleared forests
> of poisoned water,
> the spores mutate from deep within
> then burn with pressure
> with green threads that I sniff like a sick dog
>
> lapping at their sources—
> another ulcerated spring explodes
> encircled by toxins, by trunks
> uprooted in the flow;
> my material chemistry
> rushes into yours as they renew themselves
> together in the flames that still remain—

The poet has never overcome his existential despair, his nausea at the nothingness we are and become as we encounter ourselves full of appetite and morally imperfect. This is what makes his vision uncompromising and lacking in all sentimentality. He searches for "the perfect Justine" who will play the "masochist" to life as he sees himself a masochist tempted into desire by an non-answering creation which only forces more non-answering creation from us.

There is not one ounce of mawkishness, only aversion to the addictions of being alive, a flame burning with desire for mere desire's sake. Yet, there is a wry smile, a sardonic wit at work here, for de Palchi makes the erotic delectably inviting and pleasurable at the same time that he is repulsed by his addiction to it and thus the apt title *Addictive Aversions.*

Writing in his native Italian, de Palchi has been translated into sharp-witted English by Sonia Raiziss, Michael Palma, I.L. Salomon, Alethea Gail Segal and nicely edited by Michael Palma. The cover of the book is beautifully designed by Zuma with a colorful illustration by H. Matisse, 1950. The introduction by Alessandro Vettori of the University of Virginia is insightful in its appreciation and the laudatory explanation of the poet's work is well deserved. De Palchi's work has won much praise for its "dark exuberance, bright anger, cutting cynicism which hammers us to the other side of apathy." That is the very point of this poet's vision, to awaken apathy, to challenge us to a profoundly cosmopolitan view of ourselves in the vast cosmos of creation, so that we might truly become the paragon of animals if only we will see ourselves for the beasts of prey that we have proved ourselves to be through the bloody course of our history here on this voluptuous and pleasurable earth, full of human suffering wrought by man's inhumanity to man, his greed and appetite.

This is an epic view, not a narrowly confessional one, but a broadly universal theme that encompasses all creation. If there is a Dantesque harshness, there is a Montalean sorrow, even as there are glimpses of redemption and self-insight that break through with a typically Italian, sardonic tone, but Alfredo de Palchi is original in his voice and style— neither as ornate or Baroque as Dante, not ensconced in a religious motif, nor as lyrical or soft-hearted as Montale. He is a poet all his own in the "anonymous constellation" of his *Addictive Aversions*—minimalist, stark, uncompromising, and wonderfully exuberant in the clarity of his brief but flowing imagist verses, linked one to the other by his search for a morally perfectible life. A purer love, not merely sexual in this brutal and savage world in which we must listen to our own lonely spirit, is the only hoped for salvation.

> .... yours is the voice you hear submerged....

> —here I wait for the coming of an incorruptible
> *Justine.*

by Daniela Gioseffi

Fishing in American Waters for Italian and Italian American Writers

EMANUELA CARNEVALI, edited by DENNIS BARONE • MILO DE ANGELIS, *translated by* EMANUEL DI PASQUALE • CAESARE PAVSI, *translated by* GEOFFREY BROCK • LEWIS TURCO • KIM ADDONIZZIO • GRACE CAVALIERI • MARIA TERRONE • GERRY LA FEMINA • PETER COVINO • MARIA FAMA • MARIA LISELLA • GIL FAGIANI • FRED MISURELLA • PAOLO CORSO • HELEN BAROLINI • VINCENZA SCARPACI

CRITIQUES BY DANIELA GIOSEFFI OF ITALIAN AMERICAN AUTHORS

*1. **Furnished Rooms** by Emanuel Carnevali, ed. 2006, with Afterword by Dennis Barone*

Anyone interested in the roots of American immigrant poetry between the two world wars should buy and read this excellently edited book with a fascinating afterword by Dennis Barone. Emanuel Carnevali was a very important figure in American poetry in his day. Born in Florence in 1898, he died in Bazzano in about 1941 or '42 in a hospital after suffering a long and painful illness. He is a mythological figure, but how many have actually read his works? How many are aware that he edited *Poetry* magazine for a spell—the most prestigious of American poetry magazines in this and his day? How many realize how admired he was by the well-known and respected Edward Dahlberg, for just one example? Dahlberg, according to Barone, remembered a pilgrimage he had undertaken: "I was so enthralled by *A Hurried Man* [the one book Carnevali published during his lifetime] that I went to Bazzano, a hilly medieval town, two and a half hours by steam train from Bologna, to visit" the older and ailing Carnevali.

Though an immigrant, Carnevali had extensive correspondence with important figures of American culture. He was taken seriously by many accomplished figures of literary achievement, including Sherwood Anderson, Louis Zukofsky, Ezra Pound, and William Carlos Williams who devoted four pages of his autobiography to Carnevali, as Barone explains in his afterword. He translated Rimbaud from French into English in the February 1931 issue of *Poetry* magazine, and mastered his second language well enough to be appointed an associate editor of the same magazine in 1919, before illness forced him to leave that job. The poet's life-long friend, Kay Boyle, prepared another book of Carnevali's after his death;

this book included some of the poet's prose, essays, correspondence, reviews, and biographically based fiction, as well as poetry.

When Carnevali first appeared in *Poetry* in March 1918, the prestigious American magazine based in Chicago, at the youthful age of 20 years old, the editors described the immigrant poet as one "who was born in Florence twenty years ago, was educated in Italian technical schools, and came to America at sixteen. Since then, he has earned his living in various difficult ways, studied English, and written his first poems (in his new language.)" Carnevali's story is an utterly amazing one, considering the poverty and monumental suffering he endured and overcame to be a respected man of letters in America. He suffered encephalitis among other debilitating ailments by February 1931, by the time his first book had been published. His mother died when he was merely ten years of age. He attended a number of technical schools in Italy, and then to escape a hated father, ran away to America by himself. He worked, when he could get work, mostly as a waiter, and, at least, one of his poems is about that experience. "In This Hotel" deals with the irony of his having to smile politely and say "Nice day today!" to his restaurant cliental while he is burning inside with the passion and suffering of a poet who wishes to speak more deeply of true feeling (19–20).

The first section of *Furnished Rooms* is an introduction, which Carnevali titled "The Book of Job Junior." It is an astonishingly insightful essay by the poet on his attitudes and his understanding of the function of art. It is a wonderfully honest and down-to-earth exposé of the problems of creating and critiquing art that stands true for all generations. Carnevali sees, with irony, through all the pretentiousness of the art world as well as through all the shallow lies of politics, and this makes his essay is absolutely refreshing to read. "Did a man ever know what art is?" He writes:

Not know, but sense it, men surely did. And all their lives and every minute of their lives, were spent in saying it. A work of art is. It is the only human 'manifestation that is exclusively, violently, intolerantly itself and nothing else…the only human manifestation that can define its existence in terms of its sheer being; that is what an artist, Giovanni Papini, means when he says that 'art is the only depositor of the Absolute.' One cannot say what art is otherwise than by producing a work of art. A work of art is an attempt to say what art is, its only scope is that. If it is art and you understand it, then you will have gone as far as its maker in his attempt to know what art is, and, in that particular contemplative moment by means of that benignant, imbecile unconcern that you assume when you say; art is this, art is that…. Only a mood, your own, personal, individual, holy mood will give you a glimpse, or more than a glimpse, into the comprehension of art.

At the beginning of this fascinating and ironic essay, Carnevali writes:

In the beginning a man grunted, 'I am hungry,' and sat in ambush for the first saurian that happened along. Now, there is socialism, bolshevism, capitalism, surplus theories, submerged tenth, Italian table d'hotes, Mr. Fletcher, cafeterias…. In the beginning, there was a lonely Phidias that made statues and hardly knew, if at all, why or wherefore. Now every irreverent mongrel who lifts his hind leg to leave a desecration of ink on clean paper talks of technique.

It's interesting to read this immigrant poet from the earlier part of the 20th century who gained his height in 1925. He deserves a revival among us, and Bordighera Press has done us a great favor to bring him to us as a forbearer of all immigrants writing excellent poetry in America. He is a Modernist and an experimentalist by craft and declaration, who writes in colloquial free verse, heralding all of those who came to do so later in the century, and his poetry stands up well for today's readers. Carnevali's is, indeed, a remarkable immigrant story, as Barone outlines it in his afterward to *Furnished Rooms*—a book that everyone should read for the heart and soul and inspiring poetry it affords.

This reviewer's favorite poem of the collection is titled "The Return," and is dedicated to Dorothy Dudly Harvey, a woman who was helpful to Carnevali, corresponding with him and sending him money for much needed medicine and books while he was hospitalized in Bazzano at the end of his painful life. It describes Emanuel Carnevali's feelings and thoughts as he returns to his homeland through Gibraltar's rocks and enters again the Mediterranean:

> ....
> I come from America, the land that gathers
> The revels, the miserable, the very poor;
> The land of puerile and magnificent deeds;
> The naïve skyscrapers—votive candles
> At the head of supine Manhattan.
>
> I remember Manhattan Island crowned with docks.
>
> I come from America, where everything
> Is bigger, but less majestic;
> Where there is no wine.
> I arrive in the land of wine—
> Wine for the soul.
> Italy is a little family;
> America is an orphan
> Independent and arrogant,
> Crazy and sublime,
> Without tradition to guide her,
>
> Rushing headlong in a mad run which she calls progress.
> Tremendously laborious America,
> Builder of the mechanical cities.
> But in the hurry people forget to love;
> But in the hurry one drops and loses kindness.
>
> And hunger is the patrimony of the emigrant;
> Hunger, desolate and squalid—
> For the fatherland,
> For bread and for women, both dear.
> America, you gather the hungry people

And give them new hungers for the old ones.

Where the skyscrapers grow, O America,
You have yelled your name to the four winds;
An ungracious, unkind yell—
That of a sour youth.

Were more prophetic words ever written by an American poet, considering the situation America finds itself in today in the eyes of an angry world? This poem goes on for several more pages of truthful emotion and observations by a poet who deserves a revival and this book is one we all need to read and relish for inspiration and understanding of our immigrant heritage. It is one that any child of immigrants can enjoy, identify, and empathize with. Emanuel Carnevali remains a profound poet and thinker for all seasons, one whose unpretentious style and Modernist free verse is as interesting today as when he wrote it.

2. Between the Blast Furnaces and the Dizziness: A Selection of Poems, 1920–1999, by Milo De Angelis, translated and introduction, 2003 by Emanuel di Pasquale.

Though Milo De Anglis is not an Italian American, but an Italian who writes in Italian, he has many readers here in America where his work has been translated into English. Born in Milan in 1951, De Angelis is one of the most acclaimed and significant figures in Italian poetry today. Eraldo Affininati, Italian scholar and critic, writes in his afterward that "[i]t would be difficult to find a poet so totally modern."

Indeed, some of the imagery would fit well in Modern paintings like those of Magritte or De Chirico, but there is a greyness of city life to De Angelis's poems: "machinery hums, trains arrive, windshield wipers move, electrodes touch, the apple is dead...." And the mood of his poems is one of disconsolation. It is so like the cover photograph of a naked trolley yard with its electrical wires above, its barren landscape of silhouetted train-cars in shades of grey; the moon appears slightly visible and is the only light in the photo on the cover. The photo aptly captures the mood of De Angelis poetry.

Eraldo Affinati also writes, "From the first dazzling collection *Somiglianze,* 1976, up to *Biografia sommaria,* 1999, his utterance has become more precise and efficacious... a superior vision, capable of reaching the heights of extraordinary lyrical persuasion." There is indeed a persuasiveness about these poems that draws the reader into the mood of the poet, often quizzical and ironic. De Angelis's words are made luminous by his genuine emotions and refreshing imagery. He may well appeal to American readers who like to be challenged by what they read.

If one is looking for a poet of transcendent exuberance or joy, it is not De Angelis. His is a learned mind. He has translated many French poets and classical Greek poets as well. The French surrealists and symbolists have had their influence upon his work—often somber and imbued with a sense of the absurd that achieve as mood generally melancholy and questioning. For example, in his poem titled "The Part," De Angelis writes,

> Some decision
>
> even among the beans in the attic
> needs to be taken: one cannot
> ask things
> or why in the world an anticipation
> it is not enough to lazily pile up
> husks, in this sack
>
> but here
> you are seated on a box
> and you look at your shoes,
> over countless years. (27)

In his more gracious moments, his poetry gives life to our modern age in which the human and the machine seem to merge into one body of activity and being. Often his feeling of existential nausea is Sartre-like and so complete that the poet expresses a sense of disorientation or "dizziness" as in the title of the volume with its attempt to get beyond the "blast furnaces" and man's inhumanity to man.

Perhaps this collection is symbolic of the despair felt by Europe after World War II and the monstrosities suffered due to Hitler's fascism. World War II made Europeans acutely aware that the machine could be of benevolent or evil use and our mechanical and scientific intelligence used for humane purpose or heinous evil.

There is the echo of this realization throughout De Angelis's poetry. His tone of despondency and disorientation takes on a ghostly mode of nonsensical abstraction—as if the poet were with Samuel Beckett, *Waiting for Godot*. De Angelis manages to lament the passing of life as a loss of death in his poem "Semifinal":

> Dying then is losing even death, infinite
> present, no appeal, no music of a personal call.
> Other than that the veins that were rite
> and residence, milligram and announcement, infinite cry
> of joy or help, no one ever
> beyond this veins. It's simple, boys, no one." (193)

This is the poetry of a brave free thinker, who does not hide behind the hope of otherworldly salvation— a man who knows that we are morally accountable *here and now* to each other.

This handsome, bilingual edition is the first volume in a new publishing venture by Chelsea Associates, Inc., a not-for-profit corporation that, for forty-five years, has published *Chelsea* magazine—a literary review that has always been interested in promoting international poetry along with American writers. The new series is edited by Alfredo De Palchi, editor-in-chief of *Chelsea*. De Palchi has produced an attractive volume of 200 pages of De Angelis selected lyrical poems, on high quality paper.

3. Disaffections: Complete Poems, 1930-1950 by Cesare Pavese, Trans. by Geoffrey Brock

Cesare Pavese is an Italian poet widely translated and read in English in America, especially among Italian Americans. Though Pavese's poetry has been available in English translation, Geoffrey Brock's new translation seems to be of a more colloquial quality—especially in the early works where Pavese's language and the simple, appealing cadence of his music carries the narrative along. Combined with the reissue of several of Pavese's novels, American readers can now get to know Pavese in a new version, and perhaps in a greater depth, because of the work of Geoffrey Brock.

Cesare Pavese was born in a country village near industrial Turin and grew up in the city. His childhood summers were spent back in his native village. The strain Pavese experienced in these changing environments is felt in his poems; his early poems, Brock writes, "are inhabited by characters who seem to have been drawn to the city by its economic promise, only to encounter varying degrees of disappointment and isolation." The poem-story of Gella, who works in the city, but returns each night to her family farm, is one example:

Gella's fed up with going and coming, traveling at night,
living neither among buildings nor out in the vineyards.
She wishes the city were up on those hills,
luminous, secret: never again would she leave it.

When Pavese began publishing his work in the early 1930's, Italian fascism was burgeoning. Everything about fascism, including its staunch and arrogant nationalism, was repulsive to Pavese's worldly sensibility. The fascists arrested him because of his anti-fascist activism and sent him to a small town in southern Italy for three years. Cesare Pavese's first book, a sequence of narrative poems titled *Lavorare stanca* (included in *Disaffections*) is one of the most remarkable collections of Italian poetry in the 20th century and is important to Italian intellectual life in that it helps to prove how much the artists of Pavese's day resisted the idiocy and folly of Hitler's fascism.

As Brock explains in his introduction, Pavese's style in the first section of *Disaffections* was very different from the leading trends in Italian poetry of the 1930s. When *Lavorare stanca* was published in 1936, the term "hermetic" was being used to describe the mode of the leading Italian poets of the time: Eugenio Montale, Giuseppe Ungaretti, among them. Adopted from the French Symbolists, no doubt, the hermetic style was impenetrable, inward, and elliptical. It generally speaking avoided the matters of everyday life or concerns of the work-a-day world.

But Pavese, in the 1930's, wanted to write like a man aware of ordinary life in its attempt at survival around him in an uneasy time of growing fascism. His cadence is more equivalent to a Whitmanesque one or like that of William Carlos Williams's American diction, closer to free verse American poetry into a more colloquial tonicity. Perhaps, because he lived in exile from the urban intellectuals, his seventy-seven vignettes of *Lavorare stanca*, almost all of them about one page in length, deal with basic human themes, erotic love, family life, aging, hunger, youthful exuberance, passion for it's own sake as a feeling that gives joy in life, and drinking to avoid a sense of loss, the misery of being forced into apathy and dullness. They smack of the cynical depression scientifically associated with too much alcohol. But, in the earlier part of the century, poets did not stop to think how much the mood of their verses could be influenced by alcohol as a drug. It's passé to fall into ones cups in verse now, but not then: "Is it worth the trouble for the sun to rise up from the sea and begin the long day? Tomorrow the warm dawn will return with its diaphanous light and, just like yesterday, nothing will happen."

To tell his "poem-stories," or narrative poems, Pavese followed a technique that seems to avoid any emotional dishonesty he may have felt in the prevailing "hermetic" forms. He invented his own individual style of narrative:

> One day I found myself muttering a certain jumble of words in a pronounced cadence that I had used for emphasis ever since I was a child, when I would murmur over and over the phrases that obsessed me most in the novels I was reading. That's how, without knowing it, I found my verse.

Pavese named the meter "the rhythm of my daydreaming." In Italian it might be called *cantilenante*, singsong, Brock explains. This cadence sounds as if the poet is merely talking as he goes along—not stopping to laboriously compose his words. Sitting in the dark tavern, Pavese longs for the normal life of his country-side before the fascists helped to plunge the world into turmoil: "[t]he sky outside could be brilliant with stars, beyond autumn's fog and the scent of pressed grapes. Even now, the ragged songs of the harvesters could be rising from the emptied fields on the hill."

Pavese's rhythms in *Lavorare stanca* seem to sound like a jazz bass fiddle keeping a constant metric sameness under his free verse narratives. What bass players call "walking it." His poems are metrically simple and appealing, because they hold his thoughts on easy target for the reader and require little effort of interpretation. They enter the mind with the ease of a folk song or a jazz lyric: "We're walking one evening on the flank of a hill in silence. In the shadows of dusk my cousin's a giant dressed all in white, moving serenely, face bronzed by the sun."

But, the final section of this collection contains Pavese's more lyrical love poems. Written at the end of his life, they resemble the 20th century poetic style he had rejected in the earlier narrative poems. The last twenty or so love poems in the collection, suggest that Pavese is proving he can do what Montale or Ugaretti do, and his theme depicts woman as the great force of life that drives man to all meaning and desire—as if a woman's body were a life force of nature that makes a man want to live.

These translations by Geoffrey Brock—close to the literal meanings of their Italian originals—seem accurate to Pavese's intent. They do not seem to poeticize too much in their English renderings or add interpretive values. There is very little change from the original in the translator's versions in American English. There may be a few missing nuances, but as far as one can tell, Brock's translation seem to capture Pavese's tone quite accurately—especially in the earlier "poem stories" written in the 1930's. This is a volume worth the price of reading. And, of course, Pavese is a poet well worth knowing.

4. Fearful Pleasures: The Complete Poems, 1959–2007 by Lewis Turco, 2007

Is there anyone in American poetry quite like Lewis Turco—a prolific and highly versatile writer in all genres, a renowned teacher, translator, and a consummately skilled craftsman who also brought us *The Book of Forms*, that instruction in poetics that sits on almost every poet's shelf in the country? It is a manual he has reissued and revised, adding more and more accuracy over the years. The plaudits were well overdue when Star Cloud Press published *Lewis Turco and His Work: A Celebration* in 2004. Now, Star Cloud has brought us *Fearful Pleasures: The Complete Poems, 1959-2007*, and what a stupendous work it is!

Turco for many years has written and published formalist poems under the name of his alter ego, Wesli Court, even though Lewis Turco is often found writing in free verse, prose, and other genres, including memoir, literary criticism, and polemic, as well as plays and stories. Having published more than forty books, he is one of America's most prolific and versatile poets. A thick volume, *The Collected Lyrics of Lewis Turco/Wesli Court, 1953-2004*, also came out from Star Cloud Press in 2004.

Donald Jusitice wrote in celebrating Turco:

> Whenever I see in a magazine now a certain kind of poem—one witty and formally inventive and perhaps light-hearted, with verve and fizz and a few surprises—and if this poem is signed by a name unfamiliar to me, I tend to suspect that I may be reading the work of still another Turco spin-off. How many Turcos there really are I shall probably never know, but a whole townful would be all right with me.

Felix Stefanile has observed, "Turco seems to have the whole of the English lyric tradition at his fingertips." *Fearful Pleasures: The Complete Poems* certainly proves that statement correct. Turco has an ear for every sort of poem, meter, rhyme, and form, and no poet writing today can outdo him in skill. He can be exquisitely lyrical and marvelously witty and inventive. Obviously a wide reader, worldly and learned, he draws on many cultural traditions from Rabelais to Swift to gypsy balladeer. He writes poems with Asian forms and Zen concepts, asks existential questions, and composes with Lorca-like musicality, as the preface to his *Complete Poems*, written by Rhina P. Espaillat, explains:

> How fortunate the reading public is to have this wealth of writing by one of the country's most interesting poets now in one volume.... It belongs on the bookshelf of every reader willing to risk the joy and anguish of hearing the world, having it speak to him as vividly, ambiguously and honestly as it speaks to Lewis Turco.

At the end of "Millpond," a poem written at Yaddo in 1959, Turco wrote,

This is the place where peace rests
like ferns beyond lilies.
The trick is to wear it
as a mantle, but to know
cloaks for cloaks, shelter for shelters.
Beneath this reverie of surfaces, fish wait
for the dragonfly's mistake.
The trick is to not lose, but to own.

As a poet, Turco wears his mantle of peace, and while losing himself in poetry, he has come to own it completely. This latest collection is arranged chronologically from *The Sketches* (1962) through *The Green Maces of Autumn* (2002) and takes us through *A Book of Beasts, A Book of Fears, Seasons of The Blood: Poems on the Tarot, American Still Lifes* and *The Compleat Melancholick*, among other sections. There are poems and centos based on lines from Emily Dickinson's letters, because Turco can do anything and everything and has, from mournful poems of lost love and youth to verses that roundly face death without sentimentality, to observations of the natural world and all its strange creatures bestial and human, to wisdom that runs deeper than many poets ever reach.

Why he has not been awarded a Pulitzer Prize or a National Book Award has more to do with the politics of poetry, and perhaps with his Italian name, than with his talent and knowledge of poetics. Like John Ciardi and Lawrence Ferlinghetti, Turco has also worked in translation, and like Ciardi and Ferlinghetti, he is an artist who deserves more recognition than he has received. He is the granddaddy of the New Formalism while being consummately capable of the craftiest free verse.

There is nothing this writer cannot write, it seems. Lewis Turco is a poet for all seasons, and we have all grown up under his tutelage, with his books on forms and genres on our shelves. In fact, he is an institution of American poetry. As Dana Gioia has written, "Lewis Turco is one of the most diversely talented Italian American poets. [But why not just say 'American poets?'] What a pleasure to read him...." And what a pleasure to read *Fearful Pleasures*!

CRITIQUES BY DANIELA GIOSEFFI OF ITALIAN AMERICAN POETS

*5. Comparing **The Philosopher's Club** 1994 by Kim Addonizio with **Poems New and Selected** 1994 by Grace Cavalieri*

Grace Cavalieri's tone in *Poems New & Selected* is often similar to Kim Addonizio's *The Philosopher's Club* in its reasoned acceptance of losses created by the passage of time and death. Her imagery, too, is often of house, garden, kitchen, family gatherings, and relationships. Her subject matter, like

Addonizio's, also involves profound feelings for children, in this case daughters, the expressions of a protective mother's yearning. These two collections contain some of the finest poems to or about daughters to be found in contemporary American poetry of late.

Yet, Cavalieri has her moments of high-strung bliss, which add variety of tone to her seventh collection. An example occurs in "Upon Dreaming A Proposition That All Truth Is A Conversion From Negative To Positive":

> As if touched by God, I,
> At night
> Saw that all
> Which exists comes through a
> Transmutation
> From dark....
> And I am right at this moment
> Crying
> With the thought of it and how
> Happy I was
> Burning *with* it waking up on that most
> Ordinary Summer morning of my life.

And, Addonizio portrays moments of candid sensual pleasure which transcend the merely philosophical, as in "First Poem to You." Gerald Stern—in his introduction to Addonizio's poems, which appear in "The New Poets of American Series," from BOA Editions, customarily introduced by an established poet—aptly states: "There are some poets who write with a kind of fore-knowledge—I'll call it that—and it is what gives these poets their strange power. It's as if all life has already happened—as it happens—and they give in knowingly, even as they still struggle with desire and hope. Kim Addonizio is one of these. She is someone who knows, somehow, and this knowledge itself gives strength and pity and tenderness, sometimes even terror, to her poems."

But, *The Philosopher's Club* is aptly titled as reasoned discourse. Passionate wonderment or anguish does not characterize Kim Addonizio's first collection of poems. Neither she nor Grace Cavalieri are the sort of artists who would paint a wild and swirling "Starry Night" of mad obsession or tear off an ear. Addonizio's voice can be relied upon to sail reasonably along, never shrill, never crying out in sorrow, making quiet observations with intense accuracy. She captures nuanced moments with a style that leaves them suspended quietly in the reader's imagination. Both of these poets belie the stereotype of their ethnic names as neither is overly emotional or hysterical as Italians are often portrayed by the media. Their poems do not talk with their hands, gesticulating wildly, but rather contain emotions, which are controlled and yet deeply felt, as in the Baroque Classical music of a Vivaldi or Monteverdi. If such a metaphor is allowed, their poems are not symphonic rhapsodies or Verdi arias, but mellow concerti for harpsichord, flute, and violin.

Kim Addonizio is wise and crafty in her observations and her portrayal of sensual love, filial feeling, death or loss, yet there is, perhaps, a sameness of tone to the book which may dissatisfy some readers looking for those bursts of elation or explosive feelings which can add variety to a mature acceptance, resignation or quiet sensuality. Says Addonizio, in "Conversations in Woodside":

> Joe insisted that life is extreme,
> but Nadia and I argued for dailiness:
> The stove's small flame under the kettle,
> The lover who, turning over in bed
>
> reaches for an absence....

Grace Cavalieri, the more seasoned of the two poets, is the author of six other books of poetry, the most recent being *Trenton* about which Reed Whittemore said: "Bliss is strong but relaxed and easy-strong." Daniel Berrigan called her, "Truly a seer and a sayer of words that pierce and hear at once." And, he is right about that. Cavalieri is known nationwide for the longest running poetry show on the radio airwaves. For twenty-five years, she's hosted and interviewed nearly all of the contemporary American poets of our time on *The Poet and the Poem*, syndicated from Pacifica Radio, WPFM in Washington, DC. She has, through her radio show, amassed the country's largest audience for poetry and she has, no doubt, learned a great deal about the art of listening and asking questions as she does concerning craft. She interviews each poet about his or her work, which is broadcast on many affiliates throughout the country.

Cavalieri is at her best when she writes from the heart about lost children, or aspiring love, human relationships, and emotions with clarity and lucidity. When she drifts toward an abstract expressionist tone, and her subject matter becomes nebulous in the mode of the French symbolists, the reader is less engaged, less moved or captivated. Some of her most satisfying poems are her most concretely felt. "Death of a Cat," "The Lost Children," "Father," "The Orphanage," "The Offer of Friendship," and "Requiem Mass" are just a few examples of Cavalieri at her best.

Addonizio is most profound when she's philosophizing about the transient quality of life and its central realization of mortality. There is a wistful pain of loss in our most tranquil and beautiful moments, she seems to say, as they must pass into oblivion, and we are "tethered to each other by the slenderest and brightest of ropes." And, "The Last Poem About the Dead":

> Sounds like this: a long sweet silence
> the next soul breaks as it drops,
> the way a fish flops back
> slapping the quiet water,...

Both of these skillful poets possess a mature voice deserving of our attention, as there is much to learn from their poetic musings, their ability to pierce through the surface of daily life to its subtle meanings. Both exude a knowing air, which stimulates the reader to accept all that life offers in its profound but simple domestic, social and familial dailiness—even its final ending. As Cavalieri writes, in "How to Obtain":

> You will show them what you need
> And tell them what you want
> And of dying you will say
> "Is this all there is to it"
> You'll have known it all the time.

6. *A Secret Room in Fall* 2006 by Maria Terrone

A Secret Room in Fall was awarded the McGovern Prize. It is prefaced by Gerry LaFemina in an insightful introduction. As La Femina points out, Maria Terrone's poems are well crafted. Her language is carefully wrought and nicely cadenced. She writes with a precise physicality and imagery. The title poem is an apt choice for this collection, as it sets a contemplative mood that runs throughout.

Terrone is a lifelong New Yorker who graduated with a B.A. in English Literature from Fordham University. Many of her poems speak of her life as a New Yorker, acutely aware of her urban landscape: for example, "Omega Train" or "Dead Man Riding" wherein she observes the daily life of riding the subways of her city with the eye of a poet aware of irony. She sometimes assumes different personae, as in the later piece where she speaks in the voice of a dead man written of in a New York newspaper who rode the train for three hours before it was noticed that he was deceased. Indeed, a multiplicity of voices are assumed throughout the collection—as the Alice in Wonderland queen at "The Mad Tea Party," or as in "The Slain Wife of the Lighthouse Keeper Speaks" or as "A Poet in the Customs House"—in poems that are acts of transcendent imagination. Terrone often represents female laborers at work in the background of life, as in "The Pedicurists Club," but she gives each a moment of empathy that sheds light on their existence.

Her poems are accessible without being simplistic. She's a master of the understated or nuanced moment. She sometimes writes in short narrative form or in sonnet form as in "The Egyptian Queen Gives Death the Slip," which uses subtle rhymes and assonance, demonstrating her control of craft. Though her mood is contemplative and restrained, her poems often end with a twist that delivers surprising conclusions, as in the later, which ends:

> Taking flight is my talent. Let Death play solitaire,
> or else play with you his eternal, stinking
> game of boredom. That's not for me. I'm everywhere
> and nowhere, which is why you found my casket bare.

The Ashland Poetry Press has produced a handsome book in deep bluish and red tones with a cover illustration that fits the title and captures the contemplative mood of the book. This is a book of careful craft, worth the reading. As the poet says,

you, too, can make a home
in this once dazzling quarter
always on the verge
of corruption.
There are worse places
to live with your secrets.

7. *The Window Facing Winter: Poems,* 2004 by Gerry LaFemina

There is a lovely urgency to this new collection of poems in the Green Rose
Series from New Issues Press. In *The Window Facing Winter,* Gerry LaFemina
always manages to find some glory or splendor amidst the decay and death of an
urban landscape. A Japanese garden is a manicured refuge—a foil for the ugliness
of what man has wrought—as in the poem, "Chinese Scholars Garden, Staten
Island Botanical Gardens":

Dusty gray of brown prints of leaves, fossil-like
litter the asphalt path
away from the building which once housed retired sailors

and their tired stories toward new bamboo
rising thick and dreamy, the thousand tiny flags
of their leaves billowing. November.

and nearly 70 degrees,
the whole world seems to meditate.... (24)

LaFemina is not afraid to confront the realities of a grimy life, but there is hope in
the dawning of a new day if our creative intelligence can prevail.

There is no sentimentality, but rather an exacting insight expressed with preci-
sion both tough and sensitive. A human warmth and graceful irony charges these
poems with meanings that engage. His themes are loss, desire, nostalgia, and ironic or dreamy disorientation to the surreal aspects of life, but always there is hope
and the necessity of love as the ultimate healer of all despair.

An urban landscape is evident—sometimes in decay—in much of LaFemina's
work. Windows are a theme that runs through as a metaphor for the longing to
escape the humdrum into a deeper world of poetic understanding of the human predicament or freedom from it. There's a warmth, a grace, a forgiveness rather than
an anger to his sardonic wit. Sometimes a serenity or a poignant nostalgia is found
in the innocence of young love as in "Calla Lilly" or "Spring Equinox," and effective tonicities are often created from ordinary events as in "The Domestication of
Cats" or "What the Rain Does," which contains a deliberate echo of e.e.cummings:

...with fleeting vibrancy—
the air shimmery...

Umbrellas open around us, most of them black
but a few are bright red, green, white—
exuberant flowers unfolding. Their petals flip backward,

straining against the thin metal veins that give them shape
& a few blow inside out into uselessness, & the wind,

the wind has too many hands. (14)

Perhaps the poet should watch out for a word like "shimmery," but note how carefully he constructs his tactile and visual imagery.

These poems are anchored in reality, sometimes full of the grime of real life, but they are tender and affectionate about our folly, and often subtle in their observations as the poet travels through worn cities where he hears fragments of language or interprets what confronts him. An illustration of this is found in "Poem With the Morning Sun Reflected in Freshly Shined Shoes":

There's the wind pushing its invisible broom
& taxis filled with drunk tourists perusing the emptying avenues.
The night like a book read a long time ago—
a fuzzy memory with a storyline you could tell,

not precisely, but well enough to make your meaning plain.
A night like this

its belly full of wind & the wind
in the wake of those automobiles, one might find a sliver
of the absolute. A haze of skyline
beckons the eyes of a homeless man in the park
who nightly sleeps under the statue of a man on horseback
& dreams visions of being trampled to death

or riding away on a palomino from this place...

....

What is madness if not

perception? He hears a voice in the wind singing
what was once their song: he believes the cooing of pigeons
          & how much

it sounds like the vibrating purr of a cat. He's amazed
by the old men who come out each morning to shine shoes as
          the halogen sun
just begins burning the city's grim epidermis: he sees them

kneeling at their labors, hands gesticulating, as if seeking benediction. (18–19)

The Window Facing Winter creates a restive feeling, equivalent to the anxieties of our times, but transcends the urban blight that confounds our civilized existence with humor and discernment. Gerry LaFemina secures our interest with these poems of passion, loss, and fate, engaging us with his poetic powers of discovery. These are sometimes lonely poems of a restless nature, anxious to find passion and meaning in the absurdities of life. An example of the poet's imaginative use of language to convey feeling is found in the title poem, "The Window Facing Winter":

Before she left our house, she wept. I was there:
I saw her, but realize I didn't cry then, just rested

my forehead against a window facing winter,
nothing to say.
                    Then her car, laden with lies
we'd told ourselves, leaving the driveway.

....

I didn't want to return to the hunger of my house,
to watching water slide
the stalactite lengths of icicles. Still,

time kept turning the pages of these narratives....

Happiness is often expressed in the memory of loss, and there is always the poet questioning his own dreamlike or surreal state of reality but often, there's some kind of resolution or feeling that brings hope, as in "Manifesto" the poem that closes *The Window Facing Winter:*

...they'd make love right there on the shoulder
of a Michigan state highway because they've been separated
for so many days of hours that seemed like days
and because passion should always be that sporadic & urgent
and always, necessarily, always revolutionary. (62)

This poet is well worth watching and reading, and this is not his first book. It was preceded by chapbooks and two other full-length collections, the most recent of which was *Grafitti Heart,* which won the Mammoth Books Poetry Prize (2001). He has edited an anthology titled, *American Poetry: The Next Generation,* and published in *Colorado Review, Nimrod, Quarterly West, Connecticut Review,* and other periodicals. He directs the *Controlled Burn Seminar* for Young Writers, and is a member of the Board of Directors of the Association of Writers and Writing Programs. Gerry LaFemina possesses the sincerity and dedication that it takes to make good poetry out of real life occurrences, and the talent for a craft that appeals to those who seek meaning from experience. His is the sort of poetry that is honest and enduring, that speaks accessibly to mind and heart as well as art.

8. *Cut Off the Ears of Winter: Poems* 2005 *by Peter Covino*

Cut Off the Ears of Winter by Peter Covino is an impressive first book with an original tone. Dark stories of the family and child abuse are handled movingly without becoming maudlin. Covino uses techniques that are both descriptive and narrative to achieve his poetic balance.

There is something akimbo and abashing about these poems as they travel from confessional autobiography to worldly matters of art and history and embrace a larger world than that of the wounded child to become universal in their energy. For one example, as Covino writes about a painting of Judith and Holofernes, he says:

> ... he of the familiar scowl—
> these jealousies overwhelm me
> at the most inopportune moments,
> and I cannot say for sure
> whose severed head she holds....

There is a restive energy in these poems as in the title poem, which begins:

> Cut off the ears of winter
> they have overhead too much,
> where incinerators burn,
> where rubble-strewn streets
> are covered in dust
> ....
> This is my last dollar,
> last cigarette, last match.

Or as in "Two from Past Channels" spoken in the voice of Antigone, and then, Caesar:

> Small noise at night
> Voice, a river lying down
> Into itself
>
> This burden I carry.
> I sleep inside....

Covino, who was born in Italy and educated there and in the United States, has earned an MS from Columbia University in Social Work, and spent ten years as a child welfare social worker and in AIDS services. He is earning a Ph.D. in English and Creative Writing at the University of Utah, and is a founding editor of *Barrow Street Review*.

He seems to be a poet who, with his first book, has healed himself through original poetry and moved on to broader horizons that hold great promise for his art. "Tonight the Survivor," the penultimate poem of the book is followed by the contemplative "Ice Lake" which ends with "How can we explain the pieces of detail, vanishing?" As his painful past vanishes, Covino is a poet born into a new light of spiritual grace, beyond "Telling My Story"—one of the best narratives in the book along with "Clinic X." It is worth taking the trip to new heights through his restless poems with him to come to the place where details of the past blend and vanish in the soothing landscape of "Ice Lake."

When choosing Peter Covino's book as "First Runner Up" for the Bordighera Poetry Prize Sponsored by the Sonia Raiziss-Giop Foundation, in 2001, W.S. Di Piero wrote,

> These poems are acts of discovery. They deal with tough, risky—what academics now call "transgressive"—subject matter. There's a strangely exhilarating desperation in most of these poems that's compelling. Covino uses words as a medium, as materials, not as descriptive or narrative vehicles. I also like the angular unsettling humor threaded into nearly every poem.

This handsomely published first book is wide in scope and ambitious. It is not simply in the confessional autobiographical vein, but encompasses narratives of family, friendship, thought, philosophy, history and art. *Cut Off the Ears of Winter* is an admirable debut book for Peter Covino. He is obviously knowledgeable about his art and crafty in its production.

9. *Looking for Cover* 2008 by Maria Fama

Maria Fama's collection of poetry, *Looking for Cover* will bring smiles to your face as you read it. It might also at times bring tears. She is one of Italian America's most folksy and humorous poets, yet there is a deep spirituality and passion in her work—both in the sense of Catholicism with a big and a little "C." Maria seems like a deeply religious writer, but at the same time, she is fully aware of the irony in some of the beliefs Catholicism bestows. She sees the humor in people with religious morality at heart who often are practical in nature and believe in their religiosity to survive.

Perhaps, living in a Little Italy of Philadelphia has given her insight into the ways of her people that those of us who live outside such a milieu cannot see so lucidly. This is a second-generation, clear-headed view of a first generation style of life. It is neighborly with ethnic awareness and profound all at the same time. Her skill as a writer makes that combination possible and loveable. Fama has, as Mary Jo Bona noted, reclaimed the tradition of Italian story telling. This makes her poetry entertaining as well as vital.

Her use of immigrant stories and of saints' names and prayers is compelling, as in her "over-the-top" incantation for Saint Antonio whom she addresses in every imaginable form of his name from Anthony to Toni and beyond, begging for his help for "a job." That final incantatory prayer closes the book and goes on in chanting rhythm for more than four pages, as the *finale* among her performance pieces in the last section of her collection. It brings down the house when Fama recites it in person.

Other sections of the collection are titled: *Shields and Shelter, Doorways and Crossroads*, and *Spirit World*. Poems bear titles like "Nonna Mattia," "Pear Trees," "Bananas," and "*Pasta e Piselli;* Lunchtime Memories," in the delectable tradition of Italian women, kitchens, and food. Others are about the difficulties of being Italian in an American culture, i.e. "I Am Not White," "Civil Rights, Grade School." Still, others capture memories of immigrant life witnessed by a second-generation daughter who observes her family with keen clarity. The pieces in *Spirit World* are of love and death and painful loss: "August Heat," "Why I Don't Play the Guitar Anymore," and "Anita on the Telephone."

Though the music of her language is that of an Italian woman, there is a little of Gertrude Stein ringing in her poems. Often, Fama uses simple repetitions to make a powerful point and to summon emotion, and this device works well for her. Just one illustration among many of this stylistic element occurs in the poem "Jean Jacket:"

> I know you are dead
> Hanging clothes, packing clothes
> Folding and sorting clothes
> I know you are dead
> I open the drawer   you are dead
> I close the drawer   you are dead
> In the closet out of the closet you are dead.... (68)

The words the poet chooses are often simple and direct, but the rhythmic repetition of her phrases creates emotion that penetrates with power. This device Fama uses masterfully throughout her deceptively simple poems to achieve emotion strongly conveyed through artful diction. Fama writes lyrically and accessibly with imaginative detail, passing on from one generation to another a very Italian style of folk wisdom communicated with passion as in telling the stories of the immigrants from which she is descended in poems like "Table Back" or "Pear Trees" with their Sicilian landscapes.

Fama's is not a book readers will struggle to understand. Accessibility is its strength. One finds humor and seriousness in *Looking for Cover*. In its pages one discovers the courage of a people to endure against difficult odds and changing mores. Fama is perhaps our most Italian of Italian American women poets. She exemplifies the art of immigrants in America and their best character. Her work offers transcendent hope and crafty achievement. Maria Fama's poetry is in a word: *Charming!*

10. *Amore on Hope St.* 2009 by Maria Lisella

Amore on Hope St. is Maria Lisella's second chapbook of poetry. She is a keen observer of people and places who has made a living as a travel writer. Her range is geographically wide from the blue Adriatic Sea to the Borghese Gardens of Rome, from the steamy shores of Havana to a foggy day in Venice, and back to her home and love in New York.

Lisella's narratives are imbued with richly detailed images as in "Demons,"

... a shaft of cool moon light throws
the boyish curve of your man's face
into relief.

I breathe in your essence
in one long, deep breath
to absorb your peace.
Just before sleep takes me
under the weight of
your solitary palm,
you cup the pulse I surrender. (25)

The perceptions and lyrical nuances of Lisella's poetry reflect humanity with its foibles and triumphs, its love and its despairs with moving memories and longings. She is skillful in choosing the appropriate words and cadences that bring her descriptive poems to life. For example, she does so in this excerpt from "Salt Stings,"

My legs pedal through February's morning mist
The sky wears a Virgin Mary blue cape.
The aroma of aged bulkheads rife
with salt of the Long Island Sound.
Layers of tar seam the splintering
planks, keep the cliff from sliding
into the sand. The iodine smell
of dried seaweed, its briny taste,
my father said what we'd discover
would be worth eating.... (15)

Lisella's themes are the ironies of reality and the power of love to heal, the pride of the immigrant, the stalwart survival of the oppressed, the loss of loved ones, the customs of the exotic. Though she states: "I am from gnarled hands that sew and tailor, iron and wash, cook and make all places where I come from," she has travelled far from her second generation Calabrese beginnings to become a keen observer of all she encounters in her worldly travels.

Her chapbook offers a diversity of emotions and observations well worth exploration. Maria Lisella who co-curates the Italian American Reading Series at the Cornelia St. Café in New York City, demonstrates, with this loving and hopeful collection of poetry, that she is a poignant and talented poet capable of ironic observations, a writer with a worldly sensibility who has travelled widely and seen the world through a finely focused poetic lens.

11. A Blanquito in El Barrio, 2009 by Gil Fagiani

With careful details in this streetwise collection full of Latino expressions and rhythms, the speaker of these poems—*a blanquito,* a white guy, who learns the lingo of *El Barrio*—paints an accurate, sometimes brutal, picture of life in the Spanish Harlem to which he has come—an Italian American college drop-out from a middleclass Connecticut suburb. The fascination with Spanish Harlem is palpable in the voice and tone of the narrator, *el blanquito,* as he observes the throbbing living and dying around him in colorful minutiae. The narratives are often gut wrenching poems told with both affection and revulsion for the loveable and the pitiably desperate lives of *el barrio.*

At first, *el blanquito* is an observer of the life around him in these vivid narrative descriptions, but as the fast paced, street-talking verses progress, the white guy who has come to Spanish Harlem to serve as a social worker evolves into an addict and dope dealer, deeply ensconced in the worst part of life of *el barrio* with its struggling characters for whom he has both sympathy and, at times, disdain or pity. Through it all, Fagiani never views the neighborhood people from a high and mighty perch, but leaves the reader to make his or her own judgments of the characters in these colorful narratives with their curiosity provoking titles: "Shooting Dope with Trotsky," "Caucasian Cool," "The Bathroom at the Village Gate," "Diddy Bop," "Sweet Streams in Spanish Harlem," "Dopefinedery," "Righteous Fiend," "Junkie's Alarm Clock," "The Depusification Chamber," and others.

In his adventures and misadventures, he meets the good, the bad, and the pitiable. There's the noble humanitarian, an old woman, called *La Capitana* who brings the neighborhood children to protest at City Hall the cuts of their ghetto summer street programs:

> Seventy-three year old
> Iris Espinoza,
> *La Capitana* for a local
> antipoverty agency,
> received official notice.
> Her petitions appealing
> the cutoff of funds for children's
> summer street program
> have been denied.... (27)

With dripping ice cream cones and mustard laden hot dogs bought for *los ninos* by her panhandling ingenuity, *La Capitana* brings the children of *el barrio* to face down the bureaucrats of city hall at their shiny desks with a common slogan shouted with the children: *"Hasta la victoria!"* Then she declares: *"Los ninos* want their money!" Iris Espinoza seems triumphant facing the stunned bureaucrats whom one imagines recapitulating before her righteous ferocity.

There's the pitiable streetwalker, the cutthroat drug dealers, the drugged men nodding off and collapsing in the street, even as they attempt to dance to bongo rhythms of the neighborhood street musicians—Latino music always present throughout the narratives. There are the rats in the trash-laden gutters, and the starving, but prideful, young men who seek cast-off pizza crusts under the ferris wheel in the garbage-strewn amusement park. There is the shame of poverty, and the deadly profiteers of drug deals who numb that poverty and hopelessness into oblivion, and there are some noble attempts to transcend it all and live with dignity.

Fagiani is never above it all but a suffering participant who falls prey to the false pleasure that drugs momentarily offer. He too, despite his middleclass upbringing in Connecticut, becomes a drug-bum of the gutters and alleyways of Harlem's *el barrio*. He describes his tribulations with dauntless and gutsy accuracy, sparing himself no dignity. His collection of poems is the story, told with blistering honesty, of his fall into, and his rise from, the gutters and alleyways of Spanish Harlem. The poet is a survivor who has managed to relate his descent into hell, and his rise from the horrors of a drug infested reality, in succinct and vivid narrative verses that spare the reader no false niceties.

These poems are crafted narratives of a candid reality told by a white junkie who comes to El Barrio to help as a social worker and ends up a victim of despair in a neighborhood where every kind of illegal drug is easier to come by than a job or a life of purpose and productivity. These verses are horrifying stories of pitiable and disgusting addictions, peopled with memorable characters, who lead desperate lives in scenes that are starkly portrayed in the pulsing rhythms of Latino dance.

Gil Fagiani is a poet gifted with an eye for accurate observations and meticulous details who paints pictures of suffering, joy, love, and sorrow with words that are as real as the mouth from which they come. This is a book of poetry from a wise man who has lived with impoverished and struggling immigrants, become one with them, and emerged, alive and well to tell the tale, like an Ishmael, a survivor out of hell.

Fagiani has also published a chapbook, *Grandpa's Wine* in 2008, from Poets Wear Prada Press, that deals with his Italian American background. Its inspiration is the immigrant generation of his own family. The chapbook tells stories and legends of *la famiglia* come to life with personal observations and memories. Fagiani explores the angst facing immigrants everywhere as they attempt to assimilate and discover opportunity in the new land. As Robert Viscusi has accurately surmised:

Grandpa's Wine is written where people make a life among the ruins of a shattered world.... Gil Fagiani's poems inhabit this world's poignancy, searching its sorrows with unimpeachable candor and a spare language that perfectly fits its straightforward tastes and its undervalued satisfactions.

The same skill for unimpeachable candor is found in *A Blanquito in El Barrio*, for example in "Manteca":

Shoveling heaps of greasy white powder
up my sneeze box with Lefty
under an umbrella in the park on 108th Street,
the rain falling, our knees buckling,
Dizzy Gillepsie shouting in my head

Man-teca!

Loamy smell of wet sidewalks
seeps into my lungs,
soft waves of warm summer shower carry me to Park Avenue and 114th.
The El gleaming like onyx, trombones and saxophones celebrating
the first time I've taken a taste
of *man-teca*.... (55)

Gil Fagiani is a straight talking, accessible poet who makes no moral judgments regarding the characters he portrays in all their varied foibles and humanity. He leaves judgments to the reader, and is utterly honest about his own character flaws, terrible mistakes, and weaknesses. His style is narrative, clear, and unpretentious. The reader will be enlightened and edified by Fagiani's skillful and frank poetry, and the story of his fall into, and his rise out of, being *El Blanguito in El Barrio*, the white guy in Spanish Harlem.

CRITIQUES OF ITALIAN AMERICAN FICTION BY DANIELA GIOSEFFI

12. *Short Time*, 1996 by Fred Misurella

Short Time is the 8th volume in a series of books to come from VIA Folios of Bordighera, Inc. Since this reviewer is also a VIA Folios author, it is important that the following point be made. As a long time member of the National Book Critics Circle fostering ethics in reviewing, I must report— candidly—that I would be thrilled with Mr. Misurella's book even if I were not an author connected to VIA and VIA Folios.

Thank goodness—given the situation—that I was happily pleased with the fine quality of Misurella's writing. If I'd not been, I would have quietly and politely demurred to say anything about it in print, as my own reputation as a critic is at stake. Gladly, I quote Milan Kundera to back up my own opinion in this endeavor. "What a pleasure to read this little novel by Fred Misurella! In it I recognize so much that I admire: sensitivity, a heart open to ordinary people who are vulnerable and weak, weak before chance occurrences that give their own meaning and direction to events we think we master." It could not be said better. That is exactly Misurella's talent: to take the lives of ordinary people and portray them with sensitivity and quiet awe.

In *Short Time*, Fred Misurella portrays an Italian American soldier returning home after a bloody encounter as a troop leader in Viet Nam—one in which he is forced to become a murderer. The descriptions of the soldier on duty in the jungles of Viet Nam ring true to the reader. The existential predicament of the protagonist is subtly evident every step of the way. The deadly violence that ensues keeps us absorbed—even if we are not lovers of war stories.

Misurella's vision is not facile, but intricately woven of philosophic and poetic detail. At the same time that he is worldly in a sophisticated way, he manages a delicate balance of humility as the author of this often-told sort of tale. Yet there are original twists at every turn. His descriptive powers keep us focused on every lucid page of the involved story. There is clarity and steady pacing so that we want to read every word carefully and feel ever present in the evolution of the ultimately, sardonic tale.

Short Time is part of an unpublished book of stories entitled *Body Lessons*. One hopes that Mr. Misurella's entire collection will find an appropriate publisher, because his prose is so accessible and artful at the same time, much more so than much of the minimalist sensationalism, or Baroque experimentalism, touted as art in our time. Misurella is not an artsy writer who will turn away the every day reader; he is the sort of stylist who will make new readers and new fans for entertaining and enlightening literature—literature in which we recognize our selves, our sisters, and our brothers. There is not much that is experimental in technique in Misurella, yet there is an originality of tone. His characters are invested with everyday humanity and three-dimensional quality, in their search for meaning. The leading character finds the ironies of life as old world family values conflict with contemporary America's fast-paced and puzzling culture. The Italian American reader will light up with moments of identification.

Short Time is a most readable and worthy little book, and I highly recommend it to those who wish to explore some of the best qualities our writers have to offer our culture. The reading is painless, but the story ironic and full of sardonic and ordinary, as well as universal, truths. Fred Misurella, like Ben Morreale, is among the best of Italian American male writers of fiction, the sort that our American culture should pay attention to as the tellers of the real stories of Italian American life, rather than the Mafia sensationalists who have made fame and fortune from selling out their people to Hollywood fakery. His work is reminiscent of the young Mario Puzo who starved writing his best early works, like *The Fortunate Pilgrim,* prior to his notorious success in the only genre Hollywood has wanted from our men—that cheap, romanticized stereotype that continues to haunt us daily in the powerful and wholesale, visual media.

13. *Giovanna's 86 Circles: And Other Stories,* 1997 by Paola Corso

In her first collection of short fiction, *Giovanna's 86 Circles,* Paola Corso mixes naturalism with magic realism. She is ultimately a fabulist with a sense of psychological realism. Most of all, she's a good storyteller who holds your interest in the tradition of Italian fairytale makers. One can find elements of such tried-and-true tales throughout her book, probably because like most of us, she was raised on stories like *Cinderella, Snow White,* and *Pinocchio.*

Corso has a poet's eye for metaphorical language and her images are usually original and engrossing. Occasionally her desire to make similes and figures of speech runs away with her story. For example, in the story "Between the Sheets," she is describing the hot atmosphere of a hospital laundry room and writes: "I knew exactly when Bonita took a load out of the dryers. I felt the current of air, lava-like molecules escaping with the momentum of a heard of elementary school kids stampeding through the doors of the playground when the recess bell rang." This image, or implied metaphor, takes us out of the laundry room into a school-yard of noisy children and out of the atmosphere of the steamy laundry room. It is too involved and not organic to the scene she is creating. For a moment, our atten-tion is draw away from the sensual quality of the scene she sets, and we have to climb through a window out of the schoolyard, so to speak, to reenter the laundry where heat is escaping the dryers. But these sort of imaginative lapses might also be part of Corso's charm.

More often, her imagery keeps us in the story, and it is integral and organic to it, and establishes the atmosphere she is artfully creating. For example in the same story, she begins,

> The morning low was ninety-two degrees, but the temperature in the hospital laundry room started to rise as soon as steam escaped from the open lids of washers faster than smoke out of a chimneystack. The steam spread when the wet loads were carried over to the dryers, and soon the laundry was floating in the middle of a cloud passing through. (12)

Or, further on, she writes:

> The steam and heat combined sometimes took my breath away. I had to fight to get it back by inhaling as if I were diving underwater to the bottom of the deep end of a pool. I watched my waist expand and contract. I didn't like to breathe through my mouth in the laundry room because it made my throat so dry. I tried it once. It felt as if a cotton ball was stuck down there and I couldn't swallow it. No matter how much water I drank, the cotton ball came back. (13)

These are simple examples of how Corso's imagery is direct and innocently art-ful as well as part and parcel of the story, stimulating the reader's senses with word pictures that live in the mind's eye to create a voluptuous experience of atmosphere organic to the scene. It is her brand of richly descriptive prose full of sensual imagery that makes Corso a captivating writer. She simply needs to put a reign on an occasional Baroque image that takes us away and out of the scene, but her skill is palpable and engrosses us with clarity.

There are many corporeal moments in the collection: *Giovanna's 86 Circles* that make us live through the everyday experiences of her characters. Corso's stories are mostly set in working-class river towns like Pittsburg where she grew up. She has drawn on her Italian immigrant heritage to bring the folklorist's eye for wonder to a barren Rust Belt region of America. The book of ten stories lifts us out of the humdrum into a world of unpredictable and sometimes miraculous happenings symbolic of emotional experience. The everyday is given a touch of magic. These are not stories for skeptical readers but for those who wish to find psychological truths in symbolic wonders. It is for those who want to transcend the ordinary through the imagination.

The first story in the book is about a woman who donates her mother's clothes to a thrift shop only to return to find herself as her mother in her mother's coat before the dressing room mirror, magically transformed into a woman who can make good things happen from the ordinary. The story is symbolic of how empathy, or identity with another, helps us to understand their quirkiness and therefore to come to an emotional state of love and acceptance. Another example of many of Corso's descriptive powers occurs in this story as she describes the aura of the thrift shop the protagonist of "Yesterdays News" is visiting:

> The smell of cedar drifted through the air. Wrinkles on the garments seemed to disappear. Creases vanished. Clothes on racks rose up from their flattened state as if an invisible body were inside each one. Every top, bottom, overcoat, and undergarment floated on its hanger, defying gravity. Yet they all were evenly spaced, lined up like singers in a choir. (4)

There is plenty of irony, too, in Corso's tales. For example, there is a story about an innocent ten-year-old girl, who struggles with the realities of human sexuality as she observes her neighbor attempting with difficulty to become pregnant while, at the same time, her teenage sister finds pregnancy a state too easily come by.

The title story, *Giovanna's 86 Circles*, is typical of other tales in which drab reality is displaced by magical happenings. It is human emotion that transcends dull urban naturalism and gives life it's magic. The magical "green thumb" of Giovanna, a legendary neighborhood gardener, makes a young couple finding puppy-love in their first kiss to cause ghostly flowers to sprout wondrously from absent pots that have left rings of life, evidence of loving care, behind. It is what we love to do and whom we love that gives life it's meaning. The magical happening, as in a Chagall painting like "The Birthday," is a fabulous moment, but true to the *emotional life* of the lovers. Corso's fanciful devices suddenly grow surprisingly out of drab reality to make everyday life poetic. One imagines that Corso has learned to survive by making the colorless life of a Western Pennsylvania city grow richer through the courage of imagination as an elixir.

From grandmother to mother to daughter, friend to stranger, the women of *Giovanna's 86 Circles* redeem the garden-variety world with the power of poetic imagination. This is an appealing collection of short fiction written at a time when Corso's immigrant culture is fast assimilating and the filial values of the Old World are ever more vulnerable to American materialism in a world of crony capitalism and greed. The immigrant heritage from which Corso draws many of her characters is rapidly disappearing, and perhaps, that is why her stories are important as they preserve the dreams and struggles of that passing generation of laborers working to make a better life in the New World. Yet, the milieu these stories create is natural, real, and fantastical, familiar and magical, all at once. The collection affords an enjoyable and easy read, as well. At a time when books have heavy competition from other media, it's good to find one that heartily entertains as well as creates transcendence.

Corso demonstrates a level of literary accomplish to be proud of in an era when many writers want only to be experimental for experiment's sake. No wonder she is the recipient of the Sherwood Anderson Fiction Prize (2000) and was nominated for a Pushcart Press Editors' Book Award. A New York Foundation for the Arts poetry fellow and author of a book of poems *Death by Renaissance* published (Bottom Dog Press 2004)—as well as a two-time *first* runner-up for the Bordighera National Poetry Prize (2004 and 2005)—Corso has created a first collection of stories that shows talent for clear, yet imaginative, prose writing. This is old-fashioned storytelling at its best and newest.

14. Their Other Side: Six American Women & the Lure of Italy, 2006,
Essays by Helen Barolini

As a student, Helen Barolini, an Italian American whose *forte* is writing fine essays, spent years in Italy after World War II, married an Italian, and lived a good deal of her life there. These Italian years of her life have given us her best book of essays, yet. Well conceived and artfully written and researched, Barolini explores the wanderings of six American women who found their heart's desire for emotional freedom and expression in the land of sunlight and art. The women are (in order of appearance) Margaret Fuller, who longed most of her life to live in Italy and finally did, who met the love of her life there at nearly age forty and became involved in the *Risorgimento*; Emily Dickinson, who traveled there only in her imagination; Constance Woolson, who lived and died in Venice; Mabel Dodge Luhan, who was always in search of her personal south; Yankee Principessa, Marguerite Caetani; and Iris Origo, who was to the manor and manner born.

This reviewer found the chapters on Fuller and Dickinson most interesting, and the one on Fuller quite edifying and fascinating, as well as tragic. Fuller's only truly happy years were in Italy. She met her sad death at the peek of her powers, shipwrecked and drowned just off the Northeast coast upon her return to America with the manuscript she had written abroad lost in the ocean depths with her. One finds oneself at the end of the essay on Fuller, wishing with all one's heart that she had stayed in Italy continuing to send her dispatches back to *The Dial* and *The Tribune* for what both she and we lost upon her journey home.

Barolini makes us fully aware of the fact that for nineteenth century English and American intellectuals, Italy represented an emotional expressiveness and freedom from dogmatic ways. *Italia* was the place to go if one wanted to create and fulfill all passionate potential. This concept was what constituted Italy's mythic appeal prior to Hollywood's destruction of thoughts of all fine things Italian with its cruel over emphasis on the Mafia stereotype. In the nineteenth century prior to World War II and the Fascist fiasco of the fickle Mussolini, Italians were respected by intellectuals from all over the world for their artistic temperament, liberal expressiveness, their love of fine music, visual art and architecture, good food and fine wine, as well as their great struggle for freedom and independence from Medieval ideas of aristocracy and the "divine right of kings." The *Risorgimento* was seen as a noble revolution to be supported by all who believed in democracy and intellectual freedom.

The *Risorgimento* attracted Elizabeth Barrett Browning's involvement as well as Margaret Fuller's. The Brownings had fled to Italy earlier from England to find their freedom from Elizabeth Barrett's father and to pursue their poetry. Fuller met Elizabeth there, and they became friends. Both Fuller and Dickinson were great fans of Elizabeth Barrett Browning's poetry and *Aurora Leigh*, her novel in verse, which championed the lives of the likes of both Margaret Fuller and George Sand who were members of Browning's salon. *Aurora Leigh* was Emily Dickinson's favorite book, a novel written in verse that heralded women's freedom and emotional life.

Dickinson, like Fuller, longed for life in mythic Italy for it also represented to her the freedom to feel passion and ardor. Barolini quotes Dickinson's verse that speaks of a longing to escape Yankee propriety for a place of emotional truth.

> Our lives are Swiss—
> So Still—so Cool—
> Till some odd afternoon
> The Alps neglect their Curtains
> And we look farther on!
>
> Italy stands the other side!
> While like a guard between---
> The Solemn Alps—
> The siren Alps
> Forever intervene!

The Dickinson poem became emblematic for Helen Barolini of the pull of Italy and the theme of her latest book. She writes, as she did in her introduction to *The Dream Book: An Anthology of Writings by Italian American Women*, another of her finest essays:

> It is interesting how many English or American women turned from the Anglo tradition and toward the idea of Italy as a freeing of their human qualities and an enriching of life. The Brownings went off to live in Florence; Margaret Fuller, in her thirty-seventh year, arrived in Italy as the leading American woman writer and intellectual of her time and found love and motherhood there, writing, "Italy has been glorious to me." And Emily Dickinson, from Amherst, thought of Italy as the loosening of trammels, some absolute freeing of the spirit.

Barolini quotes Fuller, a highly cultured woman of many languages and worldly knowledge, about her longing to live in Italy:

> "Once I was almost all intellect; now I am almost all feeling. Nature vindicates her rights, and I feel all Italy glowing beneath the Saxon crust. This cannot last long: I

shall burn to ashes if all this smolders here much longer. I must die if I do not burst forth in heroism or genius."

Fuller would finally arrive in Rome at the age of thirty-seven, in 1847, to find love and fulfillment there.

As Barolini explains in her introduction to this engrossing and enjoyable book of essays, each a cameo of a fascinating woman,

> So much of the writing on Italy is not from long-lost or strayed children of the Motherland, the Italian American, but from those who have adopted Italy as a generous foster mother. In fact, until the mid-century, it was not Italian-Americans, but the Anglo-descended elite and intellectuals who went to Italy, who formed Dante Societies at home, who learned Italian and translated *The Divine Comedy*. It was the fashion to love Italy.... Still Italy was assumed to be a man's dream. "*Italia, O Italia*, Thou who hast/ the fatal gift of beauty!" declared Lord Byron on his pilgrimage. And Robert Browning's words are engraved in the Venetian palazzo where he died: "Open my heart and you will see/ Graved inside it, Italy."

With this splendidly interesting and well-written book of essays, Helen Barolini proves fully that Italy was not only a man's dream, but hers, and the dream of great or liberated women of America who found in Italy the emotional articulacy or artistic perspicuity that they had longed for.

For anyone who has felt the pull of Italy, this book explains it all. For Italian Americans, it is an eye-opener and helps to explain why an Italian cultured with the motherland's mode might not feel as at home in this Anglo-style world as in the mythic land of emotional and artistic eloquence.

15. *The Journey of the Italians in America*, 2008 by *Vincenza Scarpaci* with a Foreword by *Gary R. Mormino*

Vincenza Scarpaci's *Journey of the Italians in America* is a charming pictorial history book and a matter of ethnic pride for its author.

The book travels forward in time with each of its chapters. The second chapter titled "Spanning the Miles" describes the difficult passage of Italians to the United States. Between 1880 and 1924, nearly four million Italians arrived in the US. The Italian population was mostly situated in the industrial Northeast, but the growing numbers of immigrants began to spread out across the country in search of lucrative labor and affordable land. These immigrants transformed the communities with which they came into contact, as they brought their mores, customs, lifestyle, art, and cuisine with them.

The journey continues onward to describe in pictures the struggles of early immigrant life in The New Land. Scarpaci focuses on every manner of existence from religious customs to lifestyle, cuisine to assimilation and accomplishment. Her major focus is heritage. There are precise and insightful captions for the many photographs and illustrations that give the book its nostalgic, ethnic charm and make it a volume many of us might treasure as a pictorial documentation of our culture.

Through the use of over 400 photographs, drawn from both private and public collections, Scarpaci charts the journey of the Italians in America telling both intimate stories of family life and as well as enterprising commercial ventures that brought prosperity to some. She offers comprehensive reflections on past immigrant accomplishments as well as featuring Italian American celebrities of our time. One might wish she could pay even more attention to the authors of literary works than she does, but there is, perhaps, only so much one can cover in such a pictorial history. Some of the standard writers are celebrated, i.e., Pietro di Donato, Gay Talese, Helen Barolini, Ben Morreale, John Fante, Rita Ciresi, Robert Viscusi, Mario Puzo, Fred Gardaphe, and (full disclosure) yours truly. Yet, it would have been good to see more of the contemporary women authors like Josephine Gattuso-Hendin, Maria Mazziotti Gillan, Mary Ann Mannino, or Paola Corso, and more of the younger men, too, like Tony Ardizonne or Richard Vetere for just two examples. And, where are Emanuel Carnevali, our illustrious early immigrant poet, or Jospeh Tusiani, who has brought many Italian classics into English for the American audience, or our very popular, Lawrence Ferlinghetti of the influential City Lights Bookstore of San Francisco, or John Ciardi, who was so important in bringing literary art to the American media?

Still, Scarpaci, one must be sure to say, pays more attention to our writers than many other such pictorial histories of our culture have. One supposes there is just so much one can cover in 319 pages of a vast historical journey of more than a century of the Italian in America. The political sphere from Caro Tresca, through Mario Cuomo to Nancy Pelosi is well documented, as are other endeavors of culture, especially music, fashion, craftsmanship, sports, and movies, as well as social justice, where the Italians have excelled in America. Indeed, for the most part, this pictorial history is better executed than many others that have preceded it. The history it covers is more profoundly detailed and carefully captioned than other such picture portrayals.

Images cover the entire United States from Utah to Los Angeles to New York's Little Italy to New Orleans and across the ocean to the Old Country. Every photograph occasions a story, as for example the biography of Dr. Umberto Buffo, a pioneer who came to Oklahoma, then still Native American territory, to minister to Italian miners. There is the family in Massachusetts who work from their kitchen and interact with native-born American groups. The photographs when taken together afford a history of our Italian American culture, painting a full picture of our influence upon the culture of the United States. Scarpaci takes us through World War I and II, offering the experiences of Italian American families through those traumatic years. She celebrates the common men and women, alongside the notables, as well as heroes and heroines who were empathetic to their plight like well-known, New England poet, Edna St. Vincent Millay, who wrote her famous poem, "Justice Denied in Massachusetts," in support of Sacco and Vanzetti and marched with such other literary luminaries as Katherine Ann Porter and Upton Sinclair in the cause of the noted immigrant laborers. Millay is pictured holding up a sign that reads, "Free Them and Save Massachusetts American Honor! Jus-

tice Dies with Sacco and Vanzetti!" It is always heartening to remember that many
American intellectuals realized that Sacco and Vanzetti were treated unjustly because they were discriminated against as Italian immigrants.

A New York native, Vincenza Scarpaci graduated from Rutgers University in
1972 with a Ph.D. in history. She has taught United States and immigration history at various universities across the country and her expertise is obvious in this
book. She has been award by the Sons of Italy in recognition of her work documenting the Italians of Baltimore. She is now a resident of Eugene, Oregon, but
her love of New York is evident in her descriptions of New York's Little Italy—a
neighborhood now threatened with extinction by the encroachment of other ethnic
groups, particularly Asian. Scarpaci's photographs are a treasure to behold and
her book affords knowledge and nostalgia for all lovers of Italian American mores
and customs as well as those who wish to learn, visually and graphically, about the
influence of our group upon American culture.

by Daniela Gioseffi

The Love of Italy in Emily Dickinson's Poetry
Emotional Symbolism and Womanly Rebellion

Appeared in www.iitaly.com, 2012.

Most Emily Dickinson scholars would agree that the iconic American poet's emotional life can be better reconstructed from the content of her poems than from imaginative research by scholars or critics into the details, many unknown, of her biography. In the fervour of inquiry that changes according to the sensibilities of each scholar or literary critic, the core of Dickinson's poetic inspiration can be lost in the subtleties of complex prurient and turbid psychoanalysis.

Regardless of all interpretive biographies, some quite compelling, the essence of the iconic American poet's art remains timeless in its observations, wisdom, and emotional verity. It's interesting to note that her poetry contains a variety of verses in which Italy and its geography play an important symbolic role. As Judith Farr explains in *The Gardens of Emily Dickinson*, the poet, "who liked to think she saw 'New Englandly,' was, though Puritan in her disciplined upbringing, profoundly attracted to the foreign and especially to the semitropical or tropical climes that she read about in *Harper's* and *The Atlantic Monthly*—Santo Domingo, Brazil, Potosi, Zanzibar, Italy...."

Even if it were possible to demonstrate, with incontrovertible documentation, that the mythic solitude of the poet of Amherst hides an enigma conflicting with the ethics of her Puritanical Calvinist society, the discovery wouldn't alter the relevance of that solitude for the poet herself. Her years in a white dress, confining herself to her father's land, the relative seclusion in her room after the age of approximately thirty-three years, the ebullient activity of her poetic spirit, like a pearl forming in a seashell, still shines with the ineffable genius of her singing—beyond all of us frogs croaking in our ponds.

Emily Dickinson learned to look at the vicissitudes of life and its natural creatures and objects with an analytical eye, as she lived her deepening emotional life. Every detail of what goes unnoticed by many, in the din of passing days, stimulated her to discoveries, affording an emotional or intellectual response in verses often dashed off and habitually left unfinished or unedited. In her art, she seems to have re-evaluated her early education, challenging notions into lyrical transfigurations. Geography, history, astronomy, botany, ornithology, philosophy, and theology contained realizations that deepened her spiritual life based on the realities of science and nature. She is indeed one of the more scientifically orientated poets that America has produced. Many have noted the science and scientific terms peppering her texts, as well as her references to the Italian peninsula. We can surmise that she was quite aware of the geology and geography of Italy, and the studies of mountains and volcanoes in its landscape, as well as the inroads made there by Galileo, the Father of Science.

During the poet's lifetime, there were developments in science and technology, from advanced microscopes to improved telescopes, which afforded new revelations and ways of looking at nature and the world. Darwinian ideas were burgeoning, so that religion became, more than ever, in conflict with scientific discoveries, as it had been for the Father of Science, Galileo, in the Italy of old. Dinosaur fossils were discovered in the Amherst region and displayed at Amherst Seminary by Professor Hitchcock. Science courses were turning the seminary into a respected college of secular learning. New Englanders witnessed the Northern Lights, a phenomenon that augured Armageddon for some who were driven to take the route of "born again" Christianity in the Great Revival sweeping the poet's Pioneer Valley.

Others turned to Darwin and Emerson and began to feel that the natural world was the proper study of humanity, more than was scripture. Many New England Protestants embraced scientific phenomenon as miracles of nature and evidence of divine power. The conflict between conservative religion is nearly as alive today in our contemporary world as it was in the days of Galileo, Darwin, or Dickinson who wrote of the conflict in her own way. Science, as much as religion is evidenced in Dickinson's writings and its discoveries embedded in her poems, in both metaphoric symbolism and in aspects of structure and epistemology. The idea of Dickinson as scientist is not at all an unfounded one. We know from her eminent biographers that the sciences of botany, chemistry, and geology enthralled her. We shall see how the lure of Italy and its culture, as well as geology and geography, entered the imagery of the iconic American poet's mind and become a way of expressing emotional ideas and ideals.

Since she had a limited audience beyond friends and correspondents with whom to share scientific realizations in verse, her questioning mind found answers in emotional truth, stimulated by the Transcendentalist philosophers of her region. For contradictory or erroneous ideas or social premises, her genius was able to offer humane and original lyric intensity and elevated thought as well as questioning. Her compass was divination through words as musical notes beyond music itself, in images that live more fully than their symbols. Words and images associated with Italy, her "Blue Peninsula," are mentioned in several of her lyrics as symbolic of emotional truths, aspirations, and ideals.

This essay intends to present Dickinson's lyrics concerning Italy, or things related to it, as symbolic of her beliefs and aspirations. Detailed notions about Italy are not present in Dickinson's poems so much as emotional qualities associated with her "Blue Peninsula" and its volcanic and geographical structures, its volcanoes so symbolic of erupting emotions, flowing like lava down mountainous terrains.

As poet and scholar, Joseph Tusiani, wrote in his essay, titled "*L'italia nella poesia di Emily Dickinson*," that

.... at home in Amherst, and at the Amherst Academy or Mount Holyoke Seminary, in books of history, geology, and geography, the young poet learned of Italy as a valued European country of cultural and artistic expression, a peninsula whose northern neighbor was Switzerland with its more austere aspect of propriety— boarded by the Alps in the north and crossed by the Apennine Mountains, a land of two large volcanoes, Etna and Vesuvius, and the homeland of Dante, Columbus, Galileo, and various accomplished painters of renown.

Also, members of the intelligentsia of Dickinson's New England social circle had begun to travel to and be educated in Europe. With the invention of the steamship and ocean liner, the mid-century saw more and more ocean travel, and the rural aristocrats of Dickinson's Pioneer Valley began to journey abroad and be educated in fine European universities, bringing home tales of foreign lands and customs that were inviting to those repressed by the more extreme dogma of Puritanical Calvinism.

Professor William Smith Clark of Amherst College was educated in Europe and travelled in Italy on more than one occasion, as did other professors of Amherst Seminary, which was next door to Dickinson's homestead, and founded by her grandfather. According to Maki and Jones, William Smith Clark, while attaining his European doctoral degree, travelled the Continent, and wrote home to Amherst to Dickinson's neighbors, their cousins in common, the Sweetsers. At table with her Sweetser cousins, Dickinson might well have heard of Clark's travels and firsthand observations of Italy's artistic attributes, natural wonders, social mores, and architectural artifacts.

It's also interesting that Clark's affectionate style of letter writing was similar in tone to Dickinson's, where as her father's and brother's tones in correspondence were more reserved and unemotional—adding to the possibility that his Italian travels and freer emotional nature were an influence upon the poet. This a point expounded upon by Ruth Owen Jones, mentioned earlier, in her essay, which is titled: "Neighbor—and friend—and Bridegroom—," after a line in a Dickinson poem.

As Farr, Jones, Sewell, Habegger, Wolff, and other Dickinson biographers have explained that prior to her years of seclusion, Dickinson might have heard descriptions of Italy in the salons, next door in the Evergreens, held by her sister-in-law and friend of many years, Susan Gilbert Dickinson. The Evergreens, erected in Italianate style, as was popular among cultured Americans of the day, was the relatively luxurious house Emily's father had built a stone's throw from hers for her bother, Austin Dickinson, and his bride, Susan, upon their marriage. Both Susan and Austin were educated and refined and commanded some knowledge of European culture and art. Susan Dickinson held salons in the parlor of the Evergreens that welcomed well read and travelled cosmopolitan guests.

Austin owned many art books containing paintings of European masters. Various intellectuals—like Samuel Bowles of Springfield, and professors at the seminary, as mentioned earlier, Dr. William Smith Clark most eminently—travelled to Europe and, therefore, Italy, recounting their journeys through Italy at salons held in the Evergreens. Italy was a land considered by many mid-nineteenth-century minds to be the ideal place to escape to for a life of unbridled artistic development and emotional freedom. No doubt, stories of other writers' travels met Dickinson's eyes in the magazines she frequently read, *The Atlantic Monthly, Harpers,* and later, *Scribner's,* where she was acquainted with such esteemed and widely cultured editors as Thomas Wentworth Higginson and Joshua Holland, whose wife, Elizabeth, was one of Dickinson's favorite correspondents.

George Sand, Margaret Fuller, as well as the Brownings, among others, were known to have travelled to live in Italy to unleash their creative powers and escape the constraints of Victorian-style culture, felt to be emotionally constricting and full of the sort of propriety still alive in the Puritan Calvinist society of Amherst in Dickinson's day. Victorian demeanour was still the social norm for rural New England aristocracy.

Helen Barolini explains the attraction to Italy as a common mid-nineteenth-century phenomenon in her charming and astute book of essays, *Their Other Side: Six American Women and the Lure of Italy.* Barolini describes the travels of Margaret Fuller, Constance Woolson, Mabel Dodge Luhan, Marguerite Caetani, and Iris Origo, as well as Emily Dickinson's desire to travel in Italy, though she never did. After the Civil War, when New Englanders like Harriet Beecher Stowe and the painter Martin Johnson Heade began to travel and live in Florida, they called that oblong peninsula their *Italy* for the sunshine, blue skies, and flora and fauna there discovered to their delight. This phenomenon is described by edifying art and the literary critic of Mount Holyoke, Christopher Benfey, in his captivating book about the American intelligentsia of the nineteenth-century, *A Summer of Hummingbirds; Love, Art, and Scandal in the Intersecting Worlds of Emily Dickinson, Mark Twain, Harriet Beecher Stowe, & Martin Johnson Heade.*

In any case, ideas associated with Italy surely crossed Dickinson's mind because of the example of a life spent there in pursuit of sublime poetry by the woman poet she most admired: the English author, Elizabeth Barrett Browning, who had eloped to Italy with her husband, Robert. Florence, a seat of the Renaissance, held its allure for many ex-patriots of the day, Robert Browning among them.

The parallel study of Dickinson's letters and poems in chronological order with R.W. Franklin's *Collected Poems of Emily Dickinson,* wherein he analyzed her holographic texts with reference to changes in her calligraphy throughout her writing life, offers some sense of the poet's emotional development. Intimate confidences in her letters are often connected to poetic exaltations or feelings of depressions in her poetry. We can determine, for obvious reasons, that verses composed for the death of Elizabeth Barrett Browning were written in or about the year 1861 when Barrett Browning perished in her home in Florence. Consequently, Italy is mentioned in the following poem as the desirable and best resting place for Dickinson's beloved poet:

Her – last poems –
Poets ended –
Silver – perished – with her Tongue –
Not unto Record – bubbled Other –

Flute – or Woman –so divine –

Not unto it's Summer Morning—
Robin – uttered half the Tune
Gushed too full for the adoring –
From the Anglo – Florentine –

Late – the Praise – 'Tis dull – Conferring
On the Head too High – to Crown -
Diadem – or Ducal showing -
Be it's Grave – sufficient Sign –

Nought – that We – No Poet's Kinsman –
Suffocate – with easy Woo –
What – and if Ourself a Bridegroom –
Put Her down – in Italy?

In this sorrowful elegy in which an initial exaltation blends with a final tenderness, it's not yet possible to find the introspective, mystic, and tragic intensity of the poet, because the phase of "the White Election" has not yet begun. "Mine - by the Right of the White Election!" is a Dickinson poem that seems to have been written at the peak of an inner torment that none of her biographers has been able to fully explain—except perhaps, Jones who proposes William Smith Clark was Dickinson's "Master" figure. According to Jones, Colonel Clark was thought killed in the Civil War, at around about the time that the poet wrote, "Mine - by the Right of the White Election!..." Jones explains that the enigmatic poem could well be Dickinson's emotional claim of her right, as his true lover, to Colonel Clark's body for burial memorial, should his body be found and returned to Amherst—a plausible interpretation of the poem.

Prior to that period of intense emotion, following what biographers agree was some sort of trauma, Dickinson, we know, read Elizabeth Barrett Browning's works. More than any other major Victorian poet of Dickinson's day—Elizabeth Barrett Browning, during her ex-patriot days in Italy, explicitly confronted political issues concerning *women*—issues that would have interested Dickinson and her sister-in-law, Sue. Like many other writers of her time, Barrett Browning became a disciple of Shelley and other Romantics whose mode was visionary and committed to the politics of social justice in domestic and international affairs. Romantics like Byron and Shelley went to Italy, during the *Risorgiomento,* to express emotional and humanitarian ideals during the fight for democracy there.

Barrett Browning's "The Cry of the Children" (1843) is an example of such work prior to her eloping with Robert Browning to Italy, where she took up the cause of Italian democracy and nationalism, a subject which also compelled Margaret Fuller of New England and other Transcendentalist authors, as a struggle for democratic ideals against outmoded aristocracies. Barrett Browning's *Casa Guidi Windows* (1851) and *Poems before Congress* (1861) are both thematic of the Italian *Risorgimento,* as was *Mother and Poet*, subtitled *Turin, after News from Gaeta*, is a lyric spoken by the Italian poet and patriot, Laura Savio, upon learning that both her sons had died in the cause of Italian liberty. It constitutes the British poet's interest in the problem of women's constraints and the role of the female poet, as well as the cost and pain of the struggle for independence. Barrett Browning also wrote two poems (1844) in praise of George Sand and other tributes to women authors. Such concerns were at the center of her masterpiece, a novel in poetry, *Aurora Leigh* (1857), known to be a favorite of Dickinson's according to her various biographers.

Aurora Leigh, the story of a young poet who held back by Victorian constraints and the plight of women's lack of human rights—lives in Victorian England, with a strict, Puritanical aunt, somewhat like Dickinson's father, Edward, after the deaths of her *Italian* mother and British father. The poem employs contemporary settings to which Dickinson responded because the social issues were the same as her own in terms of gender and "The Woman Question" of her day. It dramatizes modern woman's need for ancestral role models who nurture literary females. It should be noted that, the orphaned Aurora Leigh chooses her Italian mother's sensibilities over her English father's temperament, adding to the concept we shall see taken up by Dickinson that Italian temperament allows more freedom of emotional expression.

In writing of the development of a woman poet, Aurora Leigh, Barrett Browning shows that women inhibit themselves by internalizing patriarchal concepts of themselves. Only when both woman and man can break free from the conceptual structures that oppress them, can they fully become partners in love. This theme is central to *Aurora Leigh*. In offering Dickinson a heroine who achieved poetic and personal liberty, Barrett Browning created a female literary tradition by alluding to her own predecessors, drawing from elements of Charlotte Brontë's *Jane Eyre*, another favorite book of Dickinson, that portrays a self-actualized heroine.

Also, *Aurora Leigh* employs gynocentric, as opposed to an androcentric, imagery, and substitutes female, rather than male, archetypes from the Old Testament. These analogies and images used by Barrett Browning, living amidst and set free by Florentine culture and the democratic ideals of the *Risorgimento* associated with American Democracy, were an important influence upon Dickinson, causing her to see Italy as elemental to artistic expression and emotional freedom where a woman could escape the constraints of Victorian cultural models.

It was probably around 1865, the year of Abraham Lincoln's assassination and after the end of the Civil War, that Dickinson began to wear her white housedress, most permanently, and it's after that year that she wrote of her decision to make her father's lands the limit of her travels. (Incidentally, it's the year that Dickinson scholar, Ruth Owen Jones, poses that Clark and Dickinson broke off their affair.) It's thought that Dickinson always, thereafter, wore her white dress until her last day, May 15th 1886—but why really? Could the wearing of that white dress also have been influenced, among other factors, by her reading of the Italian classic, *La Divina Commedia?*

Some have decided the wearing of white was to see herself as or feel like a bride or a pure virgin waiting for her bridegroom, or maybe even to bury under her "snow," as she called her poetry (perhaps influenced by Higginson's 1858 essay, "Snow," in the *Atlantic Monthly*)— the secret of her grieving heart? More recently scholars like myself, and others, have written of various possible explanations for the wearing of her white-pique housedress, not really a gown for social outings.

For one thing, she loved to garden and was often the family baker. Heavy brocades, satins, and taffetas of the day would not suit such activities. Therefore, many women wore white, washable housedresses at home, and such was the custom. Satins and brocades would not do for rambles through the woods in search of wild flowers with her big, black New Foundland dog, Carlo, named after the dog in *Jane Eyre*.

Carlo was a constant beloved and trusted companion with whom Dickinson is known to have wandered the fields and woods around her home until Carlo's death in 1866, another logical reason for her confining herself to her father's lands. According to Daniel Lombardo's "Poetry in the Air, Rabid Dogs and Typhoid in the Street," abandoned, feral, and rabid dogs wandered the streets of Amherst in Dickinson's day, and perhaps, she, devoid of her protective canine companion, Carlo, no longer felt safe on rambles through meadow and town. Since the Elizabethan color of mourning was white, and Dickinson was a great reader of Shakespeare, was she also wearing white to mourn the loss of her most faithful companion, Carlo in 1866?

Or, was Dickinson, like Bronson Alcott, wearing *Transcendentalist* white to boycott the dye-factories where workers were fainting into boiling vats of color, succumbing to death and illness because of long and inhumane hours of arduous labor without relief? Also, labor strikes were beginning in laundries where collars were washed and starched in hot vats by fainting women for upper class gentlemen, just as fabric-dye factory laborers were suffering inhumane working conditions. Dickinson read the newspapers, and perhaps, she quietly joined the strikers of labor movements as did orator, Bronson Alcott who was Ralph Waldo Emerson's and Margaret Fuller's, inspiring associate and a leader of Transcendentalist ideals. We know Dickinson wrote poetry empathizing with the working classes, and that she had a close relationship with Irish workers who labored on her father's estate: particularly Tom Kelly, handyman, and Maggie Maher, day servant. Yet, there are other possible reasons, and, perhaps, many combinations of reasons why she wore her mythic white dress.

As Judith Farr has pointed out in *The Passion of Emily Dickinson,* the Pre-Raphaelite paintings so popular in the poet's day, and no doubt in the European art books of Romantic paintings in her brother's, Austin's, library next door in the Italianate Evergreens, which we know she frequented prior to the last fifteen years of her life, may also have inspired her wearing of white. Romantic paintings of the day often contained huge, voluptuous, and mysteriously lit landscapes inhabited by one tiny white-clad figure, a nun, an angel, Christ, a wood nymph of some Romantic sort, against vastly impressive vistas of a gorgeous natural world so venerated during the American Enlightenment of New England. Higginson, mentioned prior, in his 1891 *Atlantic Monthly* essay, "Emily Dickinson," quotes as emblematic of her wearing of white, a rather Italian-Catholic poem of Dickinson's, which he titles, "The Saint's Rest."

> Of tribulation, these are they
>   Denoted by the white;
> The spangled gowns, a lesser rank
>   Of victory designate.

> All these did conquer; but the ones
>   Who overcome most times,
> Wear nothing commoner than snow,
>   No ornament but palms.

Finally, perhaps, there's yet a further reason for the poet's wearing of white, one inspired by an Italian poet. A well known lyric of Dickinson reminds us how she travelled in books to far off lands: "There is no frigate like a book/ to take us lands away...." A book is a "journey" that everyone can take with no oppression of cost or repression of spirit. Another lyric where Italy as a *land away* is evoked by verses about an antique book read with pleasure contains ghosts of many centuries ago. The book is not inanimate or motionless, but mutates into a friend who confides in us precious secrets of remote times. Herein, are cultural and literary immortals like Sophocles, Sappho, and Dante's Beatrice, a pure-hearted girl in a *white* gown.

> A precious, mouldering pleasure - 'tis -
> To meet an Antique Book,
> In just the Dress his Century wore;
> A privilege - I think -
> His venerable hand to take -
> And warming in our own -
> A passage back - or two - to make -
> To Times when he - was young -
> His quaint opinions - to inspect -
> His thought to ascertain
> On Themes concern our mutual mind -
> The Literature of Man -
> What interested Scholars - most -
> What Competitions ran -
> When Plato - was a Certainty -
> And Sophocles - a Man -
> When Sappho - was a living Girl,
> And Beatrice wore
> The Gown that Dante - deified.
> Facts Centuries before,
> He traverses - familiar -
> As One should come to Town
> And tell you all your Dreams - were true -
> He lived - where Dreams were born.
> His presence is enchantment -
> You beg him not to go -
> Old Volumes shake their Vellum Heads

And tantalize - just so -

Was the white dress that Dante made celestial perhaps adopted by Emily Dickinson—and wasn't it for Dante?—a sweet mirage symbolizing the unattainable love of his blessed and pure Beatrice? Could Emily's white dress symbolize, as for Dante, an unattainable love as written of in her three "Master Letters?"

In one of the three famous and mysterious "Master Letters," Dickinson wrote:

"Vesuvius don't talk – Etna - don't – [Thy] one of them – a syllable – A thousand years ago, and Pompeii heard it, and hid forever – She could look the world in the face, afterward – I suppose – "Tell you of the want" – you know what a leech is, don't you – [remember that] Daisy's arm is small – and you have felt the horizon hav'nt you – and did the sea – never come so close as to make you dance?

Love, when left unattended or in silence, can explode forth and be felt by the soul. Isn't the volcano Dickinson's symbol for the rage of repressed passion that kept under pressure, like lava, explodes from burning depths? Her Master's lack of response causes her to write of suppressed love and desire as Dante did. There is more about volcanic images to which we shall later return.

The land of Dante, of the Apennines and Alps, offers geographic details that the poet transforms into lyric visions of happiness and of unconditional surrender to an inscrutable fate. To sight the land of Italy from the sea, or to imagine seeing it, is not so difficult as reaching that "Blue Peninsula." From a far off vantage point, it is more delirium than shore, more ideal than reality. The poet explains, in a poem that begins, "It might be lonelier / without the Loneliness – I'm so accustomed to my Fate -" that not everyone is able to survive the ecstasy of finding happiness and freedom. The last verse of the poem states:

.... It might be easier
To fail - with Land in Sight -
Than gain - my Blue Peninsula -
To perish—of Delight -

This quatrain is typical of Dickinson's laconic lyrics, but is that "Blue Peninsula," dreamt of in vain by the poet from Amherst, really Italy? All doubt fades away, as Joseph Tusiani explains, if one thinks of those admirable verses in which Italy, compared to the immovable solemnity of Switzerland, is felt to be the ultimate dream of happiness, emotional freedom, and released creative impulse, the consequence of escape from an implacable destiny:

Our lives are Swiss -
So still - so Cool -
Till some odd afternoon
The Alps neglect their Curtains
And we look farther on!

Italy stands the other side!

While like a guard between -
The solemn Alps -
The siren Alps
Forever intervene!

Dickinson saw Italy as a horizon free of constraints, a place of longed for passion fulfilled. Though confined to her provincial life in Amherst's Puritanical and austere society ruled over by her Calvinist father, and though she's never sailed the sea, she can imagine the waves and their rush. Though she's never visited snowy mountain peaks, she glimpsed the vastness of a freer life beyond their curtains. After all, it was the style in her Victorian day for Americans to love Italy. As Barolini explains, Henry Adams had written dispatches of his travels in Italy for the *Boston Courier*, and in his autobiography, he described his sister, Louisa,: "like all good Americans and English, [Louisa] was hotly Italian." Until the mid nineteenth-century, as Barolini, pointed out in her introduction to *Their Other Side; Six American Women and the Lure of Italy,* it was the Anglo descended elite of American intellectuals who travelled to Italy, who learned Italian and translated Dante's *La divina commedia* and formed Dante Societies.

Yet, until Margaret Fuller and other American women travelled there, life in Italy was a male's idealistic aspiration. Lord Byron in his romantic pilgrimage wrote: "*Italia!* O *Italia!* Thou who hast / the fatal gift of beauty." And British poet Robert Browning's words are engraved in stone in the Venetian palazzo where he succumbed to death: "Open my heart, and you will see / Graved inside of it, Italy."

Certainly, Emily Dickinson would have heard of the French intellectual feminist, Germaine de Stael, and her novel, *Corinne, ou l'Italie,* a book that fixed Italy in the Cosmopolitan mind as the land where the imaginative woman "of genius" could self-actualize her gifts. George Eliot, so admired by Dickinson, as is understood by her biographers, makes various references in *The Mill and the Floss,* to Corinne. Also, as Barolini explains: Elizabeth Barrett Browning, so admired by Dickinson, writes of "My Italy of Women" having read with admiration *Corinne, ou l'Italie* more than once.

Margaret Fuller (born in Cambridge, a leader of the New England Transcendentalists, friend of Emerson and Thoreau) felt she had finally come into her creative stride upon her arrival in Italy during the *Risorgimento.* Once there, she met and married the impoverished, Italian revolutionary, Giovanni Angelo Ossoli, a marquis who had been disinherited by his family because of his support for Mazzini, a champion of the movement.

Margaret Fuller, as the first important woman journalist of America, sent dispatches to *The New York Tribune* and *The Dial* about the Italian *Risorgimento.* These were likely read by Dickinson in her sister-in-law Susan's library in the Evergreens next door. As is known by Dickinson biographers, Susan Dickinson subscribed to many magazines of the day, to say nothing of the fact that Fuller, before going to Italy, had published the first important and notorious feminist tract read in America, *Woman in the Nineteenth Century.* Sue's library might well have had a copy of the book, or Emily might have heard about it from her Norcross

Cousins of Cambridgeport who later in life were members of Emerson's literary salon.

Fuller's volume described the abominable lack of human rights granted to women of Dickinson's day. They were unable to own any property, even that left to them by their fathers automatically became their husband's. Women died often in childbirth and were worn out by a lack of legal birth control. They had no lawful ability to vote or earn a living wage, or to be free from abuse, either mental or physical, by the men in their families. They had no right to an education or the ability to determine their own destiny. They were literally *chattel* owned by men of their families. As Barolini writes:

> It is interesting how many English or American women turned from the Anglo tradition and toward the idea of Italy as a freeing of their human qualities and as an enriching of life. The Brownings went off to live in Florence; Margaret Fuller, in her thirty-seventh year, arrived in Italy as the leading American woman writer and intellectual of her time and found love and motherhood there, writing, "Italy has been glorius to me." And Emily Dickinson thought of Italy as the loosening of trammels, some absolute freeing of the spirit.

The Alps and Apennines of Italy inspired other lyrics of Dickinson. Their high peaks covered in immaculate snow held inviolate secrets. As mentioned earlier, Dickinson referred to her poetry as her "snow," pure truth falling from her spirit. Immortal and unreachable mountain peaks, like the Alps, are topped with snow and are mysterious because they are ancient and unattainable. Here were the Alps against which the questioning dream of Dickinson struggled for answers or response. Perhaps, the poet sees herself as a Daisy at the foot of a high and mighty, worldly and unattainable "Master" when she writes:

> In lands I never saw - they say
> Immortal Alps look down -
> Whose bonnets touch the firmament -
> Whose sandals touch the town;
>
> Meek at whose everlasting feet
> A myriad Daisy play -
> Which, sir, are you, and which am I -
> Upon an August day?

In the following verses of five parallel lines, she wrote another love poem to a divine being, or earthly and unattainable lover, using Alpine Heights as a lofty spiritual devotion that needs something as pure as poetry, "services of Snow," to attain it:

> I cannot be ashamed
> Because I cannot see
> The love you offer —
> Magnitude

Reverses Modesty
And I cannot be proud
Because a Height so high
Involves Alpine
Requirements
And services of Snow.

The Apennines suggested, a tender, fragile levity of joy after tears, as the Italian poet, Carducci, saw them in his *Rime Nuove*:

… But from afar
Your hillocks with their vanishing mists
And the green plain land smiling in the morning showers
Speak only of peace to my heart.

Dickinson, unlike Carducci, did not stop along the path of mere description, but rather, created a symbolic, elevated to a philosophical universality. The Appenines seemed to symbolize worldly discovery or realization:

The thought beneath so slight a film -
Is more distinctly seen -
As laces just reveal the surge -
Or Mists - the Apennine -

Within a conundrum, an idea becomes clearer when the misty film is seen through to a higher thought—a discovery, a release of the mind into a clearer rational.

All that mattered yesterday becomes trivial in the light of a new morning. The highest mountain peaks contain tracks one can travel through to larger horizons, as feelings and concerns of yesterday are compared with greater realizations or understandings to come:

We see - Comparatively -
The Thing so towering high
We could not grasp it's segment
Unaided - Yesterday -

This Morning's finer Verdict -
Makes scarcely worth the toil -
A furrow - Our Cordillera -
Our Apennine - a knoll -

Perhaps 'tis kindly - done us -
The Anguish - and the loss -
The wrenching - for His Firmament
The Thing belonged to us -

To spare these Striding Spirits
Some Morning of Chagrin -
The waking in a Gnat's – embrace -

Our Giants - further on -

"Our" Cordilleras, "our" Apennines, our high and spiritual strivings, might bring us to a place wherein we are small and finite, and yet, those who contemplate the world in a worldly spirit are citizens of the infinite further on.

Besides the Alps and the Apennines, it was Italy's volcanoes that capture Dickinson's imagination. But, her Vesuvius was inside herself, it seems. It was fashionable for gentlemen and ladies of the nineteenth-century to visit Vesuvius and climb her promontory. The exploration of volcanoes was in vogue. "Sir William Hamilton's treatises on Vesuvius gave rise to popular excursions," explains Barolini. People from around the globe were travelling to climb mountains like Vesuvius, and the excavations of the classical sites of Pompeii and Herculaneum were of the period, too. Goethe had come to explore, as had Mme. de Stael who staged a dramatic scene in *Corrine, ou l'Italie* on the slopes of Vesuvius. Corinne's lover, Lord Nelvil, explained why his father disapproved of his courtship of her by saying that as a woman she would take any husband away from England because, "only Italy would suit her" passionate and liberated nature.

Dickinson found her Vesuvius at Home, in Amherst where she both felt imprisoned, and also was inclined to stay, living her life in the emotional depths and passion of a poet:

Volcanoes be in Sicily
And South America
I judge from my Geography—
Volcanoes nearer here
A Lava step at any time
Am I inclined to climb—
A Crater I may contemplate
Vesuvius at Home.

There are other possible interpretations of the emotional meanings in the Italian geographical symbols used by Dickinson. Perhaps, her "Vesuvius at Home" was Squire Edward, her father, who is known to have had a fierce temper at times, in a fit, "beating his horse because he didn't look humble enough" according to Lavinia, Dickinson's sister. Or, the poet's own life at home was a volcano of emotions and passions held in, but released in her poetry? The poem containing the line "a Lava step at any time" is one of resigned determination, a somber feeling that blossoms into a corolla of light. The verse lingers between meditation and vision.

The only quatrain in which Mount Etna was mentioned offers symbolic imagery of how, "still waters run deep," and passions demonstrated loudly, can be better understood than those that seethe beneath the surface. Dickinson again used an Italian symbol to make her emotional point that "Security is loud...." Etna, also called *Muncibeddu* (beautiful mountain) in Sicilian, was known to be the largest active volcano in the world, and Sicilians were thought to be of volatile nature, even as the Bay of Naples, of the Kingdom of Two Sicily's, was thought to be a peaceful refuge in its sublime beauty.

> When Etna basks and purrs
> Naples is more afraid
> Than when she shows her Garnet Tooth -
> Security is loud -

As Judith Farr, in *The Passion of Emily Dickinson*, points out: Susan, the poet's sister-in-law, also explained by biographers to be of a volatile nature, though enthralling, was often associated in the poet's mind with volcanoes, and vibrant, torrid emotions. Though we cannot go into that complex relationship here, Farr and other biographers have explored it fully.

Joseph Tusiani, familiar with modern Italian poets, finds much of Emily Dickinson's poetry to have a *hermetic* nature, inviolable, shifty; but intimate and modest, made of attractive reticence, of internal echoes that seem to prove themselves eternal. Her life at home is a volcano of emotions and passions held in, but released in her poetry where emotional truth is revealed and levels all with lips that never lie, lips like an avid poet's lips speaking emotional truth.

> A still - Volcano - Life -
> That flickered in the night -
> When it was dark enough to do
> Without erasing sight -
>
> A quiet - Earthquake Style -
> Too subtle to suspect
> By natures this side Naples -
> The North cannot detect
>
> The solemn - Torrid - Symbol -
> The lips that never lie -
> Whose hissing Corals part - and shut -
> And Cities - ooze away -

Dickinson's irony is subtle, but powerful. Though, a gun is doing the talking; the image of life is transparent in the initial noun and gives a sad tone to the verses: an oscillation between irony and tears from the first until the last verse, a suspension between drama and tragedy. Again, Vesuvius is used to signify the pleasure of emotional release or ecstasy erupting. The final powerful aphorism dissolves into tragedy, the grief of losing a person profoundly loved before one can die oneself: "For I have but the power to kill, / Without - the power to die -."

When Emily Dickinson withdrew from the world of her "encounters with fate" in the relative solitude of her paternal house, Italy had already gone from the melancholy of Piedmont to the glory of Rome. Austria was still, in the mind of Italians, a symbol of oppression, a trap. The poet was interested in the political destiny of her "Blue Peninsula," as stated in a short lyric, whose last verse is not easy for the American mind to understand, but is very clear to the Italian one of her time.

> The wind drew off
> Like hungry dogs
> Defeated of a bone
> Through fissures in
> Volcanic cloud
> The yellow lightening shone –
> The Trees held up
> Their mangle limbs
> Like Animals in pain
> When Nature falls upon herself
> Beware an Austrian

Here, the history of Italy was analogous to the history of the world, and the individual: Austrian represents not the subtle enemy of the independence of a nation, but is symbolic of the eternal, omnipresent danger of every hoping and struggling soul.

Patricia Thompson Rizzo wrote a review, titled "Emily Dickinson and the 'Blue Peninsula:' Dickinson's Reception in Italy," regarding the publication by Marisa Bulgheroni of *Emily Dickinson: tutte le poesie*:

> It must be said from the outset that the volume represents the culmination of the growing interest that Italy, more than any other European country, has shown in the Amherst poet. Because of the impact that it will no doubt have for the next few decades of Dickinson studies in this country, the handsome Mondadori volume edited by Italy's foremost Dickinson scholar deserves to be both praised and closely scrutinized. As a preliminary note informs us, there are 1174 translations by Silvio Raffo, 392 by Margherita Guidacci, 185 by Massimo Bacigalupo and 27 by Nadia Campana.

Perhaps, the above Dickinson poem, "The wind drew off..." endears her to the hearts of Italian poets, along with her desire to travel in their land to release her pent up emotions from their Calvinist prison in other verses. As part of the American Enlightenment of New England led by Alcott, Emerson, and Fuller, Dickinson longed for the land where enlightenment first blossomed out of the Dark Ages into the Venetian and Florentine Renaissance so admired by Romantic poets of the nineteenth century.

Sometimes it's an Italian name that excites Emily's fantasy. The Etruria of antique Italy, which inspires us with treatises of erudition, also inspired Dickinson with a magic adjective, powerful and unalterable. "Etruscan" is equivalent to "mysterious," or "ineffable," and it's not applied to a terrestrial civilization but to the celestial and indefinable life of heavenly bodies. There's a boldness in living life *now* to the fullest that Dickinson turns into an image of awe and a song of transfiguration.

> The Moon upon her fluent Route

Defiant of a Road
The Star's Etruscan Argument
Substantiate a God -
How archly spared the Heaven " to come" -
If such prospective be -
By superseding Destiny
And dwelling there Today -

The same adjective is used in another poem with a seductive meaning. Here 'Etruscan,' referring to early Italian civilization so idealized by D.H. Lawrence and other authors to come after Dickinson, means "admirable," "irresistible," "definitive":

Unto like Story-Trouble has enticed me -
How Kinsmen fell -
Brothers and Sister - who preferred the Glory -
And their young will
Bent to the Scaffold, or in Dungeons – chanted -
Till God's full time -
When they let go the ignominy – smiling -
And Shame went still –

Unto guessed Crests, my moaning fancy, leads me,
Worn fair
By Heads rejected - in the lower country -
Of honors there -
Such spirit makes her perpetual mention,
That I - grown bold -
Step martial - at my Crucifixion -
As Trumpets – rolled –

Feet, small as mine - have marched in Revolution
Firm to the Drum -
Hands - not so stout - hoisted them - in witness -
When Speech went numb -
Let me not shame their sublime deportments -
Drilled bright -
Beckoning-Etruscan invitation -
Toward Light -

Did Emily Dickinson know the Italian language? There are no documents to prove it, but knowing Latin and Greek, and people who travelled in Italy, she may have had a measure of exposure to it, and likely found some in her reading. She could taste its flavor from a study of Latin. In the verses containing "the gown that Dante made celestial'"—the name "Beatrice" is seemingly used with *four* syllables [Bee-ah-TREE-che] and not three as in English—that is if one pays attention to the rhythm of the original seven-syllables. This might mean that Dickinson pronounced Beatrice in the Italian way rather than in the English manner [BEE-ah-tres.] In two other poems, there's a show of Italian words. The word *"Signor"* is used in one to mean divine being or lover:

The moon is distant from the Sea –
And yet, with Amber Hands –
She leads Him – docile as a Boy –
Along appointed Sands –

He never misses a Degree –
Obedient to Her eye –
He comes just so far – toward the Town –
Just so far – goes away –

O Signor, Thine, the Amber Hand –
And mine – the distant Sea –
Obedient to the least command
Thine eye impose on me -

The Italian word, *Madonna* is used in another to signify sacred light, like a taper burning in a darkened cathedral shrine:

Only a Shrine, but Mine -
I made the Taper shine -
Madonna dim, to whom all Feet may come,
Regard a Nun -

Thou knowest every Wo –
Needless to tell thee there - so -
But can'st thou do
The Grace next to it - heal?
That looks a harder skill to us -
Still – just as easy, if it be thy Will
To thee - Grant Me -
Thou knowest, through, so Why tell thee?

The description of the stunning beauty in a sunset scene, in the following poem, demonstrates an awareness of Italian art. The choice of words is so precise as to make us see the colors as in a painting.

How the old Mountains drip with Sunset
How the Hemlocks burn –
How the Dun Brake is draped in Cinder
By the Wizard Sun –

How the old Steeple hand the Scarlet
Till the Ball is full –
Have I the lip of the Flamingo
That I dare to tell?

Then, how the Fire ebbs like Billows –

Touching all the Grass
With a departing – Sapphire – feature –
As a Duchess passed –
How a small Dusk crawls on the Village
Till the Houses blot
And the old Flambeau, no men carry
Glimmer on the Street –

How it is Night – Nest and Kennel –
And where was the Wood –
Just a Dome of Abyss is Bowing
Into Solitude –

These are the Visions flitted Guido –
Titian – never told –
Domenichino dropped his pencil –
Paralyzed, with Gold -

Another poem for its delicate tone suggest Italy with limpid images and Venetian vistas. It's one of the Dickinson's most skillful, and, we know from her biographers, one of her most edited and carefully crafted early works:

Safe in their Alabaster Chambers –
Untouched by Morning –
And untouched by noon –
Sleep the meek members of the Resurrection,
Rafter of Satin and Roof of Stone –

Grand go the Years,
In the Crescent above them –
Worlds scoop their Arcs –
And Firmaments – row –
Diadems – drop –
And Doges – surrender –
Soundless as Dots,
On a Disc of Snow.

Joseph Tusiani finds an echo of Italian history in the poem: the fall of Venice is accurately carved in the second to last verse and symbolized by the surrender of a ruler of mere human power. The dead, "meek members of the resurrection" live on in Biblical lore forever while earthly powers come and go under the stars and turning firmament. Terrestrial glories, crown jewels, drop into silence as kings surrender. Dickinson paints the movement of history with her precise and tuneful "snow."

As Barolini explains, the poet—late in her life, at the age of forty-five, with the greatest of intensity, and with her most fecund years behind her—cut from *Scribner's Magazine* a reference to the poetry of Vittoria Colonna, the sixteenth-century Italian poet of the Island of Ischia who maintained a correspondence with Michelangleo. Dickinson, herself, was most published in the scribal sense with her correspondence. She wrote often to Elizabeth Holland, her Little Cousin in Cambridgeport, to Samuel Bowles, to Helen Hunt Jackson, to Thomas Wentworth Higginson, and very likely to William Smith Clark who had travelled to Italy and no doubt brought back with him to salons held by her sister-in-law at the Evergreens, his stories of travels in Italy, the land believed to be, as Mme. DeStael's *Corinne* believed it to be, synonymous with living openly, freed for self-expression in the arts, liberated from constricting emotional proprieties. Italy was the land where the arts were appreciated, and the sweet life, *la dolce vita*, not constricted by dogmatic hypocrisies, or held at bay by a the Puritan work ethic of more industrially advanced nations.

Italy seemed the land most welcoming to women of artistic talent and temperament. It was a country where the first Doctorate of Theology was attained by a woman, namely Saint Catharine of Sienna, who became, along with Saint Frances of Assisi, the High Patron Saint of Italy, anointed as such for service to the poor and a love of nature. It was the country where the first woman to publish a collection of poetry in Europe was Vittoria Colonna. It was the land where the first important *woman* painter of the Early Baroque era, was Artemsia Gentileschi, the premier *female* to become a member of the *Accademia di Arte del deSegno* in Renaissance Florence. It was a land where Dickinson's most admired English poet, Elisabeth Barrett Brown, lived in an ex-patriot life in Florence and wrote of Dickinson's favorite, self-actualized heroine, *Aurora Leigh*, who chose her mother's *Italian* sensibilities over her English father's temperament. It was the land to which Elisabeth Barrett Browning fled from Victorian England, and the constraints of her father, to elope with her poet lover, Robert Browning.

Dickinson's "Blue Peninsula" harbored the first prominent American feminist intellectual and defender of women's rights, Margaret Fuller, who discovered the fruition of her work, and her love in the person of a soldier of the *Risorgimento*; the "Blue Peninsula" was the nation to which *Corinne,* the celebrated and liberated heroine of Mme. De Stael, so unafraid of love without marriage, so able to assert her own identity, had also found herself, a woman like George Sand and George Eliot (Marianne Evans) another of Dickinson's admired authors. Marianne Evans lived her life with a married man, boldly expressing emotional freedom and self-expression, as William Smith Clark did around Amherst on his return from Europe, shocking Amherst with his affectionate greetings, hugging and kissing as Italians do upon meeting, and insisting upon celebrating Christmas with feasting and the spirit of generosity and gift-giving symbolized by Saint Nicolas whose reliquary is housed in a cathedral Bari—defying austere Calvinist customs of self-denial, sedateness, and fasting. Italy was where the Renaissance had bloomed, as the American Enlightenment was blooming in New England

Dickinson was re-reading Shakespeare's *Romeo and Juliet,* a tragic love story that takes place in Italy's Verona, just before she died. Finally, saying in her poetry, using symbols of Italy to actualize the idea that emotional freedom to love art, poetry, and lover, "is all there is" and "its own rescue." As Barolini explains, she drew her incantation of Sicily in the symbol of beauty and truth, the rose, the flower that represents perfection, the transcendent design of Dante's *Paradiso* as *candida rosa.*

> Partake as doth the Bee -
> Abstemiously -
> The rose is an Estate –
> In Sicily.

Italy and the island at its toe resided in Emily Dickinson's spirit—representative of a quality of independent artistic truth and beauty, her own rebellious creativity, her inviolate "snow" at the top of her Alps and Appenines, her erupting passions, her Vesuvius at home, her poetry full of emotions that have outlived their maker for well over a century.

by Daniela Gioseffi

REMEMBERING LOSING JESUS TO SCIENCE AND POETRY: A PERSONAL ESSAY

Part of an unpublished memoir: "Wild Days: Immigrant's Daughter"; first appeared in www.Ragazine. com, Jan. 2013.

Memory gives continuity to living. Without it, we are aimless ships adrift on endless seas. Memory is the current that carries us from shore to shore and toward new horizons. It is what brings us home to love—allowing us to learn, and, sometimes profit, from past mistakes. How terrifying it must be to suffer amnesia, or Alzheimer's disease, or "short-term memory loss"—all too common as an affliction of severe senility. Without memory, we can't be sure of who we are and how we came to believe what we espouse as truth. Thoroughly dependent on past experience, love itself, the greatest solace of human suffering, can be lost with lost memory.

I remember clearly an event that, early on, shaped my spiritual life. At sixty-five, I can recall fully how I, as an adolescent, was swept by fate towards the shores of pantheistic humanism as the final resting place for my spirit. I keenly recollect how I lost my ardent childhood faith in Jesus along with the hope endowed by a belief in the benevolence of a loving God. I had reached the tender age of eleven, and had just begun to menstruate, when I was forced by fate to discover a cruel world through maturing eyes. The fact that providence is often random, and innocence and love frequently unrewarded, struck me with devastating force, shaking my new found faith, too naïve and ardent to endure.

In 1952, at age eleven, I was a Pied Piper of Little Falls, New Jersey, babysitting for many kids in the neighborhood. They loved my stories and songs and would follow me about whenever they saw me. We moved there when I was ten to escape the poverty of our Newark Italian ghetto. It had adjoined the poverty of the African American ghetto to one side and the Polish-Jewish ghetto to the other side of the teeming city of Newark. And so, I tended the children of our new suburban haven, and they seemed to like me even if my big sister Lucy never would. I sang lullabies to them, and told bedtime stories, ones I made up myself. I had fun with the kids I babysat for, pretending to them that I was Dorothy from *The Wizard of Oz*, just returned to Kansas on the wings of a tornado to tell wild stories of my life "Somewhere Over the Rainbow." I was lonely when my older sister Lucy eloped, because her friends had always dominated our yard and front porch when she had lived at home, which made it difficult for me to learn to make my own. My younger sister, Camille, was a popular tomboy who immediately made lots of friends in our new suburban development. She was always out somewhere riding

257

her bike around the neighborhood, or playing baseball with a bunch of athletic kids while I was babysitting, reading, and doing my homework, alone.

After Lucy ran away and left me alone, I was happy not to be bullied by her. Alone, I dropped Roy Rodgers as my hero. He had really been hers anyway. I decided to bond, instead, with Jesus Christ as my secret friend. My parents did not give us religion. My father was a scientist, busy at his laboratory all day, and my mother though raised a Catholic had been molested in a confessional by a priest. Then, a nun who was her teacher in the seventh grade, smacked her hard with a ruler on her swollen hand, wounded and festering from a piece of broken glass that had become imbedded in her palm. When the nun smacked that aching hand with a ruler because my mother was whispering to a schoolmate in the next desk, about what page the assignment was on, my mother jumped out of her seat and ran out of the school, never to return. She forged working papers that claimed she was sixteen years old, and got a job working in a factory. "Thanks to that mean nun who beat my swollen hand, and the dirty priest who grabbed my breast in The Confessional, I never went back to school again!" That was how she told the story, many times over. "Now, I have no good education like your father has!" she would add, dejectedly.

I was on my own when it came to finding faith in any god. I bought a white plastic-framed portrait of Jesus at Woolworth's in Newark just before we moved to Little Falls and just after Lucy ran away with Billy Matteo. In my plastic portrait, Jesus was handsome as a movie-star, gentle-eyed and red-bearded with long wavy hair. He gazed beatifically heavenward. I threw away Lucy's cardboard picture of Roy, which I confiscated when she eloped, and put Jesus in Roy Rodger's place on my beside table in my new suburban bedroom. This would prove, because of Lucy's new married life, to be a very sad. Eventually, Lucy, a pretty woman, would marry four times and never really be happy. She always blamed all of her life's failures on me. She had some idea that I got more than she from our parents. Later in life, I would come to realize that I was born in what Freud would have explained as her "Electra Complex phase" when she was nearly six years old. She would forever see me as the "favored baby" who took my father's attention away from her. She'd grown for nearly six years, without having to share a thing, particularly our parents, with anyone, until I came along to displace her as the new baby and the center of attention. Then right at that juncture in our lives, my father became ill with lung disease, and my mother contracted breast cancer. All fun ceased for quite awhile until they were finally out of the hospital, and Lucy associated the end of all pony rides and Daddy's attention with me.

As a result, she'd forever feel that our parents had given me a better life than hers. Lucy simply refused to notice that I worked—babysitting all over the neighborhood for fifty cents an hour while doing my homework religiously—to get myself through public high school with A's in every subject and achieve valedictorian of my class. She also never noticed that in order to buy books and clothes, I graduated from babysitting to grocery check-out clerk, drugstore delivery girl, Howard Johnson's soda jerk, and Country Club coat-check girl. With such odd jobs I put myself through the local New Jersey State Teachers' College, now

Montclair University. In the early 1960's, one could attend for a mere $95 a semester, plus books and transportation.

After escaping Newark's ghetto to Little Falls, following Lucy's elopement at fifteen years of age with a guitar-playing construction worker, we lived in a cracker-box development house. My industrious mother promptly repainted the little shingled house white with yellow trim and covered it with red rambling roses and shrubs to individualize it from the other development houses. She had a greener thumb for growing plants than for raising children, and she knew how to do outdoor work harder than two men—ignoring us, her kids, to do so. Because Billy Matteo played the guitar and sang with her, Lucy had picked him to run away with at the tender age of fifteen, but she didn't really love him. He was eighteen, so if my parents had annulled the marriage, he'd have gone to prison for statutory rape. "What if she's pregnant? We can't annul!" My mother argued. "Let her stay married and work!"

"But she's too young! She should finish school!" My father argued sadly. He'd worked carrying newspapers on a lame leg, emptied coal buckets, and tended parking lots all night to put himself through college and earn Phi Beta Kappa from the Alpha Chapter of that prestigious honor society, and he was one of the first immigrants with an Italian name to do so. Because of his college degree—with honors from Union College, Schenectady—my father thought that America would be his oyster. Then in 1929, when he'd been graduated and went onto Columbia University for a Master's Degree in chemistry, not only had Sacco and Vanzetti recently been electrocuted by Judge Thayer of Massachusetts as "Dirty Guineas" for their labor organizing, but the beginning of the Great Depression had set in.

Companies like RCA hired him to pick his brilliant brain, giving him only a modest salary with no benefits. In fact, he set up RCA's first chemical laboratory for electronics—only to have the boss put his white Anglo-Saxon Protestant son in charge of the lab after my father had it running smoothly. Then, along came World War II when 600,000 innocent Italian immigrants were dubbed "aliens" as were many Japanese and Germans. And, my father went on to work for the Sylvania Corporation. He invented "The-Blue-Dot-for-Sure-Shot" and "Softlight" for the Sylvania Corporation in their electronics laboratory—from which the company made millions. He was paid a mere dollar for his patents earned on salaried, company time.

"It's because you're a lame little greenhorn *guinea* that you let them use you so!" My tired mother complained in despair, as she continued to work long hours as a seamstress in a Paterson factory, taking the bus early every morning to work. By the time Billy Matteo ran off with my sister, Lucy, my father had been through the job mill and was fairly tired and discouraged. So, was my mother, who had survived a radical mastectomy due to her breast cancer, even as he had survived serious lung disease and had a part of his lung removed. They were both worn-out immigrant survivors, he Greek Albanian Italian by birth, she Polish, perhaps a Jewish war orphan, looking for a little peace and quiet in their middle age.

My mother continued her argument: "Lucy and Billy love to play the guitar and harmonize. They sound just like Less Paul and Mary Ford when they sing,

'How High the Moon?' Let them stay married! Lucy plays hooky all the time any-way." She finally persuaded my father, "Billy's parents will be hurt if we annul the marriage, because the boy will have to go to jail for statutory rape. Do you want to send the boy to jail and ruin his life?"

"Lucy plays hooky because she says she gets mugged in the halls for her lunch money at that awful Springfield Avenue School over in the Ironbound section! We've got to move to the suburbs to have a better school for the kids!" my father rejoined.

"Lucy's a conniving liar!" My mother insisted. "She's buying cigarettes and sodas with the money and cuts classes for fun. She's always arguing with me and making trouble for me. She costs too much. Let her stay married and out of my hair," my mother shot back. "Or I'm leaving, and you can take care of the kids by yourself!" And, my father gave in, thinking that Billy Matteo's family seemed pretty stable and owned their own home in a nice area of Summit, a more upscale town in the suburbs of the city.

Lucy had taken to playing Billy Eckstein records, and my mother was always yelling at her, "Turn that disgusting nigger off! How can you stand the sight of him?" Billy Matteo with his dark little moustaches, except for having skin a shade or two lighter, looked a lot like Billy Eckstein, the African American crooner of the day. Billy Matteo sang "Blue moon, I saw you standing alone, without a love in your heart, without a dream of your own…" to Lucy, and played his guitar for her. She'd met him at a singing club near her high school. So they decided to elope with the result that Lucy was married and pregnant by age fifteen, and miserably bored with being stuck as a mother at home—not knowing how to become a singer like Ella Fitzgerald as she'd dreamed she'd be when Billy Matteo played the guitar for her.

Despite my mother's opinion, I thought Billy Eckstein sounded good with his rich voice and smooth diction, and his photo on the album was very handsome, even if his skin was dark. I saw Lucy's point in liking his records. He looked like somebody who already had a tan and didn't have to bake and burn in the sun to get it like we did, and his voice was very deep and smooth and mellow. Secretly, I sat on the floor outside Lucy's door and sang along with her Billy Eckstein records, but my mother kept accusing Lucy of liking "nigger music!" and being a "nigger lover!" I knew this hurt Lucy, and I felt sorry for her, but she wouldn't let me in to listen with her. She hated me for being born, and taking attention away from her, and she always would.

My red-haired Polish mother didn't like Lucy's friend Connie Germano either, because Connie was what they called olive-skinned and very dark. Connie wore earrings in her earlobes, pierced by her mother with a needle stuck in a cork and sterilized over the stove's gas flame. I guess the needle wasn't sterile enough because the newly made holes that held the earrings in Connie's earlobes were often red and festering with puss. My mother thought it was disgusting to pierce your ears and make them all pussy and then put earrings in them. It was an Italian immigrant custom, not a Polish one.

My mother, Josephine, a war orphan, perhaps Jewish, was raised by a Polish woman, named Rose Buzevski who had taught her to speak Polish as a child. My mother used to call my father a "Greenhorn Guinea," when she pushed him away. He would get hurt and call her a "Dumb Polack" in return for not wanting his embraces or attentions. This made me very lonely. I was neglected and retreated from their arguments as well as from Lucy's taunting. I tried to bond with my younger sister, Camille, but little Camille, to escape our unhappy household, became a tomboy who was always off somewhere playing sports. When we were left alone at night with me as her babysitter, I'd try to read her stories, but she'd fall asleep disinterested. She didn't like my stories the way the other kids I babysat for did. I couldn't understand how she could sleep through Nancy Drew's exciting detective adventures, *The Mystery in the Old Attic* and such, but after running around the neighborhood all day climbing, jumping, and playing, she slept well.

Meantime, Lucy began to be afraid of earrings and jewelry, and she would never let my mother come near her when she wore jewelry. Maybe she thought it would make her fester, too, like Connie's earlobes. Lucy hated her high school, and my mother wouldn't let her have a store-bought graduation dress. She had to wear a homemade dress that didn't quite fit right to her at her grammar school graduation. Even Connie Germano with her dark olive-skin and festering earlobes had a nice store-bought dress that fit her well. Lucy was mortified. She was also petrified of the older black boys in that Newark Public High School who did mug younger students for their lunch money.

My mother wouldn't let us go out on Halloween in our Newark ghetto by ourselves to "Trick or Treat" for candy like the other kids on Hunterdon Street, all dressed up as ghosts with pumpkin heads, witches with black pointy hats and green faces, princesses with cardboard glitter crowns and high heeled shoes, gypsies with scarves on their heads and lots of plastic beads and hoop earrings from Woolworth's 5 & 10 cent store. "Those niggers rape young white girls out alone at night," my mother told us. She'd grown up on Long Island as a migrant farm worker, and she was afraid of "colored people" as she called them when she was being more polite. I see now that "projection" of her own fears of poverty and starvation was the problem, and it rubbed off on Lucy, but I didn't know that then.

On Halloween, we had to go around the block with "Mommy" escorting us. We never got as much candy as the other kids, because she would only go a few blocks and then be tired. She had to get up to go and sew in the factory in the morning. When I think about it, I realize that she made Lucy scared of the black boys at school, so Lucy used to hide in the school bathroom and smoke cigarettes or play hooky with Phoebe Flood who lived upstairs with her drunken father, "Ole Man Flood," and her two sisters. My mother said that Ole Man Flood abused his daughters when he was drunk. She really made Lucy scared of men, I think. Maybe that's why Lucy married four times and never seemed to affectionately care for any of her husbands.

The Polish woman who raised my orphaned mother, Josephine, used to barter sex for groceries and *schnapps* after she arrived steerage passage in America. My mother hated all the men who used to visit her guardian, Rose, in the bedroom, locking her out, leaving my mother alone and hungry and waiting to be fed. Rose had come alone, dejected, and starving, steerage passage from Poland, after burying her husband and sons—dead of small pox when an epidemic swept through Europe. She had to dig their graves in the earth with her own hands on a farm she'd worked with them. She had to be tough to survive, and she taught my mother to be a tough survivor who could not allow herself to feel deeply. Rose had loaded up a horse-drawn wagon with her two living sons, and all they could carry of their worldly belongings, and made her way along the Polish corridor to Dansk.

Along the way, a grieving widow, driving her wooden wagon alone, she'd been accosted by Cossacks whom she'd had to entertain to survive. She sang songs to them, cooked them food, and amused them by being able to pee into an empty whisky bottle placed under her many long skirts, without spilling a drop on the earth. She'd had to drink and dance with the soldiers under the moon to survive and make her way to the port city from which she took a ship to America, steerage passage, with her two lice-ridden boys in tow. She'd arrived and made her way through Ellis Island, to Newark, where she rented a cold-water flat, de-liced her two sons with harsh brown laundry-soap in the kitchen washtub, and gone to work in a boarding house. As a lonely, grieving widow with children to feed, she drank lots of *schnapps* and partied with the working men of her Polish ghetto who gave her groceries, clothes, shoes in return for her sexual favors. She finally had five children to feed, including my orphaned mother whose father had never come home from World War I.

"I was born in 1910, the year the Titanic sank," my pretty blue-eyed, straw-berry-blond mother would laugh and sometimes cry, "and I've been sinking ever since!" She looked just like Maureen O'Hara in the 40's movies with peachy smooth skin and a radiant smile. She sewed stylish clothes to make herself look like a Hollywood star in the mode of a Jean Harlow. We loved when she would, once in a while, stay home from the sewing factory and make us doll clothes. She'd sing to us and pull us on a sled through the snowy streets. Once, she even visited my classroom on "Parent's Day," and all the kids thought she was so beau-tiful in the green dress and hat she'd made for herself, her blue eyes smiling and red hair shinny like Maureen O'Hara's.

"Your Mom's pretty!" they all remarked, making me feel special for a change. Even the teacher said, "What a beautiful mother you have, Daniela!" I felt so proud of her and wished she would come to school more often, but it was just that once that I can remember. In any case, she'd changed her name from Sophia Victoria Buszevski to "Joyce Burke" when she'd met my father, working in his electronics factory, and he'd courted her thinking she was an Irish lass. It wasn't until after he fell in love with her and they had eloped that he found out she was from a poor Polish ghetto and a war orphan with no father she'd ever known. Later, she told us that her father was a Jewish-American soldier, and because he'd borne her with a *shicksa* his Jewish family didn't want her after he was killed in the war. He'd left her with Rose Busveski to raise when he'd been drafted into World War I. In return, Rose had received his war pension for the child. This was my mother's memory of her childhood.

By the time we moved to Little Falls, Lucy—a pretty, dark-haired teenager who looked like my father's Italian family, but more like a young Elizabeth Taylor because of her pale skin—was pregnant and living in an attic apartment in Summit with Billy Matteo. As I grew to look more and more like my Polish or Jewish Polish mother, she had become a pretty married teenager who was very unhappy, and slept all day, and never took out her garbage. As I look back remembering my youth, I realize that she was very depressed and practicing "avoidance" by sleeping all the time. We all went to see Lucy and found so many bags full of garbage in her attic apartment, that we had to spend hours carrying them down the stairs and putting them into overflowing cans in the alleyway for her. She must have called up my parents and threatened to kill herself, so we all went over to help her and found her sleeping in bed, neglecting her baby.

Lucy had a little baby named Danny after my father, not me. My father's American name was "Daniel," though he'd been born "Donato Gioseffi" in Italy. It had been changed by an Irish official at Ellis Island who couldn't spell "Donato." Lucy was probably having a fit of postpartum depression, but no one knew of such things in those days. Baby Danny was blond and blue-eyed like my mother and me, not dark and brown-eyed like Billy Matteo and his family. He had a face like my mother's, so my mother liked him and Lucy and Billy used to leave him with us when they wanted to go to a nightclub and listen to singers and guitar players. I used to help my mother babysit for Baby Danny when Lucy left him with us in Little Falls. In our development house, I had my own little bedroom for the first time. Baby Danny stayed in my room when Lucy left him with us. He was company for me. The railroad went by about two hundred yards from our backyard, and even though I liked the sound of the mysterious train whistle in the night, and the patterns the train lights made on our walls as it ran through Little Falls, but it also scared me. I would hold Baby Danny so he wouldn't cry.

To keep us safe, I had my secret friend, Jesus, nearby. Jesus's photograph, that small glossy, semi-profile of a handsome, young, red-bearded man gazing beatifically upward, was always on my beside table in a white plastic frame where Roy Rogers had been. I showed him to Baby Danny whenever Baby Danny stayed in my room, and I babysat for him. I sang him Billy Ekstein and Ella Fitzgerald songs that I learned from Lucy's records as he cooed and smiled. "See, this is Jesus Christ, and he likes children and lives in heaven in the sky, and he takes care of us," I told Baby Danny. "He won't let Godzilla, The Creature from the Black Lagoon, The Thing, or the Wicked Witch from Oz get us."

My father never made us go to church, and he didn't go either. Other kids made fun of me because I didn't go. They said that I would fry in Hell for not going to Catechism after school like they all did. My mother didn't want to go, because Rose, the woman who raised her, had prayed and gone to church too much before she died. She had made my mother go to Catechism and Holy Communion, but after my mother had those misadventures in Catholic School, mentioned earlier— with the nasty ruler-wielding nun, and lecherous priest—she never wanted to go to church again.

My father never went because his father, Galileo, said the priests in Italy were *mariuolo*, or swindlers who want your money and your children to work for the Church instead of for *la famiglia*. My father told me later, that where he lived in

Candela, Provincia de Puglia, the only schools were run by priests and nuns who would demand money of the village families and then try to get their children to leave home and serve the Church as priests and nuns—rather than help the family tend the fields to grow food. The Church, *la Chiesa,* was an institution of *il Vaticano,* and of the Pope in the north of Italia, not in the *Mezzogiorno*—the poorer south of the peninsula where the farmers toiled for little pay to produce food from the "bread basket of Italy." After taxes, they had little left to feed their own families. The Church and the North had always abused and used *Mezzogiorno,* my father said. So, Grandpa Galileo would have none of it. My father grew up without religion and was a cynic about "the blood bath of history," which was largely, he learned, caused by religious conflicts.

All through my youth, he made many sacrilegious jokes, especially about the Crusades and the Inquisition, which he said were excuses for butchery, torture, and stealing. I had no religion to comfort my loneliness; rejected by both of my sisters, and a pensive youth, I watched the dramatic story of The Crucifixion and Jesus of Nazareth on television at Easter time, in black and white movies made in Hollywood, and secretly became devotedly religious, sure that my belief would save me from all the unhappiness my parents and Lucy endured. I had saved my pennies to buy my glowing plastic-framed Jesus photo. I kept it always close at night on the table near my bed and imbued it with magical significance. I took to praying to it constantly to save me from all the scary monsters of the movies like Godzilla.

My mother, traumatized by her childhood poverty, never let us have a nightlight. "Electricity is too expensive!" she scolded. My active imagination caused me many sleepless nights of worry as the shadows in my room became varied and evil Hollywood characters—Dracula with his thirst for blood; the Creature from the Black Lagoon who was an ugly beast, half-fish and half-man, who rose out of the dark water to murder and devour people; the Beast with Five Fingers, a disembodied hand that crawled about the house at night to strangle its inhabitants. The Thing was the worst; it was a large vegetable creature from outer space with claws that tore people apart. The Thing was almighty and could only be killed by cooking him—searing him like a carrot—with fire; he couldn't be stabbed or shot like the bad guys in cowboy movies who always lost to Roy Rogers. But, Jesus was more magical than Roy Rogers (whose place on my nightstand He had replaced). He could change water into wine, cure leprosy, and raise up from the dead to Heaven! And do it all without a gun or a horse!

Jesus Christ, with his kind eyes and lovely red beard, flowing hair and handsome young face like a movie-star's, would save me from all those horrible creatures, not the least of whom was the Wicked Witch of the East from *The Wizard of Oz,* green faced, pointy-chinned, and cackling, who had tried to kill pretty little Dorothy, her friends, and her cute little dog, Toto. I lived most of my nights in terror of these Hollywood creatures, unable to fall asleep in the dark, thinking my vigilant stare into its deep precipice would save me from harm. I could at least scream if I saw a shadow move or heard a voice, but now, I had magical Jesus, my secret friend, to protect me, and I fell asleep in comfort after my prayers for grace and salvation were complete.

That is, I had Jesus until Lucy's baby, Danny, suddenly got very sick for no reason at all that I could understand. I remember clearly my mother gasping as she spoke to Lucy on the phone. "We'll be there soon as possible. I'll call Daddy." My mother and father left immediately, as soon as he drove home from the chemical laboratory where he worked and beeped the horn in the driveway. They didn't come back all day and night. I decided that I could save Baby Danny, no matter how grave his illness. All I had to do was pray hard to Jesus Christ.

I knelt beside Jesus's magical photo, shining in its white plastic frame. I prayed and begged for Baby Danny's life.

He's only a little baby, six months old, Jesus, and he hasn't even had a chance to be bad or steal anything. He hardly even cries, and he smiles a lot just for a rattle or a song. I know his head is kinda flat in the back, but Mommy says it's 'cause Lucy doesn't pick him up and turn him over enough. She sleeps all day and doesn't take out the garbage. That's not Baby Danny's fault. I know you know that, Jesus, and you love children, so please, please let him live! His father Billy smokes and works a lot, and he doesn't pick him up either. Lucy says she's unhappy, but that's not Baby Danny's fault. He's just a baby, and he doesn't know much, so I know you will look after him—because I heard you love children, even though you make them suffer to come unto you as *The Bible* says. Lucy found out that running away and getting married and having a baby is not as much fun as going to Springfield Avenue School in Newark even. She's sad because she doesn't want to be a mommy. She wants to be a singer like Ella Fitzgerald or Mary Ford, but that's not Baby Danny's fault, so please, please let him live and be well, Jesus, Son of God. Please. I know you will take care of him, just like you protect me from the Creature from the Black Lagoon, and the Thing, and the Beast with Five Fingers, and Godzilla, and the Wicked Witch, too. They didn't get me and kill me and Danny since I've been praying to you every night, Jesus. Thanks Jesus, Son of God! Thanks a lot for taking care of me and Baby Danny....

I kept on praying and must have prayed harder than any human ever had, all day and night, without stopping once for a drink of water or to go to the bathroom or anything. I was sure I was saving Baby Danny from all harm. All day and into the night, praying on my knees, until I fell asleep on the floor prostrate before Jesus's magic photo, his kind eyes looking heavenward, his handsome, red-bearded face that looked kinder than a movie star's. I dreamed of him standing there in my room by the bedpost in a white gown, his hands spread at his sides to welcome me. His face quietly smiling like a mother happy to see her child. He faded into a ghostly white light that shimmered around my bedpost just where the moonlight hit it.

"Wake up and get in bed, Daniela! What are you doing here on the cold floor, you crazy kid?" My mother grabbed me up by the arm, waking me from my prayers. "The baby's dead," she said. I started to whimper climbing into bed half-awake. "Go to sleep! There's nothing you can do about it! No one can to anything about it." She spoke matter-of-factly, reverting to her toughness so that she wouldn't have to feel too deeply, trying to make me tough, like Rose had made her tough to survive, as she pulled the blanket up over me. "We'll have to have a funeral for Baby Danny and bury him in Summit tomorrow. Get some sleep or you can't go with us for the ride in the car."

After she left the room, turning out all the lights to save electricity, and leaving me in the scary dark, I mulled over what she said. Then a big sob shook free from my throat, and I defiantly turned the light back on just long enough to knock Jesus off the bed table with a punch. I never prayed to him again. If he couldn't help a little baby like Danny who never hurt anybody and couldn't even talk or walk yet, one with blue eyes and blond hair that Mommy said was better, too—a little baby who never did anything bad to anybody—he surely wasn't going to help me. I sometimes stole bread and cake from the kitchen when my mother wasn't looking. I wasn't good like Danny, and if Jesus wouldn't save Baby Danny, he surely wouldn't save a sinner like me from the horrible movie monsters of the night. Maybe, they were not real either. Not as real as the fact of death had suddenly become to me.

Some years later, in my teens, I read and learned about the Doctrine of Original Sin, the idea that we are all born "defiled" or "dirty" from the sinful act of sex. The idea that sex was a dirty thing, and all men wanted from women, had already been imbued in me by my mother's teaching, but I knew she was wrong. Somehow, I knew that the act that makes us all living, breathing humans, the sexual union from which we come, is not dirty or evil except that people make it so. Somehow, to me the idea that sex is dirty is one of the most evil ideas on earth, causing horrible perversions and troubled people. Somehow, I knew that my father wanted love as much as he wanted sex from my mother, maybe more, and she would give neither. That I sensed from early childhood—the way she was always pushing him away and he was always trying to hold and kiss her. They were never nice to each other like Fred Astaire and Ginger Rodgers. I vowed when I married that I'd never push my husband away and make him unhappy as my mother had my father.

The Doctrine of Original Sin would be the final reason that I would forsake Catholicism, and finally all religion for science and its actual wonders. If we are all born dirty and in sin, then why bother having us all grovelling here alive trying to earn a bit of happiness along with our bread from this earth? No, I couldn't buy it.

There is too much beauty in the goldfinch and cardinal's song for them to be born in filth, too much sweet innocence in a small child for him or her to be born of dirty sin. I decided at the age of sixteen, after reading Edna St. Vincent Millay's *Renascence, and Other Poems,* Walt Whitman's "Song of Myself," and Shakespeare's *Tempest* that the Doctrine of Original Sin couldn't possibly be The Creator's idea. It was the Calibans of the earth that ruined sex. It was the great poets from whom we learned emotional truths, not religion. I still liked to read Christ's "Sermon on the Mount," his greatest piece of poetry, but I did not like the story of the Cruxificion, so full of sadism. Christmas, the child born of the mother in innocence in a manger of straw, is a beautiful piece of poetry that I like to celebrate, but Easter for me, I decided, would always be the celebration of Estarte, ancient goddess of fertility and spring, *prima vera.*

Once I became a teenager showing a real interest in reading and books, and bringing home A's on my report card, my father—with his dramatic diction and passionate recitation—read me, *Romeo and Juliet.* He wept at the sad ending.

Next, he read me Cervante's *Don Quixote*, saying he felt like Don Quixote at the finale. He said his Italian mother, Lucia, had told him stories of *Cinderella* and *Pinocchio,* animating them with her voice and gestures, as he sat with her by the coal stove in their Newark home, darning covers on baseballs from the baseball factory with his many brothers and sisters. For each finished baseball, they earned a penny with which their immigrant mother could buy bread.

Once Lucy had run away and married, and Camille was always running around on her bike like a tomboy, my father started reading to me, and I stopped being so afraid of the dark. I would dream of the characters in my father's favorite books at night, instead. Unwittingly, he got me started along a better path, poetry—a path that asks important questions without giving easy answers, only emotional truths. After Shakespeare, I found my way to Walt Whitman's "Song of Myself," and oh, how I wept alone in my room after reading it through. Next, I found Edna St. Vincent Millay, and then, Emily Dickinson, and I've been surviving on the emotional truths in poetry, ever since.

Some crazy, misogynist priests who hated women—the type who would castrate Abelard for loving Eloise—*they* made up that Doctrine of Original Sin, I decided. It was in antipathy to all the natural beauty I saw around me, rain falling on leaves, sun streaming through my windows, children laughing as they played happily—the wondrous gift of our animal joy, too purely sensational—man and woman combining in love to produce a child as I wished my parents had! It was all too astonishingly beautiful—too perfect a plan for it to be wrong, dirty, a sin!

I eventually forgave Jesus for getting mixed up with all those priests and their crazy ideas of sex as sin. "The Sermon on the Mount" is true and good, I told my Christian friends, but Christianity is one thing, "Christiandumb" another! I decided, finally, that Jesus had loved Mary Magdalene, that Mary Magdalene's gospel had been lost and subverted with *The Gnostic Gospels*, the way Elaine Pagels says in her book, and that Jesus himself did not think of sex as sin, and He would not have condemned Baby Danny to eternal Hell or Purgatory for not being baptised. The Doctrine of Original Sin was surely the idea of some women-hating priests who wanted to make all the boys celibate so the boys would join the monastery and so they could have the boys all to themselves.

Anyway, what did celibate priests know of life, love, babies, or nature's glories? Why did children have to suffer to come to Christ? That was their idea, not his. Just like it was the idea of mortals that people of different color skins should be segregated, and people of the wrong religion should be killed in the name of God, and so I gave up Jesus and gained a fervor for social justice and the wonders of science, nature Herself. I studied the tenants of all the great religions of the world which all embrace the Golden Rule: "Do unto others, as you would have then do unto you!" What a great Golden Rule that is if only men who make wars and murder would listen to it! (I was to have my run in with the Ku Klux Klan at twenty in Selma Alabama, in the days of the Freedom Riders and Sit-in's— but I didn't know that then and that's a whole other story.)

"What could be more extraordinary than all those unseen molecules spinning around their nuclei, the schemes of *photosynthesis* and *atmospheric balance* that most live daily unaware of?" I thought. How often, when chopping down trees or rain forests, do men or corporate hacks think of the romance of Photosynthesis— the first link in the food chain that weds us all to Mother Earth? That spectacular wonder by which plants convert sun to energy for the entire animal kingdom! How often do we think, in our daily lives, of the trees giving off oxygen as we breathe out offering them carbon dioxide in the balance of planetary breath?

What is more awe inspiring than the mystery of endless space, stars shining light years away in the galaxy; what more spiritual than the music of the spheres as we spin in an expanding universe too vast to know; what more phenomenal than the red and blue colors of the sunset which continues to out do itself year after year; or the flight of a tiny ruby-throated hummingbird thousands of miles south and north in its yearly migration to breed?

What more religious a prayer is there than the cry of a baby born from a womb, bloody and wet, into the light of spectacular seeing and phenomenal hearing—all come from the wondrous gift of pleasurable sexual union? If there is a god, and he had a mortal son, he knows that he made it just exactly right when he dreamed up the scheme of sperm and ova from which we miraculously blossom from a mother's and father's love. If there is a Holy Trinity, if there is a Father and a Son, then "The Mother of Us All," must be the "Holy Ghost!" The memory of how I found my way to "Her" is the story of my life's work in poetry nurtured by my awe of science as revealed by natural wonders of this mysterious universe.

PART IV: FOUR DYNAMIC ITALIAN AMERICAN WOMEN:
THE POWER BEHIND AMERICA'S LITERARY ARTS

LEE BRICCETTI: "I DWELL IN POSSIBILITY…"
THE CALM POWER BEHIND A GREAT HOME FOR POETS

Interviewed by *Daniela Gioseffi*

Introduction: **LEE BRICCETTI** is the long-time Executive Director of Poets House in New York City. She has helped to shepherd it from a small facility to a grand and fabulous library and auditorium with both an adult program and a children's program accessible to all. Under her leadership, Poets House developed the Poets House Showcase, an annual exhibit of new poetry books, as well as Poetry in The Branches, a national outreach program that assists public libraries throughout the country in providing poetry services. Lee Bricetti has received a New York Foundation for the Arts Award for her own poetry and been a Poetry Fellow at the Fine Arts Work Center in Provincetown. Her first book of poetry, *Day Mark* was published in 2005 by Four Way Books in New York.

Daniela Gioseffi [DG]: You have shepherded Poets House through enormous changes. Can you briefly outline those changes and tell us about the challenges involved in their fruition? What challenges still remain?

Lee Bricetti [LB]: Now that Poets House has been lovingly "repotted" into a larger facility, everyone involved is engaged in its nurture and care so that it takes root and grows, welcoming more and more local users as well as visitors from all over the world. Really, this is a way of saying that the new building is a starting place for the next phase of community building—an invitation—and that the life we make together through our artistry and conversations is ongoing and evolving.

[DG]: I've read your poetry, and I feel that it must be very difficult to be both an executive director of a grand facility like Poets House in Battery Park, Manhattan, *and* be a sensitive poet with your own personal concerns for your work at the same time. How do you manage that and what are the difficulties involved, if you might say?

[LB]: Poets House has been at the center of my creative life for twenty-two years. Though making an organization will always be more public and collaborative than making a poem, both activities have a craft. My life at Poets House has demanded intense collaboration, a long view, strategic thinking and has routinely exposed me to new poetries. During the capital construction period—which was tantamount to the poets being in the gladiatorial arena with the real estate industry—the pace of business at Poets House created a less than balanced personal equation. Sometimes it is necessary to give everything to make a project work. But now I am finally making new poems and, as I tell my friends, rebuilding the person who can write my poems. I like to think of this period, as Dickinson writes (or almost) as a "midsummer in the mind...her polar times behind."

[DG]: You've hosted so very many great poetry programs by accomplished poets. Do you find that being so utterly steeped in contemporary poetry makes it difficult to write your own? In other words, aside from time constraints, does listening to and reading so many poets almost daily inhibit your ability to write freely without feeling threatened internally by accomplishments of others?

[LB]: Tuning one's ear to great poetic voices from across different cultures and times only expands one's sense of what language can do and what a poem can be. Personally, I have a need to make poems. Being engaged in this larger conversation with poets from different parts of the world has inestimably enriched my sense that we make our home in language.

[DG]: I've interviewed, Jane Ciabatarri, President of the National Book Critics Circle and Grace Cavalieri, host of the country's most widely syndicated public radio show on poetry The *Poet and the Poem* of the Library of Congress, sponsored by the NEA. As an Italian American woman, how did you escape *la vita della cucina*, the traditional Old World role of the women tied to the kitchen, and how did you become executive director of Poets House, what background prepared you for it?

[LB]: At some point, years ago, I drove by my old high school and saw a sign for the 15th Annual Lasagna Dinner benefiting the school's literary magazine. When I did the math, I realized that I had started the tradition. You never know what will be worthy; and I never knew in high school that what I was doing—directing plays or running the magazine, inventing community dinners to support them— could become a practical, professional path.

Later, I picked up tools as a town planner in upstate New York and as an urban planner in New York City working on low income housing issues. A generous supervisor took me under her wing and showed me how to write my first grant, and that, and the engagement with long-range planning, gave me an unusual starting place for my Poets House work.

But surely, the most important, incipient training for a life in public service has been coming from an enormous extended Italian-American family—juggling loyalties and negotiating with the many personalities and voices.

[DG]: Are you currently working on a project of your own writing?

[LB]: I am currently working on a new book of poems and writing more critical prose.

|DG|: What is your hope for the future of Poets House?

|LB|: All over the country non-profit organizations are built by boards and do-nors—by people who care—to create deeper civic engagement. Non-profit or-ganizations like Poets House create options in the cultural landscape, and the cultural imagination, that would not otherwise exist in the market economy.

Since Poets House has a sixty-year lease at its new home in Battery Park City, my rose-colored glasses see it thriving far into the future; and thriving will al-ways mean inviting the broadest spectrum of people possible into a deepened relationship with the art of poetry and engaging communities in the support of this mission-based work.

What do I hope for Poets House? That it may give joy to many even as it changes, as poetry changes, and that it will continue to bring together diverse practitioners, making a place brimming with conversation, in Battery Park City and online.

During the opening of Poets House's new space, almost from the beginning, people sat down to read in the library as if they had been thirsty. For me, seeing this engagement with the collection, with reading, in our new home was joyous. I had an even keener sense of arrival when I saw a teenager with tattoos and a nose ring studying Giaocomo Leopardi all afternoon.

|DG|: I imagine that being steeped in all the philosophical thoughts and imagina-tive worlds of poetry, day after day, makes for a very rich inner life. Though there are time restrictions on your own writing life, I imagine that being Executive Di-rector of Poets House is a rewarding life? Would you like to say something about that? Hasn't it given you a stupendous and learned education in the art of poetry?

|LB|: That "precarious gait some call experience" can also be called an educa-tion. Poets House's programmatic focus for the last twenty-five years has been on poets reading and discussing other poets…and it has been a remarkable educa-tion—learned, friendly and based in exchange. Soon, much of the Poets House programmatic archive will be open to everyone, no matter where they are in the country, through our new website.

A program in 1990 that Susan Howe presented on Emily Dickinson changed my reading life and introduced me to the radical consciousness of Dickinson. Our many years of co-sponsoring The People's Poetry Gathering with City Lore helped me understand more about poetry's roots in oral tradition, chant and song. But throughout the years, Poets House's international programs continue to make my world bigger. Stanley Kunitz, (along with Elizabeth Kray, the co-founder of Poets House) said, I paraphrase: Poetry is the most remarkable historical record-ing device, telling us what it feels like to live in a certain time and place.

JANE CIABATTARI: ENERGETIC POWERHOUSE OF THE NATIONAL BOOK CRITIC'S CIRCLE

Interviewed by *Daniela Gioseffi*

Introduction: **JANE CIABATTARI** is the author of the critically acclaimed short-story collection, *Stealing the Fire*. Her short stories have been widely published and nominated for O'Henry and Pushcart awards. Ciabattari served as president of the National Book Critics Circle from 2008 to 2011 and currently is Vice President/ Online for the NBCC, in charge of the *Critical Mass* blog and social networking. She also serves as an executive board member and secretary of the Overseas Press Club, and is former board chair of *Women's eNews*. A past president of the Women's Media Group, and a member of the Authors Guild, PEN, and The Century Association, her articles and book reviews have appeared in the *New York Times,* the *Guardian, Bookforum, NPR.org, The Daily Beast, Salon.com, The Paris Review, Los Angeles Times, Washington Post, San Francisco Chronicle, Chicago Tribune, Ms., Poets & Writers Magazine, The East Hampton Star, Kirkus Reviews, Three-penny Review, Psychology Today,* and *Columbia Journalism Review.* Ciabattari has been awarded fiction fellowships from the New York Foundation for the Arts, the MacDowell Colony, and The Virginia Center for the Creative Arts. She's taught for Bennington's Low-Residency MFA program; Knox College in Galesburg, Illinois; Columbia University's Graduate School of Journalism; New York University; and at numerous writers' conferences, including the Squaw Valley Community of Writers and the Taos Summer Writers Conference. Ciabattari was a longtime Contributing Editor to *Parade* magazine and has been editor in chief of DIAL, the public television magazine; a Senior Consulting Editor in Fiction at *McCall's,* and a reporter and columnist for the *Montana Standard* in Butte. For *Parade* she traveled widely interviewing luminaries like Isabel Allende, Halle Berry, Sandra Bullock, Jimmy Carter, Michael Douglas, Aretha Franklin, B.B. King, Sylvester Stallone, Margaret Thatcher, Archbishop Desmond Tutu, and Renee Zellweger.

Daniela Gioseffi [DG]: You've had and still have a very impressive and varied career as a writer. It is mind boggling, all that you've done. How did you escape the traditional role of the woman and become a writer, and editor, and literary critic, and how did you come to be president of The National Book Critics Circle?

Jane Ciabattari [JC]: I was raised in a traditional family in the Midwest--I'm a fifth generation Kansas descended from abolitionists. I went to public school and won a National Merit Scholarship to Stanford, where I studied creative writing and married Mark Ciabattari, an Italo-Finn from Butte, Montana who was a bit older. (Happily, he's also an author, and still my husband.) Mark and I were adventuresome. We essentially swapped roles for thirty years or so. I was the major breadwinner, working as an editor, a journalist, a *Parade* columnist, and always writing fiction; and he was raising our son Scott. It worked for us--I was interested in the world of work, which seemed exotic, given my mother's role as a homemaker, and Mark was a nurturing dad while doing graduate work (he has a Ph.D. in American intellectual and cultural history) and writing (three books of fiction and a social history of the 1940s).

Fast forward: In 2001 I was writing for *Parade* and about to launch my first book of short fiction, *Stealing the Fire*, with great pre-pub reviews (*Kirkus* called me a "master of transformation"), when I was in a taxi accident. My injuries made it difficult for me to continue my journalistic work (I was in physical therapy and in bed for half of the time for months). I turned to reading fiction, my love at Stanford and at San Francisco State, where I got my master's at night while working full-time as managing editor of the Sunday magazine of the *San Francisco Examiner and Chronicle*. I was the top ranking woman at the time. Not always easy. And I decided it would be fun to review a new Alice Munro collection, so I emailed Steve Wasserman at the *Los Angeles Times*, who I knew slightly from his time as an editor in New York, and offered. He ran my review on the cover. And so I set out to shift to book reviewer. Of course, the last decade of reviewing books has led to shifting sands at all turns. (My take on the subject, 4,000 words, is in the September/October 2011 issue of *Poets and Writers*.)

I often attended the National Book Critics Circle awards ceremonies in New York, and always enjoyed them. I come from a family of folks who pitch in, so I ran for the NBCC board once I had been reviewing for several years (regularly for the *Los Angeles Times, Kirkus, the Washington Post* and others). After elected, I chaired the Autobiography and then the Fiction awards committees, served as VP/Membership, and helped then president John Freeman and tech VP Rebecca Skloot launch *Critical Mass*, the blog. I was elected president by the board in 2008. (I served three years, was elected twice.) I'm now back to *Critical Mass* and keeping an eye on NBCC Facebook and Twitter.

[DG]: Do you find that your executive positions take tremendous energy and time away from your writing, or did it help to fertilize your own work? I'm sure that both are true in a measure, but what would you say about this issue? How do you find time to write your own fiction and still participate in all you do?

[JC]: Of course I lost writing time. No question. I wrote most of my early short stories and the novella that was my thesis (and published in *Redbook*) on Saturdays. I've had tremendous support from writers' colonies like MacDowell and the Virginia Center for the Creative Arts. I still have weeks at VCCA in the fall that are sheer heaven, working continuously. On the other hand, I've witnessed all sorts of human behavior in the course of my work. My stories often are inspired by place, and I've traveled all over. Examples of a couple stories in my new collection: my story "Aftershocks," published online at *KGB Bar Lit*, was inspired by a business trip I made for *Parade* for the Golden Globes (I did Oscar predictions). I ended up in the Northridge earthquake. And my story "Shanghai Blues," which Dawn Raffel published in *The Literarian*, the Center for Fiction's literary quarterly, was informed by several overseas reporting trips to China. I hope to have more writing time now...

[DG]: Is it more difficult to be a woman in a directorship or editorship than it is to be a man, do you think, or do you find that a superfluous question?

[JC]: I wish I could say that's a superfluous question. At the *Examiner,* as a woman in my early twenties, I was surrounded by traditional guys, most of them in their forties and fifties. Some of them made my life tough; others saw my merits and promoted me and supported me. I learned a lot. (Among other things I learned to empathize with women AND men of all ages, and I learned to be flexible.) Later, on the road as a *Parade* columnist, covering international affairs, Washington politics and the movies, I sometimes seemed to surprise the heads of state, politicians, and film stars I was interviewing when I showed up (in particular I recall a group of NATO leaders, including a Norwegian general and the German secretary general at the time, who seeming bemused that I was asking them such knowledgeable questions; the secretary general asked who had been briefing me.) But I had the clout of 80 million American readers behind me.

[DG]: Ah, ha! Why do you think you enjoy reviewing books so much? Does being a reviewer make you hypercritical of your own writing do you think?

[JC]: I love good literature. Always have. I grew up reading books from the library, my parents subscribed to *The Sunday New York Times,* so I was reading book review sections in our local paper (the *Emporia Gazette,* where I got my start writing a weekly column when I was 14), the *Kansas City Star,* and the *NYTBR* all the time I was growing up. Being a reviewer helps me see what works and what doesn't. As a fiction writer, I've been thrilled to recognize (and learn from) the work of NBCC award finalists and winners like Jennifer Egan, Jayne Anne Phillips, Bharati Mukherjee, Jane Smiley, Roberto Bolano, and dozens of others.

[DG]: How do you feel about the new digital electronic age in publishing? Are you happy about it? Does it provide more opportunity for writers or less? How does it effect their making a living?

[JC]: I don't think we'll be able to turn back the tide. I just try to keep up with the currents. The past decade has been earthshaking, no doubt about it. But we're still a nation of passionate readers, and we still need gatekeepers or curators to guide us toward what's worth our time. I have talked a lot about these changes over the past six years at writers' conference, at NBCC events, at the BEA, on university campuses, and every six months the picture changes. As I put it in my Poets and Writers piece, "Five years ago, Twitter was just another start-up, and the iPad was a gleam in Steve Jobs' eye..."

|DG|: You are currently Vice President working on the NBCC blog, *Critical Mass*. What does that entail in terms of daily workload? What exactly do you do in editing it

|JC|: I chair the online committee, and post to the blog several times a week, usually the work of NBCC members, former finalists and winners. I post information about NBCC events, and cover them if I'm in town. There's a wide range of work on *Critical Mass*: www.bookcritics.org/blog

|DG|: You've done so much to revitalize the National Book Critics Circle with interesting and vital forums and events. What are some of the changes you've instituted, and what is your hope for the future of the NBCC in this digital age?

|JC|: I'm pleased to have been part of the founding of *Critical Mass* in April 2006 (as I mentioned, then president John Freeman and then tech VP Rebecca Skloot were the moving forces in the early years; Eric Banks, now NBCC president, was blog chair when I was president). The NBCC has been an online-only organization ever since I've been on the board, so I see digital as a huge advantage for a tiny nonprofit funded almost entirely by membership dues (top dues are $40 for working reviewers; associates—anyone who loves books can join for $25, student memberships are welcome for only $15 at www.bookcritics.org/membership).

Also, during my tenure, I hired David Varno, the NBCC's unbelievably effective and versatile web manager, who came highly recommended by board member John Reed of the *Brooklyn Rail*. And, I developed NBCC discounts for members from literary quarterlies and other places. We started doing that this past winter, beginning with *Granta, Pleiades, Poets and Writers, TinHouse*, now expanded under new president Eric Banks to include the *Paris Review, New York Review of Books, Open Letter Books*, and I just brought in *Selected Shorts*). Setting up a Wiki for the members-only *NBCC Guide to Freelancing Markets*, updated annually by former board members Steve Weinberg

The National Book Critics Circle got its first ever NEA grant while I was president, and that's something I worked hard on. Ditto: expanding the events nationwide, in the wake of John Freeman's energetic barnstorming as president. I tried to keep up that momentum with NBCC events at AWP, BEA, PEN World Voices, and book fairs and festivals all over the country, from Brooklyn to Portland to Virginia and Texas and at iconic bookshops like Canio's, Prairie Lights, City Lights, and others. Upgrading the website, under Tech VP Lizzie Skurnick. Hosting three years of NBCC finalists' announcements and awards finalists' readings and awards ceremonies, with the incredibly hard working Barbara Hofffert as awards chair. And all the hours of online and in person book discussions. There is nothing like arguing passionately with 24 fellow critics.

|DG|: What projects are you working on now? What is your hope for your own writing life in the future?

[JC]: I'm finishing up a second collection of short stories, named after the title story, "Arabella Leaves." Most all have been published. And a novel my agent wishes she had yesterday. It's about a small-town Illinois couple descended on his side from a runaway slave and on her side from the town's founders, who ran an underground-railroad station. Abby and Zeke fall in love in high school, marry, have a child, and then Zeke disappears. Abby moves in with his parents to raise their son, who begins to get in trouble (using, then selling drugs) in his early teens. The present day story is set in 2004, when Abby is living in New York after graduate school, and her son calls her from prison to say his girlfriend is pregnant. With twins.

[DG]: By the way, are you Italian American by birth and ancestry, or is Ciabattari your husband's name? It doesn't matter, as you've made your way in the world of writing with an Italian name. Just curious, please! (Actually, I am of very mixed heritage with an Greek, Albanian Italian father and a mother orphaned by WWII and raised by a Pole.)

[JC]: I'm a triple Celt--Scots, Irish, Cornish--with some Swiss-German and Delaware Indian (my mother's father). I got my Italian name from my husband. I was invited by Helen Barolini to be in the groundbreaking anthology of Italian-American women writers, *The Dream Book*, after she saw my story "Gridlock" in *Redbook*. ("Gridlock" is in my first collection; *Redbook* nominated it for a National Magazine Award). I told Helen I wasn't eligible because I wasn't "really" Italian American. Years later, I discussed this with Fred Gardaphe, who said it seemed fair to say I have been "acculturated" as an Italian American. I've certainly been visualized as an Italian American via my byline. I was once told by a prestigious New York newspaper that my byline belonged in the *Daily News*. And the name is not easy to pronounce or spell....:)

[DG]: *Si, si! Capisco!*

GRACE CAVALIERI: POET/PLAYWRIGHT AND GRACIOUS RADIO HOST TO ALL AMERICA'S POETS

Interviewed by *Daniela Gioseffi*

Introduction: GRACE CAVALIERI is the author of 15 books and chapbooks of poetry, the most recent are: *The Poet's Cookbook* (Bordighera Press, 2009,) *Anna Nicole: Poems (Goss:183* Casa Menendez, 2008,) *Water on the Sun* (Bordighera Press, 2006,) *What I Would Do For Love* (Jacaranda Press, 2003,) *Cuffed Frays* (Argonne House Press, 2001,) *Sit Down Says Love* (Argonne House Press, 1999). *Pinecrest Rest Haven* (The Word Works,1998.) She's also written texts and lyrics performed for opera, television and film. Her 21st play "Quilting the Sun" was presented at the Smithsonian Institution, and received its world premiere at Centre Stage, S.C. Grace teaches poetry workshops throughout the country at numerous colleges. She produced and hosted "The Poet and the Poem," weekly, on WPFW-FM (1977-1997) presenting 2,000 poets to the nation. She now presents this series to public radio from the Library of Congress via NPR satellite.

Grace has received the Pen Short Fiction Award, the Allen Ginsberg Poetry Award, The Corporation for Public Broadcasting Silver Medal, and awards from the National Commission on Working Women, the WV Commission on Women, the American Association of University Women, and more. She won a Paterson Prize for *What I Would do for Love*, and The Bordighera Poetry Prize for *Water on the Sun.* She received the inaugural Columbia Merit Award for "significant contributions to poetry." She writes full-time in Annapolis, Maryland where she lives with her husband, sculptor Kenneth Flynn. They have four grown daughters.

Daniela Gioseffi [DG]: What got you started in producing the country's most widely syndicated radio show with poets and poetry, The Poet and The Poem from The Library of Congress, and how long was it before you managed to garner support from The National Endowment for the Arts and the Witter Bynner Foundation?

Grace Cavalieri [GC]: Well, I co-founded a radio station (WPFW-FM) in 1977 partly with a mere $40,000 grant form NEA Literature Division to put poetry on the radio (plus 8 other art programs a week) but it was not until the 1990's when I had more support from NEA. Then in 2004, a $5,000 grant from NEA when Dana Gioia saw the value of poetry on air, and along the way I applied for personal state arts and humanities grants that I always poured into radio. Witter Bynner came in, 1989, with a single grant to send my regional series national from the Library of Congress (a trial balloon.) Then when I went to the Library from retiring the 20-year show on WPFW in 1997, Witter Bynner FDN. started supporting the series annually. Each year I reapply. I am not a line item on anyone's budget.

[**DG**]: You now have your interviews online at the Library of Congress website, don't you? When did that begin to occur and are all your interviews online there in mp3 or audio files? on "The Poet and the Poem,"

[**GC**]: I have interviewed/presented approximately 2,500 poets in 34 years (as of 2011.) Only recent shows are on the LOC website. There are 1000 at the George Washington University Special Collections (Grace Cavalieri Papers.) Approximately 500 are held at Pacifica Archives & Program Service. And most of the shows raw (not produced) done form the LOC are at the LOC on hard drives and tapes.

[**DG**]: For how many years have you been doing the show and how widely syndicated is it. Can people lobby their local stations to carry it?

[**GC**]: The show will celebrate 35 consecutive years on-air in Feb 2012. A big landmark! It is given free to all public radio stations and I have no idea who takes it. Station carriage changes, but I imagine from 30 to 50 stations carry it. There is no way to chart it, because some stations tape it for educational use, some download and play at random, some take series as sent, some miss the feed and write me to get CDs ...It is something I cannot control. Now NPR distribution is all automated so it is a computerized set up where stations can pick programs from "Content Depot" as grapes from a vine. Each season, I send shows up weekly and they hang there for 6 months for the taking.

[**DG**]: When did you yourself start writing and publishing poetry, and how much have you published of your own poetry?

[**GC**]: As we all know, poets are born brain-wired a certain way and every poet I know wrote as a child. I'm no exception. I sent poems out as a young adult, but not until my fourth child was born did I write and send poems out every day. That was 1964.

[**DG**]: Amazing how you do all you do! Does doing the radio show interfere with or fertilize and encourage your own writing?

[**GC**]: Well you know more than many, Daniela, how public service cuts into personal creativity. They are streams from the same river but with different destinations. I get a huge energy transfusion from listening to poets read their works. But that does not belong to me. I go into a different room in the house inside myself to plunder my own secrets and language for poems. If anything, hearing another poet is a sacred experience I enter, but I can honestly say this does not influence my own work.

[**DG**]: How many poets have you interviewed to date, and which were your most notable interviews, as well as the ones you enjoyed most.

[GC]: More than 2,000. Probably 2,500. Ginsberg was the most difficult as he had been up all night marching in a protest and was cranky (1977.) Also being a woman from the suburbs with children and being a Navy wife did not bring me much love from his world. I might have been politically aligned, which I was, but I could not carry a sign proving it. We became friends later. The poet Wilfred Cartey from Trinidad was a blind poet and he was the last of the "Negritude movement." When he finished talking with me, we were both in tears. I've loved all the Poets Laureate. They are happy to share themselves in the bright light of that appointment. W.S. Merwin's interview this year was a highlight of my life as a radio host.

[DG]: Have there been some funny incidents that stand out in your mind, or some embarrassing moments that you'd like to correct or share?

[GC]: A million mistakes! On WPFW, Henry Taylor was on-air. The wiring got fouled up and the front door buzzer and speaker came over the air. So everyone who was trying to get in the station, came through on my show and Henry braided it all into his poetry. It was fantastic performance art. Brodsky started every sentence with *Nyet!* and *No!* Then he'd agree with me. So, I edited out all the *No's* and had a reel of 50 *No's*; and on the final program, he sounded quite affable. Everything that can go wrong, in 34 years, of course, did. At one time, our radio station was located in China town in D.C. and Chinese Year interrupted my audio. Even a sound proof studio could not shut out the fireworks. A.R. Ammons showed up for an hour interview and reading without his books (Thank Heavens I had his.) This happened quite a lot. I never arrived empty handed again.

[DG]: How much preparation do you have to do for each show, and where do you tape them, on location, or at a radio studio in your area?

[GC]: If I am interviewing a U.S. Poet Laureate, I read every single word written: prose, memoir, poetry. I do that all summer as these interviews occur each October. This is enjoyment for me. As for other poets, I know their most recent book(s) and probably former works. All shows are in the Library of Congess studio. 10% of shows are done on location with broadcast equipment (which worries me the whole time.)Sometimes the audio needs special attention for these. But all are national quality. My husband, Ken Flynn, is Associate Producer and is a great help in timing, engineering and setups on location. The first 20 years of "The Poet and The Poem" were in WPFW's studio in Washington, D.C.

[DG]: Lately, I note you've been working on having your plays produced. Tell us about those, where they've been done, and what has pleased you about their productions.

[GC]: Well, I am a product of the "Hippie" theater movement of the 60's. In 1968 I had my first play produced in Baltimore's Corner Cafe (a branch of Café La

Mama.) It was the heyday for theater, even using storefronts and cafes for stages. I had 10 plays produced in succession, all one-acts... which was the vogue then... along with Sam Shepherd, Leonard Malfi, many interesting writers. I had one show billed with Joe Orton (the late great cult figure) at WPA Theater Off-Broadway in 1977. (WPA is still going strong today.) But, with 4 children I could not play in that sandbox, continuously. It takes hands-on attention and I had to meet the school bus each day at 3pm. In mid 70's I saw my first full-length play win a national award, produced several times on both coasts. Then a hiatus until the mid 80's with that same play in NYC. (It has just been published in "Scene4 International Magazine of the Arts:" The Sticker Tree," all these years later.) In the 1980's I formed an association with NYC's Xoregos Performing Company, and through my writing grants, several plays have been mounted with professional actors. I have had 23 plays produced/staged since 1968 all over the country. They usually are tried in NYC such as "Hyena in Petticoats" in 2006 --then it went to Durango Colorado. "Quilting the Sun" After trials went to Greensville S.C. and now being produced in different SC city in NOV 2011...With preparation for Spoleto (S.C. Festival.). Also harking back to the 70's and 60's I have worked with Baltimore composer Vivian Adleberg Rudow in writing texts and lyrics for songs and opera that continue to be produced and recorded.

[DG]: Also, tell us about your latest books and projects. What are they? Also, what first started you writing poetry?

[GC]: I started writing poetry because language was how I understood the world. It was a paradigm that made everything matter and in forms that were safe to hold what I felt.

In 2010 I had two books of poetry published: *Navy Wife* (a chapbook,) and *Sounds like Something I Would Say* (both from Casa Menendez Press.) In 2008 *Anna Nicole: Poems* was published by Casa Menendez and it won a Paterson Award for Literary Excellence. Although some of the intelligentsia sneered at the subject matter, I guess the London Opera's new show on Anna is proving that wrong. My current process is that I write a book of poems and then the characters won't go away so I write a play from that. This is the case with my last 5 plays. They were books of poems first. Yet, the play becomes nothing at all like the poetry. However, the characters have been born there.

But, before we close, may I please say that all you do for poetry, Daniela, and your support for others' work has been essential to my own career. Thank you for all your work in the field for so many years.

[DG]: Thanks, Grace. You're always gracious!

NOREEN TOMASI: EXECUTIVE DIRECTOR OF NEW YORK'S BUSTLING NEW FICTION CENTER

Interviewed by *Daniela Gioseffi*

Introduction: NOREEN TOMASSI became Director in 2004 of the exciting Center for Fiction, the latest new bustling institution for literary art in New York City. She began her career in Play Development department at McCarter Theatre in Princeton and was director of the Literary Arts and Theater programs at the NJ State Council for the Arts and a past president of Arts International. Her books are *Money for International Exchange in the Arts* and *American Visions/Visiones de las Americas*. She was co-creator (with Jane Alexander and Birgitta Trommler) of *What of the Night,* a theater piece based on the life and work of Djuna Barnes, produced by MCC Theater at the Lucille Lortel in Spring 2005. She earned her Bachelor of Arts at Skidmore College. She resides in Harlem and has one son, the jazz pianist Keenan McCracken.

Daniela Gioseffi [DG]: How did you come to be director of the Center for Fiction, and how did the Center for Fiction come about as an institution and facility?

Noreen Tomassi [NT]: When I took the job as executive director in fall 2004, The Center was still called The Mercantile Library of New York. The "Merc" was founded in 1820 by a group of merchants who wanted to create a library for the use of their clerks. I believe I was hired because in my interview I laid out my vision for a Center for Fiction in New York City and this perfectly aligned with the Board's interests in moving the organization into the 21st century.

[DG]: Please describe the facility's functions and programs for us in brief? Its *raison d'etre?*

[NT]: The Center for Fiction is the only nonprofit in the U.S. solely dedicated to celebrating fiction, and we work every day to connect readers and writers. *Time Out* calls The Center one of the top three reasons to stay in Manhattan for literary events, citing the innovative panels, lectures and conversations that take place in our beautiful building on East 47th Street. We also feature workspace, grants, and classes to support emerging writers, reading groups on classic and contemporary authors, and programs to help get kids reading. We recognize the best in the world of fiction through our annual awards, and we operate one of the few independent *fiction* bookshops in the country. We are also an important piece of New York City history, continuing to build our renowned circulating fiction collection, begun before the advent of the public library system.

[DG]: As a woman with an Italian American surname, can you say how you escaped the traditional feminine role of *la vita della cucina* (the Old World role of the woman in the kitchen as the center of *la famiglia*)? Were your parents and family encouraging of your education in literary arts?

[NT]: I not only have an Italian American surname, I am Italian American. My grandmother spoke almost no English and a number of my cousins were born in Italy and still live there (in Milan and Rome). My mother was Irish American, thus the name Noreen. Neither my mother nor my father, nor any of nearly 40 aunts and uncles on either side, were college-educated. So, no, I can't say that anyone encouraged me to continue my education in any field, though they seemed more or less glad that I graduated high school. That said, my mother was a voracious reader and wrote quite good poetry, mostly on religious themes, and encouraged me to read.

Because most of the adult men I knew in my extended family worked seasonally in the trades as masons and stonecutters or carpenters, nearly all of the women worked outside the home to provide a basic steady income. My mother learned bookkeeping and worked in the office at a car dealership. Many of my aunts worked the assembly lines at the GM plant or as grocery store cashiers, and a few worked as motels maids at the places along Route 1 between Newark and Perth Amboy. So I don't know that I had much of a sense as the woman as keeper of home and hearth. It's true that these women made homes, created holidays rich with tradition, were the primary care-givers to their children and did all that in addition to working, unlike their husbands. But, I don't know that that was specific to Italian American families of the time.

Did I escape the notion of the woman in the kitchen as the center of *la famiglia?* Maybe. It's clear that early on I decided to learn how to be financially self-sufficient always and to find a way to do work I would love. I have a career. I take care of myself. I've traveled around the world. I value my time alone. But, check in with me on any Christmas Eve and you'll find me in the kitchen furiously cooking my grandmother's beloved recipes for my son and nieces and their families. I doubt there's anything I love more than sitting at that long table among high chairs and toddlers and teens and my son and nieces and their partners with my glass of red wine and a meal I cooked for them on the table. *La vita della cucina*, indeed!

[DG]: Was your degree at Skidmore in literature or arts administration?

[NT]: Literature, though I was very interested in philosophy and wrote a senior thesis on the aesthetics of reception, which relates to the experience of reading literature as well as to theater audiences. Maybe not too interesting now, but riveting to me then.

[DG]: Does being director of the Center for Fiction inhibit your own writing time and do you still do writing of your own?

[NT]: Yes, it really affects it. I'm not a terribly structured writer and am full of admiration for people who say they write x words or x pages a day without fail. I have to have an idea or project I love. I was wildly in love with Djuna Barnes for three years. Thought about her day and night, couldn't stand to be away from her. I do note that *What of the Night*, my last big project, ended just as I was taking this job, so it's possible that the amount of energy and passion I put into The Center is getting in the way of my next big literary love affair. (Though I am having a little flirtation right now, so who knows?)

[DG]: I imagine that the richness of programs the center offers is advantageous to your inner life. Can you say something about that?

[NT]: Well, I hope so. But I mostly hope that the programs mean something to our audience, are advantageous to their inner lives. There have been a number of books lately, the wonderful *Montaigne, or How to Live; Tolstoy and the Purple Chair, A Jane Austen Education* to name just a few, that suggest that great literature can teach us how to be better human beings. I'd like to believe that's true, that anyone who reads Jane Austen can't be a bad human being, but there's lots of evidence to the contrary, isn't there? Think of the writers who disprove it. Naipaul, for example, is a fine writer and obviously a thoughtful reader, but it clearly hasn't been advantageous to his inner life. Pound read Dante and Leopardi, but was a wreck of a human being. Still, still . . . It's a good question.

Why spend 60 or more hours a week, week in and week out, if you don't believe reading makes for a better, richer inner life? I guess the truth is that despite the evidence I do believe it. I have faith. Reading is better than not reading, books can be sacred objects and libraries sacred places, and my inner life, such as it is, and certainly my outer life, my everyday existence, are made better by fiction.

[DG]: What are the biggest challenges in shepherding the Center for Fiction's work and existence? I imagine it is difficult in these hard economic times.

[NT]: It is hard—and has been especially hard for all non-profits since 2008. But it's hard for everyone. The goal is to find enough people who love the art of fiction enough to support a center—the only Center for Fiction in the entire country—in these rough times. Charitable giving is always a very personal choice and when money is tight, the trick is not to convince random people to give, (That never works!), but to find the institution's "family," in our case the people to whom writing and reading matter terribly, who really very much want to help writers and get kids to read and to whom it feels natural and right to help maintain a meeting place and oasis for fiction lovers. We find more and more people like that every year, and that's heartening.

[DG]: What do you like best about your position, and what are it's greatest challenges?

[NT]: I love writers. They are endlessly fascinating to me and for the most part are a pleasure to be around. So the programming is my greatest joy, matched only by working on the awards we give—The Flaherty-Dunnan First Novel Prize and the Emerging Writers Fellowships in particular. I can't begin to explain how satisfying it is to sit down with the first 25 pages of a debut novel submission and think—"Ah, this is it, the real thing, this is a writer I'll still be reading with great pleasure 20 years from now." I also love talking about books, which makes lingering with audiences after events and leading book groups a lot of fun.

And I love my Board. There, I've said it, committed it to paper. I hope other executive directors don't hate me too much, but I honestly do think I have one of the greatest Boards ever—committed, thoughtful, supportive, and full of humor and grace. My Board Chairman in particular (Peter Ginna of BloomsburyUSA) is a godsend.

The biggest challenge? It continues to be how to do all we do with such a small staff. People are generally amazed to hear that there are only five full-time people working here. They are all talented, dedicated people, but still . . .

[DG]: Do you write creatively yourself, that is to say do you write *fiction* in particular, or are you an appreciator of literature who enjoys shepherding the art to greater fruition for the community of readers and writers?

[NT]: I don't write fiction, but I'm a devoted reader of it and love bringing writers and readers together.

[DG]: What is your future vision for the Center for Fiction?

[NT]: I would like The Center to be known nationally and internationally as the pre-eminent place for lovers of fiction, both readers and writers, on-line and here in NYC. I'd like to be able to support more writers early in their career. I'd like to have a residency program for accomplished writers. I'd like us all to think about fiction more expansively—novelists writing for TV, as Tom Piazza does for *Treme*; multi-media work and innovative ibooks; immersive fiction/gaming, and more—and I'd like The Center to be known for having unbelievably great, earth-shatteringly great, literary programming here in our building, at other sites, and in all media.

[DG]: Is there something else you wished I'd asked you that you'd like to expound upon? I always ask this at the end of an interview. Please feel free to add anything else about your work and life that you'd like to articulate in closing.

[NT]: It's a nice way to end an interview, so thanks for asking. The question I'm most often asked at dinner parties seems to be whether I think people will still be reading books twenty years from now, whether the next generation will have the ability to, and the interest in, to immerse themselves in a novel. My answer is a resounding yes. More people are reading on this planet than ever before and new technologies will make great books even more available around the globe. Not everyone will want to become a voracious reader or a person who "lives by fiction" as I, and many members of The Center, do. But that's always been the case. Some people care more about music or dance or finance or painting— or golf, or baseball. But the fact that more people are literate and more people have access to the written word means that more people *will* fall in love with reading. Whether books, in their current form, survive is a different question and I don't have an answer for that. I don't think anyone does. I do know that as much as I love real books, paging through them, the smell of them, the look of type on paper and the beautiful covers, it really is what's inside them that counts. The stories matter, not the form in which they're delivered. And, I don't have any doubt at all that people will keep telling stories and reading them as long as there are people around.·

·These four interviews first appeared in *Rain Taxi Review of Books* and in another version in *VIA*, 2012.

PART V: ADDITIONAL RESOURCES:
LETTERS TO DANIELA GIOSEFFI

CITY LIGHTS
BOOKSELLERS & PUBLISHERS
261 COLUMBUS AVENUE
SAN FRANCISCO, CALIF. 94133

8/12/84

Dear Daniela Gioseffi —

I didn't mean to encourage you to send mss. to City Lights for publication, since we are absolutely inundated with good poetry someone should publish. We are, as they say, over-committed — and can't consider more ....Anyway, I did read your Animal Intimacies and I can see why you have been published extensively — perhaps more than any other Italo-American woman poet — It was a pleasure to read, and I shall keep your phone number !

Thank You Lawrence Ferlinghetti

291

Geraldine A. Ferraro

September 27, 1985

Dear Ms. Gioseffi:

I was delighted to receive your letters and the copy of your book of poems, Eggs in the Lake.

I apologize for being tardy in responding to you. Since I saw you at the NOIAW luncheon I have been constantly traveling with little time in the office. And when I am in the office I was finishing my book.

You expressed interest in reviewing the book. Please contact Stuart Applebaum of Bantam Books, (212) 765-6500 who is handling the publicity for the book.

I enjoyed your reading at the luncheon. We are both pioneers in two different careers ...but I think your talent is the true gift.

With best wishes,

Cordially,

Geraldine A. Ferraro

Ms. Daniela Gioseffi
GPO Box 197
Brooklyn Heights, New York 11202-0197

108-18 Queens Boulevard • Forest Hills, N. Y. 11375 • 1-718-793-8811

STATE OF NEW YORK
EXECUTIVE CHAMBER
ALBANY 12224

MARIO M. CUOMO
Governor

November 21, 1986

Dear Ms. Gioseffi:

Thank you for enclosing the short story with your letter.

Poetry and fiction are demanding art forms and the reviews
you have received for your imaginative works are impressive.

Philosophical arguments and laws are not the only ways to
end prejudice. Works of art with themes such as yours can also
help bring about greater understanding among different groups.

Sincerely,

Mario M. Cuomo

Ms. Daniela Gioseffi
Communications and Speech Arts
St. Francis College
180 Remsen Street
Brooklyn, NY 11202

STATE OF NEW YORK
EXECUTIVE CHAMBER
ALBANY 12224

MARIO M. CUOMO
GOVERNOR

July 3, 1986

Dear Professor Gioseffi:

Thank you for your letter and thank you for
using your talents to editorialize against ethnic
prejudice.

The use of the word Mafia as a synonym for
organized crime is hurtful to all Italian-Americans
and offensive to everyone who wishes to be judged
on the basis of his or her character.

Sincerely,

Mario M. Cuomo

Professor Daniela Gioseffi
Communications and Speech Arts
  Department
St. Francis College
180 Remsen Street
Brooklyn, New York 11202

28 November, 2000
Daniela Gioseffi
   Montague St.
Brooklyn Heights
New York City

Dear Daniela,

What marvelous energy your book, GOING ON has! I have been
dipping into it as I find the time, and each time I do certain poems leap out. THE YOUNG GIRL is so small and so
powerful. The pathos and menace of AUGUST WHEN SPIDERS
SPIN. WATCHING AMERICAN TELEVISION with its bold mixture of
anger and detail heating up the poem : I imagine this delivers
well on the stage. I could go on. Thank you for sending the
book. I am sure it will attract readers.

I am honored deeply that you wish to present some of my
poems on the Italian American Writers website. You have my
permission, of course, and you don't have to worry about
changing titles if you come to that. I can't think of a better
host for my work. Please accept this paragraph as full consent.

Please don't worry about reaching the age of sixty. Your
poems keep you young. Your idiom is contemporary, and at the
same time universal.

Keep well and enjoy the holiday season. Your passion will
never fade.

                              Sincerely and with gusto,

                              Felix Stefanile

Excerpted from a 1985 Correspondence between John Ciardi and Daniela Gioseffi
Published in *The Selected Letters of John Ciardi*, Edited by Edward M. Cifelli .
[Fayetteville, Arkansas & London: Arkansas U. Press: © 1991]

John Ciardi
Metuchen, New Jersey
September 9, 1985

Dear Daniela,

.... Thanks for the poems. I respond to these much more richly.... They take the time to be rather than to mean. No matter that they are more elevated than my low mind: they are poems, captured and made, not assertions, and to that I can answer and do answer. Thank you....

Yes, the forties are a right time for ambition, and I wish you all the good of yours. But if I have learned anything, I think it is that poetry is an instrument. As the Sweet Singer of Michigan once wrote, "Literary is a work very difficult to do." It is a joyously difficult instrument, and the most difficult instrument forgives least.... The instrument won't respond to claims about it. It must be wooed. One submits to it humbly and hopes it may be moved.... Either what comes in memorable and sticks to memory (and even perhaps to the memory of this crazy species) or it is forgettable and get forgotten. ...every reader is a Pope within himself, and wholly authorized to publish required damnations. I wish there were some other ground rules, but I don't know what they might be. I have never known any others....

If it pleases you to have Galway Kinnell call you "visionary and full of vitality." Take a bow.... W. D. Snodgrass says your style is "splendidly clean and straight." Snodgrass can write, ... I grant you without reservation the pleasure of taking pains.... If I send you love you ain't got much. If you are a glutton for punishment, send me more poems.

Earnest love, my sweet equality,
affectionately,

Bibliography of Works Cited, and Further Reading

Barolini, Helen. *The Dream Book*. New York: Schoken Books, 1985. Rpt. Syracuse, NY: Syracuse UP, 2001.

___. *Their Other Side: Six American Women & The Lure of Italy*. New York: Fordham UP, 2006.

Barrett Browning, Elizabeth. *Aurora Leigh*. London: Chapman and Hall, 1857.

Benfey, Christopher. *A Summer of Hummingbirds: Love, Art, and Scandal in the Intersecting Worlds of Emily Dickinson*. New York: Penguin Books, 2008.

Bernal, Martin. *Black Athena: Afroasiatic Roots of Classical Civilization, Vol. 1: The Fabrication of Ancient Greece, 1785–1985*. Rutgers UP, 1987.

Bingham, Millicent T. *Ancestors' Brocades: The Literary Debut of Emily Dickinson*. New York: Harper & Brothers, 1945.

Bloom, Allan. *The Closing of the American Mind*. New York: Simon & Schuster, 1988.

Boelhower, William, and Rocco Pallone, eds. *Adjusting Sites: New Essays in Italian American Studies*. Stony Brook, NY: SUNY, Filibrary Series, 1999.

Bona, Mary Jo. "'But Is it Great?': The Question of the Canon for Italian American Women Writers." *Multiethnic Literature and Canon Debates*. Ed. Mary Jo Bona and Irma Maini. SUNY Series in Italian/American Culture. Albany: State U of New York P, 2006. 85–110.

___. "Recent Developments in Italian American Women's Literary Traditions." *Claiming a Tradition: Italian American Writers*. Ed. Mary Jo Bona. Carbondale: Southern Illinois UP, 1999. 163–98.

___, ed. *The Voices We Carry*. Toronto: Guernica, 1993.

Bona, Mary Jo, and Irma Maini. Introduction. *Multiethnic Literature and Canon Debates*. Ed. Mary Jo Bona and Irma Maini. SUNY Series in Italian/American Culture. Albany: State U of New York P, 2006. 1–17.

Broadway Danny Rose. Dir. Woody Allen. Perf. Woody Allen and Mia Farrow. Orion, 1984.

Capps, Jack L. *Emily Dickinson's Reading, 1836–1886*. Cambridge: Harvard UP, 1966.

Caputo, Philip. *Means of Escape*. New York: HarperCollins, 1998.

Camaiti, Anna, and Anthony J. Tamburri, eds. *Screening Ethnicity: Cinematographic Representations of Italian Americans in the U.S.* Boca Raton, FL: Bordighera P, 2002.

Carnevali, Emanuel. *The Autobiography of Emanuel Carnevali*. Ed. Kay Boyle. Horizon,1967.

___. *Furnished Rooms*. Ed. Dennis Barone. Bordighera P, 2006.

Cavalieri, Grace. "Pointing Beyond Language." Rev. of *Word Wounds and Water Flowers,* by Daniela Gioseffi. *Poet Lore* (1996).

Ciongoli, A. Kenneth, and Jay Parini, eds. *Beyond the Godfather: Italian American Writers on the Real Italian American Experience*. Hanover: UP of New England, 1997.

Corso, Paola. *Giovanna's 86 Circles: And Other Stories.* U of Wisconsin P, 2007.

Covino, Peter. *Cut Off the Ears of Winter: Poems.* New Issues Poetry and Prose, 2007.

Cyrus, Virginia. "Power, Racism, and Ethnocentricity." *Experiencing Race, Class, and Gender in the United States.* California: Mayfield, 1996.

"Daniela Gioseffi." *PEN American Center.* 5 May 2008. <http//www.pen.org/MemberProfile.php/prm/ProfileID/19901>.

De Angelis, Milo. *Between the Blast Furnaces and the Dizziness: A Selection of Poems, 1920–1999.* Trans. Emanuel di Pasquale. Chelsea Editions, 2003.

De Palchi, Alfredo. *Additive Aversions.* Trans. Sonia Raiziss and others. Las Cruces, NM: Xenos Books, 1999.

___. *Anonymous Constellation.* Trans. Sonia Raiziss, Las Cruces, NM: Xenos Books, 1997.

___. *The Scorpion's Dark Dance.* Trans. Sonia Raiziss. Las Cruces, NM: Xenos Books, 1993.

___. *Sessions with My Analyst.* Trans. Isidore Lawrence Salomon. October House, 1971.

DeLillo, Don. *White Noise.* New York: Viking, 1985.

Di Donato, Pietro. *Christ in Concrete.* Esquire, 1937.

Di Prima, Diane. *Loba.* New York: Penguin, 1998.

___. *Memoirs of a Beatnik.* Olympia P, 1969.

___. *Recollections of My Life as a Woman: The New York Years.* New York: Viking P, 2001.

___. *Revolutionary Letters.* San Francisco: City Lights Bookstore, 1971.

Dickinson, Emily. *The Complete Poems of Emily Dickinson.* 3 vols. Ed. Thomas H. Johnson. Cambridge, MA: Belknap/Harvard UP, 1955.

___. *The Letters of Emily Dickinson.* 3 vols. Ed. Thomas H. Johnson and Theodora Ward. Cambridge: Belknap/Harvard UP, 1958.

Diehl, Joanne Feit. *Dickinson and the Romantic Imagination.* Princeton: Princeton UP, 1981.

DiStasi, Lawrence, ed. *Una Storia Secreta: The Secret History of Italian American Evacuation and Internment During World War II.* Foreword Helen Barolini. HeyDay Books, 2001.

Du Bois, W. E. B. "Prospect of a World Without Race Conflict." *American Journal of Sociology* 49.5 (Mar. 1944): 450–56.

Emerson, Ralph Waldo. "Nature." 1836. *Selected Writings of Ralph Waldo Emerson.* Ed. William H. Gilman. New York: New American Library, 1965. 186–22.

Erkila, Betsy. "Emily Dickinson and Class." *American Literary History* 4.1 (Sept. 1992): 1–27.

Fagiani, Gil. *A Blanquito in El Barrio.* Rain Mountain P, 2009.

Fama, Maria. *Looking for Cover.* West Lafayette, IN: Bordighera P, 2008.

Farr, Judith. "Emily Dickinson's 'Engulfing' Play: *Anthony & Cleopatra.*" *Tulsa Studies in Women's Literature* 2 (Fall 1990): 231–50.

___. *The Gardens of Emily Dickinson.* Cambridge, MA: Harvard UP, 2004.

___. *The Passion of Emily Dickinson.* Cambridge, MA: Harvard UP, 1992.

Ferlinghetti, Lawrence. *A Coney Island of the Mind.* New York: New Directions, 1958.

___. Letter to Daniela Gioseffi. 12 Aug. 1984.

Ferrara, Geraldine. Letter to Daniela Gioseffi. 27 Sept. 1985.

Franklin, R. W., ed. *The Master Letters of Emily Dickinson.* Amherst College, 1986.

___. *The Editing of Emily Dickinson: A Reconsideration.* Madison: U of Wisconsin P 1967.

___. "The Emily Dickinson Fascicles." *Studies in Bibliography* 36 (1983): 1–20.

___, ed. and introd. *The Master Letters of Emily Dickinson.* Amherst College, 1998.

___, ed. *The Poems of Emily Dickinson: Variorum Edition.* Cambridge, MA: Belknap/Harvard UP, 1998.

Gambino, Richard. *Blood of My Blood.* New York: Doubleday, 1974. Rpt. Toronto: Guernica, 2002.

___. *Vendetta: The true story of the worst lynching in American, the mass murder of Italian-Americans in New Orleans in 1981, the vicious motivations behind it, and the tragic repercussions that linger to this day.* New York: Doubleday, 1977.

Gardaphe, Fred L. "Breaking and Entering: An Italian American's Literary Odyssey." *Beyond the Godfather: Italian American Writers on the Real Italian American Experience.* Ed. A. Kenneth Ciongoli and Jay Parini. Hanover: UP of New England, 1997. 175–89.

___. Conclusion. *Leaving Little Italy: Essaying Italian American Culture.* Ed. Fred L. Gardaphe. SUNY Series in Italian/American Culture. Albany: SUNY P, 2004. 151–61.

___. *From Wise Guys to Wise Men: The Gangster and Italian American Masculinities.* Routeledge, 2006.

___. Introduction. *Leaving Little Italy: Essaying Italian American Culture.* Ed. Fred L. Gardaphe. SUNY Series in Italian/American Culture. Albany: SUNY P, 2004. xi–xix.

___. *Italian Signs, American Streets: The Evolution of Italian Amererican Narrative.* Durham: Duke UP, 1996.

___. "Linguine and Lust: Notes of Food and Sex in Italian American Culture." *Leaving Little Italy: Essaying Italian American Culture.* Ed. Fred L. Gardaphe. SUNY Series in Italian/American Culture. Albany: State U of New York P, 2004. 137–49.

___. "Mythologies of Italian America: From Little Italy to the Suburbs." *Leaving Little Italy: Essaying Italian American Culture.* Ed. Fred L. Gardaphe. SUNY Series in Italian/American Culture. Albany: State U of New York P, 2004. 37–50.

Gattuso-Hendin, Josephine. *Heart Breakers, Women and Violence in Contemporary Culture and Literature.* Palgrave Macmillan, 2004.

___. *The Right Thing to Do.* New York: Feminist P. 1999.

___. *Vulnerable People: A View of American Fiction since 1945.* New York: Oxford UP, 1978, rpt. 1979.

Gillan, Maria Mazziotti, and Jennifer Gillan, eds. *Unsettling America: An Anthology of Contemporary Multicultural Poetry.* New York: Penguin, 1994.

Ginsberg, Alan. *Howl and Other Poems.* San Francisco: City Lights Pocket Bookshop, 1969.

Giordano, Paolo A. "Bibliography of Italian Studies in North America." *Italica* 73.2 (1996): 295–311.

Gioseffi, Daniela. 2006. *Poet and the Poem Webcasts.* Library of Congress, Washington. 5 May 2008 <http://www.loc.gov/poetry/poetpoem.html>.

___. *Blood Autumn: Poems New and Selected.* Boca Raton: Bordighera P, 2006.

___. *Earth Dancing; Mother Nature's Oldest Rite.* 1st ed. Harrisburg, PA: Stackpole, 1980.

___. *Eggs in the Lake.* Brockport, NY: Boa Editions, 1979.

___. *Going On: Poems.* West Lafayette, IN: Bordighera P, 2000.

___. *The Great Amer. Belly Dance: A Novel.* 1st ed. Garden City, New York: Doubleday, 1977.

___. *In Bed with the Exotic Enemy: Stories & Novella.* Greensboro, NC: Avison, 1995.

___. "Lover of Science and Scientist in Dark Days of the Republic: Solving the Mystery of Emily Dickinson's 'Master Figure." *Chelsea Literature Review* 81 (2006): 109–41.

___. *Symbiosis: Poems.* New York: Rattapallax P, 2002.

___. *Wild Nights, Wild Nights: The Story of Emily Dickinson's "Master," Neighbor and Friend and Bridegroom.* Austin, TX: Plain View P, 2010.

___. *Wildlife of Northwest New Jersey: An Introductory Guide.* Andover, NJ: Ladybug, 1994.

___. *Word Wounds and Water Flowers: Poems.* West Lafayette, IN: Bordighera P., 1995. Full text also available in the *Contemporary American Poetry Archive (CAPA)* <http://capa.conncoll.edu/gioseffi.ww&wf.html>.

___, ed. *Gioseffi.com: Daniela Gioseffi.* <http://www.gioseffi.com>.

___. *Italian Amer. Writers.com: Contemporary Italian American Writing.* <www.italianamericanwritiers.com>.

___. *On Prejudice: A Global Perspective.* New York: Anchor/Doubleday, 1993.

___. *PoetsUSA.com.* <www.PoetsUSA.com/.

___. *Wise Women's Web: A Mag. of Women's Literature* <www.Poets.USA.com/>.

___. *Women On War: Essential Voices for the Nuclear Age from a Brilliant International Assembly.* New York: Simon and Schuster, 1988.

___. *Women on War: An International Anthology of Writings from Antiquity to the Present.* 2nd ed. New York: Feminist P at the City U of NY, 2003.

___, and Enildo A. Garcia, trans. *Dust Disappears: Carilda Oliver Labra.* Latin American Writers Chapbook Series 1. Ed. Stanley H. Barkan. Merrick, NY: Cross-Cultural Communications, 1995.

Gould, S. J. *The Mismeasure of Man.* New York: Norton, 1981.

Green, Rose Basile. *The Italian American Novel: A Document of the Interaction of Two Cultures.* Fairleigh Dickinson UP, 1974.

Grillo, Jean Bergantini. "*Arrivederci* Kitchens: Four *femme forte* shake up the Madonna Myth." *IAM: The National Magazine for Italian-Americans* 1.1 (1976): 40–43.

Guida, George. "Gioseffi, Daniela (b. 1941)." *The Italian American Experience: An Encyclopedia*. Ed. Frank J. Cavaioli, Salvatore J. LaGumina, Salvatore Primeggia, and Joseph A. Varacalli. New York: Garland, 2000. 267–68.

Habegger, Alfred. *"My Wars Are Laid Away in Books": The Life of Emily Dickinson*. New York: Modern Library Paperback Edition, 2002.

Harding, M. Ester. *Woman's Mysteries: Ancient and Modern*. Longmans Green & Co., 1935. Rpt. Pantheon, 1955; Harper, 1971; and Shambhala, 1990.

Harrison, Barbara Grizzuti. *Italian Days*. Atlantic Monthly P, 1998.

Haw, Richard. *Brooklyn Bridge: A Cultural History*. Rutgers UP, 2005.

Higginson, Thomas Wentworth. "An Open Portfolio." *Christian Union* 42 (Sept. 25, 1980): 392–93. Rpt. *The Recognition of Emily Dickinson*. Ed. Caesar R. Blake and Carlton F. Wells. Ann Arbor: U of Michigan P, 1964: 3–10.

Howe, Susan. *My Emily Dickinson*. Berkeley: North Atlantic Books, 1985.

Howard, William. "Emily Dickinson's Poetic Vocabulary." *PMLA* 72 (March 1957): 225–48.

Isaacs, Jason. "Elizabeth Barrett Browning, Women's Issues, and Aurora Leigh." *The Victorian Web: Literature, History, and Culture in the Age of Victoria*. 1992. <http://www.victorianweb.org/authors/ebb/al3.html>.

James, Henry. *The American Scene*. London: Chapman & Hall, 1907.

Johnson, Thomas H. *Emily Dickinson: An Interpretive Biography*. Cambridge, MA: Belknap/Harvard UP, 1955.

___, ed. *The Poems of Emily Dickinson*. Cambridge: Belknap/Harvard UP: 1955.

___, and Theodora Ward, eds. *Letters of Emily Dickinson*. Cambridge: Belknap/ Harvard UP, 1958.

Jones Library: Special Collections. Vertical files of various documents on William Smith Clark, Samuel Williston, Emily Dickinson's Amherst, etc.: Amherst: MA.

Jones, Ruth Owen. "Neighbor—and friend—and Bridegroom—." *The Emily Dickinson Journal* 6.2 (Winter 2002).

Jong, Erica. Letter to Daniela Gioseffi. 24 Apr. 1986.

Joyce, James. *Finnegan's Wake*. Faber and Faber, 1939.

Keroac, Jack. *On the Road*. New York: Viking P, 1957.

Kirk, Connie Ann. *Emily Dickinson: A Biography*. CT: Greenwood, 2004.

Korzybski, Alfred. *Manhood of Humanity*. 2nd ed. Institute of General Semantics, 1950.

LaFemina, Gerry. *The Window Facing Winter: Poems*. New Issues Poetry and Prose, 2004.

Lamb, Charles. "Imperfect Sympathies." *London Magazine* (Aug. 1821).

Lawrence, D. H. *Sketches of Etruscan Places and Other Italian Essays*. Ed. Simonetta de Fillippis. Cambridge UP, 2002.

Leyda, Jay. *The Years and Hours of Emily Dickinson*, 2 vols. New Haven: Yale UP, 1960.

Lisella, Maria. *Amore on Hope St*. Finishing Line P, 2009.

Little Caesar. Dir. Mervyn LeRoy. 1931.

Lombardo, Daniel. "Chapter Three: Poetry Was in the Air: Rapid Dogs and

Typhoid in the Streets." *Hedge Away: The Other Side of Emily Dickinson's Amherst.* Northampton, MA: Daily Hampshire Gazette Press, 1997. 37–55.3

Longsworth, Polly. *Austin & Mabel: The Amherst Affair & Love Letters of Austin Dickinson & Mabel Loomis Todd.* New York: Holt, Rinehart, Winston, 1984.

___. *The World of Emily Dickinson.* New York: W.W. Norton, 1990.

Love, Barbara J. "Gioseffi, Daniela." *Feminists Who Changed America 1963–1975.* Chicago: U of Illinois P, 2006. 175.

Lowe, John. Foreword. *Multiethnic Literature and Canon Debates.* Ed. Mary Jo Bona and Irma Maini. Albany: State U of New York P, 2006. vii–xi.

Maki, John M. *William Smith Clark: A Yankee in Hokkaido.* Japan: Hokkaido UP, 1996.

Mangione, Jerre, and Ben Morreale. *La Storia: Five Centuries of the Italian American Experience.* New York: Harper, 1993.

Mannino, Mary Ann Vigilante. *Breaking Open: Reflections on Italian American Women's Writing.* West Lafayette, IN: Purdue UP, 2003.

Mazza, Cris. *How to Leave a Country.* Coffee House P, 1992.

McCourt, Frank. *Angela's Ashes.* Scribner, 1996.

Messina, Elizabeth G. "Perversion of Knowledge: Confirming Racist Ideologies Behind 'Intelligence' Testing and the Impact on Italian Americans." *Real Stories, Discrimination of Italian Americans.* Rutgers UP, 2007.

___. "Psychological Perspectives on the Stigmatization of Italian Americans in the American Media." *Saints and Rogues: Conflicts and Convergence in Psychotherapy.* Ed. Robert B. Marchesani and E. Mark Stern. Binghampton, NY: Hawthorne P, 2004.

Meyer, Howard N. *The Magnificent Activist: The Writings of Thomas Wentworth Higginson, 1823–1911.* Cambridge MA: Da Capo Press/NY Perseus Books. 2000.

Misurella, Fred. Rev. of *In Bed with the Exotic Enemies: Stories,* by Daniela Gioseffi. *VIA* 9.1 (1998): 206–08.

___. *Short Time.* West Lafayette, IN: Bordighera Press, 1996.

Moonstruck. Dir. Norman Jewison. Perf. Cher and Nicholas Cage. MGM, 1987.

Morreale, Ben. "Eyes for Seeing Inward." Rev. of *In Bed with the Exotic Enemy* by Daniela Gioseffi. *Small Press Review* (1998).

Morrison, Toni. *The Bluest Eye.* New York: Washington Square Press, 1972.

Murray, Aife. "Miss Margaret's Emily Dickinson." *Signs: Journal of Women in Culture and Society* 24.3 (Spring 1999): 697–732.

Order of the Sons of Italian. *Italian American Crime Fighters: A Brief Survey.* 2005.

___. *Italian American Stereotypes in U.S. Advertising.* (Summer 2003).

Orsini, Daniel J. "Emily Dickinson and the Romantic Use of Science." *Massachusetts Studies in English* 7.4/8.1 (1981): 57–69.

Ovid. *Metamorphoses.* Trans. David R. Slavitt. Baltimore: Johns Hopkins UP, 1994.

Pagels, Elaine. *The Gnostic Gospels.* New York: Random House, 1979. Rpt. 2004.

Palma, Michael. "Daniela Gioseffi Wins the John Ciardi Award for Lifetime Achievement in Poetry." *Italian Americana* 25.2 (2007). 170–71.

Parenti, Michael. *The Culture Struggle*. New York: Seven Stories Press, 2006.

___. "The Italian-American and the Mass Media." *Ethnic Images in American Film and Television*. Ed. Randall M. Miller. Philadelphia: Balch Institute, 1978.

___. *Make-Believe Media: The Politics of Entertainment*. Wadsworth, 1991.

Pavese, Caesar. *Disaffections: Complete Poems, 1930–1950*. Trans. G. Brock. Copper Canyon Press, 2002.

Peel, Robin. *Emily Dickinson and the Hill of Science*. Fairleigh, MA: Dickinson UP, 2010.

Petrino, Elizabeth A. *Emily Dickinson & Her Contemporaries: Women's Verse in America, 1820–1885*. Hanover, NH: UP of New England, 1998.

Pollak, Vivian R., ed. *A Historical Guide to Emily Dickinson*. New York: Oxford UP, 2004.

Puccio, Valerie. "Daniela Gioseffi on New Mother Earth." *Phoenix* (10 Apr. 1979): 2.

Puzo, Mario. *The Fortunate Pilgrim*. Atheneum, 1965. Rpt. New York: Random House, 1997

___. *The Godfather*. 1st ed. New York: J. P. Putnam's Sons, 1969.

Prizi's Honor. Dir. John Hurston. Pref. Jack Nicholson, Kathleen Turner, and Anjelica Houston. ABC Motion Pictures, 1985.

Reed, Ishmael. *MultiCultural America, Cultural Wars, Cultural Peace*. New York: Viking Press, 1997. 2006.

___. *Writin' is Fightin'*. Antheneum, 1988.

Rizzo, Patricia Thompson. "Emily Dickinson and the "Blue Peninsula: Dickinson's Reception in Italy and Marisa Bulgheroni's Emily Dickinson: *Tutte le poesia*." *The Emily Dickinson Journal* 8.1 (Spring 1999).

Robertiello, Dr. Richard C., and Diana Hoguet. *The WASP Mystique*. New York: D.I. Fine, 1987.

Scarpaci, Vincenza. *The Journey of the Italians in America*. Pelican, 2008.

Sewall, Richard. *The Life of Emily Dickinson*. New York: Farrar, Straus & Giroux, 1974.

Shark Tale. DreamWorks Animation, 2004.

Stampino, Maria Galli. Rev. *Word Wounds and Water Flowers*, by Daniela Gioseffi. *Italian Americana* 17.5 (1999): 228–29.

Talese, Gay. "Where are the Italian American Novelists?" *New York Times Review of Books* 14 Mar. 1993.

Tamburri, Anthony Julian. "Beyond 'Pizza' and 'Nonna!' Or, What's Bad about Italian/American Criticism?: Further Directions for Italian/American Cultural Studies." *MELUS* 28.3 (2003): 149–74.

___. "In (Re)cognition of the Italian/American Writer: Definitions and Categories." *A Semiotic of Ethicity: In (Re)cognition of the Italian/American Writer*. Ed. Anthony Julian Tamburri. SUNY Series in Italian/American Culture. Albany: SUNY P, 1998. 3–20.

___, Paolo Giordano, and Fred L. Gardaphe, eds. *Writings from the Margin: Writings in Italian Americana*. West Lafayette, IN: Purdue UP, 1991. Rpt. 2002.

Terrone, Maria. *A Secret Room in the Fall*. Ashland Poetry Press, 2006.

Tricarico, Donald "GUIDO: Fashioning an Italian-American Youth Style." *The Journal of Ethnic Studies* 19.1 (1989–1990).

Turco, Lewis. *Fearful Pleasures: The Complete Poems, 1959–2007.* Star Cloud Press, 2007.

Tusiani, Joseph. "L'italia nella poesia di Emily Dickinson." *Parola del Popolo.* 26 (Jan. 1957).

"Venus of Willendorf: Exaggerated Beauty." 22 June 2006. *A KCET/BBC Co-Production.* 5 May 2008 <http://www.pbs.org/howartmadetheworld/episodes/human/venus/>.

Vignale, Catherine Giambanco. "In Search of an Italian American Woman of Letters." 1989.

Viscusi, Robert. *Buried Caesars and Other Secrets of Italian American Writing.* SUNY Series in Italian/American Culture. Albany: SUNY P, 2006.

___. *An Oration Upon the Most Recent Death of Christopher Columbus.* West Lafayette, IN: Bordighera Press, 1998.

Winwar, Frances. *George Sand and Her Times: A Life of the Heart.* New York: Harper, 1945.

Wolff, Cynthia Griffin. *Emily Dickinson.* Reading, MA: Perseus Books, 1988.

VIA FOLIOS
A refereed book series dedicated to the culture of Italians and Italian Americans.

MARIA FAMÀ, *Mystics in the Family*, Vol. 84, Poetry, $10

ROSSANA DEL ZIO, *From Bread and Tomatoes to Zuppa di Pesce "Ciambotto"*, Vol. 83, Italian American Studies, $15

LORENZO DELBOCA, *Polentoni*, Vol. 82, Italian Studies, $20

SAMUEL GHELLI, *A Reference Grammar*, Vol. 81, Italian American Studies, $20

ROSS TALARICO, *Sled Run*, Vol. 80, Fiction, $15

FRED MISURELLA, *Only Sons*, Vol. 79, Fiction, $17

FRANK LENTRICCHIA, *The Portable Lentricchia*, Vol. 78, Fiction, $17

RICHARD VETERE, *The Other Colors in a Snow Storm*, Vol. 77, Poetry, $10

GARIBALDI LAPOLLA, *Fire in the Flesh*, Vol. 76, Fiction, $25

GEORGE GUIDA, *The Pope Stories*, Vol. 75, Fiction, $15

ROBERT VISCUSI, *Ellis Island*, Vol. 74, Poetry, $28

ELENA GIANINI BELOTI, *The Bitter Taste of Strangers Bread*, Vol. 73, Fiction, $24

PINO APRILE, *Terroni*, Vol. 72, Italian American Studies, $20

EMANUEL DI PASQUALE, *Harvest*, Vol. 71, Poetry, $10

ROBERT ZWEIG, *Return to Naples*, Vol. 70, Memoir, $16

AIROS & CAPPELLI, *Guido*, Vol. 69, Italian American Studies, $12

FRED GARDAPHÉ, *Moustache Pete is Dead! Long Live Moustache Pete!*, Vol. 67, Literature/Oral History, $12

PAOLO RUFFILLI, *Dark Room Camera oscura*, Vol. 66, Poetry, $11

HELEN BAROLINI, *Crossing the Alps*, Vol. 65, Fiction, $14

COSMO FERRARA, *Profiles of Italian Americans*, Vol. 64, Italian American, $16

GIL FAGIANI, *Chianti in Connecticut*, Vol. 63, Poetry, $10

BASSETTI & D'ACQUINO, *Italic Lessons*, Vol. 62, Italian American Studies, $10

CAVALIERI & PASCARELLI, eds., *The Poet's Cookbook*, Vol. 61, Poetry/Recipes, $12

EMANUEL DI PASQUALE, *Siciliana*, Vol. 60, Poetry, $8

NATALIA COSTA, ed., *Bufalini*, Vol. 59, Poetry

RICHARD VETERE, *Baroque*, Vol. 58, Fiction

LEWIS TURCO, *La Famiglia The Family*, Vol. 57, Memoir, $15

NICK JAMES MILETI, *The Unscrupulous*, Vol. 56, Humanities, $20

BASSETTI, ACCOLLA, D'AQUINO, *Italici: An Encounter with Piero Bassetti*, Vol. 55, Italian Studies, $8

GIOSE RIMANELLI, *The Three-legged One*, Vol. 54, Fiction, $15

CHARLES KLOPP, *Bele Antiche Stòrie*, Vol. 53, Criticism, $25

JOSEPH RICAPITO, *Second Wave*, Vol. 52, Poetry, $12

GARY MORMINO, *Italians in Florida*, Vol. 51, History, $15

GIANFRANCO ANGELUCCI, *Federico F.*, Vol. 50, Fiction, $15

ANTHONY VALERIO, *The Little Sailor*, Vol. 49, Memoir, $9

ROSS TALARICO, *The Reptilian Interludes*, Vol. 48, Poetry, $15

RACHEL GUIDO DE VRIES, *Teeny Tiny Tino's Fishing Story*, Vol. 47, Children's Lit, $6

EMANUEL DI PASQUALE, *Writing Anew*, Vol. 46, Poetry, $15

MARIA FAMÀ, *Looking For Cover*, Vol. 45, Poetry, $12

ANTHONY VALERIO, *Toni Cade Bambara's One Sicilian Night*, Vol. 44, Poetry, $10

EMANUEL CARNEVALI, Dennis Barone, ed., *Furnished Rooms*, Vol. 43, Poetry, $14

BRENT ADKINS, et al., ed., *Shifting Borders, Negotiating Places*, Vol. 42, Proceedings, $18

GEORGE GUIDA, *Low Italian*, Vol. 41, Poetry, $11

GARDAPHÈ, GIORDANO, TAMBURRI, *Introducing Italian Americana*, Vol. 40, Italian American Studies, $10

DANIELA GIOSEFFI, *Blood Autumn Autunno di sangue*, Vol. 39, Poetry, $15/$25

FRED MISURELLA, *Lies to Live by*, Vol. 38, Stories, $15

STEVEN BELLUSCIO, *Constructing a Bibliography*, Vol. 37, Italian Americana, $15

ANTHONY J. TAMBURRI, ed., *Italian Cultural Studies 2002*, Vol. 36, Essays, $18

BEA TUSIANI, *con amore*, Vol. 35, Memoir, $19

FLAVIA BRIZIO-SKOV, ed., *Reconstructing Societies in the Aftermath of War*, Vol. 34, History, $30

TAMBURRI, et al., eds., *Italian Cultural Studies 2001*, Vol. 33, Essays, $18

ELIZABETH G. MESSINA, ed., *In Our Own Voices,* Vol. 32, Italian American Studies, $25
STANISLAO G. PUGLIESE, *Desperate Inscriptions,* Vol. 31, History, $12
HOSTERT & TAMBURRI, eds., *Screening Ethnicity,* Vol. 30, Italian American Culture, $25
G. PARATI & B. LAWTON, eds., *Italian Cultural Studies,* Vol. 29, Essays, $18
HELEN BAROLINI, *More Italian Hours,* Vol. 28, Fiction, $16
FRANCO NASI, ed., *Intorno alla Via Emilia,* Vol. 27, Culture, $16
ARTHUR L. CLEMENTS, *The Book of Madness & Love,* Vol. 26, Poetry, $10
JOHN CASEY, et al., *Imagining Humanity,* Vol. 25, Interdisciplinary Studies, $18
ROBERT LIMA, *Sardinia Sardegna,* Vol. 24, Poetry, $10
DANIELA GIOSEFFI, *Going On,* Vol. 23, Poetry, $10
ROSS TALARICO, *The Journey Home,* Vol. 22, Poetry, $12
EMANUEL DI PASQUALE, *The Silver Lake Love Poems,* Vol. 21, Poetry, $7
JOSEPH TUSIANI, *Ethnicity,* Vol. 20, Poetry, $12
JENNIFER LAGIER, *Second Class Citizen,* Vol. 19, Poetry, $8
FELIX STEFANILE, *The Country of Absence,* Vol. 18, Poetry, $9
PHILIP CANNISTRARO, *Blackshirts,* Vol. 17, History, $12
LUIGI RUSTICHELLI, ed., *Seminario sul racconto,* Vol. 16, Narrative, $10
LEWIS TURCO, *Shaking the Family Tree,* Vol. 15, Memoirs, $9
LUIGI RUSTICHELLI, ed., *Seminario sulla drammaturgia,* Vol. 14, Theater/Essays, $10
FRED GARDAPHÈ, *Moustache Pete is Dead! Long Live Moustache Pete!,* Vol. 13, Oral Literature, $10
JONE GAILLARD CORSI, *Il libretto d'autore, 1860–1930,* Vol. 12, Criticism, $17
HELEN BAROLINI, *Chiaroscuro: Essays of Identity,* Vol. 11, Essays, $15
PICARAZZI & FEINSTEIN, eds., *An African Harlequin in Milan,* Vol. 10, Theater/Essays, $15
JOSEPH RICAPITO, *Florentine Streets & Other Poems,* Vol. 9, Poetry, $9
FRED MISURELLA, *Short Time,* Vol. 8, Novella, $7
NED CONDINI, *Quartettsatz,* Vol. 7, Poetry, $7
ANTHONY TAMBURRI, ed., *Fuori: Essays by Italian American Lesbians and Gays,* Vol. 6, Essays, $10
ANTONIO GRAMSCI, P. Verdicchio, Trans. & Intro., *The Southern Question,* Vol. 5, Social Criticism, $5
DANIELA GIOSEFFI, *Word Wounds & Water Flowers,* Vol. 4, Poetry, $8
WILEY FEINSTEIN, *Humility's Deceit: Calvino Reading Ariosto Reading Calvino,* Vol. 3, Criticism, $10
PAOLO GIORDANO, ed., *Joseph Tusiani: Poet, Translator, Humanist,* Vol. 2, Criticism, $25
ROBERT VISCUSI, *Oration Upon the Most Recent Death of Christopher Columbus,* Vol. 1, Poetry, $3

Published by Bordighera, Inc., an independently owned, not-for-profit, scholarly organization that
has no legal affiliation with the University of Central Florida and the John D. Calandra Italian
American Institute, Queens College/CUNY.

CPSIA information can be obtained at www.ICGtesting.com
Printed in the USA
BVOW011907200213

313818BV00006B/36/P